Business Psychology in Practice

Business Psychology in Practice

Edited by

PAULINE GRANT MA, MSc, CPsychol
YSC Ltd

assisted by

SARAH LEWIS MA, MSc, CPsychol
Gemstone Consultancy Ltd

and

DAVID THOMPSON PhD, CPsychol, AFBPS
Royal Mail

Association of Business Psychologists

W
WHURR PUBLISHERS
LONDON AND PHILADELPHIA

© 2005 Whurr Publishers Ltd
First published 2005
by Whurr Publishers Ltd
19b Compton Terrace
London N1 2UN, England and
325 Chestnut Street, Philadelphia PA 19106, USA

British Library Cataloguing in Publication Data

A catalogue record for this book
is available from the British Library.

ISBN 1 86156 476 7

Typeset by Adrian McLaughlin, a@microguides.net
Printed and bound in the UK by Athenæum Press Ltd, Gateshead, Tyne & Wear.

Contents

Contributors

Kylie Bains joined organizational capability consultancy YSC Ltd in 1994 and is now a Director. Graduating in organizational psychology from Queensland University, Australia, she worked in IT recruitment and in product development and marketing for a UK business psychology firm prior to joining YSC. She is responsible for YSC's public relations in addition to her consulting role. She has a particular interest in political behaviour inside organizations and how women achieve leadership success in business.

Ellen Bard is a consultant at SHL UK Ltd. After completing her Master's degree in organizational psychology at UMIST she worked for PSL, focusing on selection and assessment. Her work at SHL involves the design, implementation and delivery of assessment and development centres through to following up with participants via feedback and coaching.

Helen Baron has many years' experience in the design and implementation of effective employee selection and assessment systems, both paper based and electronic. She is involved in training and consultancy to help organizations audit their assessment procedures and formulate equal opportunities policy. As a leading member of the SHL research and development team she developed many psychometric tests and published widely in equal opportunities and selection issues. Now an independent consultant, she continues her research and development work and presents in conferences internationally.

Trevor J Bentley has many years' experience as a personal and professional development coach with chief executives and executive teams. He has a PhD in organizational development, and is a Fellow of CIMA and a chartered member of CIPD. Trevor leads training programmes for executives and consultants in applying a Gestalt approach in the UK and

Australia. His 'inspirational leadership' and 'winning teams' approaches have guided his clients to significant business success. Trevor has written over 30 books and numerous articles.

Ellie Boughton is the Regional Product Director, Asia Pacific in SHL where for several years she has consulted in the UK, Europe and Asia Pacific. She has created competency models for manufacturing, fast-moving consumer goods, mining, retail sales and the public sectors. She studied psychology in Sydney and gained a Master's in organizational psychology from the University of New South Wales. Specific interests include using 360-degree competency questionnaires in development and how Internet technology helps this process to be run more efficiently.

Paul Brewerton is managing director of business psychology consultancy Blue Edge. Paul's consulting work focuses on change and development at individual, team and organizational levels and includes coaching, training, team building, diagnostic research and psychometric development. He often works in the areas of organizational culture change and leadership development, the two frequently going hand in hand. Recent assignments included a global culture change programme for a mobile telecommunications company, high-performance coaching for senior executives in the technology sector, and delivery of the Cougar leadership development programme across a range of industries. Paul authored *Organizational Research Methods*.

Simon Brittain is a partner and director of Kiddy & Partners. He specializes in strategic talent management, assessment/development centre design/implementation and one-to-one assessments for senior executives and high flyers. His experience crosses a range of sectors including financial services, automotive, professional services, consultancy, FMCG and hi-tech. Simon joined Kiddy & Partners from a major test publisher, prior to which he worked with a number of consultancies and the Post Office where he was a manager in the occupational psychology unit.

Michael Burnett joined SHL in 1999 and has managed the development and deployment of a range of Internet, PC and pocket PC assessment products. He is now director of production and operations. He previously worked in the UK software industry. At EDS, Michael managed a group providing human factors, change management, training and integrated logistics support to clients on some of the largest IT integration projects in the UK for corporate and public sector clients. Following his graduation in psychology in 1978, Michael worked as a psychologist for the Royal Air Force.

Nadine Burton is a chartered occupational psychologist with considerable consulting experience. She has worked across a variety of sectors, including financial services, retail, FMCG, manufacturing, government and charitable bodies in the UK, Central and Eastern Europe and Canada. Nadine specializes in designing and implementing rigorous yet pragmatic assessment and development solutions for executives and managers. Project work has included the identification of factors that drive effective performance, executive selection, high potential talent assessment and performance management. Nadine has been a director with two leading UK business psychology firms.

James Bywater has worked as a business psychologist since 1990, using his background in finance and psychology to implement unique assessment and development solutions for clients. He specializes in the banking sector and in utilizing technology and the Internet to make the solutions that he suggests scaleable for national and global clients.

Sue Clayton is lead partner of *the space between (UK)*, a consultancy practice with an associated partnership in Australia. Sue's Gestalt style raises awareness of individuals and teams to levels that dramatically improve their contribution to the organization. She is co-founder and co-leader of the not-for-profit partnership, Gestalt in Organizations, teaching Gestalt to leaders, managers and professionals. Sue is a representative for the UK on the board of the Marion Woodman Foundation, an international charity for developing women, based in the US. Having published four books on people and organization development, she is now researching a PhD on business leadership.

Roy Drew is a partner of Drew Associates, a business psychology practice specializing in organizational design, development and change. He supports executive boards in the process of identifying, initiating and implementing improvements in business performance by developing those organizational capabilities demanded by corporate or operational strategies. Roy's work in managing organizational change has incorporated major public to private sector transitions in transport, energy and defence, strategic change assignments in manufacturing and financial services and research on the organizational implications of technological change for the Commission of the European Communities.

Kieran Duignan is principal of Enabling Space, and a member of the Institution of Occupational Safety and Health, the Ergonomics Society, the European Academy of Occupational Health Psychology and Personal

Construct Psychology Education and Training. He specializes in interactions between the occupational health of employees and business performance and contributes to assessing and managing risks as chartered psychologist, counsellor, registered ergonomist and safety practitioner. He has written guides to career management, information management and technology and auditing systems for managing occupational stress as well as a handbook on recruitment.

Pauline Grant is a Director of the organizational capability consultancy YSC Ltd. Pauline qualified and worked as an educational psychologist before moving into the corporate world. Now she consults to sectors including finance, retail, construction and fast-moving consumer goods, in some cases working internationally. Often the focus is development: coaching individual leaders or top teams, workshops and consulting around change. She also finds time to do *pro bono* work and chair an ethics committee. She is the author of *Careering Upwards* and was the first Vice-Chair and first conference speaker for the ABP.

Howard Grosvenor is a senior consultant at SHL UK. As well as delivering the core components of SHL's business (training, product and consultancy), Howard has special responsibility for technology-based assessment and the UK portfolio of ability tests. He has experience in both technical and occupational psychology-focused roles. He has worked with a broad range of clients on everything from the design and delivery of development interventions to the implementation of online selection systems.

Anne Hamill is a Director of Strategis Ltd, a consultancy that equips people to cope with rapidly changing work environments. She started her career at ITRU (the Belbin unit), then spent 9 years working across virtually all sectors on government-financed research to identify the highest performance in various job roles and design practical selection and development tools. A past Chair of the Occupational Division of the BPS, Anne's key interests lie in enabling people to manage ambiguity and rapid change and in creating self-directed, highly effective learners.

Malcolm Hatfield has worked for many years as a psychologist in business with EMI, P&O, Chloride, Saville & Holdsworth and partnership, Hatfield Jefferies and is now an independent consultant. He is widely experienced in assessment at all levels from customer facing staff to CEOs and has developed tests in the UK and the Middle East. His current interest is in defining and managing the human requirement needed to support strategic objectives in different types of organizations.

Jo Hennessy is a business psychologist specializing in the development of people at work. A partner in Human Qualities, she previously headed executive development at Brathay & Penna Change Consulting. Her expertise centres on large-scale development programmes and she has extensive experience of identifying the people requirements of a business change, then applying interventions to facilitate the transition. She has worked nationally and internationally in such areas as visionary leadership, motivational management and customer relationship management. Having begun her career at SHL, she is also an expert in assessment methodologies.

Janey Howl is a leadership coach specializing in senior executives, top teams and entrepreneurs. Recognition of the impact of personal issues on organizational performance led Janey to qualify as a life coach. The result is a considerable track record in successful client career transitions and enhanced leadership capability. Howling Success Ltd (www.howlingsuccess.co.uk) is committed to the creation of working lives with passion and purpose. Workshop themes include 'raise your game', 'sustainable development', 'team performance' and 'manager as coach'. Howling Success Ltd also provides master classes in coaching expertise for in-house development staff.

George Karseras is a chartered occupational psychologist and change manager in Atos KPMG Consulting's change and programme management business consulting team. George has built his internal reputation as an expert in designing and facilitating launch events for AKC project teams. He combines business psychology training, particularly systems thinking and family therapy techniques, with project management and his experiences as a sports psychologist to Premiership football to design and facilitate highly pertinent, challenging and involving launch events for newly engaged project teams across the AKC delivery network.

David Lane had an early career in banking and in legal practice, then education and academia with periods as visiting professor at Syracuse and Middlesex Universities and honorary posts at University College London and City University London. He has acted as a professional coach for senior management and consultant on organizational development for major corporations, and has provided research forum and benchmarking projects internationally. He has been a non-executive director and is currently director of the Professional Development Foundation.

Sarah Lewis is managing director of Jemstone Consultancy Ltd, specializing in delivering team, management and individual development activities. She is particularly interested in approaches that work through an understanding of the power of cognitive processes to affect our behaviour through beliefs, values, stories and accounts. She is also interested in the developing and emerging field of positive psychology. She finds that taking an appreciative inquiry approach to organizational, team or individual issues draws on both these interests and is fun and effective.

Mark Loftus has many years' consulting experience and expertise in the fields of emotional intelligence and relationship development. After graduating from Oxford University in philosophy and psychology, Mark trained at the Institute of Psychiatry in London. In 1993 he co-founded the Oxford Consulting Group, now OCG Ltd, a successful consultancy inspiring change and vitality in individuals and organizations. In addition to his role as managing director, Mark also leads OCG's Assessment and Talent Management practice and is a trusted coach to senior figures in industry.

John Mahoney-Phillips is a chartered occupational psychologist and global head of Human Capital Performance for UBS, a leading financial services firm. Working out of the corporate HR function he is responsible for performance management, psychometric testing and assessment standards, staff surveys and succession/talent pipeline metrics. Previously John was head of leadership and management development for UBS Private Banking, and a managing consultant with SHL Group.

Penny Markell is a consultant at SHL UK Ltd. She worked in human resources before taking her MSc and moving into occupational psychology. Her work includes designing and implementing development and assessment centres, more recently on a large international scale, as well as conducting feedback and coaching sessions with participants.

Helen Marsh is a senior consultant at SHL UK Ltd. Her work involves the design, delivery and project management of assessment and development centres. Areas of particular interest and expertise include the development of competency frameworks, simulation exercise design, management development, feedback and coaching.

Siobhan McKavanagh, consultant with 7days Ltd, is an experienced organization development, talent management and change management specialist. She was a managing consultant and team leader for Ernst & Young UK Ltd from 1996 to 2002, and also took an active role in the service offers and thought leadership around HR transformation and e-HR. She previously worked for Hay Group after starting her career in 1989 with Coopers & Lybrand (PriceWaterhouseCoopers).

Charles Mead, Director of organizational capability consultancy YSC Ltd, trained at Oxford and London Universities in experimental and occupational psychology. He worked as a corporate psychologist for RHR Inc and then held senior HR positions in J. Walter Thompson, Booz Allen & Hamilton and Nabarro Nathanson. For 7 years he was European Personnel Director for Sotheby's and from 1995 to 1998 he was head of human resources for Coutts & Co. Charles's main professional interests currently are in performance management, leadership and motivation in professional and financial services firms.

Kate Oliver has been working as a consultant occupational psychologist since 1993, both in the UK and overseas. In this time she has worked with many leading, blue-chip organizations to help them manage talent and get the best from their people. She is a Partner in Human Qualities, where she specializes in the use of embedded learning for leadership and organizational development. She has a particular interest in applying the skills and techniques of occupational psychology in a commercial setting, to achieve enhanced business results.

Richard Plenty is a business psychologist with particular interest in helping to create sustainable high-performing organizations. He works with top teams and human resources leaders on issues associated with culture and change, often on a global scale. He is founding Director of 'This Is...', a consultancy which works with organization leaders to help shape identity, vision and culture. Previous experience includes coordinating and facilitating strategic change programmes in Europe, Asia and North America with Shell International as an HR Leader and Organization Development Manager. He is a guest lecturer on organizational issues at King's College, University of London.

Shane Pressey is a founding partner at Human Qualities. As an occupational psychologist, she has provided consultancy services for businesses in all sectors for many years and has extensive experience of working with international organizations. Her expertise centres on facilitating integrated team and individual development interventions. Particular areas of interest include executive coaching and management team facilitation. She has worked as a coach with many senior executives, helping them explore their inner motivation and unlock their full potential, through her supportive, challenging and business-focused interventions.

Amin Rajan is the chief executive of Centre for Research in Employment and Technology in Europe (CREATE), a network of researchers advising the UK government, City institutions, multinational companies and international bodies. He is a visiting professor at the Cass Business School, London Metropolitan University, and the Exeter University's Centre for Leadership Studies and is President of the Scientific Committee at Audencia, Nantes Ecole de Management. He has appeared on radio, television and published widely on leadership, business cultures, socio-economic forecasting, globalization, new technologies, and new business models. In 1998 he gained the Aspen Institute's prize in leadership.

Christopher Ridgeway has practised for over 20 years as a business psychologist and has worked with several leading organizations globally. He initially had an academic career teaching and researching at Bradford Management Centre, and moved on to be an HR manager and then director in both the UK and the US. He has published prolifically throughout his career and is a regular contributor to *The Occupational Psychologist*. He is also a counselling psychologist and executive coach.

Rachel Robinson is a director of the organizational capability consultancy YSC Ltd. She joined YSC in 1999 and has worked across the spectrum of YSC's work advising organizations on how to release the potential of their people, so that they can meet their strategic goals. She has been on both sides of the consultant–client fence having previously worked for GlaxoSmithKline plc and Pilkington plc and having sponsored the work of consultants within these organizations.

Joanne Share-Bernia is a management consultant and trainer as well as mentor and coach to leaders in industry and commerce. Joanne is a commentator for CNN television on business psychology. With many years' experience in business consultancy, she works with a range of blue-chip organizations as well as the public and SME sectors. Specializing in change management, team building and Investors in People National Standard, she has undertaken many projects in the measuring-up process and training in change management from individual, team and organizational perspectives.

Sylvana Storey has significant international experience across sectors including oil, nuclear, telecommunications and transport and has consulted on assignments in both the private and public sectors. Her key areas of expertise and experience lie in strategic transformation and facilitation, business psychology processes, and change management and organizational strategy. She has contributed to the implementation of a service strategy within the transport sector, the development and implementation of a focused differentiation regional strategy in the oil sector and training programmes tailored for these projects.

David Thompson heads the group of psychologists working on assessment within Royal Mail. He carried out university careers advisory work before moving into graduate and managerial recruitment. Much of his time is spent designing and running assessment centres for selection purposes and he also retains his involvement in career development through activities in talent management and the identification of managers and professionals with high potential. He is involved in examining occupational psychologists for Chartership and presents papers on assessment.

Rod Vincent is a chartered occupational psychologist. He founded Human Qualities in 1993 and has since grown the business to its current position as a leading occupational psychology consultancy. His 16-year consultancy career has included work across Europe, the US, the Asia-Pacific region and the Indian subcontinent. He was co-editor of *Selection and Development Review* published by the British Psychological Society from 1993 to 1999. Previously he worked with British Steel in a central organizational and management development role, and with SHL where he managed projects for major clients in various market sectors.

Mark Williams is a senior consultant within the SHL Assessment Strategy Team. He is responsible for the design and delivery of assessment and development centre products and initiatives within a broad array of clients, from both the private and public sector.

Maria Yapp is the managing director and founder of business psychologists Xancam Consulting Ltd. With a strong focus on assessment as a core specialism she also consults on performance management, executive team development and coaching for role transitions. She works with blue-chip clients across a range of sectors in the UK and overseas, relating interventions to clients' current and future commercial priorities. She also has a strong interest in the assessment of longer-term potential, having both researched and practised widely in this area.

Rob Yeung is an independent business psychologist working in the areas of assessment and development. He previously worked at the Boston Consulting Group and Kiddy & Partners. He has written seven books on management topics – two of which have been updated and reprinted as second editions. He is frequently asked to contribute to print media including the *Financial Times* and the *Guardian*, as well as broadcast media ranging from CNN and ITN news to *Big Brother*.

Foreword

In the year 2000 a number of psychologists working with businesses decided to come together in a series of meetings to discuss the possibility of creating an association of like-minded individuals. We were all united by three things.

First, we believed that the services and approach we provided our clients were special and different from the traditional offerings of psychologists, and we wanted to create a learning forum to develop these further.

Second, we knew that what we had to offer was hugely valued by the commercial and private sector organizations with which we worked, that they regarded it as distinctive and that it represented a new approach to the application of psychological principles to the challenges of the business world.

Third, we wanted to create a coherent professional identity to demonstrate to the world that a new field of practical psychology was emerging and to develop the market for new entrants and new clients.

Out of these meetings emerged the Association of Business Psychologists (the ABP). This association is now a thriving organization with a very active membership, a full programme of annual conferences, seminars and knowledge-sharing events. Practitioners with a wide range of experience rub shoulders with client and academic members to exchange ideas and collaborate on work projects. One of the results of the ABP's efforts is the introduction of new master's degree programmes in business psychology, which have been set up to cultivate the next generation of practitioners.

Business psychology is a young profession, with its roots in such diverse fields as organization development and learning, 'quality of working life', change-management, complex systems theory, human resource development, assessment, team building, group-facilitation and personal coaching. The practitioners have equally diverse backgrounds embracing many branches of applied psychology. The uniting force behind this new profession is the desire of each business psychologist to help organizations and their people *realize their full potential* – by applying the insights that psychology brings to individuals, teams and organized communities.

The philosophy behind business psychology is quite straightforward: it is a *practical* profession. We use our knowledge both of the business world and of psychology to challenge and help organizations and their people. Our 'interventions' – or activities within an organization – are *systemic.* That is, we understand that we are working with sophisticated human beings and communities in a complex organized commercial world to deliver pragmatic business benefits.

Business psychologists are:

• knowledge sharers;
• enablers;
• critics;
• organizational 'agents provocateurs';
• process designers and guides.

Our work can range from helping a chief executive and the management board of a multi-billion pound organization wrestle with developing their strategic leadership agenda, through to providing developmental coaching for an up-and-coming marketing manager facing major personal and organizational challenges.

This book is another result of the ABP's collaborative spirit. What you see here is the collective creative energy of some of the best and most experienced practitioners in our field, a project launched with enthusiasm and commitment by two of our founder principal members, Pauline Grant and Sarah Lewis. Indeed all the authors are principal members of the ABP. Here you can find a real sense of what business psychology is about. This book is among the first in the field to give you a flavour of our new profession's activities. I hope it enthuses you, and helps guide your practice and understanding of business psychology. For further information about the ABP and membership details, see www.theabp.org.

Dr Brian Baxter
Founding Chair, Association of Business Psychologists

Preface

When reflecting on the work involved in putting this book together, a metaphor came to mind: one of those wonderful tapestries compiled by many hands. My role has been to encourage and admire some pieces so beautifully done that they mustn't be touched, to rework, gently and carefully, some of the complex and less tidy elements and to find opportunities for individual talents to be displayed. The end-result has, in my view, and I hope in yours, fully justified the work involved.

There were doubters when the ABP started. After all, business psychologists earn their living by their ability to add something special to their clients – something that these clients are willing to pay for. Why should they share that with other people who are competitors? Was it courage or folly to include in our community those who bought our services, thereby removing any mystique about what we do? And would all these people have the time and inclination to collaborate? The venture was an optimistic experiment – one that depended on the confidence of practitioners to share their skills and experiences, warts and all, in the spirit of helping the profession to progress and thereby become even more valuable. This confidence has been shown to exist, and is at least in part underpinned by the knowledge that the market we operate in is both growing and changing constantly, and that together we enhance rather than restrict the opportunities.

The decision to include a category of membership of the ABP that allows non-psychologists and psychologists who are non-practitioners to join the community reflects another important principle: that of learning *from* as well as *with* each other. Our practitioner members benefit from having human resources professionals and other interested managers, academics and specialists from other branches of psychology to provoke thought, add different perspectives and offer diverse experience. The affiliates, those with an interest in business psychology although not themselves practitioners, benefit from having full access to the learning community that feeds that interest.

What follows in this book fulfils the brief that Sarah Lewis and I first put together – that of providing a window on what we do, the body of knowledge and theory that underpins it, and the continual development of practice through experience. Business psychologists cannot wait for research to tell them what to do in the unique and complex situations they are asked to advise on and intervene in. They sometimes have to learn with their clients. You will therefore find in the following pages some candid descriptions of interventions that contribute to the development of better practice and are at the leading edge in the sense of building on, rather than copying, what has gone before. There are also case studies that bring to life what might otherwise seem to be idealistic or speculative approaches. You will find helpful journeys through theory that serve to explain the thinking behind practice and the rationale for it, and some new models and perspectives derived from experience. However, you will also discover some provocative pieces that might stimulate you to challenge some accepted practices and perceptions. This book was never intended as, nor ever could be, a comprehensive account of business psychology but, seen as an exploratory probe, it provides insight into the profession and its practice.

I would like to acknowledge the contributions of:

- Sarah Lewis, with whom the book was scoped and who was a true partner in the editorial endeavour over the major part of the journey from concept to print;
- David Thompson, the willing volunteer to whom Sarah passed the baton for the final editorial stages;
- Stuart Francis, who gladly picked up stray tasks and delivered them with alacrity.

I would also like to pay tribute to my colleagues at YSC Ltd for their continued support and interest. I am truly proud to be part of an organization that, despite being busy, has sustained its commitment to the profession as a whole, a demonstrable example being the flexibility to enable me to work on this book.

The encouragement and advice of Peter Herriot and Adrian Furnham has also been much valued. Both showed their belief in the book from early stages and helped in our quest for a publisher that shared that belief. Colin Whurr and his colleague Margaret Gallagher have been a pleasure to work with.

Finally, the ABP will benefit from the sale of this book as the royalties will be assigned to the Association. The authors have thereby levered the gift they have made to the learning community by their contribution to the book. If that gift provokes thought, encourages self-reflection, gives cause for admiration, stimulates debate, provides acknowledgement of a job well done or reminds us that we extend ourselves, in Newton's words, 'by standing on the shoulders of giants', it will have been well received.

Pauline Grant

PART 1
CONSULTING

CHAPTER 1
Introduction

PAULINE GRANT

Consultants? 'They are the people who borrow your watch to tell you what time it is and then walk off with it.' So said Robert Townsend (1970). This oft-quoted and, let's face it, frankly derogatory view of consultants makes one wonder why anyone employs them and, even more surprisingly, why anyone would choose to become one. Consultants provide professional advice for a fee. If it's as transactional as that, why all the fuss about building relationships? Well, the fact is that, just as medical consultants would regard the job as incomplete if they just provided advice, so business consultants generally intervene as well as proffer guidance. They are valued for the results they contribute to as well as, and perhaps more than, the accuracy of their opinions. I could obtain the same advice from two sources but might only value it from one. That's the one I'd work with. That's the one I'd trust to care enough to help me make it work.

It is not always apparent why we are chosen for some assignments and yet miss other opportunities. It can take courage and, of course, time – time that we might prefer to spend on the work we have to deliver, to collect feedback and discover what went wrong. Often this reveals that the initial conversation has changed clients' thinking and that what they now want to do is substantially different from what they originally said. Wouldn't it therefore be preferable to concentrate on having the kind of relationship that allows us to engage in conversations during this time of shifting sands and moving goal posts?

One of the first pieces of work I successfully pitched for, over a cup of tea at a Little Chef with a human resources director I hadn't previously met, was won not because of what I knew, but because I was honest about not knowing. The human resources director had already received proposals from other potential providers but had felt they were dealing with things at a level that was too superficial. The neat, stepwise processes they were suggesting made logical sense but didn't convince her that they would bring the required change in her environment. She was therefore more attracted by the idea of a starting point that allowed time to get to know the organization and the people.

Whether working internally as an employee of an organization or as an externally commissioned consultant, business psychologists use their expertise as psychologists in an organizational environment. This might seem obvious but I have had many discussions with colleagues about whether we are being psychologists when we work and why what *we* do is special and different from people with expertise in different areas. The reality is that the best business psychologists are being psychologists at all stages and are not restricting this expertise to either the advice or the intervention. Indeed, as psychologists we know that all our interactions, even those over tea at a Little Chef, are also interventions. This section helps all consultants benefit from taking a psychologist's perspective on their interactions with their clients.

We start this section with an overview of what clients want, offered by business psychologists who are effectively poachers turned gamekeepers – Mead and Robinson are consultants who have been on the client side and have substantial experience of commissioning external experts. They offer an insight into clients' requirements. All consultants would benefit from attending to this. Their analysis allows us to understand why some consultant–client relationships work well and others flounder, and that this distinction is not always to do with expertise. Hamill then invites us to take a deep dive into the first meeting with a potential new client and helps unpack the psychological aspects of that interaction. She encourages us to reflect on the potentially different expectations that each party brings to that first meeting and offers practical guidance on how it can be managed effectively. Not surprisingly, the skills of posing questions and summarizing are of paramount importance.

McKavanagh continues with a detailed model of consulting throughout the relationship that will be of special interest to those at early stages in thinking about how they can best deal with clients, or indeed those who tend to muddle through without a coherent framework. She shares experiences of dilemmas and pitfalls that can derail otherwise effective consulting interventions, and provides guidance in avoiding them. We follow this with Loftus's view of the consulting relationship, which provides a further stretch of thinking. He describes a three-phase model with an emphasis on building trust.

The chapter by Loftus confronts the uncomfortable reality that we sometimes let our clients down and that these occasions can be poignant moments in the relationship. I recall a time when I had let a client down and was expecting to be hauled over the coals for a mistake that was likely to have unfortunate ripple effects. Instead, I was met with a mature 'these things happen' response and appreciation of the way I'd handled revealing the error to them. The relationship was actually strengthened by this event. Loftus's realistic, business-minded overview importantly covers endings as well as beginnings. Finally, Clayton and Bentley provide a thought-provoking discourse that helps us to challenge assumptions and work with organizations as they are and consult in a way that allows authentic dialogue to form the basis of interventions. They remind us that self-awareness is an important component of successful consulting and that there will be some clients we might appropriately decide we should not work with.

We make no apology for the inevitable overlap in the models that different experienced consultants have derived to drive their practice. Indeed, the fact that such overlap exists in the thinking of people who have arrived at their *modus operandi* independently gives some comfort. However, the different nuances and emphases are also of interest and you will find that you have been offered some options. These options are generously described by people who have undergone the pain of learning from experience as well as doing the legwork to discover what they now consider the best approach. Perhaps it is too obvious to say that following their recipes for success carries no guarantee, but skilled consultants who have the potential and motivation to provide a truly valuable service for their clients, and indeed clients who want the best from their consultant relationships, might reflect on how this potential can be wasted by failing to attend to some of the messages in this section.

CHAPTER 2
What clients want

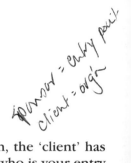

CHARLES MEAD, RACHEL ROBINSON

When delivering business psychology to an organization, the 'client' has to be defined at two levels. First, there is the individual who is your entry point into the organization. This person should perhaps more accurately be referred to as the 'sponsor'. The client is also the organization in which the sponsor is given the licence to operate, whether that is a department, subsidiary or whole company.

As two former sponsors who now work as business psychologists, we thought it would be useful to share our experiences of working with consultants, and in particular business psychologists, in sectors as diverse as pharmaceuticals, fine arts and financial services. We have endeavoured to capture what we valued in consultants and what we looked for when appraising potential suppliers.

So what is it that sponsors look for? Ultimately we were looking for, and subsequently engaged, those consultants who we were convinced would deliver successful assignments. Consultants who deliver have the capacity to enhance the client sponsor's reputation and credibility as well as their own in the process. The real measure of success for the consultant is to be asked back to do more, hopefully in an even more professionally challenging context.

So what are the factors that lead to appointing consultants who can deliver successful assignments? Reflecting on our different experiences as sponsors, we realized that we used three simple criteria. We wanted business psychologists

- who have the right *capability* – the people who are the best at what they do;
- who have the right *chemistry* with us personally and with our organization – the ones who are able to work in a way that is acceptable and influential;
- in whom we had *confidence* – the people who deliver what they said they will.

These three 'C's are the basis of successful business psychologists' consulting and inform our own practice of business psychology as a basic checklist.

Capability

[handwritten annotation: "want examples...) (stories of"]

Sponsors engage consultants for what they do, what they deliver. The link between these two facets is the acid test of capability as far as the client sponsor is concerned. It is not enough for consultants to be the best psychometricians or team builders. This will probably only get them as far as the door of the sponsor's office. As sponsors we want to hear from the psychologists – and, just as important, from other sponsors they have worked for – about the results of what they have done for other organizations. We want to hear from consultants about their understanding of their client organizations, the challenges they helped their client organization frame that raised the bar in terms of the organization's performance, the judgements the consultant made, the advice given to client organizations and, most important of all, the outcome of the intervention and the benefit the organization derived from it.

Understanding

[handwritten annotation: "J Ahead the moves and compl ASK THE RIGHT ?'s."]

The sponsor wants to assess business psychologists' capability both in terms of their specialist knowledge and also their consulting skills. The skilled business psychologist should start with understanding. The initial steps in building the relationship with the sponsor are as much about asking the right questions as sharing information about previous assignments. It is difficult for business psychologists to frame their professional knowledge and ability unless they build understanding both of the business issues with which the sponsor is dealing and the related organizational context – and test that understanding as they go. In terms of demonstrating capability, the sponsor wants to hear the right questions rather than any answers. They want to be sure a consultant understands the unique requirements of their organization and that the consultant gives due consideration to what are often complex, personal and sensitive assignments.

Ability to challenge

The second important capability that we looked for in consultants was the ability to challenge us. Sponsors do not want consultants who will tell them what they already know or what they think they want to hear. The best consultants are those who will give us what we don't already know, or don't want to know, as a means to creating a more effective organization. Part of the business psychologist's contribution is to leverage their experience about what is necessary, what is realistic and what is best practice. The best consultants will help their sponsors to think more clearly about the issues they face and help them identify new opportunities to move their organizations forward.

Making judgements

The final element of consulting capability that we looked for in the best consultants was the ability to make judgements about the organization and the issues as a start point for developing solutions and the quality of their advice as to what their solutions might be. Business psychologists need to demonstrate their judgement in offering hypotheses about key factors at work in the organization as well as a range of models, experience, techniques and advice about potential solutions. Consultants who lack opinions, who are reluctant to offer an hypothesis or who present pre-packaged nostrums and conventional solutions clearly do not add the value that justifies their fees!

What our experience suggests about the best business psychologists is that their professional capability is not enough. They possess a parallel capability as consultants based on skills in understanding, challenging and making judgements about the sponsor's business that they exercise from the first time they meet their potential sponsor.

Chemistry

If capability gets a consultant to the door of the sponsor, then it is the chemistry they create between themselves and the sponsor that leads to them being asked back. In particular, great consultants are shrewd about how they build and manage relationships, initially with their sponsor and subsequently with the organization at large. If the client enjoys working with them and the consultants enjoy working with the client, then the chemistry is right. Consultants will do their best work when they are enjoying it.

For a business psychologist this is the key opportunity to demonstrate a core capability – the ability to read other people. In our experience the best consultants read us, our interests and needs, from the word 'go'. They formed hypotheses about our personal needs and, when confirmed, use these hypotheses as the basis for building the relationship and going forward. The most impressive consultants make the terms of the relationship explicit. They create a contract with their client, characterizing the

Make terms of relationship clear & explicit

relationship in specific terms and reviewing the progress of the relationship against that contract. This ensures that both parties know where they stand at any time.

As sponsors, we also considered chemistry at a second level, namely the chemistry between the consultant and the organization at large. The best consultants managed the politics of organizations in an open and realistic manner. Three indications of the consultants' ability to do this emerge early in the consulting relationship.

Research reputation & performance of org'n

- First, the best consultants share their observations of the organization and its dynamics early in the relationship. Well-briefed consultants will have started researching this subject before the initial meeting. They *offer* will have some view about the dynamics of the organization based on *Observa-* the reputation and current performance of the client and their experi- *tions.* ence of similar organizations. They will offer their observations as hypotheses early in order to check them. In our experience as business psychologists, organizations are fascinated by objective, outside perceptions of them and intrigued by consultants' experience of other organizations (within the bounds of confidentiality, of course). The best consultants use this as an opportunity to build the relationship with their sponsor and client, using it at the same time to develop and check their reading of the organization's dynamics.

- The second indication is that these consultants discuss *how* the assignment will be best carried out and demonstrate real curiosity about the degree of acceptance, commitment and readiness of the wider organization to engage in the assignment. In our experience, they explore in a realistic way the opportunities and threats to the assignment with the sponsor; at first, to assess the degree of difficulty and likelihood of success of the venture and, later, to share their experience and actively manage the conduct of the assignment to ensure its success.

- Third, the best consultants mould their own approach to fit the organization. They ensure that their own behaviour is congruent with the organization's priorities and preferences. They demonstrate agility and flexibility in style, picking up on the cues of how the organization prefers to work. Getting the right chemistry does not mean solely following instructions, becoming the sponsor's best friend or compromising one's own values. Rather, it means being shrewd about the nature of the relationship required between consultant, sponsor and broader client organization and actively shaping its development.

In our experience, a key tension for business psychologists to manage is the relationship with human resources and line functions. Frequently, business psychologists have strong relationships with either line managers or human resources professionals. If introduced by the line, the human resources function can often feel usurped or threatened. If introduced by human resources, the business psychologist is dependent on the credibility and clout that human resources has with the overall business. The best business psychologists build and then maintain relationships with both and are sensitive to the power dynamic between these two parties.

Confidence

The final 'C' in what clients look for in consultants is confidence. This is the characteristic that allows them to move from the sponsor's office through the door into the wider client organization. The sponsor needs to trust and respect consultants to feel confident in referring them further into the organization. Establishing their capability with sponsors will go a long way to establishing their respect. Managing the chemistry in an open and deliberate way will establish trust. The third element required for complete confidence in a consultant is the sponsor's experience of delivery. Again, this starts early in the relationship with simple things. The sponsor will expect commitments that are made, however simple, such as returning telephone calls and making sure invoices are accurate and issued in a timely manner, to be met from the start. The key elements in establishing confidence are partnership, open communication (being 'user friendly') and self-management.

Partnership

Our experience of the best consultants was that they worked with us in partnership. The degree of confidence that we invested in consultants was in direct proportion to the extent that we felt comfortable with them as partners. Being a consultant affords the consultant the privilege of concentrating on the intervention, which is a luxury that busy sponsors and others in the client organization rarely have. In our experience, good consultants established a clear and explicit understanding of the roles they would play, also the roles of the sponsor and the role of others in the organization. So, clients look for consultants who define the partnership that is required and, once defined, deliver on their commitments as partners.

Open communication

The best consultants are easy to work with. At no time did we feel that we did not know what they were doing; at all times we had clear expectations

[handwritten margin notes: know what they're doing all the time; use know/exp of sponsor to test solution chance success]

of what they were going to deliver in both the short and the long term. If we needed something, we knew who to go to and how to get it quickly. The best consultants were open and non-judgemental with us. They shared the good news and, more importantly, the bad news when things might not be going as planned. They shared their observations and involved us in developing their judgements and solutions. And they used our experience of the organization to test and refine them.

Self-management

[handwritten margin notes: monitor own perf; have checks/measures in place; take resp.]

Again, looking at it from the sponsor's point of view, engaging a consultant is different from employing an expert. Employees require managing; they are part of the organization and have loyalties and responsibilities to others in the organization. Indeed the employee expert may become part of the problem. By contrast, consultants manage themselves and manage their clients to make their interventions run well. They monitor their own performance and have their own checks and measures in place. They take responsibility for improving performance when necessary and don't rely on their sponsor to tell them something or someone isn't working.

[handwritten note: Know bef sponsor if something isn't working]

An illustrative example

In distilling our experience of engaging consultants, including business psychologists, to produce the most important attributes of the best organization consultants above, we are struck by one overriding attribute of the best. It is their ability to tell us something normally uncomfortable to accept, difficult to hear or challenging to our self-concept or our organization in a way that gains our complete attention and ends up creating an opportunity for us or our organization, or both.

A simple example of this occurred in one of our previous organizations, where the chief executive insisted on using 360-degree feedback as part of selecting his leadership team in a major reorganization. The head of human resources (one of us!) was adamant that this was contrary to best practice in using 360-degree feedback. A standoff between CEO and head of human resources ensued. They agreed to engage a firm of business psychologists to advise them. The head of human resources interviewed three different potential consultancies who had all held the same view of best practice, which was concordant with his own. He therefore believed that they would put forward this view and recommend suitable options.

After initial discussions with the CEO, head of human resources and some of the senior executives who would be part of the selection process, the consultants presented their findings to the head of human resources. Not only were they convinced that the CEO's idea was appropriate, they had changed their position about the use of 360-degree feedback! They had found that the CEO had done such a good job in selling the concept to those who were affected that the senior executives concerned were not just reconciled to the idea – they actively welcomed it. This was uncomfortable news for the head of human resources! However, in their advice to the CEO, they were able to confirm the head of human resources' opinion about best 360-degree practice and reassure the CEO that the head of human resources was acting from professional, not personal, motives. All parties concerned adjudged the subsequent selection process a great success.

The business psychologists concerned would not have been able to manage the complex net of relationships concerned – CEO, head of human resources, senior executives – without demonstrating their capability, establishing the right chemistry and giving all parties confidence in them by displaying many of the attributes above.

CHAPTER 3

Make or break – structuring the initial meeting

ANNE HAMILL

How can a business consultant use the first meeting effectively, to create a situation where it is possible to operate strategically, adding real business value?

In first meetings with a client, each party comes to the table with different aspects of both the problem and the solution:

- Clients bring the problem, but they also know the history, the operational constraints, and the politics that are critical to producing an effective solution.
- The consultant brings professional expertise about solutions but will also often contribute to the understanding of the problem based on experience of similar situations elsewhere.

One of the most delicate of all meetings to handle is therefore the first meeting at which an issue is discussed. Business psychologists are likely to have an advantage in understanding the psychological contracting, reading body language, and so forth. However, they may not always be skilled at the confident structuring of the first meeting.

Over the years, Strategis has analysed what experienced consultants actually do to achieve successful first meetings, resulting in the following practical guidelines on how to manage expectations, achieve the task of uncovering the problem, and create the possibility of adding value through strategic reappraisal.

A common problem with initial meetings is that the consultant initiates the relationship with the client from a position of being an expert. A real-life example may illustrate this. The client (a large utility company) telephones to arrange a meeting to discuss team building in one of its regions. At the first meeting, the client says that there is an urgent need to introduce team building for a large number of people across a region in the next 2 months. It has to be done over the next 2 months due to operational constraints.

The natural expert approach to this situation is to find out as much as possible about the problem, probing to understand which team building approach might be most appropriate. However, this questioning may miss some key issues.

- The person we spoke to isn't the budget holder and decision maker but is a human resources consultant who has been delegated the task of briefing suppliers.
- A key line decision maker defines the need as being to improve cross-functional teamwork in responding to customer problems by creating '10-minute teams' of people from different areas to solve customer problems.
- The primary driver for the work is that 'improving team working' has been set as one of the objectives handed down to the regional chairman. It is therefore imperative to produce hard evidence that 'team working' has improved.
- The extremely tight deadline is only a problem if the solution involves taking large groups off line.

These critical pieces of information are much more likely to emerge if the consultant approaches the initial meeting as a business problem solver, rather than a team-building expert.

In our experience of training thousands of people from many disciplines in consultancy skills, we find that people can sometimes be *more* effective in fact finding at the first meeting when they have little expert knowledge in the problem being presented by the client.

This is because, faced with a technical problem, experts can rarely resist diving into the problem and asking a series of technical questions to find out 'Is this the problem? Is that the problem?', based on their past experience of solving similar problems. They are keen to be efficient in their questioning so they also often fail to summarize what they have learned. As a consequence, they come across as having achieved a much less solid understanding of the whole business situation and requirements.

Diagnostic exercise

Carry out this exercise to diagnose your current approach. This will enable you to identify additional ideas to add to your toolkit to make your first meetings more effective.

You receive an email (below) from a potential client, outlining a problem that she would like you to look at and requesting a meeting. Read the email, and quickly brainstorm all the questions you would ask at the first meeting. Don't try to prioritize or plan your questions – just list any questions you would want to ask, whatever the subject.

Email

I am the sales director of ABC Corporation, and I've been recommended to talk to you regarding the performance of our customer services department.

This fast-growing department employs 40 people in teams of six, who deal with their clients entirely by phone. The team leaders have been on a number of technical training courses and are highly skilled at customer service. However, I am concerned that they are spending too much time on the phones, joining in with the work of their teams, and not enough time managing. Can you help?

Write down all the questions that you would ask at the first meeting.

Questioning at the first meeting *Incorporate Here*

The objective of the first meeting is to get an outline of the technical problem, but equally importantly, to clarify the parameters within which the problem must be solved. There will be other chances to explore the technical detail, after you have discovered key information about the nature of the overall project.

Over 20 years, we have built up a bank of questions that experienced consultants have found useful when taking a brief. These cover six key areas of ambiguity that must be probed at the first meeting:

- the nature of the problem;
- preferences about the solution;
- resources;
- stakeholders;
- the client relationship;
- practicalities.

The nature of the problem

This is the background to the situation – what is currently happening, why this is a problem, and what the client is trying to achieve. *If you don't probe this well, you will be in danger of offering an inappropriate solution.*

If you completed the diagnostic exercise, work out what percentage of your questions fell into this category. In a one-hour first meeting a good guideline is to spend 30 to 40 minutes probing the nature of the problem but, critically, the remaining time should be spent probing the other five areas of ambiguity. You may like to consider whether the distribution of your questions reflects this time split. Probing the nature of the problem includes questions like:

1. Why is the department growing fast?
2. What is the nature of the calls the customer service team is handling?
3. When do the supervisors become involved, and why?
4. What performance measures do you have?
5. What training have the teams had?
6. What managerial training have the team leaders had?
7. Are the team leaders aware of what you want them to do?
8. Are the teams aware of what the team leaders should be doing?
9. Is staffing adequate?
10. How can there be 40 people in teams of six?

Note that some of these are relatively closed questions with an expert bias (numbers 5 to 9) – the consultant has a hypothesis and is asking these questions to test 'Is this the problem? Is that the problem?'.

In contrast, many of the most useful questions posed by experienced consultants can be applied to almost any business problem in a range of disciplines, because they are open questions addressing these situations. For example:

• Why do you want to take this initiative?
• What is your overall aim in doing this project?
• What problems are you aiming to solve?
• How did you become aware there was a problem?
• Can you give me some examples of the kind of problems that are arising?
• What are the main business drivers for tackling this issue?
• Apart from (xyz), are you hoping to address any other issues at the same time?

Preferences about solutions

These include what has already been tried, what clients have in mind and why, and what they don't think would work and why. *If you don't probe this, you will have trouble selling your ideas because you will be uninformed about the client's existing thinking about solutions.*

• In the ideal world, what sort of result would you want?
• What solutions have you already tried? What did you think of those solutions?

- Have you seen any approaches that you liked? What did you like about them?
- Have you seen any approaches that you didn't like? What did you dislike about them?
- How complex/perfectionist/hi-tech do you want the result to be – Rolls-Royce or Mini?

Many consultants do not probe to discover their clients' ideas about solutions because they know from bitter experience that this may lead them into a situation where every stakeholder has firm views on what the solution should look like. The project then becomes a hotly debated compromise with little freedom for real strategic input or innovative solutions.

Stakeholders with very different ideas on the solution

There is a very simple way of using questions to find out clients' ideas about solutions while opening up their minds to new possibilities and obtaining permission to come up with very different solutions. This is to get them to talk about their ideas for a solution, and then ask 'why?' – to find the underlying reasons for preferring this solution. *focus on reasons*

In recording clients' or stakeholders' success criteria it is very important to record the underlying reasons, not the methodology they suggest. In this way, you can create freedom to think strategically by removing the need to negotiate between two mutually incompatible methodologies.

Stakeholder A: 'I think we should produce a "train-the-trainer" pack so that the managers can train their direct reports.'
Stakeholder B: 'I think we should create an expert system on the intranet that the manager and staff member can work through together.'

By focusing on why the stakeholders prefer these methodologies, we can move to:

Stakeholder A: 'It is important that line managers are seen as owning the process and take responsibility for making it work.'
Stakeholder B: 'It is important that the message is put across consistently.'

The consultant should also ask a specific question – 'So you would be happy to consider other solutions, as long as part of the process is that managers demonstrate their ownership of the process to their direct reports?' This creates much more freedom for the consultant to offer new, strategic solutions. When documenting (see the discussion of the project brief, below) it is the reasons, and not the methods, which should be recorded as the criteria of success.

Resources

Time, money (how much and whose budget?) and operational constraints on solutions. *If you do not probe here, you will not be able to create an effective solution, as you have little understanding about what resources are fixed and what is negotiable.*

- Do you have a budget allocated for this? Who is the budget holder/decision maker?
- Can you give me an idea of the budget limitations I need to work within?
- What is your deadline for a finished product? What are the reasons for this?
- Is there any leeway in the deadline? Can a solution be introduced in two stages – a prototype, then a final product?
- How much time can I spend on this – my time, your time, other people's time?
- Are there any operational constraints I need to be aware of in proposing solutions?
- Scale/quantity – how many will be required?

Stakeholders

These are the people who initiated or are driving the project and anyone who needs to be consulted, approve of the result, provide information, or change the way he or she works. When considering stakeholders one also needs to take into account other organizational initiatives that may be taking place, which your project needs to reinforce. *Failure to probe here is the most common cause of projects stalling or failing to be implemented. You need to know all the stakeholders so that you can involve them from the first day and ensure that their criteria of success are built into the solution, otherwise you will later find yourself trying to sell your solution to key stakeholders who may not buy in.*

- Who initiated this project, and why? Who is driving it?
- Who will use the system?
- Who else will the system affect?
- Who will need to provide help or information for the project to be successful?
- Who else would you like me to involve?
- Is there anyone else who needs to be pleased with the solution?
- Are there any sensitivities I should be aware of?
- Do you foresee any problems in introducing this project?
- How does this project need to fit in with other initiatives?

Client relationship

The role of the client and the consultants in the project, reporting methods, working methods and guidelines. *Probing this area will enable you to establish an effective working relationship right from the start, rather than learning by your mistakes.*

- How do you see your own role in this project? How do you see my role?
- How do you like people to run projects for you – what do you like? What do you dislike?
- Can you give me any guidelines about how you would like me to work with you?
- How shall I communicate with you? Email/phone/formal report? How often?

Immediate practicalities

You need to consider the next steps. What type of proposal is required? By when? What is the date of the next meeting? What are the deliverables for that meeting? *This will give you instant credibility by ensuring that your first steps are error free.*

- What priority does this work have, compared to other work I am doing for you?
- Can we agree the action plan for the next steps? (Suggest a course of action, including writing up a project brief with criteria of success from this interview, an outline of any investigative work to be taken with other stakeholders, and a time for delivering a proposal/plan.)
- What type of proposal do you want – a short note with key ideas for your eyes only, or a longer and more detailed proposal that you can use to persuade others? If the latter, who needs to be persuaded, and what are their 'hot buttons'?
- When shall we next meet? (Suggest an agenda for the next meeting.)

Creating strategic solutions

Another important issue in first meetings is how to create the space and time to consider what the consultant needs to create a strategic solution. Consultants must address the client's expectation that they will come up with solutions at the first meeting.

If you feel that you have to provide instant solutions, half of your attention will be on 'What am I going to suggest?' rather than on 'What is the larger business framework within which the problem must be solved?'.

Moreover, if you provide instant solutions you will almost never provide innovative, strategic solutions because these require reflection. Instead, you are likely to pull rabbits out of the hat – rabbits you had in your hat before you came to the meeting.

Before and at the initial meeting, experienced consultants create a clear agreement with the client that the initial meeting will be used to establish a full understanding of the business problem, with ideas for solutions coming later. This allows you to create the opportunity to take the problem away, think about it, challenge assumptions, and redefine the problem to provide the best possible solution. This is the root of strategic consultancy.

Giving yourself time to think also allows you to consult a range of technical experts back at base. If necessary, you can bring these technical experts into later conversations with your client.

Unfortunately, most clients expect to hear solutions at the first meeting. This meets an emotional need to test the consultant's credibility and to feel that progress has been made. Managing clients' expectations is only the first step. We also have to meet their emotional need for a sense of progress.

Creating a sense of progress for the client

While consultants spend the first meeting questioning, and feel a sense of progress because of greater understanding, clients often feel that they have just been going over a problem they have been living with for some time.

The easiest way for the client to feel progress is to agree a solution that the consultant will then implement. However, at this stage we don't want to commit ourselves to a solution. What if we go and talk to another stakeholder, and find out that the picture is far more complex than the client has represented it?

We need a way to gain credibility with clients and make them confident that we have taken up the challenge, and that we are now going to take action to resolve the problem.

Consultants can gain great credibility in the first meeting through the quality of their listening and questioning. Our objective should be to ask good questions (ones that may cause clients to think through issues that they have not considered). We should also summarize the problem very effectively. Our summary must be concise and must mention the key issues – the real heart of the problem.

The skill of taking effective notes and delivering an accurate summary of the critical issues at the end of the meeting is a very powerful way to create credibility and a sense of progress for the client. This is therefore a very important foundation skill for all consultants.

Having impressed the client by our grasp of the situation, we now need to impress him or her with our action orientation. It may not be desirable to write a proposal immediately because it may be essential to check the views of key stakeholders and understand their criteria of success before proposing a solution.

We have found that a useful strategy is to ensure that, within 24 hours, there is an email or one-page document on their desk that summarizes:

- *Background* to the project (with any factual information you were given – especially numbers, costs, amounts – and all the key issues outlined, expressed in a neutral way that will be acceptable to all stakeholders).
- *Criteria of success* for a solution. These need to be stated in terms that don't define the methodology (see section on stakeholders).
- *List of stakeholders* (to ensure it is complete and to remind you who must be kept in the loop).
- *Next actions* (what you will do in the following one or two weeks; what you will deliver for the next meeting).

We call this short document the *project brief*. It acts as a holding mechanism, creating a feeling of instant progress for the client while providing time to talk to other stakeholders (involving them from the start, so that their criteria of success are elicited before the solution is designed). It also provides a breathing space that increases the chance of creating a strategic solution that really adds business value.

As an external consultant, this project brief may be a summary email sent after a meeting, with the proposal sent a week or two later. It may be necessary to arrange a second meeting or a telephone conversation with the decision makers before the proposal can be developed. If this is not possible, the proposal will obviously need to make provision for consultation before design and delivery takes place.

Summary

In summary, then, some of the key skills in managing initial meetings successfully lie in

- taking a broad approach to business problem solving (leaving technical detail until later);
- ensuring that all suggested methodologies are probed by asking 'why?' to reveal the underlying criteria of success;
- managing client expectations;
- establishing a sense of progress for the client (through summarizing and a project brief).

CHAPTER 4

The consulting project lifecycle

SIOBHAN MCKAVANAGH

Synopsis

There are a number of factors at play during key stages along the consulting project lifecycle that have particular relevance for the business psychologist working in an organization. Practical experience is used to highlight techniques alongside the critical skills, experience and insight that business psychology lends to the consulting process, from securing work through to delivery and the ongoing management of the relationship.

Introduction

Within a business context, a simple definition of consultancy might be 'helping an organization solve a business problem or make an improvement'. This is typically in the form of a project with agreed outcomes and an expectation of completion within an agreed time frame. Projects can be delivered by either an internal or an external source; if help is externally sourced, a commercial contract typically underpins the project relationship. A great deal of research has been carried out on the factors that contribute to the successful delivery of projects within organizations – see Kotter (1996) for a synopsis of the key issues. Within this, it is widely recognized, and personal experience backs this up, that dealing with the 'human factor' is one of the key risk areas to be managed in any project – see also Bridges (2003) for another very helpful perspective in dealing with the human factor during change. In relation to this, business psychologists can get involved in a wide range of projects from discrete interventions on specific areas such as training or assessment through to advising on the organizational and people issues involved in implementing wide-scale organizational change.

Why organizations use consultants

As the consulting market has grown and matured, consultancies (in-house and external) and the organizations that engage their services have become increasingly adept at managing the relationship between them, not only commercially but also on how best to make use of externally sourced expertise.

Organizations use consultants for a variety of reasons:

* to access specific knowledge, experience and/or expertise;
* to bring outside challenge and fresh perspective to a business issue;
* to plug a resourcing gap within their own available resources.

As consultants, business psychologists typically find themselves engaged in client situations involving a strong element of organizational change (e.g. changes to working practice, from who does what through to how the work is done). They can be hired to provide specific technical expertise, for example selection and development of talent, designing new organizations and jobs, and so on. They can be hired to provide broader organizational development support, working with the organization as a coach/facilitator to jointly diagnose a given business issue and identify potential ways forward. They can also be brought in to help realize a change in business strategy, advising on the people and organizational consequences of that change and how to implement new ways of doing things.

In organizational settings, business psychologists work independently, with colleagues or as a member of a multidisciplinary team, providing specific expertise on organizational and people issues. Irrespective of the way in which the support is provided, work that has a heavy 'people' element, not surprisingly, can often be particularly challenging to implement and can create some interesting ethical dilemmas to be managed, some of which are described below.

Some consulting 'dilemmas'

Consider the following real-life situations.

You have been commissioned to carry out a staff opinion survey across an organization. You have taken all the necessary steps up front to ensure that the survey objectives are well communicated and have the visible endorsement of senior management. You've also ensured that senior managers are well aware of the potential for the survey to result in some unfavourable feedback but that this can be handled effectively as part of the communications process. As it turns out, the survey results are much more negative than you – and indeed the management group – had been hoping for. They want to pull the communications plan. What would you do?

Take another example. You have been working with company x for a few months on an organization development programme. This has involved you working with a number of senior managers. You think that you have established good working relationships with them all and they have been very open in sharing their views with you about what the issues are and what the business needs to do to create change. The chief executive calls you in after a meeting towards the end of your work there – he would like your opinion on his team and has in mind a need to do some restructuring to 'weed out some of the weaker players'. He knows that you have grown to know them all quite well. Providing this type of feedback wasn't part of your brief – or so you thought. What would you do?

These examples involve issues of role clarity and role boundaries as well as the more obvious issues around project scope and objectives. They highlight the 'softer' implicit aspects of the consulting relationship, which, unless carefully handled, can lead to conflict and unhelpful tension in your working relationship with that client and damage to your professional reputation.

Managing the dynamics of the consulting project lifecycle

Figure 4.1 sets out the typical stages involved in securing and delivering a consulting project, whether that's done as an internal resource or as an

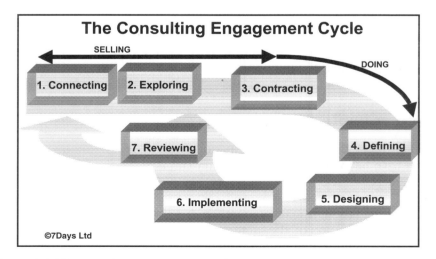

Figure 4.1 The consulting engagement cycle.

external one. This model, which we use within 7Days to capture the key stages of the consulting experience, is also intended to show that the process is holistic: the activities and processes involved in finding work are closely integrated with project implementation.

In practice, of course, there are many variations around this core process: different organizations may use different labels to describe the steps involved, there may be different entry points (for example, you may be engaged to deliver a new piece of work on the back of a previous project, you may be competing with others for the work, or you may move straight to implementation for a project involving more prescriptive methods such as psychometric testing).

The following paragraphs set out the main dynamics at play during each of these stages, covering explicit content as well as the underpinning psychological process and suggested tactics for successfully working through them.

Finding work – Selling

Assuming you've defined the range of services that you intend to offer to prospective clients, at the highest level finding work starts with marketing those services to create initial interest, targeting prospective 'buyers' for what you are offering and then homing in on a specific opportunity, ideally culminating in a project contract. At this point, particularly where a prospective client has issues but lacks ideas on the way forward for addressing them, you may be collaborating to create and shape the project. Alternatively, clients may have defined the problem and know what they want to do to address it. For external consultants in particular, this can involve competing with others to win the work.

Building relationships – Connecting

This is a typical starting point. It involves establishing and nurturing contacts through networking or referrals and then building a positive relationship with those individuals. Your intention going into this phase is to build rapport, trust and respect, particularly in the context of building a peer-to-peer professional relationship (a more transactional approach can be used if you are offering discrete, product-type support, as long as professional standards and ethical practices are still adhered to, to protect your reputation and, for external consultants, your brand). Particularly where the relationship is new, there is a fine balance to be maintained between 'promoting' the support you can provide and how it would benefit the organization but avoiding 'hard sell' sales tactics. When you peel back the layers of the securing work process, clients tend to want to work with people they like and with whom they are able to establish strong rapport. Aggressive selling can interfere with this process.

Table 4.1 Specific tactics

Where the client is	Tactics	Watch out for
Not sure if they have a problem or if what you are offering is of interest as a potential solution	• Exploring their current business situation, threats and opportunities • Sharing insights from your experience • Encouraging disclosure – 'tell me more about' • Suggesting potential ways forward: light touch, 'food for thought' • Collaborative approach, on the assumption that the organization has, if elicited through skilled facilitation, the inherent capability to identify and resolve its own issues	• Pushing a solution too early in the discussion • Selective hearing • Assuming you are talking to the person who has the ability to purchase • Dragging the 'exploring' discussions on for too long
Have a clearly defined problem they'd like help in addressing	• Fact-finding questioning style • Understanding the drivers for doing something – what will create concern/inspire excitement • Providing content on potential approaches, methods • Assertive and authoritative advice on the way forward – more likely to be the case that you are offering a defined solution, for example training versus offering a process for getting to the right solution, for example workshop-based organization design	• Being overly prescriptive on what the best way forward may be • Proposing an approach that only deals with symptoms not the underlying problem • Balancing expertise and prior experience with open mindedness
Responding to a future opportunity or potential threat – may or may not have formed their ideas on a response	• As above, but with greater emphasis on helping them lay out the potential consequences of the situation facing them – problem solving and analytical skills	• As above • An expertise-driven approach may be more relevant here versus a process-driven approach, particularly if the time frames for taking action are tight

Relationships can be built in a number of ways. There are the more straightforward aspects of relationship building that need to be effectively handled. Can you effectively build and maintain a network of contacts? Do you have effective interpersonal skills that enable you to interact well with others? And so on. Beyond this there are some specific tactics that can be helpful to you depending on where the client is starting from. These are outlined in Table 4.1.

Establishing need – Exploring

Establishing a need for consulting support is one of the desired outcomes from building an effective relationship. (Obviously you can dive straight into this phase if you are known to the organization, you are recommended by someone else or if they approach you directly.) The challenge here is to keep an open dialogue, with a clear eye on directing that dialogue to reach an agreement to carry out a piece of work. Across this spectrum of situations, well-developed questioning, problem-solving and listening skills are essential to maintain rapport, trust and respect. There is also a range of consulting styles that you can draw on to create effective interaction with the prospective client. A number of these are summarized in Table 4.2.

?g; prob solving; listening; analytical?

Table 4.2 Consulting styles

Style	Benefits	Risks
Reflective, listening	• Encourages clients to talk and hence helps you find out as much as possible about their issues in order to effectively respond • Some people like the opportunity to talk to an 'outsider'; can build trust and rapport	• Difficulty in narrowing in on an opportunity; time wasting • Missed opportunity to specify how you could help
Advice giving	• Demonstration of expertise and experience; show how you can help, where you've done it before • Suits task-oriented individuals • Works for clients who think they know what the problem is and just want it dealt with	• Home in too quickly on what you can 'sell'; may not fully get at underlying concerns • Can sell a quick fix
Directive, confrontational	• Demonstrate your experience, expertise and insight into the client situation, issues and so forth • Can work in crisis situations	• Client doesn't like being challenged, even if your points are valid

In practice, the style you adopt will depend on a number of factors:

- Fit with the other person's style (you can quickly pick up clues on this from your early interactions with them).
- Fit with your own preferred style.
- If you work as part of a team of consultants, internally or externally, fit with the preferred 'house style' (which is usually addressed as part of the recruitment process).

As with any application of style, some of these will more closely fit your preferred way of operating than others (your comfort zone). It is best to be as authentic as possible in how you deal with others; having a broad repertoire of styles to draw on, however, will enable you to be more adept at dealing with different situations. Explicitly communicating your consulting style/preferred way of working – for example, by describing how you typically like to work and the principles and values that you adhere to – can also help you to find work, particularly in a competitive situation or where the organization is a sophisticated (experienced) buyer of consultancy and may have had some prior poor experiences. The following is an example of how this might be:

Our approach to working with clients can be characterized as . . .

Pragmatists not purists – real people, real scars.

Focused on getting the right results – supported by, but not religious about, a robust methodology and tools (which we leave behind).

Expert – insights based on a blend of theory and real practical experience.

Commercial and flexible – sensitive to the commercial drivers in your business and able to work with changing needs and flex our involvement according to where you're at.

© 7Days Ltd

Contracting

The successful conclusion of this phase of work is the agreement to deliver a specific project – *contracting*. If you are externally hired, this typically means creating a commercial contract: what will be delivered, for what reasons (the business benefits), for what cost and how, including explicit reference to how much effort it will take to deliver, typically covering both your effort as a consultant as well as the effort you also expect the client to invest. Ideally, if the initial relationship-building phase has gone well, this step almost becomes automatic in the sense of confirming and finalizing an agreed commitment to work together.

As well as this tangible content, it is also useful to consider the implicit nature of the contract between both parties (the psychological contract). It involves coming to a mutual agreement about a transaction: *as a client, I want you to do X; I expect you to do that in this way, for a cost and by when; as a consultant, I commit to delivering you the desired result, assuming you provide me with the working conditions I have stated I need in order to carry out my role successfully.*

Delivering work – Doing

This includes *defining, designing* and then *implementing* the work (the *what* and *how* of what you are being commissioned to deliver and what will be achieved as a result). Delivery technically marks the end of the finding work process but clearly becomes the next step in the relationship you are actively building with a particular organization or individual.

Defining

Δ Issues: Ambiguous. Contentious. politically fraught.

This is primarily about project planning. Often described as scoping, it includes: agreeing desired outcomes, objectives, major activities and tasks and an estimate of the effort required to deliver the project. A version of this will typically have been created as part of the contracting phase. It is highly recommended that you ensure that you still build in a 'defining' step before you become involved in the detailed delivery of the project itself. This is particularly critical if your work will have a significant organizational impact or where you have had little opportunity during the selling process to really get under the skin of the organization to figure out what the issues and business drivers are. This risk is particularly likely in organizational change projects, where you may be dealing with ambiguous, contentious and politically fraught organization cultures.

It is important to ensure that there is as little ambiguity as possible about what you are being asked to do, for what purpose and, for example, how many people you expect to involve, the methods you will use, and so forth. The scoping piece of work typically starts during the securing work (selling) process. This is a critical stage to get right – poorly scoped projects are a major source of risk for both the consultant and the buyer of consulting support. From a risk-management point of view it is highly desirable, particularly for a complex and/or poorly defined business problem, to revisit and confirm the agreed scope of work at the start of the project before committing to details about the design and implementation of your recommended solution. It also gives clients the opportunity to drive the pace at which they take on external support – particularly, if they are hesitant about engaging support.

At this stage it is also possible that a mutually agreed decision may be taken not to proceed with the project. This can happen if you discover unanticipated risks, a lack of willingness or capacity within the wider organization to provide necessary support for the initiative, or even a realization that the client's expectations are unrealistic and cannot be met satisfactorily. Obviously, as argued above, this should ideally be addressed during the contracting process. Sometimes, however, you may find yourself in a situation where you are delivering a piece of work that may have been poorly scoped or the information you gathered during scoping isn't the full picture. Unless there is an opportunity to rescope, for example, do less if there are real time constraints, it's generally advisable to agree not to proceed (unless you want to invest the time to build the relationship; if you proceed on this basis, you will still need to ensure that you can deliver the project to quality standards).

It is highly likely that you will need to revisit some of these assumptions as you really start to 'touch' the organization during implementation. This is very likely to be the case when you are involved in organizational change projects, as you start to navigate through the political, emotional as well as logical/rational factors at play within the organization. This requires skills in influencing and persuading, managing power and politics and conflict resolution.

Setting boundaries

Another critical aspect of the project consulting relationship is the setting of clear role boundaries between yourself and the organization and individuals with whom you are interacting. This is particularly relevant for the type of work in which business psychologists will tend to find themselves involved – implementing organizational change. For change to be realized in an effective and sustainable way, individuals top to bottom and across the organization typically have to adapt new ways of working. This can be initially facilitated by external consultants but care must be taken to ensure that the changes are fully adopted by the organization, avoiding the risk of dependency on the consultant. Being an 'outsider' gives the consultant a stronger mandate to challenge, coach and advise on behavioural change. Being too much on the outside, however, can hamper your ability to build the necessary preconditions of trust, rapport and respect. Being too much of an 'insider' – particularly, a risk with long-term relationships or where you have the 'ear' of senior leaders – can mean you lose the incentive and motivation to challenge and confront and can contribute to client dependency issues.

Applying a systems thinking perspective to the concept of role boundaries illustrates the dynamic to be maintained between being both an effective partner with the organization, working collaboratively to achieve results, whilst also maintaining appropriate distance from the politics and 'machinations' of how the business works day to day (see Figure 4.2).

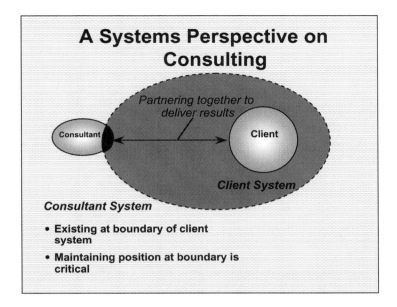

Figure 4.2 A systems perspective on consulting.

Consider the answers
to these in putting
together the proj. plan

Designing

This is the next step in the process. It includes the specific *AND*
content/approach/methodology of how you will carry out the project work. *quest'q*
You will very likely have introduced this during the 'finding work' stage; at *process*
this point, the focus for your efforts is on refining and adapting your desired
approach to the specific constraints and context you find at the client organization. The range of questions you need to ask here includes:

- How will those who are affected by the change participate in the
  process?
- How will the resources involved in the project be structured?
- What are the priorities and sequence for implementing the activities
  within the project?
- Are the roles and responsibilities defined and understood by those
  who are affected by the intended change? *← ?*
- Is there a structured process for communicating management's expectations to all employees?
  ?

Implementing the work

This is the next stage in the consulting project lifecycle. From a risk-
management point of view, particularly for big impact and/or lengthy

build in Cback *+ ask up*
in points - *Front -*
free it
contract'
content

projects, decision points can also be built in along the way to gauge client commitment and readiness to proceed. Implementation will also vary according to the nature of the work you are delivering but will typically include the following steps:

- *Mobilizing the organization:* how the organization's resources will be structured and involved in the project. You will need to form a view on what this will encompass during the contracting and defining work stage but, at this point, you move into more direct contact with the organization. For a discrete piece of work this can be limited to interacting with a small number of people; for larger-scale projects you will need to engage with a wider range of people, from those who will work with you to deliver the project to those who will ultimately be impacted by whatever your project purpose is. This doesn't mean that you need to assume responsibility for managing these audiences, but you would wish to recommend an approach to handling them that ensures the project runs satisfactorily.
- *Defining the gap between current state and future state.*
- *Designing how to fill the gap.*
- *Planning the detailed implementation of the agreed solution.*
- *Rolling out the agreed solution.*

A key aspect of project delivery is the management of risk – every organization within which you are attempting to create a change will have a unique set of risks that, unless identified and managed, have the potential to significantly delay or impede the successful delivery of your project. For example, I was involved in working with an organization on a project to restructure its UK operation. The work was seen to be highly sensitive and time critical. Balancing our preference for collaborative organization design with the business's desire to minimize distraction to the workforce during this time of uncertainly, we agreed to work with a small core team of executives in a closed working space and at rapid pace. The approach worked but also created the risk that the organization would encounter staff resistance when it came to rolling out the detailed design. During mobilization, an implementation approach was agreed that created a high level of staff involvement to mitigate this risk.

?" How are *you going to* *manage the* *environment* *change ?*

From a systems thinking perspective, during the implementation phase of the project, particularly for work that involves a significant organizational impact, the approach needs to include how you intend to handle organizational change. From a consultant perspective, specifically, there are some tools and techniques based on theories of how power and influence works in organizations that provide helpful guidance on how to handle this effectively in order to manage resistance and secure commitment to your solution.

RES:

McClelland and Burnham (2003) provide background reading in this area:

- Be clear about what it is you are trying to accomplish (project goals).
- Identify who is most impacted by your solution. Which individuals are influential and important in you achieving your goal?
- Assess perceptions and perspectives. What are their points of view likely to be? Where do you think they are coming from? How will they feel about what you are trying to do? What have they got to lose?
- Assess *their* power base. What is it based on – for example, positional power, access to resources, 'closeness' to the CEO? Which of these is more critical to them?
- Assess *your* power base. What are your bases of power and influence (this can be a challenge or an advantage if you are an outsider to the organization)? What bases can you develop to gain more control over the situation?
- Tactics. Which of the various strategies and tactics for exercising power seem most appropriate and are likely to be effective, given the situation you're faced with? How best to act?

Finishing – Reviewing

This is the final stage in the consulting project lifecycle. The ultimate goal of any consulting intervention is to deliver a desired outcome in the target organization. Although it is an important marker, achieving what you've specified in your project plan does not necessarily mean the same thing as delivering the desired outcome. This is a subtle but important distinction. Ideally, particularly if you are in the business of selling your services as an outside contractor, the desired end-game should also be the establishment of a positive and sustainable working relationship with the organization. Within this context, client satisfaction is a key measure of success, covering not only agreement that the project has been delivered to agreed specifications and outcomes, but also that the experience of getting there has been satisfactorily handled – and even enjoyed!

Conclusion

Relationship management skills are key to being a successful consultant and are an integral part of the project lifecycle. These skills carry forward from the initial stages of agreeing a specific project through to the successful delivery of that project, ensuring that expectations are continuously managed along the way. Looking back at the consulting dilemmas highlighted in the introduction they are also a way to ensure that, where possible, any such 'dilemmas' are anticipated and addressed as part of the contracting process. Where this isn't possible, at least there will be a clear project framework in place within which these challenges can be raised and ideally resolved in a constructive, pragmatic, mutually satisfactory and collaborative way. To conclude, Figure 4.3 summarizes the consulting style 'dynamic' to be managed so as to interact effectively with clients along the project consulting lifecycle.

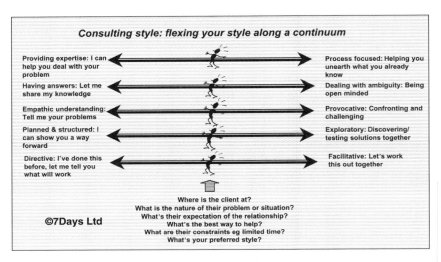

Figure 4.3 Consulting style: flexing your style along a continuum.

Recommended reading

Project management and the consulting process:

Andersen E, Grude K, Haug T (1987) Goal Directed Project Management. London: Kogan Page.
Block P (1999) Flawless Consulting. San Diego CA: Jossey Bass Wiley.
Cockman P, Evans B, Reynolds P (1998) Consulting for Real People. Maidenhead: McGraw-Hill.
Cope M (2000) The Seven Cs of Consulting. Harlow: Financial Times/Prentice-Hall.
Schein E (1988) Process Consultation: its Role in Organizational Development. Reading MA: Addison-Wesley.

Challenges of implementing organizational change:

Hammer M, Champy J (2001) Reengineering the Corporation. London: Nicholas Brealey.

CHAPTER 5
The consulting relationship

MARK LOFTUS

In the minds of many within client organizations the term 'business psychologist' can suggest a particularly unholy alliance. First, the management consultant who became one of the late twentieth century's stereotypes – shorthand for a smooth, manipulative purveyor of snake oil who would probably put close relatives for sale on eBay if offered the prospect of a meeting with senior executives in return. Second, human resources, which, as it consolidated its power base of executive remuneration and organizational downsizing, rapidly assumed the mantle of 'most feared function'. Finally, psychology, which has been almost too successful for its own good – psychologists commenting on everything from reality TV to the stress pandemic to elite athlete performance. Psychobabble commentary is rife. So when a consultant pitches up under the mantle of business psychologist, and his or her primary client base is the senior human resources community, we can be sure that consultants will need a high level of effectiveness in the way they seek to engage their clients.

The relationship becomes the primary means of both engaging with the client system and delivering the intervention. Without strong and effective relationships, the most incisive and well thought through of consulting interventions will flounder. So, the ability to create and sustain relationships with clients is one of the keys to building a successful consulting practice. This much is self-evident, and yet out of all the different kinds of relationships, the consulting relationship is one of the most difficult to get right. There are many sources of complexity, such as ambiguity about who the client is – the company that is paying the bill, or the person who is commissioning the work, or the person who will benefit from the work, or all three? And what if there are conflicts of interest between these groups? Or again, the tension between selling and consulting: we all need to sell our services, whether as internal or external consultants, but if we get this dynamic wrong, our clients can feel suspicious about whether we are selling to them or consulting to them.

The good news is that psychologists are, in many ways, ideally placed to understand and manage these complexities, given that we are typically drawn to psychology because of our interest in people and in interpersonal dynamics. My aim in this chapter is to reflect upon more than two decades of consulting experience in order to offer a guide to the important aspects of relationships.

Here are the themes I and my colleagues at OCG look to sustain our focus on.

First, the core psychology of the relationship: is the relationship characterized by trust and openness, by energy and challenge, or by emotional distance and caution? How do we create trust and deliver for our client whilst ensuring that we get our needs met?

Second, how clear are we about the client system: the network of inter-relationships, each party of which may have different expectations and needs in relation to our work.

Third, the practical and real issues that will colour and cloud the relationships, such as when to sell and when to consult, handling the procurement department, dealing with key people changes within the client, or handling difficult gatekeepers.

In this chapter, I will interweave comments on the first two themes and follow with conceptual models and a number of practical suggestions gathered from our own consulting experiences.

The psychology of the consulting relationship

We use a framework developed in-house, which we call 'Relationship Q'. This evolved from an extensive research programme into the nature and development of relationships at work. Our aim was to understand what makes relationships most effective and what can be done to facilitate the rapid development of productive relationships. Over a 5-year period we studied (through interview and questionnaire, and quantitative and qualitative analyses) thousands of managerial relationships across many of our client organizations.

One of the most important aspects of this model is that it does not seek to provide a static account of relationships but rather a picture of the way in which productive relationships change over time. The core of the model suggests that it is useful to think of a 'relationship space' within which relationships move dynamically over time. The first dimension of this space tracks how transactional or emotionally based is the relationship. The second is that of trust – whether it is reinforced or risked. The third dimension relates to energy: the amount of energy and challenge that exists within the relationship. We represent the first two dimensions in Figure 5.1, and we can envisage the development of a relationship as following a figure of eight within this relationship space.

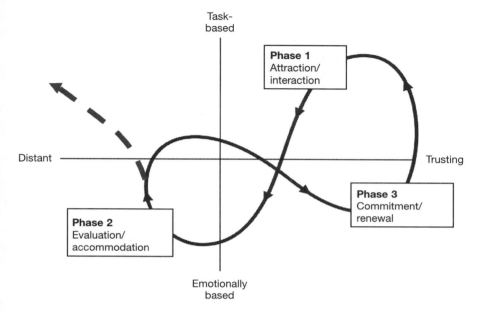

Figure 5.1 Dimensions of relationship space.

Phase 1: attraction and interaction

Typically, new relationships begin in the top right-hand quadrant (labelled Phase 1) whether they are personal, business or client relationships. In our early interactions with our client, the primary focus of the relationship will be about the task at hand but there is also often a degree of provisional trust as a basis for building rapport in the relationship.

Essentially we are trying to do two things over our early interactions. First, to tune into both the role and personal agenda of our immediate client. (What are they looking for? What would count as personal success in this piece of work? What kind of pressures and risks are they carrying?) Second, to establish an explicit 'transactional basis' for the work (to include both the commercial basis and the intended outcomes for the wider client system).

We describe this phase as 'attraction and interaction' because our evidence is that both of these dynamics need to work effectively in order for the relationship to begin to work. If we move straight to the 'interaction' without taking the time to tune in to our client, or without allowing our client to find out about us, we run the risk of shaping up interventions that will not meet their underlying needs and undermining the likelihood that a deeper level of trust can emerge within the relationship. As we engage further with the wider client system we will come to depend on a number of trusted coaches within the system who can guide us through the myriad of agendas and positions we are likely to encounter. So time spent creating the basis of mutual attraction is generally time well spent. On the other hand, if we are not sufficiently assertive about the transactional basis of the relationship, we run the risk of failing to get our needs met within the piece of work, or of failing to understand some key client expectations.

And the skills and capabilities needed? Try the following checklist of behaviours:

Do you . . .

Tuning in
Ask open, inquiring questions to get to the heart of how the other person sees the world?
Adapt your personal style and behaviour to other people?
Demonstrate understanding of their world from their point of view?
Recognize and understand underlying motives, concerns and feelings that shape the other person's behaviour?

Structuring transactions
State explicitly and realistically what can be offered and what cannot in any negotiation?
Express views and opinions backed by reasons forcefully enough to be taken seriously?
Define clear criteria by which to assess whether expectations have been met?
Not give too much too soon?
Act in an appropriately assertive way about getting your own needs met?

We need to be aware that the strongest relationships are formed when there is reciprocated incremental commitment – when an early pattern is established within the relationship of expectations clarified, commitments made and commitments met. This often happens at a mundane level (such as arranging mutually convenient meeting times and place) but the importance of generating *reciprocal* commitment is clear: all too often we can become caught in a pattern of making commitments that our client does not match, creating an imbalance in the relationship, ultimately leading to the frustration of feeling like a servant rather than offering a service as a partner.

In some situations the relationship may start in the top left quadrant where there is more suspicion and even distrust. *These can be highly challenging yet ultimately rewarding interactions.* Cognitive flexibility is our most important resource here: our ability to sustain perspective and the awareness that coolness and suspicion on behalf or our client relates to our role rather than to us personally. A strong transactional basis (clarity about expectations and commitments) becomes vital.

More commonly, we find that different elements within our client system start their relationships from different positions. For example, procurement departments very often appear to want to focus solely on the transactional basis of the relationship and, in particular, issues such as intellectual property rights, cancellation terms and travel reimbursement arrangements. It can prove challenging to sustain the awareness that these interactions are telling us important things about our client's system and how it approaches the world!

Phase 2: evaluation and accommodation

As the relationship progresses, the sense of emotional connection within it develops, although the level of trust often does not deepen significantly yet. Think of the relationship as having arrived at a stage of mutual dependency: we feel emotionally engaged but not necessarily comfortable with the sense of exposure and dependency. Yet if this sense of mutual dependency does not enter into the relationship, there is a good chance that we are not working on the right agenda – bringing about change in complex systems generally requires a level of instability being introduced into the system and it is this sense of instability that is reflected in the heightened emotional intensity of the client relationships.

Despite our best endeavours and most professional of actions, sooner or later we will let our clients down, just as they will let us down: we don't intend to, and neither do they, but it happens. When things go wrong, emotions run even more strongly, but at the same time the relationship can feel less trusting and more distant. How we and they respond to this experience will be a key determinant of whether the relationship strengthens and trust builds, or whether the relationship fragments.

In many ways, it is only when the consulting relationship goes through these more testing times that a deeper level of trust has the opportunity to grow: where each partner gets a glimpse of the humanity, fallibility and vulnerability of the other.

One of the key issues here is that we are trying to create balanced relationships of mutual commitment and it becomes as important to seek to comment upon and work through the areas where we feel that our clients have not delivered on our (hopefully explicit) expectations of them, as well as eliciting their feelings and thoughts about our delivery on their expectations. It is our belief that practitioners with a depth of psycholog-ical awareness are uniquely well placed to guide clients through these issues, and by doing so deepen their own sense of engagement with their clients immeasurably. More than this, it is often when we reflect on these experiences with our clients that we are able to help them gain new insights into the dynamics within their own organization and thereby fur-ther facilitate the change process.

And the skills and capabilities needed?

Do you . . .

Building trust/dealing with problems
Act openly and non-defensively in the face of problems?
Acknowledge when the other person's expectations have not been met?
Succeed in getting the other person to acknowledge when they have not delivered on their commitments?
Focus and build on common ground?
Devise positive outcomes for all parties?
Use problems as an opportunity to build trust?

Dealing with emotions and conflict
Actively surface tensions in the relationship?
Acknowledge emotions: your own and the other person's?
Step back from difficult situations to understand what is going on and why?
Stay positive in the face of conflict?
Demonstrate mutual interest and cooperation even in difficult circumstances?
Actively sustain contact with the other person when there are difficult problems?

Phase 3: commitment and renewal

If the difficulties and differences can be negotiated, grounded in the expe-rience of managing expectations and establishing a degree of emotional engagement, then the relationship can move towards trust – a kind of trust that is qualitatively different from that which exists early on in rela-tionships. Essentially, the move is one from trust based on assumptions (I will trust this person until I am let down) to trust based on experience (I trust this person because they have earned my trust). We can start to talk about a relationship based on mutual commitment rather than mutual dependency.

It is at this stage that arguably the consulting relationship will be at its most potent. The experience of having dealt with disappointments and

...as strengthened trust in the relationship will mean ...openness and directness in the pattern of commu- ...level of engagement between client and consultant ...act more powerfully as catalysts with the broader ...ed change. As the network of relationships that are ...plex piece of organizational consulting moves at its ...their path of development, this core consulting rela- ...a stable-base for client and consultant alike.

...at commitment, the development of the relationship ...t does, it is likely to become stale and unproductive. In ...it continues to be alive and productive the cycle is com- ...challenges and results are identified for the consulting relati... ...the process begins again. The key challenge is to recognize when this cycle is complete and either seek to disengage or to renew the relationship. If this doesn't happen, the relationship is likely to lose its catalytic potential, despite continuing as a comfortable, warm and secure relationship.

Back to skills and capabilities:

Do you . . .

Sustaining and renewing the relationship
Acknowledge changing circumstances?
Fully understand implications of changes in the other person's world?
Succeed in getting the other person to understand implications of changes in your world?
Establish fresh challenges within the relationship: move established relationships onto new levels?
Renegotiate expectations?
Create a relationship of mutual commitment?

The practicalities

There is the risk that this framework may appear to represent a counsel of perfection – one hard to follow in the pressured realities of a busy consulting life and given the commercial realities of the world we work in. To help retain a practical perspective on managing the consulting relationship, I offer the following.

1. At OCG, we have reached a view of 'sell first and then consult'. This means that we try to be quite explicit when we are selling that this is exactly what we are doing. Of course, effective sales techniques draw upon much of the same skill set as effective relationship management: most people like to be listened to and to feel that the other person has

taken the time to understand their world. Nevertheless, we have found it helpful for the transactional basis of the relationship to be explicit about when we are selling and the point at which we move into a fee-paying consulting relationship.

2. Time taken early on in the relationship to build a really clear understanding of the client's world and their expectations is rarely time wasted, even though you and your client may be facing significant pressures to swing into action as soon as possible.

3. Procurement is an increasingly important and powerful function within client organizations, whether public or private. For example, one of the significant changes widely anticipated in the public sector is that procurement will become more professional and powerful as the sector faces up to the major head-count reductions planned by the government. So one of the skills we need in creating effective relationships with our clients is to know how to handle the procurement function. Our approach at OCG is to seek to divide responsibilities amongst the consulting team, to ensure that the different stakeholders' needs are fully understood and represented in our discussions.

4. 'Trust me' is one of the most dangerous phrases in the language. Trust erodes most frequently because people are careless, not because they are not trustworthy. However, because trust is so important, we are vigilant for evidence that others are not trustworthy, just as they are vigilant for evidence that we are not; but this vigilance itself leads to an erosion of trust. People's behaviour is as much (if not more) driven by the situation they find themselves in as it is by 'trustworthiness'. In other words, put people in a situation that compromises their capacity to behave with integrity (for example, where simultaneous allegiance to both the company and the customer is not possible) and they will behave in an apparently untrustworthy way. This in turn can lead to an erosion of trust in the people/institution that put them in this situation. So place trust carefully and encourage your clients to do likewise.

5. One of the great unwritten laws of human behaviour (or is it male behaviour?) is that people hate to lose face. So whilst we all want to be trustworthy, we don't want to do it at the expense of losing face and if we inadvertently put our clients in a position where they fear that they are going to lose face as a consequence of their involvement with our project, do not expect loyalty from them. It is far better to think through the personal impact of our work on them and their reputation than to put them, yourself and the piece of work in that position.

6. 'Gatekeepers' are a fact of organizational life: people who do not have the authority to actively commission a piece of work but who do have the authority to block it happening. The most effective approach we have found is to identify and 'recruit' a coach from within our client

system who will provide advice on how best to manage these gate-keepers, and even take it on themselves to manage their concerns and objections directly.

7. Email and written communication can erode trust, particularly if the relationship is moving into phase 2 (evaluation and accommodation). If something is not working, then somebody has to risk trust and, as painful as it might appear, has to meet face-to-face with the client. Our capacity to fear the worst, to generate catastrophic negative fantasies about what will happen in such meetings, has never been matched by the reality.

8. People change within organizations, either by changing roles and responsibilities or by new people joining: welcome such changes as a stimulus to renegotiate and reinvigorate the consulting relationship.

9. It can take a brave or apparently commercially naïve consultant to face up to the fact that his or her contribution is finished. But the real naïveté lies in imagining that our client will not already have realized that this is the case. So, have the open conversation and be prepared to move on to the next piece of work and you are likely to find that your client will be only too happy to help you network your way to the next stimulating assignment.

CHAPTER 6

Values-based consultancy

SUE CLAYTON, TREVOR BENTLEY

Values are the belief systems that drive all human behaviour. Individuals carry their values with them wherever they happen to be. When people join groups, they usually do so because there is a degree of alignment between their own values and the shared values of the group. This is less true for commercial organizations where people join out of a need for financial reward as well as for a sense of connection and belonging. Efforts to bring core values to the heart of an organization have revealed that it is a tricky process, which does not fit with old ways of working.

Values-based consulting in complex systems

Every organization is a complex adaptive system of human beings woven into an intricate network of relationships and dependencies. Such human systems are self-organizing and coalesce into an 'agreed' way of functioning. (For further reading on complex adaptive systems see Stacey, 2001, and Griffin, 2002.) This process is emergent. The focus for agreement is the shared values and purpose of the system.

Using the term 'agreement' may seem strange, in that very few people in the organization are aware of having agreed to anything, let alone something as important as the values and purpose of the organization. Agreement is both tacit and explicit and through working with and accepting a set of values people are agreeing.

When consultants enter into such complex situations, they have a tendency to seek to diagnose some form of dysfunction and then to intervene to correct/improve/change the way the system works in order to eliminate the dysfunction, just as a medical practitioner might diagnose and treat an illness.

The difficulty with this approach is that every complex adaptive system is bound by its very nature to be both functional and dysfunctional. It may in fact be the consequences of the dysfunction, if indeed it is such, which create the organization's uniqueness. Removing, or attempting to remove the dysfunction may, paradoxically, critically damage the functioning of the system. An example of this is evident in organizations that are led by highly narcissistic leaders. Narcissists are especially gifted in attracting followers often through their convincing and persuasive language as well as their charismatic nature. They are innovators, visionaries who see the big picture, and are often revolutionary in their interventions. On the other hand, narcissistic people are known to be poor listeners, especially when they feel under threat; they struggle to hear feedback that challenges their self-image, they tend to listen only for the information that they seek, and are often uncomfortable with feelings – their own and the feelings of others. They typically keep people at arm's length. Organizational systems led by narcissistic leaders are adapted collectively towards the patterns of such leaders.

We saw this patterning in the culture of one of our clients. A well-known luxury brand business believed itself to be the best in the market and responded to customers on the basis that they were privileged to be allowed to buy its products. They also responded to suppliers with the attitude that it was a 'feather in their cap' to be selected as a supplier. Their projected image was highly inflated and one that they found almost impossible to live up to. All of this reflected the narcissism of the CEO.

In our business climate today where self-awareness and emotional intelligence are promoted, and high-quality interpersonal contact is valued, narcissistic leaders and the systems around them could be described as highly dysfunctional. So is it appropriate to remove the leader in order to establish a more functional system? (For further reading on narcissism in leadership see Maccoby et al., 2003.)

The workplace today is moving on from analytical consultancy practices towards ways of working that recognize human experience as a valuable component to organizational functioning. In the past many of the organizations that subjected themselves to process re-engineering studies suffered as a result of applying analytical and mechanistic approaches to living systems. We encountered this with a newly established and rapidly growing client who decided to re-engineer its processes – that is *how it did things*. Shortly after this work was completed, some managers started to realize that people were paying more attention to the processes than they were to each other. Communications and efficiency had declined. We worked with them to rekindle the quality of personal relationships.

Similarly, quality was initially treated as an intellectual exercise being 'trained in' and policed within the laws of the quality manual; it was all-encompassing. The approach to quality has changed from a corporate

[handwritten note:] Approach "quality from a personal exp and individually attributed rather than "corp exp."

event to personal experience and individual responsibility, using manuals as guidelines as opposed to absolute rules. A large Australian bank discovered this when it decided to become more customer focused by relaxing the observance of the rule books and responding, within the scope of its procedures, to the needs of the customers. The quality of its customer service approach was enhanced by this relaxation of the 'quality rules'. We can learn from this and know that embodying our values and ethics begins from the human experience.

In view of this, values-based consultancy seeks to avoid the problems of analytical diagnosis and mechanistic interventions by:

- Discovering how the system functions (*creative field enquiry*). The notion of *fields* emerges out of evolutionary biology (Sheldrake, 1988) and can be found in Gestalt psychology as a way of understanding the complexities of people in context (Parlett, 1991) and in depth psychology (Conforti, 1999).
- Then helping to develop a process of *authentic dialogue*.
- Finally, working with the system to *focus* energies in a way that fosters and builds on the organization's uniqueness; specific actions that make a difference.

Bringing values alive is implicit in this process. These three processes, creative field enquiry, authentic dialogue and focusing are the basis of values-based consultancy.

Creative field enquiry

Creative field enquiry is a process aimed at discovering what is happening – in this case how the values are operating either in accord with or contrary to the core values, following two distinct threads.

1. *How the community of people in the organization work together.* These are guiding principles in the way that people relate to each other. They are the part of the glue of the working community, of the culture.
2. *How the organization operates.* These are usually a set of principles that guide a company's actions in its day-to-day business. They can be the source of a company's distinctiveness.

We would expect these two sets of values to be aligned. In our inquiry what we look for is the unseen; what we listen for is the unheard, and what we give voice to is the unspoken. We start by exploring the currently held views and perceptions of the organization that people within the organization have. Through carefully crafted individual and group discussions we develop a heightened awareness of what is currently being experienced. From this heightened awareness we are able to construct a 'rich picture' of the organization's functioning.

We may present this picture in a variety of ways that might include storytelling, diagrammatical and pictorial representation, creative description and dramatic unfolding. There are many forms of storytelling in organizations today, if you are not familiar with working in this way, Denning (2001) offers a good basis for developing skills in this area.

For example in one organization it was hard for the CEO to see and hear that his approach was not helping and supporting his people in achieving high performance so we told him a story:

> Once upon a time, actually around about now, a king ran his kingdom with a fist of feathers. Every time there was a problem he would bang the table with his fist and feathers would fly everywhere creating a feather fog of confusion. What his people wanted was some direction and clarity, but all the king kept doing was banging his fist and creating confusion. Then one day, actually one day soon, along came . . . (Bentley, 2001)

The result of this type of intervention is that management can begin to see what it has not seen or has not wanted to see, hear what it has not heard or has not wanted to hear, and will be invited and encouraged to speak the unspeakable.

We know from our experience that solutions to intractable problems exist within the organization and are hidden by the tapestries of established practice and prejudice. We seek to look behind the wall coverings and unearth the hidden possibilities and potential.

Authentic dialogue

Within the context of the rich picture, managers are invited to connect with each other through a process of authentic dialogue that involves them in being able to share what is going on for them in the moment.

Authenticity is aspired to in many organizational values but is often not well understood. It is in fact very simple: 'Being authentic is matching our outer selves, what we say and how we say it, and what we do and how we do it [how we interact with others], with our invisible [inner] selves, our values, beliefs, viewpoint and emotions . . .' (Clayton, 2001).

As values-based consultants, a large part of our own personal work and responsibility is to deepen our understanding of ourselves, our own authenticity. That means increasing our awareness of ourselves and to know our own patterns of openness and closedness. Our ability to model transparency and to support others in developing theirs is at the core of values-based consultancy.

Through authentic dialogue people become able to see beyond the moment, to hear beneath the message and to speak their truth with confidence and without fear. People are freed to operate in accord with their own values and with the values of the organization. Ethical dilemmas become owned and explored by teams and management, increasing learning and feedback, rather than held as a personal struggle by a few individuals. We want to establish a clear and explicit, shared understanding about what values mean in practice.

Focusing

A variety of key issues emerge as awareness and authentic dialogue continue to grow and develop. These can be of all shapes and sizes and of all levels of potential impact on the organization. Many of these issues are to do with things that have traditionally not been discussed. These might be relationship difficulties, the pattern of unhealthy internal politics (for example, 'you get promotion around here because of who you know – not who you are'). There could be conflicts between people or departments or dysfunctional decision-making processes, gripes that have been brushed under the carpet, challenging leadership decisions, structures and processes that exist because of convention but have lost their purpose (for example, meetings). The extent to which staff compromise their personal values for work demands could be resulting in hidden grievances. In order to focus attention it is important to be able to relate these issues to the core values of the organization. It is also important that all levels of management, the people who are usually seen as role models, embrace the values and aspire towards practice and improvement of them.

A London-based legal firm had established a set of values, one of which was to ensure a balance between work and home demands. They were, they said, committed to this value. They also operated a commercial imperative that their front-line lawyers had to charge 50 hours per week to customers. To achieve this lawyers had to work 80 hours a week or lie on their time sheets.

Without a carefully defined set of core values, this organization was incapable of focusing attention in such a way as to ensure that there was a realistic balance between social responsibility and commercial imperative. Many organizations today are beginning to accept that there are complexities in finding this balance.

A large oil company had a published document explaining how it managed to maintain a balance between social responsibility and commercial imperatives. Almost every day it was possible to read in the press how it was failing to live up to the social responsibility side of the equation. Through discussions with senior executives they commented that it was almost impossible for managers to decide what to do when they did not have clear core values to guide them.

In this context, social responsibility covers both the internal responsibility, caring for and supporting the people who work for the organization, and the external responsibility for those upon whom the organization has direct and indirect impact.

Inevitably managers and decision makers will be faced with complex ethical dilemmas. Such dilemmas often lead management to defer to 'old practices' and put business before values when these are in conflict. There is no easy way to deal with these dilemmas. Our work as values-based consultants is to awaken management to the difficulties and encourage new and different ways of dealing with these dilemmas – ways that will not compromise values.

Taking values into the heart of the system

It is still the case that many organizations naïvely produce long lists of values and pin them to notice boards in the belief that they will then be put into practice. Others have invested vast resources in an attempt to learn values, not appreciating that:

- Values become integrated into the heart of a system through exploration, discovery and insight, rather than input. Working with values as though people can be 'taught' will not work – they need to be felt. It is not an intellectual exercise.
- Core values cannot be established effectively until management are aware and able to engage in authentic dialogue. If the attempt is made to determine core values when the organization is operating with old unseen and unspoken patterns of behaviour, the values will simply reflect what is on the surface and become just a set of words without depth of meaning or belief.
- There is no end-goal that can be achieved in values practice – we can only aim to establish values in relationship with others and to gain some sense of when we are getting there. We know when we experience those moments of real achievement – we feel it inside us. We also know when we are not being true to our values, but many people do not listen to the feelings that can inform them.
- Codes of ethics can only offer a map from which people can discover a more meaningful path if the support is available.

Of course, every organization needs to define and espouse its core values to gain the support and commitment of its people. Once it does so, every decision and action can be checked with these core values and people can act in accordance with them and feel confident they are doing the 'right thing'. They can also check to what extent their own values are aligned with, or conflict with, the organization's values and they can choose whether to stay or leave.

In a more general sense the vision and direction in which management are leading the organization can also be checked with the core values and decisions taken to keep the strategic decisions in line, or to change the core values with all that this will mean.

Once the hard work has been done and core values that truly reflect the belief systems of the organization are established, they become a focus and rallying point for finding the balance between social responsibility and the commercial imperative.

There are an increasing number of businesses that openly demonstrate these values, such as a well-known furniture manufacturer that uses English hardwoods in its furniture and has developed a whole series of schemes for managing woodlands, including careful harvesting and planting so as not to damage the local ecology. It is also mindful of maintaining the beauty of the English countryside.

Organizations are complex systems and highly influenced by the people that work in them. Our work as values-based consultants supporting organizations to achieve values integration means working in a new way. It also means that we need to have our own values operating to a high standard in ourselves and in our own consultancy practices. We do this in a number of ways: by reviewing our own practices on a regular basis, by ensuring healthy relationships within our practice and with our clients, and by checking our value systems in relation to our clients or potential clients. There are times when we may need to let go of potential work if our values and style of consultancy do not match well with presenting propositions. For example, if at an early phase of negotiation with a new client we feel that our values are strikingly different and that such a difference will compromise the quality of our work together, we will not take on that contract. This happened with an invitation for work that we were exploring with a national financial corporation. They were espousing a set of values such as openness, honesty, integrity, and good relationships with customers and suppliers. Yet in their relationship with us it transpired that they had not been open and honest. Despite our efforts to address these issues through open discussion, we eventually decided to walk away from the contract; the gap between our practised values and theirs was too wide.

There is no single solution to values, no one way. We need to be willing to learn with the client and not pretend that we have the answers, nor feel that we have to prove that we know the answers. Our ability to stay present with the client as they discover for themselves how to truly own and practise their values is the best that we can do, and in order not to compromise our own values there are times when we may need to walk away from the work offered to us.

Recommended reading

Bentley T, Clayton S (1999) Gestalt: A Philosophy for Change. This is a collection of articles on the practice of gestalt in organizations, originally published in the *Training Officer* in 1996. They can now be obtained in a booklet from the authors.

Nevis EC (1987) Organizational Consulting: A Gestalt Approach. New York: Gardner Press.

PART 2
THE ORGANIZATIONAL
LANDSCAPE

Chapter 7

Introduction

Pauline Grant

In a later part of this book you will find a provocative challenge to business psychologists to gain a better understanding of the context in which they work. Part 2 takes a small step in that direction by looking at the environment that we find within organizations. It is a series of short glimpses that make up an incomplete picture but serve to give insight into the organizational landscape and therefore the context into which we move when working with our clients.

It could be argued that only by gaining direct experience of organizational life from the inside can one become really fluent in the language of business, truly sensitive to the pressures and changing priorities that beset our clients and fully aware of the politics and disparate agendas that drive choices and decisions. On the other hand, organizations are communities and each community has its own unique signature, style and sense of direction. It can therefore equally be argued that consultants are ideally placed to gain experience of many organizations and that, over time, they become expert in describing the dynamics and suggesting the best interventions to improve them.

The truth is that both arguments have merit and yet neither is correct. When Erving Goffman put together his seminal essays on 'total institutions' (Goffman, 1961), part of the magnetism came from peeking inside, seeing things as an insider. Yet he was not an insider, but rather someone who could bring new insights because of his position as an outsider. *Barbarians at the Gate* by Bryan Burrough and John Helyar (1991) was a popular story as well as an account of organizational life. The ability to stand back from what was going on and comment on it made this more than a piece of history.

An empathic observer can gain great insight, just as a closed-minded one might derive little benefit from many diverse experiences. As Argyris points out, our actions and experiences inform our beliefs, but these actions are also driven by our beliefs. His helpful and illustrative 'ladder

55

of inference' is well known but perhaps it is easy to forget how deeply programmed we are to learn in this way and, therefore, how difficult it is to be truly objective about our own belief system. I recall my first visit to Ghana in what many might see as a dream assignment – certainly, I did at the time. My brief allowed me to spend a long time just talking to people in the client and other global organizations to discover what they did and why, what might work better and what would be culturally acceptable in terms of assessing managerial capability.

I asked a lot of questions and discovered a huge amount about Ghana, about my client company, other international players in that market and, of course, about individuals I met. But an experience that stays in my mind was being driven back to my hotel through busy Accra by a British (expatriate) manager. As in many cities, the rush hour traffic was seen as a fruitful market for street traders and we crept along with people trying to sell us just about everything you could imagine: clothes, toilet rolls, food, newspapers, electrical goods, plants, toys. My driver companion advised me not to make eye contact with the traders. After 18 months in the country, he had nevertheless retained his model of street traders from his days in Middle Eastern countries on previous postings. There he had come to the view that any interaction was taken as encouragement. In Accra, the polite traders would not hassle anyone who indicated that they did not want to buy, so eye contact with a 'no' sign released them to try elsewhere whereas not making eye contact left them unsure as to whether you had noticed what they were selling.

The popularity and success of the Dilbert cartoons (Adams, 1998) and the TV comedy *The Office* suggest that we love to poke fun at the environment in which many of us spend so much of our time. However, the skill of cartoonists and comedians comes from their ability to look at the commonplace and see it from a different perspective. The saying about not seeing the wood for the trees comes to mind. Sometimes it is easier to see things from the outside than it is to stand back from the day-to-day and challenge our own assumptions. That outside view is a privilege that consultants share with cartoonists and comedians and, when used with empathy, humility and insight, is much appreciated by clients. Indeed, often a highly valued contribution that the consultant makes is to look afresh at current practice and question it. Hopefully, readers will forgive me for starting this section with a somewhat whimsical look at reward systems and how they can go wrong even when designed with the best intentions. It is an example of how much easier it is to be objective and take a fresh view from the outside than when immersed in the business that also serves as a warning about simple solutions.

The other contributors to this section also offer their perspectives as insightful observers. Hatfield continues the theme by noticing that key decision makers can become their own worst enemies and he suggests why this happens and how to avoid it. Bains brings together her experience and a body of research around political behaviour (and not just human political behaviour) to describe and explain how it plays out in organizations. She provides a light-hearted taxonomy of political types that many of us will relate to, with the benefits and pitfalls associated with each. However, despite the frivolous descriptions she is emphatically not poking fun or making judgements but rather recognizing the diversity of behaviour that we encounter in organizations. If these chapters leave us feeling that the complexities are too much to handle, or that there is so much that can go wrong that it might be better not to try, we can be reassured by the account given by Lewis of an intervention approach based on highlighting the positive aspects of what we and our clients notice. Her description of appreciative inquiry is illustrated by a practical case study.

Chapter 8

A fairy-ish story

Pauline Grant

Once upon a time in a far-off land, a million miles away, there were some companies. Now these companies all had shareholders who were entitled to a return on their investment. The shareholders were reasonable people but constantly hungry and fickle. Each company wanted to satisfy the hunger of its shareholders so that they would sleep easily.

The companies also had employees who were entitled to pay in return for their work. The employees were reasonable people but constantly hungry and fickle. Each company wanted to satisfy the hunger of their employees so that they would return to work the next day.

Across the land there was a feeling of discontent. A cry was heard: 'How shall we satisfy the hunger of both our shareholders and our employees in the current economic climate?' Many meetings were held and many conferences convened; many papers were written and some of them read; many consultants were appointed and disappointed. Eventually a new cry was heard throughout the land: 'We must reward performance so that our employees know we value their efforts, and we must increase profit so that our shareholders know we appreciate their investment!'

The tale of the service company

Now one company was established to serve the needs of many other organizations. To do this it had to understand the needs of these other organizations and to suggest how these needs could be met within budget and to a tight timescale. The board of this company considered long and hard the issue of rewarding performance and increasing profit. Its members went away for three days and two nights to a country hotel where, individually and collectively, they engaged in the ceremony of visioning. There they experimented with the ritual of brainstorming and celebrated their achievements with much red wine. At the end of their retreat, they shook hands and congratulated each other on having come up with The Answer – *to target sales.* One of their number produced a scroll so that The Answer could be carried by herald throughout the company and proclaimed to all employees.

The herald took the scroll and promised to communicate its words accurately to all concerned. He rode through the night to the regional office and there, at a meeting of all, read the message of the scroll: 'Rejoice! Rejoice! You are to be rewarded for your efforts! It has been decreed that each of you will have performance targets and that as you achieve these targets, so will a bonus be triggered. Many riches will follow to those who not only achieve their targets, but also exceed them.'

A great cheer arose spontaneously, although a couple of employees remained strangely quiet. When the cheers had died down, one of the assembly called out, 'Tell us, good herald, what is the nature of these targets?'. The herald read on: 'You will be rewarded according to the value of new contracts. Each year you will be given a target for new contracts and each quarter your performance will be reviewed. This will enable you to reassess your sales effort and so achieve your targets.'

Then the Herald named the targets for the current year. A polite round of applause greeted this announcement. Those assembled started to talk amongst themselves, then a voice was heard from the middle of the third row. 'These are stretching targets in a difficult and competitive market. Only those with diligence, perseverance and excellent interpersonal skills will be able to meet these targets. However, I have confidence that my team possesses those qualities. We will overcome all difficulties and achieve a bonus in the first year of the scheme!' Members of her team cheered and waved their hands.

Another employee from near the back of the room stood up and called to the herald. 'Is there more, good herald? Are we not charged to deliver increased value on our existing contracts?' Then there was a silence as the herald inspected the scroll carefully. 'I can see no such reference', he said shaking his head. 'Look again, good herald – perhaps in the small print.' Again the assembly waited as the herald perused all portions of the scroll, even to the small print, to the smallest of fonts in the document. 'The board has spoken. There is no more.'

A great muttering and rumbling started in the room. 'Are we to neglect our existing contracts in the pursuit of new ones to achieve our targets?' The herald shrugged, and shook his head. 'No doubt, as professionals, you will balance your commitment to your existing contracts against your wish to achieve a bonus, and I feel sure you will make the right decision.'

Then the clear tones of the commercial manager rang out as he stood up to speak, and the assembly listened with care. He held an envelope on the back of which he had inscribed words. 'By my calculations', he began, 'the tendering process for new contracts takes on average 5 days' work, and we have a 40% chance of success. However, when we retender for existing contracts it takes only 3 days and we have a 75% chance of success.' All around the room employees told each other tales of tendering, and no doubt would have continued to swap anecdotes in support of the commercial manager for many hours had he not held up his hand to continue. 'Moreover', he declared, 'the average value of contracts for which we retender is greater than that of new contracts, although I have no research data to tell me conclusively why this should be so.'

The minutes of the meeting were quickly prepared and the herald returned to the board. 'Oh, board members, I fear the mission may turn out to be a failure.' The board members were amazed. 'Did you not explain that they were to be rewarded? Have you not told them that their efforts will bring them rich bonuses? Why are they so ungrateful?'

After a while, the members of the board decided that targeting sales was, after all, a bad idea and they told all their friends as much.

The tale of the manufacturing and distribution outfit

In the valley of this land, where the water flowed sweet and the communications network was well developed, was the centre of manufacturing and distribution of a much-needed, but short shelf-life product. The message of rewarding performance and increasing profits reached the valley on the early morning breeze, followed shortly afterwards by the disturbing news that sales targets don't work.

'We know where they went wrong, so we are well placed to learn from their mistakes', said each and every senior manager. A meeting was held and it was agreed that a new target must be devised. The senior management team then set off on a quest to find the new target. They built rafts together and hurled ropes across deep gullies. They abseiled down steep cliffs and shot each other with paint guns. They camped out under the stars and constructed bridges from Lego bricks. They learned to work together as a team, and were inspired.

When they returned, they communicated the message directly to the other employees. Each senior manager played a part in this process, and this in itself convinced all others that this was indeed The Answer: 'Friends, we have no doubt in your ability to pull together as teams – for we have done it ourselves! (And if we can do it . . .) Our aim as an organization is to boost throughput and so increase profit. Our shareholders will be satisfied and will sleep.'

The assembled employees nodded, understanding the wisdom of this aim. For surely the shareholders must be satisfied if they are to sleep and not regret their investment. Many said they had always known that they could be more efficient and get more boxes out of the door. 'Do not think that we care only for the peaceful slumber of our shareholders! We care for you, and indeed ourselves too. We will therefore set throughput targets and help you to achieve them. If they are achieved, we will all benefit from a share of the profits that this will produce.'

The throughput targets were specified and the assembly listened attentively. One of their number spoke up. 'Indeed, these are challenging targets. Only by true teamwork and cooperation in keeping the machines working and reducing waste can they be achieved. However, many of us have worked here all our lives, as have other members of our families. We will work together to achieve these targets and benefit from the profit share.' A cheer went up and after a cup of tea and biscuit all returned to their work.

For some weeks the factory was a hive of activity and all were given feedback on their performance according to the targets. Then a message was received from the warehouse manager. 'I have a problem! I cannot find room for your goods. The warehouse is at 84% capacity and getting the trucks loaded is becoming a nightmare. We are working overtime to move goods around so that the right things can leave the warehouse at the right time, and that the shelf-life is not exceeded. You must slow down production.' There followed a list of products that the warehouse had in plenty.

'What then shall we make?' asked the employees. 'How shall we achieve our throughput targets?' The senior managers were mightily worried, for if the warehouse was granting overtime to move goods around this was beyond what was budgeted. A crisis meeting was called. It was agreed that targeting throughput did not work and they told all their friends.

The tale of the financial institution

There was, in the city of the land, a mighty organization with such complex dealings that few understood what went on inside even though all had occasion to make use of it. Deep in the recesses of the fourteenth floor was a department that would lend money to those in need, in return for the provision of security and an agreed rate of interest. Each manager looked after a portfolio of loans and tried to ensure that the interest was paid.

News of the experiments with targets had reached this organization and many wise heads shook in dismay, for if companies did not do well they might not be able to pay their interest. 'We want the companies to do well. If they do well, we do well!' This mighty organization, in accordance with its custom, set up a working party to consider effective ways of rewarding performance and increasing profit. The working party was cross-functional and chaired by a very senior manager. It met each fortnight for three months, and at the end of each meeting agreed that it was moving towards The Answer.

Finally, it was convinced that it had The Answer, and it put a paper to the board. It waited with trepidation and fear. What if the board did not like the paper? Would they be discredited and another working party set up? What if the board did like the paper? Would they be acknowledged and esteemed? What about a budget for implementation?

A month later a memo was received within the department explaining the new reward system. In future, each manager would assess his or her portfolio and calculate on a quarterly basis the average rate of interest they had been able to collect. If this average was equal to a rate to be determined according to the performance in the market within that quarter, they would be rewarded by a high rating on their performance appraisal. If it exceeded that rate, they would be entitled to a share of the profit bonus – the exact amount depending on the performance of the department as a whole.

Each manager read the memo and many went straight to their portfolio to undertake the calculations in accordance with the specified formula. Shortly afterwards, an email message appeared:

> Most of us have a group of loans that are effectively dormant. The individuals or companies have had such difficulties that they cannot pay us any interest at all. They are not exactly 'bad debts' as we have not been asked to write them off, and indeed we hope and pray that one day they will return to prosperity and repay what they owe. How do we incorporate these into the formula – because, as everyone knows, if one applies a multiple of zero, then all else reverts to zero?

The reply was succinct and much appreciated: 'Ignore dormant portfolio for purposes of target exercise.'

Then came the time for appraisal and many managers were content that they had achieved the target. A few were delighted that they had exceeded it and bought their friends a drink to explain how they had been so successful. All were amazed that it had taken so long to come up with such a simple and effective solution.

Then came the appraisal of one manager who had not had time to calculate her own performance and was dismayed to find that she had been given a poor rating. 'How can this be?' she exclaimed in alarm. 'I have consistently negotiated good loans and have an excellent record in collecting favourable rates of interest. Have I done something wrong for which I am being punished?' The facts were laid before her for no one wanted to appear unfair, and all had thought her a high flier with senior executive potential, and were disappointed for her. 'These figures can't be right!' she declared.

That evening, with a supportive colleague, she went through her port-folio to uncover the truth. Far into the night they worked, writing numbers and undertaking complicated calculations. 'Look at the income I have generated', she said after some hours. 'Surely this will convince them that I am indeed achieving my target.' Her colleague had to agree that the income was truly impressive. It exceeded his own by some 12.5%, and he had been awarded a share of the bonus. 'Let's look through it all again', he suggested, 'just to be sure we aren't missing anything.'

Again, they went through the figures. This time the colleague found a loan that was yielding a pitifully low rate of interest. 'I'm proud of that', the manager explained, 'because until recently that had been a dormant loan for many months. I have managed to generate income where there was none before.' Then the penny dropped. 'That low rate, and others like it, are bringing down your average.'

The working party had sat, the paper submitted, the board decided, and the memo sent. There was nothing to be done. All managers agreed that targeting return did not work and they told their friends.

The tale of the combined sales and service organization

Across the land there were small units selling, maintaining and repairing machines for others. Sometimes in order to sell their machine they would take another in part exchange and try to sell this also. This company, too, had heard that shareholders could have their hunger satisfied so that they would sleep, and that employees could have their hunger satisfied so that they would continue turning up for work. They believed strongly that per-formance should be rewarded and profits increased. However, they had heard rumours of reward systems that did not work.

Being practical and uncomplicated people they had a half-hour meet-ing to decide how they should reward performance and increase profit. After only 20 minutes, they had The Answer on their flipchart and a sec-retary quickly transcribed it onto a word processor. It was then placed on the agenda for the next regional conference and launched just before lunch so that all could discuss its implications over a ham salad or plough-man's lunch with a glass of beer.

Each unit would have its own profit target for each of its activities. This would reward teamwork for each activity and encourage efficiency and competitive pricing. There would be a great deal of autonomy – the only measure would be the profit and none would question how that profit was achieved.

The salad was consumed and it was good. The beer was swallowed and it was good. A warm glow suffused the faces of those at the regional conference as they thought up new and exciting ideas to increase profits. 'We will cut our overhead whilst maintaining sales.' 'We will price keenly to increase market share.' 'We will advertise carefully to encourage volume.' 'We will enhance quality to defy the competition.'

Time passed, and the first mutterings of complaint were heard throughout the company. The Answer was proving divisive, for even as all were focused on increasing profit they had lost sight of the company as a whole. Thus the sales team wanted to take a machine in part exchange, and calculated the price at which they could resell. The service team estimated the cost of servicing the machine and charged them commercial rates. The sales team was appalled that its profit had been eaten into. The service team was happy that it had maintained its level of profit. Thereafter, the sales team commissioned another agency to undertake service more cheaply so that it could protect its profit, and the service team was appalled that it had lost the business. All agreed that targeting profit did not work and they told their friends.

The end?

Now this may have seemed like a fairy story but it is predominantly true – apart from the fact that the organizations are not a million miles away. They are, of course, real companies, and in some cases the stories represent more than one company. Some have accepted that their apparently sensible reward systems did the opposite of what they had wished, and made changes. Others tried to make a flawed system work better by tinkering with it.

Interestingly, these stories emerged not as a result of a specific assignment, but by being involved with clients closely enough to understand their businesses and see what was happening. In some cases, this allowed conversations to take place between consultant and decision makers that led to the issue being addressed. Of course, it doesn't have to be a psychologist who identifies flaws in reward systems, but it just so happened that in the above cases it was one.

There are many lessons to take away from these tales and this list is probably not a comprehensive one:

- We know that there is no single reward that is valued by all individuals. Equally, there is no one way of rewarding performance that works for all organizations and all circumstances. Learning from 'best practice' means learning the principles, not copying the practice. (The principle might be 'what gets measured improves' – but it doesn't tell you what to measure.)

- To establish a reward system that encourages the right performance and behaviour, it is first necessary to know what the right performance and behaviour is – and that is a dynamic, not a static entity. (Increasing production volume is a good thing until it isn't!)
- Reward systems need to be established by those with an understanding of the whole value chain. Silo thinking raises the possibility of one part improving at the expense of another – as with the sales and service example.
- Sales targets should be regarded with extreme caution. The story could have included many other examples – targets were achieved but profit reduced; marketing resource directed to increasing volume sold to satisfy head office, and the new product budget blown on short-term gains rather than sustainable growth; sales on paper that could not be delivered; complaints and cancellations rising as sales increase. Niceties like quality and diversity of sales look good in theory but require flexibility and judgement that may be unrealistic on the ground.
- Sacred cows are there to be challenged. Activities that are irrationally valued (such as winning new business being valued more highly than securing repeat business) need to be identified. The difficulty of tackling this can be enormous; the implications cover power and status as well as pay and bonus. Finding out what is maintaining the irrational belief might be more productive than designing a solution that no one will implement.

CHAPTER 9

Avoid being your own worst enemy!

MALCOLM HATFIELD

Success is more likely if you can avoid the trap of the common psychological causes of failure than if you seek to replicate the successful approaches of others.

An early and formative experience in my working career occurred during training in the use of the16PF questionnaire in the 1970s. A course attendee produced the profile of what he and his organization considered to be their 'best' manager, who had become the template for all further recruitment. Even with limited experience, this approach seemed to me to be fraught with potential problems and sowed seeds that have steadily grown. However, despite the intervening years, many aspects of applied psychology teaching may be viewed as adding a level of statistical credibility to the basic paradigm underpinning the course-attender's proposition: study the situation, identify an ideal to meet the need, then replicate the ideal in actual practice. Whether it is one profile or a multivariate specification equation, the principle is the same and, in my view, equally flawed.

Moses myopia

This seductive psychological trap captures professional psychologists as much as anyone else. And why not? Most psychologists are human too! The demand for books such as Peters and Waterman (2004) suggests that, in business, the appeal of identifying characteristics of success and pursuing an ideal remains. Belbin, in his original work on teams, described a tendency for management to try to create teams out of 'stars' in order to deal with difficult problem situations, which then failed, to their surprise.

All of this suggests that at the individual, group and organizational level there is a common tendency to look for the way forward in replicating others' past successes. However, I suggest that this *modus operandi* is questionable in concept and leads to dependency, restricted thinking and the prevalence of 'tablets of stone', which we could call 'Moses myopia': people become unable to look beyond straightforwardly defined, apparently unambiguous 'common-sense' solutions. Instead they either slavishly follow the prescription or, alternatively, smash up the current tablets of stone, only to exist in some level of panic until the next ones arrive. In the words of Marshall McLuhan, the message has somehow been lost in the seduction of the medium.

The alternative view proposed here is that humans are naturally creative, adventurous and innovative; in their anxiety, expediency or hurry they may want a prescriptive solution but for much of the time they do not need to be told how to do things well. If they fail, it is usually because of factors unrelated to their capacity for ideas but due to problems that they face on the way, which often have a psychological basis. So 'let innovation flower by avoiding failure' is a fruitful rallying cry for business psychology.

rules/steps; prescriptive advice gives comfort in uncertainty

Why does such unproductive behaviour persist?

I have the following suggestions in the absence of research specifically directed towards answering this question:

- Anxiety inhibits and distorts decision making. Fear of failure is common.
- Progress in business is complex, open ended and uncertain, therefore formulaic or quasi-scientific answers such as '10 common characteristics of successful companies and executives' offer a way forward in uncertainty, thereby reducing anxiety.
- A similar effect results from the outcomes of academic research, especially if that research is 'translated' by others into a simplified form that can be more easily applied.
- The reassurance that exists in conformity was shown many years ago in social psychological research and there is an equivalent raising of levels of anxiety involved in divergence.
- Success tends to lead to two possible traps: firstly, an inappropriate sense of invincibility, and secondly, an all too human desire to enjoy it as the result of past efforts. Both of these inhibit adaptability.

previous success ⇒ "no need to do different"
languish in success.

Illustrative examples

The personnel selection task is always important and generally difficult and is therefore perceived as a crucial element of managerial behaviour.

It also produces anxiety in those responsible as mistakes are very visible.

The role of the psychologist in selection decisions varies with different situations. These variations are little explained and researched, but there is usually a tendency to define the Holy Grail, some ideal of effective performance, and then to try and recruit as closely to this as possible. The current sophistication in human resources processes may not change the basic problem; for example, I have helped numerous organizations define competencies in terms of idealized or preferred patterns of behaviour. Having done this, conventional academic methods of predictive validation are usually too slow; organizations need answers or to have confidence in a process ever more quickly. More pragmatic methods, such as 'This test profile describes our best and therefore ideal general manager', may be faster but suffer from the flaw of assuming that replicas of one individual in one situation will necessarily generalize to another.

At a collective level, the end-game is the situation in which careful application of systematic methods makes matters worse than they would have been otherwise because an organization of clones cannot adapt to different demands and new requirements. (I was recently employed by a major European bank to increase the diversity of a group of senior managers.)

The behaviour described is driven by the psychological needs of the individuals concerned. Anxiety reduction is achieved by application of a process and by the real or illusory scientific respectability of professional statistics or other research. If there are failures, then the offending consultants, or the tests they use, can be easily replaced by new ones, probably with more impressive quasi-technical and professional credentials, without rocking the boat of the basic paradigm. Reliance on supposed scientific and expert power in trying to replicate some predefined ideal may thereby reduce anxiety, but real performance improvement remains elusive.

There are wider examples of management behaviour being affected by psychological blocks that create incompetence. The next concerns the use of company resources and strengths.

In the mid-1980s the Chloride group was a well-known international manufacturer of batteries. One of the company's major strengths and resources, made possible by its size and power, was its research-and-development establishment. Scientists and technologists within the organization knew as much as, and probably more than, their competitors about sophisticated issues in the chemistry, electrochemistry, material science and production engineering of battery manufacture. The question is: what is the purpose of such a resource? How does it add value and ensure competitive advantage?

To understand this we need to consider the market-place and customers. The traditional market had always been divided between original equipment manufacture (OEM) and replacement. Original equipment manufacture was high volume, predictable, a possible 'cash cow' in which margin and profit could be made by producing to a given specification. The replacement market was represented by a very different customer: the average motorist who bought a battery when the original failed. It was assumed that quality should and could enable the premium price to be achieved. The Chloride group had an upmarket brand name. The chief executive's strategy was very clearly focused to push the research-and-development establishment to support the brand by designing a new, advanced technology product with which no other manufacturer could compete. The company's loyalty and support for the quality image of the brand was strong and not up for debate. As a result, the capability of the research and development was directed towards a hopeful, prestige project, and not towards business competitiveness.

But the market was moving in different ways: OEM sales to manufacturers such as Ford were harder. Ford's production engineers knew only too well what it cost to produce a battery and so there was a major squeeze on profit margins at this part of the market. Vehicle electrics were also becoming more reliable so that batteries lasted longer and the replacement market moved downmarket to supply older vehicles; the demand for a premium product was in decline. Both the senior management of the company and the research-and-development staff could be seen to pursue what became a rather grand aim in the face of conflicting reality. Competitors were able to undercut at the replacement end of the market as they had fewer expensive overheads such as research and development. There was little market for a highly sophisticated automotive battery; the advantages, although present, were insufficient, and the strength of the research-and-development establishment was therefore squandered. (An alternative strategy would have been to use the research-and-development strength to take the cost out of the regular product thereby squeezing the competition.)

This is an example of resources being used in a way that reflects management's desired image and needs as opposed to what would add real competitive advantage.

The Redland Group, a more recent casualty of strategic errors, maintained a large technical centre that developed highly visible premium products. These were not core to the business, and thereby reduced resource to help manufacture and sell basic products at a competitive price.

Why? The fault here is not with intellect. Neither the Redland HQ senior management nor the Chloride management group lacked capacity to analyse the situation. However, intellect alone is not a good determinant of effective decision making in uncertain and emotionally driven situations.

Indeed, the capacity of management to rationalize, in the true Freudian sense, the pursuit of inappropriate processes will be that much greater because of their intellect.

The 'why' is likely to be multifaceted when psychological processes are involved. Having a high-visibility, high-quality, innovative, forward-looking research-and-development division is positively reassuring to management with high status and recognition needs. Accepting that it is necessary to abandon what has proven successful in the past and risk the unknown is psychologically difficult, perhaps more so to those with high aspirations.

Charles Handy (1995) encourages management to recognize cycles of business, products, organizations and the market-place, and commends us to move on to new opportunities as soon as we see the success of the current change process. In accepting the reality of the sigmoid curve there is little time to enjoy the fruits of our labours; once success seems to be apparent, it is necessary to look to the next development. This makes logical sense but is psychologically and emotionally demanding.

So this is another pitfall. Organizations have resources under senior management control that can be used in different strategic directions. Choosing which direction is hard, but the choices are not necessarily amenable to decision making on the basis of purely factual information. In the presence of uncertainty, psychological processes flourish that affect the decision – as easily for the worse as for the better. This may seem a rather negative analysis, but offers wonderful opportunity to business psychologists in being able to add further value.

Thinking traps

The 1970s cult book *Zen and the Art of Motorcycle Maintenance* (Pirsig, 1979) makes much of what the author identified as the 'gumption trap'. This is a situation in which otherwise capable, flexible, balanced and competent people fail to solve a problem simply because they are locked into modes of thinking that stop them reconceptualizing the problem from a different perspective. These thinking traps often arise from a prescription about the best way in which things must be done, which is essentially a value judgement. Parallel behaviour is often seen in business situations. It can be described as the 'dig harder' syndrome. When faced with real pressure and difficulties, the tendency is to revert to type or even to regress to prior modes of behaviour. Failure is seen as being due to insufficient application – hence the tendency for individuals placed in holes of their own making to make matters worse by pursuing decisions that worked in the past but whose applicability is beyond their sell-by date.

Further examples come from manufacturing companies. Manufacturing industry tends to develop rather specific senior production management skills related to the production and technology concerned. This leads to patterns of thinking based on the apparent uniqueness and criticality of this expertise and potentially a vicious circle of ineffective management.

One production director who, in his particular company, was seen as *the* UK expert on vitreous enamelling and of irreplaceable importance, delegated his annual strategic business plan to an inexperienced graduate trainee whilst filling all the supervisory roles with acolytes. Another ran the production side of a factory more as his own personal fiefdom. This is not to deny the specific technical or production expertise of the individuals concerned but to question their capability as senior managers. Yet their capability as directors in the companies concerned was not challenged by a series of able, resilient, confident, ambitious and otherwise successful managing directors, who nonetheless recognized the limitations in teamworking, flexibility, capacity for change, and strategic thinking in their production directors.

Why did they do nothing about it? The answer seems to have been fear, driven by overestimating the value of the specific knowledge and experience held by individuals. This is the danger of the 'black art' ('only Bill Smith knows how the system really works, so you need to have him around when it goes down'), with the result that 'Smith' has power that, over a period of years, can become perverted and dysfunctional.

In these cases, when the individuals concerned were eventually removed, the outcome was not the feared collapse because of the sudden loss of the unique expertise, but a sense of relief, freedom, flexibility and improved performance. In the absence of oppressive control other people, who also have relevant knowledge, are only too happy to share it and help the organization go forward.

The blame lies equally with the individuals and their managing directors. Dixon (1994), in his superb book *On the Psychology of Military Incompetence*, discovers that successful military commanders can and do, on many occasions, behave in a highly direct, robust and tough way; however, the crucial thing is that this is never done out of fear, insecurity, desperation or simplistic hope, but out of a calm and mature understanding and evaluation of the situation.

So, psychological issues and processes are crucial in influencing decision making at whatever level. Unsatisfactory situations, to the detriment of organizational performance, are easily papered over by senior management who are articulate, persuasive and intelligent enough to put up good arguments in defence of what they are failing to do.

Over-commitment in acquisitions

A further example of psychological processes to be avoided emerges from study of acquisitions and mergers. At the time of writing, a typical example was in the news. Safeway, the UK's fourth largest food retailer, had been on the market with several potential buyers jockeying for position and consequent uncertainty. The result was a realignment of the UK supermarket business with approval from the City and the attendant need for the winners to absorb the company operations into its own. How easy is it to merge two large organizations and sustain business efficiency? How does a company spread its culture and management competence into a new acquisition?

The answer is, of course, with difficulty. Companies typically tend to underestimate their capacity to do this. Has William Morrison, Safeway purchaser, with an organization built up on the basis of lean management, steady growth by small acquisitions and development, the capacity to absorb the cuckoo Safeway into its nest when its own management surplus is limited?

When Redland purchased Steetley in the early 1990s, there was much media discussion over the price and value paid. The determination of the Redland directors to pursue the opposed takeover became a test of power and strength, which has its own psychological underpinnings. Having 'won', the crucial issue was the capacity of the company to integrate the two businesses to produce the hoped-for results. In the event, a very interesting comparison can be made: the Redland brick manufacturing business made a huge effort to create a new company out of the two joining together, with new top management, new headquarters in a new place and new culture. The real effort and commitment proved successful in a reasonably short time. It may have been driven by the new MD's needs to prove himself, increase his recognition and status and progress his marketability in a subsequent bigger job, but the outcome was clearly effective and a good strategic decision.

In contrast, the aggregates business, continuing its individualistic and competitive culture, pursued a more simplistic, tough-minded and directive line in which there were clear winners and losers. The result was a lack of cooperation and the geographically distant centre of the original Steetley business in the north was able to resist real assimilation for at least five years.

Ironically, Redland's financial weakness following this acquisition meant that it had to sell off the brick business, which was more integrated and profitable and, hence, saleable, but the company was not able to stave off a subsequent bid by Lafarge. Lafarge, a French company with a longer viewpoint, has taken several years and put considerable effort into assimilating its UK businesses into its worldwide corporate culture and strategy.

So what is the psychological issue here? It is always easy to assume that a strong financial position enabling acquisition is the result of superior management capability, such that, like errant children, the newly acquired businesses can be brought round to better behaviour when your ways have been imposed. This depends, firstly, upon this view being correct and, secondly, that there is also surplus resource available in the acquiring company to ensure the effective change. It may sound cynical, but my experience is that, more often than not, both assumptions are unwarranted.

These examples make the point that, irrespective of the sophistication of change management in mergers and acquisitions, the real issue concerns the psychological processes of the senior decision makers in the acquiring company, their motivation and whether distortions in their perceptions have led to erroneous decision making.

Unlike the managing directors who fail to fire their unbalanced production directors, in this case it is not fear that has inhibited action. Rather it is a form of addiction to growth and acquisition, together with overconfidence; a lack of psychological inhibition or association, which leads to over-commitment.

Addiction to work is relatively common at all levels. The examples quoted are perhaps at an extreme level, but they illustrate the danger of potent motivators, potent reinforcers, overwhelming the capacity of the individuals concerned to avoid becoming stuck on the treadmill of addiction. A managing director for whom I once worked used to work himself into sleep most days, being so anxious to keep going and so driven to succeed that only when physically incapable would he allow himself to stop; otherwise there was a small possibility that more could have been achieved had he worked even harder.

That this was counterproductive was obvious to everybody around him; their advice and the implication of many academic studies were equally ineffective in getting him to change his behaviour.

The major addiction clinics in the UK treat people who are able, assertive, demanding, with a capacity for self-delusion, conventional financial and other success, a need for recognition, a lack of emotional control, and short time perspectives. Many of those under treatment are highly successful, driven people. These are characteristics shared by some senior managers.

Conclusion

So where does this discussion leave us? The suggestion is that the endeavour to repeat the supposedly behavioural predeterminants of excellence shown by others is suboptimal. It satisfies a great need in those seeking to emulate successful others and it provides business psychologists and social scientists amongst others with an effective outlet. But it is, at heart, regressive. In an evolutionary sense it implies systematic adaptation to specific environmental parameters which then give rise to vulnerability to change in the environment. How wonderfully well adapted was the tyrannosaurus – the bigger the better! The reader may like to count the number of organizational tyrannosauruses in her or his experience.

The real essence of business success is innovation and courage. The real creators of business success do not seek to emulate others – they have their own ideas. If they have a problem it is that, in pursuing their idea, they fall into a number of psychological traps – common reasons for failure or common causes of incompetence. The issues we have raised, addiction, the gumption trap, fear of failure, enjoyment of the comfort zone, fear of uncertainty, assumptions of invincibility, can all lead to major mistakes at the individual and at the corporate level, despite the considerable potential competence of the individuals concerned.

From this analysis it is suggested that, as business psychologists, our task is to seek to help our clients avoid mistakes, to identify and anticipate common causes of incompetence, which could well arise from their personalities and, indeed, from their strengths. If freed from avoidable disaster, they will probably find their own routes to innovation and success, without us or anyone else trying to tell them how.

I would contend that this has many implications for our actions. It would, for example, change the orientation of theoretical work on selection to great advantage. There is, however, rather little published that reflects this approach. A significant example is the work of the Centre for Creative Leadership (Leslie and Van Velsor, 1996) on identifying common causes of why otherwise potentially successful managers 'derail'. It does *not* tell them what to do, but more usefully identifies common causes of why people in some way do not do as well as expected – ignore this at your peril!

The study of psychology itself suggests a much closer examination of the day-to-day working of business and decision making. Only at the level of detailed involvement is it possible to engage with colleagues and clients about underlying emotion and other drivers of decision making, to understand enough about the business itself to question assumptions authentically, to have sufficient credibility to be accepted, and to avoid the intellectually rationalizing snow job that can be presented in order to get you to go away.

So these examples do not lead to an alternative grand theory of organization or suggest a new fad as a total answer to every problem. The discussion may seem to be related, to some extent, to the concept of emotional intelligence but it is more focused on individuals' behaviours, actions and reactions to specific situations, rather than making assumptions that business leaders need to possess more of a previously unidentified characteristic.

The real impact of business psychology would seem to lie in working in the nuts and bolts of organizational life, helping people to see and understand situations with clarity and humanity, to understand how their own feelings, fears, emotions, strengths and attributes influence their decisions, so that they are able to avoid incompetence and allow space for their own innate innovation.

CHAPTER 10

The political terrain

KYLIE BAINS

'In the office in which I work there are five people of whom I am afraid. Each of these five people is afraid of four people (excluding overlaps), for a total of twenty, and each of these twenty people is afraid of six people, making a total of one hundred and twenty people who are feared by at least one person. Each of these one hundred and twenty people is afraid of the other one hundred and nineteen, and all of these one hundred and forty-five people are afraid of the twelve men at the top who helped found and build the company and now own and direct it.'

Joseph Heller, *Something Happened*

The political paradox

Political behaviour in organizations is a ubiquitous phenomenon yet, curiously, very few people believe themselves to be the culprits. People often describe difficulties in their working environment to do with hidden agendas, one-upmanship, territoriality and favouritism, yet those same people often feel that they themselves play a straightforward game. Indeed, it is rare to come across someone who admits to being a political player in this great game of corporate chess. So who is doing all the politicking?

We all operate on some political level. The style may be elaborate, subtle or Machiavellian but most, if not all, of us will have some cognitive process that justifies our particular actions. Indeed, psychological paradigms like the fundamental attribution error and self-serving bias demonstrate that we are great rationalizers of our behaviour.

Political behaviour is a subjective experience or state of mind. Identical behaviours will be seen as political by some people, but not by others. We also typically perceive our own behaviour much more favourably than that of others. More precisely, if we don't agree with what someone else has said, done or achieved, we are more likely to be critical of them, or describe their behaviour as political.

At a deep level, individuals think that it is acceptable for them to be political but they don't want others engaging in political behaviour. Each of us wants the edge. We don't want to be outmanoeuvred; competition is dangerous in the corporate world. It is most advantageous for us to see situations, attitudes, emotions and agendas clearly and to know where threats or opportunities exist.

This chapter aims to help individuals to gain some understanding of the political dynamics around them and, through this, to stimulate thinking on how to secure worthwhile achievements and thrive in organizations. Indeed, to ignore the existence and benefits of political behaviour or to abstain from it entirely is self-deceptive and, at the extreme, a recipe for career suicide. However, the tactics need to be sophisticated as transparent, obvious or inept political behaviour is even worse than no politicking at all!

How people think about political behaviour

Good and bad politics

Politics has different meanings for different people. One man's politics is another man's influencing. It is therefore useful to explore how politics has been construed and defined by writers over time:

- For Aristotle, politics was seen as a productive means of creating order from the divergent interests of individuals while avoiding forms of totalitarian governance.
- Murray and Gandz (1980) describe workplace politics as: 'the pursuit of self-interest at work in the face of real or imagined opposition.' They also recognize that politics is often seen as a 'dirty word'.
- Mintzberg (1985) regarded political behaviour as typically divisive and conflictive, often pitting individuals or groups against a formal authority, accepted ideology and/or certified expertise, or else against each other.
- Ferris, Russ and Fandt (1989) defined political influence behaviour as a 'social influence process in which behaviour is strategically designed to maximise short term or long term self interest, which is either consistent with, or at the expense of other's interest'.
- Morgan (1986) in his *Images of Organization,* approached the analysis of organizational politics in a systematic way by focusing on the relationship between interests, conflict and power.
- In their study of evolutionary and psychological literature, Sloan Wilson, Near and Miller (1986) defined it as 'a strategy of social conduct that involves manipulating other for personal gain, often against the others' self-interest'.

The negative connotations associated with political behaviour cannot be doubted. They are also among the primary reasons why many people fail to develop effective political skill. However, while there is undoubtedly inept and harmful politics there are also serious and worthwhile political behaviours that can enable significant achievement for others and the wider community.

My personal view is that political behaviour is *any activity focused on harnessing the forces around you to achieve things.* It can be done either in a malevolent way, where achievements are self-serving, or in a benevolent way where the achievements also benefit the interests and needs of others.

What drives us to behave politically?

Many definitions of organizational politics allude to the motivations of individuals to optimize their own interests. Our interests can be broken down as follows:

- we operate politically to protect our jobs;
- we protect our jobs to protect our financial interest;
- we protect our financial interests to protect our basic needs and the well-being of our families;
- we protect ourselves and our families to protect our genes.

Darwinism and Stephen Dawkins's 'selfish gene' theory are testimony to the biological roots of our political behaviour.

You only have to look at animal colonies to see that political behaviour is not about human nature, but has its roots in the hierarchy. Franz De Waal (1989), in his fascinating book *Chimpanzee Politics,* observed trends of chimp behaviour that would all be familiar in many an executive boardroom. In particular, De Waal identified two basic rules of conduct among chimpanzees: 'one good turn deserves another', and 'an eye for an eye'. However, Robert Wright (1994), in his book *The Moral Animal,* states that

> for all the suggestive parallels between ape and human striving, the differences remain large. Human status often has relatively little to do with raw power. It's true that overt physical dominance is often a key to social hierarchy among boys. But, especially in adults, the status story is much more complex, and in some cultures, its political aspects have been quite subdued.

Nonetheless, our social brains have evolved relatively recently and are concerned with the business of outwitting each other and surviving other humans. Indeed, the evolutionary literature is full of interesting hypotheses on the adaptive value of manipulative behaviour.

Hierarchy

Arguably, the structural hierarchy of organizations is cohesive in the sense that it gives people role definition and clarity around their expected behaviours and responsibilities within an organization. And yet, just as with the chimpanzees, this hierarchy is inherently dynamic because individuals, in the interest of their genes, vie for the most sought-after positions in the hierarchy.

But does the structural hierarchy determine political activity? This question is particularly interesting in light of the fact that the industrial organizational model is virtually a thing of the past. We now see flatter organizational structures, virtual global teams and hollow organizations where much central activity is outsourced. Given that humans have a natural motivation and a propensity to compete against each other (hence the development of our social brains), contemporary organizational structures make the hierarchy more ambiguous and harder to see. However, there is no denying that a hierarchy will always exist even in the most egalitarian of organizations.

If we are to survive as the human race, let alone within the context of our jobs, our greatest challenge is to overcome our biological drives for self-interest and channel those energies toward the greater good.

Model of political types

Figure 10.1 indicates two dimensions, 'competitive drive' and 'overtness', which drive the different 'types' of political behaviour.

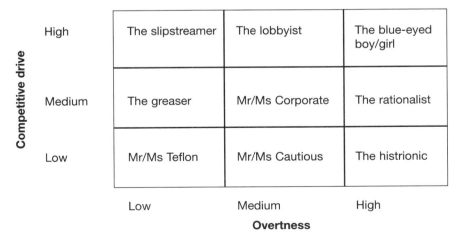

Figure 10.1 Political types.

Most of us are unable to predict, on a consistent basis, the underlying motivations of others or the outcomes of every political game. Doing so would enable us to adjust our own influencing strategies accurately to ensure we get what we want, as in a chess match for example. Consequently, we tend to develop particular game plans and hope that they will work for us most of the time. However, because of the constantly changing political landscape around us, such game plans are unlikely to be effective all of the time.

The way we behave politically has roots not only in our evolution, but also in our individual psychological makeup. The nature of our deepest insecurities, our values, the events and issues we choose to focus our attention on, and those we choose to ignore, underscored by our emotional maturity, all influence our reactions to politically charged situations.

The 'political types' identified in the political behaviour model are outlined below. Brief characteristics of each type are given. There will be some situations where the strategy of each of the types works well but there are others where it will almost certainly be disadvantageous for the individual. It is intended as a lighthearted exploration of political behaviour, although readers may find it useful for provoking thinking about their own political engagement. Outlining political types in this oversimplified manner is only productive if used as a structure for discussion or coaching and it is my hope that it will be used as such. As consultants working with or coaching individuals it is useful to help people reflect on the extent to which they see aspects of their own styles here, or the way in which those around them are behaving. It is also likely to be helpful for discussing ways of maximizing the effective outcomes for the business as well as themselves and for minimizing the negative effects.

Of course, we are all far too complex and contradictory to fit into any of these behaviours in a set way. People do, however, tend to make use of particular strategies, which they feel they can rely upon. Hence, our political behaviour is partly learned from our environment.

The slipstreamer

Characteristics demonstrated by the slipstreamer are as follows:

- a focus on building strong personal relationships with powerful others;
- using those powerful others as sponsors and political buffers;
- less likely to develop ties with people lower down in the organization;
- not afraid to use sexuality to charm;
- typically follow bosses if they move to a different organization;
- keep a low profile.

Effective outcomes

The success for this political type is fundamentally dependent on the future success of the people to whom the slipstreamers attach themselves.

Ineffective outcomes

This strategy is prone to circumstance and undoubtedly an element of luck. You need to back the right horse!

The greaser

Characteristics demonstrated by the greaser are as follows:

- crude ingratiation of superiors (for example, frequent compliments, laughing at unfunny jokes);
- exuberant interest in the boss's family and/or extracurricular activities;
- constant verbal admiration of the boss's character, intellectual prowess, business achievements, interpersonal skill, and so forth;
- puppy-like readiness to offer service in even the most rudimentary of tasks.

Effective outcomes

The greaser is likely to be very effective with an egotistical boss. He or she is more likely to appreciate endless compliments, and less likely to suspect them, than someone with lower ego needs who is fundamentally more self-secure.

Ineffective outcomes

On the other hand, greasers are highly unlikely to be popular with fellow members of the organization, particularly as greasers are inclined to expose their counterparts in an effort to make themselves look better.

Mr/Ms Teflon

Characteristics demonstrated by Mr/Ms Teflon are as follows:

- nothing sticks to them;
- when things go wrong they are not seen for dust;
- blame always seems to elude them, almost regardless of the situation;
- they are skilled at highlighting their achievements and burying their mistakes;

- they are constantly vigilant;
- they select and communicate information that justifies their decisions and ignore data that do not;
- they explain failure in positive terms or avoid information that might be interpreted as reflecting negatively on their performance.

Effective outcomes

The Mr/Ms Teflon behaviours are most likely to be effective as part of an upward influencing tactic. Mr/Ms Teflon's manager, who will not necessarily see behind the scenes but will only receive the filtered information through Mr/Ms Teflon, is likely to think positively about him/her. It is also most advantageous as a short-term strategy.

Ineffective outcomes

However, Mr/Ms Teflon may be advised to reverse his/her strategy on occasion. Many of us would become suspicious of an individual who never seems to make mistakes. Firstly, human error is inevitable and, secondly, mistakes are a vehicle by which people learn. In order to appear realistic, therefore, Mr/Ms Teflon would have to openly take the flack every now and again. If not, this strategy is likely to be risky over the longer term.

The lobbyist

Characteristics associated with lobbyists are as follows:

- they gather support from others in bars, coffee rooms and rest rooms prior to meetings;
- they are quiet, one-to-one achievers;
- they prepare the scene for group events, so that they weigh in their favour;
- they are smooth and patient in dealing with others;
- they read the scene and choose their targets carefully.

Effective outcomes

This type of covert operation has its roots not only in governmental politics, but in the secret service and national defence. It has the obvious benefit of keeping opponents guessing because manoeuvring is hidden. It is also, in many senses, a very astute and rational way of achieving influence. It provides the individual with the opportunity to gauge others' views and debate their own perspectives in a relatively safe environment. In this way, the lobbyist has no surprises in formal meetings and can use that time to the best effect.

Ineffective outcomes

Unfortunately, however, this approach sends out messages that secrecy is sanctioned. Moreover, opponents may detect such tactics.

Mr/Ms Corporate

Characteristics demonstrated by Mr/Ms Corporate are as follows:

- they recite the mission statement at every public opportunity;
- they have a firm and overt belief in the values of the organization;
- they have been known to vote for a corporate uniform, tie or scarf;
- they usually join the organization straight from school or university and remain there until retirement;
- they are belligerently critical of all competitors;
- they live and breathe the word 'professional';
- they show a profound denial of the company's weaknesses.

Effective outcomes

This type of political operating is highly effective in proud, traditional organizations with strong cultures. As such, acceptable behaviours are known and often documented as part of the company mantra. These businesses often recruit a particular 'type' of individual and those who are wrongly recruited and don't fit will very soon be aware of that. Mr/Ms Corporate can flourish in such environments, assuming, of course, that the business remains successful.

Ineffective outcomes

Clearly, the Mr/Ms Corporate approach is not going to work in businesses that value individuality or need a touch of the maverick in order to grow and succeed within their markets. Their style of engagement is likely to be at odds with smaller businesses and more fluid cultures. In addition, the degree to which Mr and Ms Corporate are able to mobilize people around them depends on them sharing those same corporate values. It is also possible that such an obedient soul may evoke suspicion, especially from peers. The 'too good to be true' syndrome is, indeed, a danger for all those who adopt the corporate tactic.

Mr/Ms Cautious

Characteristics demonstrated by Mr/Ms Cautious are as follows:

- profoundly suspicious;
- super vigilant regarding potential threats and dangers;
- fiercely competitive;
- takers rather than providers of information;
- cowardly regarding overt confrontation;
- they tend to play a quiet, low-key card.

Effective outcomes

In intensely political environments, Mr/Ms Cautious is perhaps a wise politician. It is also a useful entry point to new or unfamiliar organizations where time is needed to understand the individuals around you and the nature of the political fabric before intervening with any personal strategy.

Ineffective outcomes

This is an inherently defensive strategy rather than one that is going to drive their own progression forward at pace. In particular, Mr and Ms Cautious can be so wrapped up in their paranoia that they fail to identify and seize the positive political opportunities. Moreover, as with Mr/Ms Teflon and the greaser, this tactic tends to attract suspicion from people around those who use it. Playing an overprotective game, therefore, can tend to have the opposite effect – that of highlighting oneself for attack. A disintegration of trust from colleagues, subordinates and superiors, can also serve to undermine Mr/Ms Cautious' interest.

The blue-eyed boy/girl

Characteristics demonstrated by the blue-eyed boy or girl are as follows:

- an eye on the future;
- creative;
- overtly ambitious;
- form strong bonds with senior players and particularly their own bosses;
- question traditional ideas or practices;
- or, alternatively, espouse the virtues of traditional ideas and practice, but in a highly energetic and enthusiastic manner.

Effective outcomes

The blue-eyed boy/girl strategy can get these individuals noticed and they therefore typically have a strong chance of being given new opportunities. In turn, their chances of influencing decisions and having an impact on an organization can be significantly increased. This type can also be highly effective in sleepy organizations that want to change. They recognize the danger in their sleepiness and hold hopes in fresh new blood with the promise of salvation.

Ineffective outcomes

The blue-eyed boy/girl, however, must be wary of the favouritism stigma. Being sanctioned and encouraged from above has only limited benefits if jealousy and animosity is coming from sideways and below. Consequently, unless the blue-eyed boy/girl tactic is coupled with satisfactory capability and due modesty, it may prove counterproductive.

The rationalist

Characteristics demonstrated by rationalists are as follows:

- the non-political 'politico';
- they relate to others;
- they give a balanced insight into the political dynamics of the organization;
- they are trustworthy;
- they are able to defuse emotionally fraught situations by acting as level-headed facilitators;
- they are appropriately assertive;
- they take initiative and operate responsibly;
- they don't rock the boat;
- they are calm and predictable.

Effective outcomes

On initial inspection the rationalist would seem to be effective in almost any political dilemma. Indeed, this type usually does well in organizations – at least up to a point. Their likelihood of being promoted is relatively high because of the smooth path they make for those around and above them.

Such balanced and relatively low-key behaviour may not catapult individuals into the highest ranks but it would certainly preserve their energy in maintaining their current position. Indeed, while moving up a corporate ladder or indeed a social hierarchy takes considerable effort, simply maintaining one's position is certainly no easy task. Consequently, conserving one's effort in this regard can be quite a viable strategy.

The rationalist can also be effective in volatile climates that provoke anxiety in individuals about their job security, their reputations and their long-term welfare within an organization. Therefore, rational and level-headed subordinates are a valuable commodity.

Ineffective outcomes

On the other hand, the rationalist strategy is less likely to be effective in organizations that value competitive aggression. In these situations, rationalists are less likely to gain a high profile and be noticed by key stakeholders who could assist them in making a broader impact on decision making. It is also possible that rationalists are seen by their counterparts as relatively insignificant and ineffectual.

The histrionic

Characteristics demonstrated by histrionics are as follows:

• they are emotionally volatile;
• they have difficulty seeing beyond their own emotional needs;
• they achieve their own ends by being generally loud and pushy;
• they are partial to temper tantrums and hysterics if they don't get their own way;
• they are often behind-the-scenes gossipers and starters of rumours.

Effective outcomes

The histrionic strategy tends to work in a positive way for its players, simply due to the fact that other organizational members defer to them in order to keep the peace. Histrionics can therefore be skilled in getting their own way. They can also be effective in raising concern for difficult or delicate issues that the more rational contenders prefer to sweep under the carpet. If they see themselves as being treated badly alongside others, they can be strong advocates for the underdog in organizations.

Ineffective outcomes

The histrionic is definitely best as a short-term strategy. After a while people tend to ignore the histrionic, much like the tantrum-throwing child in the supermarket. The tantrums become intensely irritating for others, especially as they tend to prolong decision-making processes and generally make them more stressful for everyone. Histrionic tactics need to be selected carefully in order to have maximum impact. If used on a consistent basis, the result is like the boy who cried wolf. In conclusion, leave your tantrum throwing for major battles.

Conclusion

Experience tells us that 'politics' is endemic in organizational life, and whether or not we acknowledge our contribution to it, that contribution is nevertheless present. After all, political behaviour is in the eye of the beholder. The descriptions of how different political styles play out in practice, how they confer both advantages and disadvantages on the individuals concerned, will hopefully have provided a balance to the sometimes negative view of office politics. The recognition that there are both good and bad forms of politics is an important start; but inept politics or opting out is unlikely to lead to the fulfilment of individual or broader organizational interests. To use the model effectively therefore demands overlaying it with both insight and skill.

CHAPTER 11

Team development – a case study based on 'appreciative inquiry'

SARAH LEWIS

Appreciative inquiry

Appreciative inquiry (AI) is a change methodology developed by David Cooperrider in America. It is based on five key theoretical principles: the constructionist, poetic, positive, anticipatory and simultaneity principles (Cooperrider and Whitney, 2001). The key methodology is known as the 4D methodology (discovery, dreaming, design and destiny) and is illustrated in Box 1. The following describes a team intervention based on appreciative inquiry processes. Throughout the account reference is made to the 4D methodology and the underpinning principles of appreciative inquiry.

Appreciative Inquiry: Discovery, Dreaming, Designing and Destiny

Key Points

- The constructionist principle: we created our world
- The poetic principle: an organisation is more like a text than a machine
- The simultaneity principle: the question is the intervention
- The anticipatory principle: human systems grow towards positive anticipatory images
- The positive principle: it takes energy to achieve change

The 4D Model

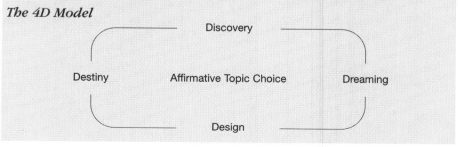

Affirmative Topic Choice: Choosing a life-affirming subject into which to inquire, that is related to the area of organisational interest

Discovery: Through interviews, surveys or other means creating and collecting embodied personal stories of the best of times in the context of the organisational area of interest

Dreaming: Imagining how life could be if more of the best times happened more of the time: building a positive anticipatory image based on what is known to be possible (the discoveries)

Designing: Thinking back from the future to how we need to be organised, what we need to be doing now to increase the possibility of attractive futures unfolding

Destiny: Doing different things or things differently in a coherent and conjoint way, inspired by the work together, energised by the positive energy generated, coordinated by the shared aspirations

Background

The initial commission was to help improve the work performance of a small team within a professional not-for-profit institute. The team was described as underperforming with poor personal interrelationships. It was made clear that the team leader's line manager, who was also the commissioner, was under pressure to consider alternatives such as outsourcing the function if performance didn't improve. The team leader's leadership skills were also under question. While the commissioner knew that some events recently organized by the team had gone badly, it was not clear that this information had been conveyed to the team. Nor was it certain that the team knew that they were under the threat of outsourcing.

Initial interviews: an 'appreciative inquiry' process

The initial step was to interview all team members individually to start to develop an understanding of existing accounts of the situation. The simultaneity principle makes us aware that this is also an intervention process, as the question *is* the intervention and so must be constructed with this awareness in mind. The semi-structured interview was divided into five parts: appreciation, changes, future, current times, and other things. Team members were also asked to give some base line measures on various features of teamwork. Under the 'appreciation' section they were asked 'When is the team at its best?' and 'When are you at your best?' and 'Describe the last time you felt good about something you contributed at work'.

It is fair to say that people were expecting to be asked directly about what was wrong and who was to blame and were very concerned about giving such accounts. The initial appreciative questions came as a pleasant surprise. Later in the interview, under the 'future' section, they were asked 'How will you have an impact on the future?'. At no point in the interview were they asked directly for their account of what was wrong and who was to blame. However, the last section 'Other things' included the question 'What else do I need to know to be able to help this team work more effectively together?'. This allowed people to say anything they had come prepared to say, were driven to say, and would have felt cheated if they hadn't been able to say.

In this way the initial interview worked to incorporate the five key AI principles. The whole interview was structured from the AI simultaneity principle that the question is the intervention. So the questions were chosen with a mind to the accounts they would produce. The positive principle informed the appreciative section of the interview. The anticipatory principle was gently present in the future section where interviewees were asked to talk about what they would like to happen in the future. Similarly, the poetic principle was inherent in the suggestion that they could have an impact on the future. (The poetic principle suggests that an organization is multi-authored – that is, everyone plays a part in its creation.) The whole interview was based on a social constructionist understanding that there are many accounts of a situation that are equally valid and that no one holds a monopoly on the truth. So the interviews were constructed to serve three clear functions:

• they were an appreciative process intervention in themselves;
• they produced data for the consultant about how the situation was currently perceived, experienced, understood and accounted for;
• they produced qualitative data for a later evaluation.

A story to start with

The following is the account that was fed back to the organization of the outcomes from the initial investigation. It has been altered slightly to preserve anonymity.

Over the last few years the team has delivered much good work and achieved many successes. The team has a good reputation, and individual members of the team have good credibility, within the organization.

However, there are signs that review, change and development are needed. Broadly speaking the staff are frustrated and disaffected, with many currently considering leaving. The team has experienced relatively high turnover during the last few years. There appears to be a lack of a clear induction programme for new staff and there is some perception that work is not distributed fairly. Staff members have many ideas for how things could be improved yet feel that nothing actually changes. It seems that the team has difficulty in making and implementing decisions and moving forward in its development.

In addition, the nature of the work seems to have changed in the last year or two. There is a sense that the group is being asked to service both more conferences and conferences of a different nature. Some recent events have attracted criticism. Some factors important to the team's ability to deliver quality events are outside their immediate control, such as the registration process. All in all, the staff are feeling powerless and angry, are demoralized, working in an essentially reactive way, and seeking to make sense of what is happening. At the same time there appears to be an energy, enthusiasm and commitment to improve service delivery, working atmosphere and business processes.

Clearly this account is tailored to its audience and context and plays down the emotional content of the accounts of the situation. Talking to the team, it was clear that emotions were running very high, with members reporting shouting matches in team meetings, tears, blaming and social isolation. This was not, at the time, a fun place to work. Team members were also very angry with their team leader, who they wanted to hold responsible for the distress they were experiencing, yet also didn't want to 'blame' because they considered her to be a very nice person. One person said, 'I would love to have her as a neighbour, just not as a manager'. The members of this team could hardly bear to be in the same room together.

A story for action

Following discussion with the team and the commissioner, the agenda of work was agreed as follows:

- establishing proactive and positive leadership and management – of people, process, boundaries, customers, and work;
- developing a sharper and empowering sense of purpose, aspiration and value;
- clarifying issues of autonomy, group coordination and teamwork;
- recognizing, registering and broadcasting success.

It was agreed that there would be three team intervention sessions, followed by an evaluation session.

A story of what happened

Once the broad outline of the work that needed to be done had been agreed, a series of three team interventions took place. The first was a full day that aimed to create a shared account of current context and core activity. The objective was that by the end of the day, the team would have:

- a shared understanding of when the team was working at its best and how its members all contribute to that;
- developed a shared account of the context within which it was expected to perform;
- identified how the team, through its context and strengths, added value to the process of organizing events (or could do so);
- begun to work on a form of words that addressed why the team exists and what it aims to become; and
- identified team and/or individual actions to take the process forward.

The process for this day was built around the appreciation, poetic and construction principles particularly. In terms of the 4D model the discovery element was the focus for this day. The other exercises were provided to help create some further commonality about their situation. Within this there was a strong focus on extending the story of what was going on beyond the 'personalities in the team' account that clearly wasn't creating positive change, to a more systemic one. In this way, the possibility is created of changing the story of 'how I come to be feeling this bad' from one of a 'clash of personalities' to a more systemically based account. As this different account is developed, so different possibilities for action are created. The focus on identifying the value added is a process to construct an appreciative account of what the team does.

Process of the first team session

Beginnings

The early part of the day was most revealing. Some people were late and then couldn't look each other in the eye. The members of the group were finding it hard to be in the same room; it was fairly evident that people were worried about the day and some had found it quite hard even to get there. It was decided to address some of this first, so as part of the process of introduction participants spoke about their hopes and fears for the day. This allowed people to express how concerned they were about what might happen in the day and what they might be asked about, and that they might reproduce their 'office' behaviour (not listening, shouting over each other, and so forth) at the event. Following these expressions, it was appropriate to move to the members of the team agreeing how they wanted to work together for the day. This initial work was necessary to gain sufficient agreement to work, to be able to go into the discovery exercise.

Discovery

Drawing on appreciative inquiry methodology, team members then paired off and shared a moment of exceptional team working. Participants were given some instruction about how to interview appreciatively. For instance, they were asked to focus on obtaining description rather than explanation (so to avoid asking 'why') and to be sure to include the emotional component of the experience. This approach works to encourage the 'recreation' of the original experience, which allows those positive emotions from the past to be re-experienced in the present – that is, it brings them into the room. During this exercise, the team discovered new things about itself. For instance two people who had paired up chose, by accident, the same episode as their example. They had had no idea that the other had felt this way about the particular episode they were both involved in.

They then fed back how they had felt doing the exercise and at the time of the experience. The feedback from this exercise produced over three flipchart sheets of data. The change of emotional tone in the room as these stories emerged was palpable. For the team members, the idea that any one of them, never mind all of them, could identify a good team experience was a revelation. They were both astonished and delighted by this evidence of good feeling within their group.

They then worked together to ascertain what made the particular event they had identified so effective in teamwork terms compared with other similar but not so good episodes. It soon became apparent that these 'good times' tended to share the theme of being offsite and involving only a few members of the team. However, it was also clear that the different nature of the work, and the feedback loops available, played a big part in creating the difference.

An important point about an appreciative approach is that the process doesn't then immediately move on to 'solve' the 'problem' of how to replicate those features in other environments. Rather, the information is left to do its process work through people's changed understanding and held in abeyance to be used to inform later parts of the process, as appropriate.

Appreciating the complexity of the context: the web of expectations

The team members then moved on to identify the different parties (stakeholders) who had an interest in what they did and to start to think about their expectations of the team and their criteria of success. Again, a wealth of data was produced. When asked to consider what they had produced, they noted the sense of relief gained by getting it all 'out there'. Some of the tensions and paradoxes evident within the system were identified, and the facilitator noted that such 'system' tensions are often played out within a group that holds an awareness of all these agendas. This observation was not explored further at this time, although some members of the group nodded in agreement.

Appreciating the work: added value

After lunch the team members moved on to specify the elements involved in putting an event together with the intention of going on to identify how they added value at each part of the process. The team demonstrated a strong shared sense of what the event elements were and organized itself very effectively to do this task. Again, the view was expressed that it was very useful to have this knowledge made explicit and 'out there'.

Appreciating the importance of purpose: what are we trying to do?

The team moved on to create statements of purpose and vision. This happened remarkably smoothly, reflecting the progress the group had made in working together and developing a shared understanding.

Appreciating personal effect: I have impact

Finally, each individual member committed to doing something different as they returned to the work environment, and some team activities were identified to move things forward.

Process of the second team session

Approximately a month later the team met for an afternoon. The aim of the afternoon was to create a shared vision for the future, and a shared understanding of how to make it happen.

Appreciating change

The session started with the team members revising how they wanted to work together, and identifying, in pairs, how things were changing for the better since they had last met. While this initially seemed challenging, they were soon able to come up with many examples. Clearly this exercise is based on the construction and appreciation principles. It is only when asked about how things are changing for the better that the account begins to be created. As ever, the question is the intervention and what we talk about is what we see. The data produced from the last session were also reintroduced and people were asked to recall how they had felt on seeing all this. This is the positive principle in action. The group are moving on to think about change and so an intervention was made to help them reconnect with the positive energy they had generated last time we were together.

Dreaming

People were then asked to pair up and interview each other 'in the future'. The future is grounded in the previous discovery, so the essential guiding principle for this vision of the future is 'how would things be if more of these good things were happening more of the time?'. The type of questions they asked each other included: 'what are you doing, where are you, who is around, what are your achievements, aspirations, hopes etc. What are people saying about the department?' This exercise generated terrific energy.

Each pair then fed back these pictures of the future. It soon became clear that this list of 'future features' could be mined for items to form a template to measure change. The group began to identify those that easily lent themselves to measurement.

Design

The pairs then returned to interviewing each other about how the transition had been made from the past to this future. 'How did some of these things start to change? Who did what?' In this way, a ladder was created between the desired future and the present by working back from the future. People then worked as individuals or in pairs on how some of these future outcomes could be achieved, and from their discussions they created 'ladders of change'. As these pairs fed back the ideas they had been working on and their aspirations for change, a very valuable impromptu discussion on the role of the leader emerged. During this feedback, the leader was given a clear directive/permission from the group to be the outward-looking, boundary-crossing, different-function-coordinating person, while they got on with the operational work. In effect, she was given a clear management and leadership mandate by the team members.

Process of the third team session

Reconnecting, getting started, a changing context

The last session was a more production-oriented day – that is, a day focused on 'what are we going to do?'. This day was overshadowed from the start by a forthcoming huge project and the amount of work that generated for the team. The team started by identifying 'changes for the better' since we had last met. People found this exercise harder than the previous time. This was put down to pressure of the big project and the danger of this sending the team back into old ways of relating. It was noted that highlighting this was useful in itself.

We then brought everything that had been done over the last two sessions, all the flips and data generated, into the room and people looked at it. The general tenor of the observations and comments was about how much they had done and the progress they had made. People particularly remembered how they had felt doing the future-oriented exercises.

Destiny

The team members interviewed each other one by one, with the others acting as a listening and reflecting team, about what they thought should be done, not worrying for the moment about who might do it. Everyone was given 10 to 15 minutes to explain their views. The many ideas were captured on flipcharts. The team then looked at all the information that it had produced and held a discussion about what it would do and how it would organize itself to do it. This discussion was facilitated and recorded by the team leader. Essentially an action plan was drawn up with names and dates against events. Unfortunately, the general agreement was that in the main these initiatives would have to wait until the project was over. It was clear that this would have a negative effect on the momentum generated by the day for further change.

Evaluation

The team reassembled with the facilitator 7 months after the previous intervention to assess progress. Initially, each remaining team member (two had moved on during the process) and the commissioner were interviewed, after which the team came together as a group to assess the progress so far.

Some effort was made to record change over time by taking baseline perceptual measures on the initial areas of concern that could then be revisited at the evaluation. The scale used for all measurement is from

1 to 10, with 1 as low. Table 11.1 shows the results. These cannot be regarded as statistically significant, however they give a clear indication of direction of change.

Table 11.1 Initial areas of concern

Objective	Mode Oct 2002	Spread Oct 2002	Mode Oct 2003	Spread Oct 2003
Holding boundaries	3	2–4	6	2–10
Sharing knowledge and skill	None	3–8	8	7–9
Importance of success	10	1–10	9	8–10
Fairness of work share	None	2–7	6	3–10
Manager skills	5	3–5	6	4–7
Leadership skills	5	1–6	None	3–7

Some more general observations included:

- the sessions had had an immediate effect on team relations and team working but these tended to fade over time;
- there had been some increased sense of empowerment amongst team members;
- decision making could still be slower than was desirable;
- the line manager's hands-on management style was helpful;
- there was less frustration within the team generally;
- the team leader was more effective and needed to become even more so;
- the work from the sessions wasn't always capitalized on as fully as it could be;
- the sessions provided a safe space;
- the team meetings were becoming learning experiences to a greater extent;
- outsourcing the design work was a good idea that was working well;
- the team members were generally working better together;
- it was good to have the new person in the team;
- there was a continuing need to focus on the future.

However, there were considered to be some issues outstanding:

- continuing to build trust and team work;
- maintaining and improving listening and communication;
- renegotiating team fit given change in team roles;
- continuing to increase professionalism and somehow continuing the safe space, focus-on-the-future, long-term consideration process.

The story continues

Change is an ongoing process. As change agents we join other people's stories of change for a short while, and the story continues after we fade out. The life of a consultant is one of unfinished stories.

This unfinished story is presented not as a template for 'how to do AI' or, even worse, 'how to do successful team development'! Rather it is an attempt to illuminate how theory always informs practice, and that practice can only be evaluated by how helpful or useful it is to a particular group in a particular situation at a particular time. And that none of these features stays constant. This is presented as an account of a particular experience of attempting to help others achieve helpful change working from the principles of AI. Was it helpful? I think so. Will it be useful to you? I hope so.

PART 3
PREDICTION

CHAPTER 12

Introduction

DAVID THOMPSON

Nils Bohr, Nobel laureate in physics, once uttered the memorably simplistic phrase 'Prediction is very difficult, especially if it's about the future.' Similarly, when Stella Rimmington, a former head of MI5, was commenting on the dreadful events of 9/11, she observed that the biggest challenge in intelligence work was in the area of 'preventative intelligence': being able to predict future events. Psychologists spend a great deal of time and effort trying to predict the future behaviour of individuals and groups but despite having developed all sorts of ways of reducing error rates, like everybody else who attempts prediction, they find it extraordinarily difficult. Contributors to this section put the process of prediction into a real-world organizational, legal and cultural context, and I start with a chapter addressing some fundamental questions about measurement.

Organizations are prepared to pay business psychologists to attempt this because of the potentially significant economic benefits; organizations deliver a product or service and good-quality staff are a necessary component in successfully doing this. Even in times of recession press articles will appear about 'the war for talent', reflecting the fact that attracting, selecting and retaining good staff is seen as a critical competitive battleground. Recruiting and hiring is also a subject of widespread fascination amongst people in general, affecting everyone who has a job; it will, for example, significantly affect how successful you are if your role involves filling jobs that report to you. Managers and psychologists are interested at both a practical and an intellectual level because a hiring decision is a prediction about the future based upon incomplete information and probabilities rather than certainties. The nature of this judgement process is discussed in Malcolm Hatfield's contribution. The size of the forecasting-related industry, from market research companies to strategy consultancies that support organizations' attempts to prepare themselves for what is ultimately an unknowable future, runs to millions of pounds. Business psychologists have as a core specialism the measurement of people and the prediction of their future behaviour. The research evidence underpinning the strong case for using assessment centres for selection is well covered here in the contributions from Rob Yeung and Simon Brittain, and by Helen Marsh et al. With the rise of the Internet, the 1990s saw an explosion of research into the different forms of technology-enabled recruitment and assessment, most of this showing very favourable candidate reaction (Lievens and Harris, 2003). The chapter by Bywater et al. contains a good example of the use of technology in recruitment by a bank.

Business psychologists are not simply compliant servants of organizations; they are a principled body of practitioners covered by a code of ethics (see Francis, 1999 and Lowman, 1998) and will always seek to ensure that individual employees are treated fairly during, and as a consequence of, any intervention. This theme is fascinatingly illustrated in practical and technical terms, in an international context, in the chapter by Marsh et al.

Maria Yapp's contribution gives us an informed insight into the critically important activity of spotting those with high potential. Talent management is an essential area for organizations, as the segmentation of the workforce by identifying those with potential usually implies preferential access to developmental opportunities and also informs succession planning, upon which very survival of the organization partly depends.

CHAPTER 13

Themes of measurement and prediction

DAVID THOMPSON

In this chapter, I will cover some fundamental questions that business psychologists and their client organizations address when considering the application of psychology to the measurement of capability and prediction of successful performance. These questions are:

- Why measure?
- What to measure?
- How to measure?

The answers from these are presented drawing on personal experience as well as research.

Why measure?

The management of organizations relies heavily upon measurement; in the past these measures were almost exclusively of financial performance and these still predominate but they have now been supplemented by an approach known as the organizationally generated 'balanced scorecard' (see Gary, 2002). This represents an attempt to introduce relevant non-financial measures such as customer satisfaction, product/service quality, sales of new products, even employee morale, as key performance indicators of an organization. These measures tend to cluster into three broad strategic themes (Gary, 2002):

- operational effectiveness;
- customer management;
- product innovation.

However, the relationship between these measures and bottom-line performance is seldom clear to the managers in organizations that adopt them. Regrettably, the way employees contribute to the bottom line is not precisely quantifiable: they obviously do in terms of effort, attitude, knowledge and innovation but measuring such cause-and-effect relationships in complex organizations is extraordinarily difficult. A rare classic study that has been able to demonstrate such a link between people measures and business performance is that of Heskett et al. (1997). One of the many problems that bedevil measurement progress in this area is the existence of non-linear relationships and interdependencies between the variables (Hatfield, 2000; Somers, 2001). Share price is important to quoted companies. The stock market valuation might be up to six or seven times greater than the combined physical and financial assets. This is derived from an assessment of their 'intangible assets', to which the skills of the workforce make an important contribution. We are, however, still some way from knowing specifically how better selection contributes to the bottom line.

Psychologists have historically been relatively successful at showing a link between a specific intervention and an outcome – a new selection procedure, for instance, and the job performance of individuals (Murphy, 2000). Assessment centres are good predictors of a range of measures such as job performance and rate of promotion. Psychologists have also investigated the impact of other human resources interventions such as appraisal, which is akin to assessment. A study by West et al. (2002), for example, showed that the extent and sophistication of appraisal systems was closely related to a very important outcome measure: that of lower mortality rates in 61 acute hospitals in England and Wales. Lower mortality rates were also linked with the sophistication of staff training and the percentages of staff working in teams. A good empirical demonstration of what television hospital drama addicts always suspected! In general, psychologists have used measurement to show which practices are worthwhile in order to help the decision makers in client organizations.

What to measure?

There is no doubt that, within human resources practice, selection is the most researched area where many have sought to prove the effectiveness of different methodologies. An obvious reason for this is that recruitment and selection cost identifiable sums of money. Most organizations have a fixed annual recruitment budget and want to spend that money wisely. In reality there is limited application in the UK of the latest advances in selection methodology, other than in large organizations (see Nobble and Bozionelos, 2001). Historically research in this area has tended to be driven by academic criteria rather than economics. Because the variables involved are easy both to identify and to manipulate it is a topic open to traditional experimental design. However, the validation of selection procedures 'in the real world' has become increasingly difficult.

In economic terms the most important type of validity is predictive validity. Is the selection procedure reliably identifying above-average performers? Gathering longitudinal performance data on employees, say over 2 years, has become virtually impossible as jobs change, disappear, or staff move on. It is also difficult to find human resources professionals able to fund such studies, as budgets shrink or other things have priority. Some help is at hand, though, through the statistical technique of meta-analysis and validity generalization, which allows psychologists to group together previous studies on a particular selection method to make an estimate of its validity coefficient (Hermelin and Robertson, 2001), and hence judge its effectiveness. An interesting by-product of these statistical analyses has been the discovery that we had previously been underestimating just how powerful many selection methods, such as interviews and personality measurement, are (see Salgado, Ones and Viswesvaran, 2001). In practice, business psychologists use validity generalization to inform their selection procedure designs, which tend to be driven by a combination of technical, practical, economic and 'internal political' considerations. Alec Rodger, one of the UK's founding fathers of occupational psychology in the 1950s, consistently argued that what psychologists propose to clients should always be 'technically sound, administratively feasible, socially acceptable and politically defensible' – a shortlist of pragmatic criteria that are still wise counsel today.

Since the 1980s there has been considerable academic interest in utility analysis, which can be used to measure the financial benefits of improved performance from human resource interventions such as training or selection. With respect to selection we find from this research firstly that staggeringly large sums of money can be saved through the use of valid selection procedures, and secondly that the benefits are proportional to job complexity and job impact. In other words, the greater the employee discretion in how the job is carried out and the greater the degree of importance of the job to the success of the organization, the larger the monetary gain from sound selection (Cabrera and Raju, 2001). This is a convincing argument for doing middle and senior management selection well and for successfully identifying those with potential. Return on investment from selection is only one of a multitude of variables on which the majority of decision makers base their decisions (Macan and Highhouse, 1994).

With constant pressures on costs, a good financial business case for changing a selection procedure is frequently required, and a diverse range of measures might be used to demonstrate value, such as:

- reduction in employee absence;
- turnover;
- accident rates;
- recruitment cycle times;
- human resources staff to run the process.

Running in parallel with the question of financial return is the legal issue of scientifically demonstrable reliability and validity. This is required of all human resources practices that can be described as 'tests' under US and Canadian law, but is a more ambiguous requirement in legal terms across the EU member states. Following both the spirit and letter of the law can often be a perilous process for the practitioner.

Human resources professionals tend to be driven by considerations of person/job/organizational fit; value for money in the recruitment and selection process; fairness and the political/legal defensibility of the process. Recruiting line managers, on the other hand, are primarily concerned about getting the best person they can into the job and the time that it will take to achieve this.

Human resources departments adopt performance measures that reflect these two sets of stakeholder concerns and for which data are readily available. So, for example, they will measure:

- achievement within budget;
- time to hire;
- average vacancy level;
- turnover levels;
- line manager satisfaction with their service.

A consequence of this is that client stakeholders will tend to judge the contribution of the business psychologist against their own organizationally relevant criteria rather than more technical measures, so it is an important professional attribute of the psychologist to be able to work towards and to value the achievement of these differing performance metrics.

It was stated earlier that assessment centres are good predictors but a great puzzle over the years has been to try to work out what they are actually measuring; the studies by Lievens and Klimoski (2001) have shown that they do not measure very well the things that we thought they were measuring. We are getting closer now to understanding this with consistent themes relating to cognitive abilities and certain personality traits (Collins et al., 2003).

Following many years of research into selection, there is now a degree of certainty about some of the things that psychologists should be measuring. General cognitive ability seems to be the best all-round predictor of job performance, irrespective of the nature of the job (Schmidt and

Hunter, 1998). What we do not know as unequivocally is the contribution made to job performance by job knowledge (Olea and Ree, 1994). A weakness of many current assessment-centre designs is the failure, where relevant, to adequately test job knowledge. One of the problems is knowing what and how to sample, as job knowledge can be implicit as well as explicit and does not have a neat boundary drawn around it, as does, for example, an examination syllabus.

In terms of personality traits, conscientiousness has emerged as the best single predictor across performance measures and occupations (Murray et al., 2001). Extraversion has also been found to be positively related to performance in sales and managerial jobs (Tett et al., 1991). However, these generalizations in turn mask depths of complexity. For example, Hough et al. (1998) showed that conscientiousness predicted work performance but not the number of job promotions or salary, which were predicted by achievement orientation. Motivation consistently emerges as a mediator between personality and performance at work, so it also has a claim to be amongst the attributes to be measured. Maria Yapp (Chapter 17) emphasizes the important distinction between *motivation* and *motives* in assessment.

Much measurement focuses upon the individual, but it is clear, anecdotally and from the literature on the weaknesses of appraisal systems, that management is a collective or group rather than an individual activity (Furnham and Stringfield, 1994). One of the many challenges in assessment is therefore to predict how an individual will work constructively with others, particularly as failure here seems to be one of the reasons for consequential staff turnover. It is estimated that up to 40% of people changing job are leaving a boss rather than leaving a job. Personality traits assist here, as they have been shown to be good predictors of both team and individual performance, in particular agreeableness and conscientiousness (Newman and Wright, 1999).

Understanding the nature of job performance is a critical part of the measurement equation as this is what we are normally trying to predict. It is obvious that job performance is different for an accountant and a sales manager. A key question is: are the similarities between job demands/performance greater than the differences? At the managerial level the answer from the academic research seems to be 'yes': Borman and Bush (1993), for example, were able to group managerial performance dimensions into four clusters:

- leadership and supervision;
- interpersonal relations and communication;
- technical behaviours (for example, administration);
- useful skills (for example, handling crisis).

Dulewicz (1989) studied middle managers and produced four 'supra-competencies':

* intellectual;
* interpersonal;
* adaptability;
* results orientation.

Identifying generic sets of competencies that provide a common language and framework for human resources interventions is a very attractive proposition to organizations. As a result, much money has been spent through the 1990s developing them, although much money was also wasted producing competencies that were not measurable. Business psychologists have been besieged by clients seeking help to rework competencies they had developed and then found to be unusable in human resources practice. Many turn out to be dog's dinner offerings, characterized by ambiguity, overlaps and conceptual confusion. There can be little doubt that using general, poorly defined competencies weakens the accuracy of prediction.

What we are measuring moves into a fascinating realm when we consider the topic of impression management in the interview, an essentially social process, in which both interviewee and interviewer try to impress in their different ways. Most of the research here has focused on candidate behaviour because of the fear that impression management might reduce the validity of the interview as a selection instrument. In general the research has shown that impression management can backfire if excessively used (Baron, 1989). However, researchers point out that some impression management is legitimate, expected, and indeed is regarded as a desirable candidate skill, although in some is seen as denoting a lack of authenticity and may involve conscious deception (Walley and Smith, 1998). The issue becomes one of distinguishing between the two and should be addressed in interviewer training programmes by getting interviewers to focus on gathering verifiable behavioural examples. Clients prize highly the ability of experienced psychologists to detect deception in amongst the 'noise of impression management'. This takes us back to the issue of judgement, covered later by Malcolm Hatfield.

How to measure?

The challenge for the practitioner psychologist is to find valid measurement techniques that generate positive reactions from those who are measured. There is little point in constructing an excellent selection system that identifies potential high performers only to find that they subsequently turn down your job offer because they have been turned off your organization by the nature of the process itself. In general, candidates regard assessment centres favourably. Our own monitoring for posts in Royal Mail shows that candidates normally see all the various exercises as fair and even enjoyable, except for the psychometric tests. There seems to be a range of reasons for this dislike of testing, boiling down to the fact that they are seen as less relevant and the results open to misinterpretation or misuse (see Chan et al., 1998). A tension for psychologists is that, for some jobs, tests are the single best predictors that they have available. Individual reactions to assessment tests and exercises are closely linked to outcomes: people who perform poorly see them as less accurate, less fair and their own behaviour at the assessment centre as being less representative of their 'real life' behaviour (Teel and DuBois, 1983). From our own experience people who hold the most 'down to earth' types of jobs, such as maintenance engineering and operational management, tend to react least positively to assessment and particularly to activities such as tests and role plays. For groups such as these a great deal of effort needs to go into creating realistic exercises that have good face validity with both candidates and assessors. The poor candidate reaction to tests suggests that a guiding principle in assessment design should be that the greater the transparency that can be achieved the better.

What people think and feel about assessment is one of the factors affecting the quality of the relationship they have with their current or potential employer. Today this relationship is very much based on negotiation around mutual benefit, with both employee and employer expecting assessment to be fair and accurate, with results openly shared. An issue right at the beginning of this relationship is that candidates look for honesty from employers in describing the jobs they have on offer, but are also sceptical, expecting a degree of marketing hype, particularly in job advertisements. We put this observation to practical use at Royal Mail and had notable success in attracting good candidates by honestly advertising one of our roles as challenging but possibly the worst managerial job in the organization! The points worthy of note here are:

- Firstly, that recruitment and assessment practices are systems, made up of interconnected and interdependent components, that have an impact on candidate behaviour.
- Secondly, that there is a social element to this process, so that it is not solely about individual differences between candidates.
- Thirdly, that this has implications not only for how things are measured, but also for what is measured.

The social and cultural dimensions of assessment were brought into sharp relief for me when first recruiting in France. Our candidates expected a decent lunch built into the assessment process, and they did not expect this to be hurried, much to the detriment of our tight assessment centre timetable. We also discovered a distaste for what they perceived to be mechanistic, reductionist, North American-inspired assessment method-ology. For these candidates knowing them as 'whole people', their background and their 'philosophy of life' was culturally important. Subsequently, we changed our assessment process to include much more eating, drinking, socializing and informal 'getting to know you' time, whilst still retaining the original elements of the assessment centre.

An important concern for many organizations is equal opportunities. In terms of attracting suitable candidates the issues usually revolve around organizational culture and the image that the organization proj-ects. With respect to assessment design the issues are usually around methodology and the attitudes of the managers involved. Most sizeable organizations have monitoring processes and some have targets and affir-mative action programmes. My own experience as a practitioner is that unfair discrimination is usually indirect and unintentional. Some years ago, I managed a recruitment campaign to find 15 managers for a nation-wide network of newly built distribution centres. The job analysis of existing centre managers showed, amongst other things, that existing managers of units of this size had in excess of 10 years' managerial expe-rience prior to appointment to these types of roles. Consequently, I chose as one of the sifting criteria 5 years' previous managerial experience. Once all the appointments were made, I reviewed the campaign statistics and found that all the appointees were men and that all 89 candidates seen through the assessment centres had been men. However, in the applicant pool there were 38 women; on rereading their applications it was clear that at least 20 of these women were well qualified in terms of relevant academic and professional qualifications and work experiences but none had met the 5 years' managerial experience criterion. This was a clear case of indirect discrimination as I had no evidence of a link between 5 years' managerial experience and work performance. I was shocked to realize that working in a predominantly male environment had blinkered my perception to such an extent that I had failed to notice the lack of any women as the assessment centre process ran and conse-quently failed to spot a need for early remedial action. This also illustrates that recruitment processes are interdependent systems; it did not matter how fair the assessment centre itself was, as the recruitment process was fundamentally flawed in one of its early steps. Ever since this experience, I have taken care with the first steps. By careful monitoring of sex ratios at each stage it is common to find women overrepresented in the latter stages of managerial recruitment procedures, compared with their repre-sentation in the original applicant pool. So, although in most campaigns

I have run there have been numerically fewer women candidates than men, they have often proved to be of higher average quality than the men, with this effect flowing through to the number of women in the final appointments.

The assessment of ethnic minority candidates needs to be done with care. Groups of white candidates, for example, tend to score on average higher on both verbal and numerical reasoning tests but this is not always so and the reasons behind these ethnic group differences are complex (see Baron and Chudleigh, 1999). Similarly, Harris (1989) has indicated that the effect of race on interview ratings seems to vary. In my view extreme caution is needed in interpreting test and exercise results, together with an open dialogue with the candidate. I have always found it good practice to discuss with candidates their previous experiences of real or perceived discrimination in selection and their expectations in this current situation as, for the majority of ethnic minority candidates, discrimination is a key aspect of their life experience. A core aspect of assessment has traditionally been about seeking to reject variability by selecting people against a tightly defined template of criteria. This is a major challenge for assessment designers in the context of valuing increased employee diversity.

It is now widely accepted that both the process and results of assessment need to be as transparent as possible. This transparency covers telling candidates not only how they will be assessed, but also against what. Sharing knowledge about the competencies at the core of the assessment is also very helpful to the assessor as good candidates will prepare in advance relevant past behavioural examples illustrating their possession of each of the competencies, so saving the assessor time and resulting in a more focused interview.

In recent years computer and Web-based testing has grown apace as the various technical problems have been solved one by one. These methodologies offer great assessment benefits in terms of cost, speed of scoring and data management, with the Web allowing remote data capture as well. With the Web there are potential problems with authenticating the test taker and cheating on cognitive tests by enlisting help, which do not have ready solutions, apart from the random retesting of a subsample of the candidate population when they attend in person at the assessment centre. Technology does offer potential solutions to some long-standing problems in testing, such as detecting candidates engaging in impression management (faking good or bad) in their responses to personality questionnaires and in measuring how long candidates think before responding to each item (Buckley and Williams, 2002). An example is the Cognitive Process Profile, developed by Maretha Prinsloo, which is able to measure 100 cognitive processes on 100 points and then interpret these 10,000 points to provide measures of both current and potential functioning. This is way beyond the scope of paper-and-pencil technology and is of particular interest to those employers who wish to attempt to predict how an individual might develop intellectually.

Because of its many benefits some large organizations, such as the supermarket group J Sainsbury and the Royal Mail, have worked on developing e-enabled assessment centres. However, care is needed so as not to completely dehumanize the process because interacting with warm human beings is an important component of assessment! There is evidence that the research base is lagging behind the capacity of practitioners to innovate in their use of technology in support of assessment (see Lievens and Harris, 2003). As a result, the area might be characterized by many empirically unproven practices, such as online application forms and electronic sifting for many years to come (see Price and Paterson, 2003). Human resources managers with experience of technology-based recruitment practices report mixed results and a host of problems such as systems incompatibility, staff training, IT upgrade costs, unreliable IT vendors, security, handling large candidate volumes and candidate cheating, to mention just a few, so this is far from being a panacea. It does, however, illustrate the range of challenges in recruitment and assessment that many find so rewarding to tackle. There is no doubt, if only on cost grounds, that this is where the future of assessment lies.

CHAPTER 14

Assessment centres: getting more bang for your buck

SIMON BRITTAIN, ROB YEUNG

Introduction

Assessment centres (ACs) were first used by the military to identify officer potential. This began in Germany in the 1930s and was taken up first by the British (through the War Office Selection Board) and then the US military (initially by the Office of Strategic Services – the OSS, which later became the CIA) during the Second World War. These early applications were the forerunners for the first use of ACs within a business setting – at American Telegraph and Telephone (AT&T) in 1956. The AT&T centres were followed up over a 5- to 7-year period and found to be accurate at predicting future success in the organization (Bray and Grant, 1966).

Since this time, AC use has increased rapidly in the US, with over 1,000 organizations using them by the mid-1970s (Cook, 1998). The proportion of UK organizations reporting that they use assessment centres is shown in Table 14.1. Boyle et al. (1993) found that around 50% of private sector organizations and 39% of public sector organizations reported that they use ACs. In addition, their research showed a large variation in their use across business sector, with food, drink and tobacco businesses included in their survey showing a usage in over 60% of organizations.

Table 14.1 Surveys of AC usage in the UK

| Authors | Year | Reported % use of: | |
		Assessment centre	Development centre
Dany and Torchy	1994	12	–
Robertson and Makin	1986	20	–
Boyle et al.	1993	39 to >60*	–
Industrial Society	1996	59	43
Shackleton and Newell	1991	60	–
Roffey Park	1999	63	43

* Rates varied by public/private sector and industry type

113

Many organizations that use AC methodologies do so for specific levels of employee within the business – traditionally for graduate entrants or moves into middle management. Since the mid-1990s there has been a rise in the use of ACs within the processes of succession planning and the identification of development needs for the next generation of senior managers. Recently, these assessments of high-potential managers (Hipos) have been gradually shifting from looking at junior managers who may have the ability to 'go far' in the organization to focusing on middle or senior managers to establish if, when and how they might be suitable for a move into the most senior positions in a business. It appears that organizations have accepted the evidence from the psychology and human resource literature that assessment centres are a useful predictor of the future performance of a manager. Indeed, organizations themselves are raising the stakes for assessment centres by using them to identify their mid-career hipos who will be developed and moved into the key senior positions – with the responsibility for making multi-million pound decisions about business activity.

We believe that the AC method has a lot to offer, although there appear to be many misconceptions about their effectiveness and the applicability of assessment centres with certain groups of managers. In the rest of this chapter we will explore the key areas of:

- what the research tells us about the validity and utility of assessment centres versus other methods, as well as the understanding of this by practitioners;
- when is an assessment centre not an assessment centre;
- guidelines on using and investing in assessment centres – typical contents, key issues and likely costs;
- ethics in assessment centre use;
- where next for assessment centres.

What the research tells us

From a practitioner's viewpoint, one of the key considerations when choosing an assessment method – regardless of the human resources process (such as selection or development) in which it is being applied – is *validity*. Within a selection context this is the predictive validity. The predictive validity coefficient is directly proportional to the practical economic value, the utility, of the assessment method (Brogden, 1949; Schmidt, Hunter, McKenzie and Muldrow, 1979). The higher the utility the higher the employee performance, when measured in terms of increase in output, the monetary value of that output and increased learning of job-related skills (Hunter, Schmidt and Judiesch, 1990).

Assessment centres have long been held up as the 'best' way of predicting performance in a particular job. Indeed, Robertson and Smith (2001) state that 'Probably the most significant change within personnel selection research literature in the last decade or so has been the increased confidence that researchers have in the validity of most personnel selection methods'. Schmidt and Hunter (1998) state that ACs have 'substantial validity'. However, this does not seem to tally with the statistics on AC usage – if they are the best, then why are they not used more in selection or development decisions? Practitioners, whether human resources professionals or business psychologists, often use the argument that they are too expensive and take too long to administer. They can appear expensive when first encountered: for instance, Spychalski et al. (1997) estimate the average cost per candidate to be $1,700 (around £1,000), which includes design, materials, and so forth, but not the indirect costs such as assessors' and participants' time. Beard and Lee (1990) emphasize that the majority of the costs associated with AC use are found in areas such as briefing participants and managers, assessor training and attending the centre itself – for both assessors and participants. So, the AC is not going to be the cheapest option to consider, but what does the research actually tell us about the effectiveness of the AC method?

There have been many reviews of the validity of ACs (for example, Cohen, Moses and Byham, 1974; Schmitt et al., 1984; Gaugler et al., 1987; Schmidt and Hunter, 1998), which have quoted validity coefficients of between 0.33 (when correlating with performance ratings by supervisors) and 0.63 (when assessing for potential). Gaugler et al.'s (1987) study reported a mean raw validity of 0.29, which was estimated to have a true validity of 0.37 when corrections were made for range restriction, and so forth.

Schmidt and Hunter (1998) took the analysis of AC validity one stage further. They reviewed 19 selection procedures and the incremental validity of each procedure above that provided by general mental ability (GMA) alone. (General mental ability is referred to by some researchers, such as Robertson and Smith, 2001, as 'g' or cognitive ability.) Incremental validity is the increase in validity gained when an additional assessment method is combined with an existing process, for example, in the Schmidt and Hunter study with previous experience or peer evaluations. They begin by restating the 'most well-known finding from 85 years of validity research', which is that the most valid predictor of future performance and learning, for people with no prior knowledge or experience of the job, is GMA – as measured through pencil-and-paper tests. They quote a validity coefficient of 0.51, which is only beaten by work sample tests (validity coefficient of 0.54) in predicting future performance. Work sample tests require the individual to have skills and knowledge already associated with doing the job – for example, a manager might be expected to conduct a review of a

GMA: gen mental ability = best predictor of success

business plan specific to the organization – but in a selection context they are likely to be unfamiliar with the finance systems in the new organization. Their findings show that when AC performance is combined with GMA there is an incremental validity of just 0.01. In other words, adding AC data to a measure of GMA gives an overall validity of 0.52. One explanation put forward for this is that ACs rely heavily on GMA and the ability to learn new tasks.

So, why not just use measures of GMA in selection? They can be administered quickly, are usually relatively cheap and are easily scored. The obvious problems associated with tests of GMA are focused around fairness issues for different ethnic groups – differential validity, predictive fairness and subgroup differences in mean scores (for reviews of these issues see Ones et al., 1993; Hunter and Schmidt, 1996; Bobko, Roth, Potosky, 1999). Indeed, Cook (1998) sees these issues as potentially being the ultimate downfall of the routine use of tests of GMA and goes as far as saying that over the next few years 'mental ability tests could be virtually outlawed'. Assessment centres do not appear to suffer from these problems. Thornton (1992) looks at the court cases in which ACs were accused of unfairness in the US and reported that there had yet to be a ruling against an AC – because they allow observation of job-related performance dimensions in job-related exercises. Other studies (such as Huck and Bray, 1976 and Ritchie and Moses, 1983) found similar pass rates for different gender and ethnic groups. The authors' own research on the assessment of senior managers across a number of UK businesses suggests that women score slightly higher than men in ACs. Our explanation for these results is that, in most organizations, women have to be clearly stronger than their male counterparts to get into senior positions – and so do better in the ACs.

We can see that ACs have a reasonable validity (0.37) in their own right, when not combined with a measure of GMA. As would be expected, the utility of the AC method is correspondingly good. For example, Feltham (1988) estimated that using the Civil Service Selection Board (CSSB – a distant successor to the WOSB) instead of an interview to select batches of 70 administrators saves the British government at least £1.8 million per batch.

There are further issues to be considered in the selection of managers and, in particular, senior managers, which the AC method can address. These centre around what some commentators refer to as organizational citizenship behaviour: organization fit on a values level and how the individual will represent the face of the business (both internally to employees and externally to customers). Organizations have become increasingly concerned that managers act in ways that are consistent with

value

alignment is

the stated values of the business. So the challenge for ACs has changed from identifying managers who can produce results to finding the managers who behave in the 'right' way *and* produce results.

Further reading in the area of AC validity suggests that a 'two-stage' process occurs within performance prediction. A number of studies (for example, Russell, 2001) have shown that competencies (or whatever the assessment criteria are labelled) relating to task completion/problem solving are predictive of initial (6 to 18 months) performance within a senior managerial role. Beyond this time these competencies become less predictive and competencies relating to people management become the key predictors of performance. Reflecting on this research, it could be that high-performing managers make an immediate impact on a new role by using their problem-solving skills to identify and introduce quick wins in their part of the business but that changing the way that their teams think and behave at work takes much longer.

What makes an assessment centre an assessment centre?

Many organizations say that they use assessment centres at some point in their business. But what do people mean when they use the phrase 'assessment centre'? The traditional business psychology definition is a 'multi-trait, multi-method' approach – it should be designed to measure more than one aspect (most often a set of competencies) of an individual and use a number of different exercises to tap into these. We explore both the multi-trait (criteria) and the multi-method (assessment exercises) issues in this section.

When we talk about ACs, we use the term generically to describe the method as applied across a number of HR processes – selecting people into an organization, promotion, high-flyer identification, benchmarking and the identification of development needs. As practitioners working in the area of ACs, one of the most common (and frustrating) misconceptions that we encounter is when clients tell us that they currently use ACs when in fact they use an extended interview method – typically a competency or biographical interview plus some tests of ability or personality. An AC must use a number of exercise formats to assess a number of assessment criteria. It will have an assessment matrix, such as that shown in Table 14.2, which will be completed by the assessors after marking exercises, and in almost every case it will involve the participant(s) being observed and scored by a number of assessors.

Table 14.2 Example of a completed assessment matrix

	Interview	In-tray	Project Meeting	Coaching Simulation	Overall
Managing change	4		3		3
Judgement	3	4	4		4
Decision Making		4	4	2	3
Managing Resources		3	2	2	2
Commercial Awareness	3	4		4	4
Interpersonal Skills	2		2	3	2
Strategic Awareness		3	4	4	4

Test Result: Numerical – 75th percentile compared to a senior manager norm	Overall:	2*

Note: the shaded boxes indicate where the competency is **not** assessed in a particular exercise. The rating scale used is 5 – excels in all aspects, 4 – clear strength, 3 – proficient and competent, 2 – some development needed, 1 – significant development required.
* The overall decision is a 2 because the role is an MD of a medium sized division of a major plc – the balance between working effectively with others and commercial skills is critical. This individual has a weakness in some elements of working with others.

The exercises – multi-method

Most exercises used in ACs fall broadly into three categories and can be 'off the shelf', customized or bespoke:

- Individual – role-play simulations, presentations or interviews; generally a good source of information about the candidate because assessors are able to manage the situation to check the information they are getting or move on to test another area of behaviour. We find that using actors in role-play simulations detracts from the data because it is not possible to control their interaction with the candidate. Role-play simulations are criticized by Woodruffe (1993) for adding to the resources required for a centre (role players) and because of difficulty in timetabling the exercises. Our experience is that assessors are more than capable of taking on the role player and assessing role, so requiring no extra bodies, and that with a little work the exercises can be timetabled. Assessors need to receive training in these skills and have clear guidelines to work to in the simulations, which are a very fruitful source of data about how participants interact with others.

- Group – leaderless, alternating chair and assigned-leader discussions. There are a number of problems with group exercises that are recognized and discussed within the research (for example, Brittain and Ryder, 1999; Woodruffe, 1993). The issues focus around the control of the situation – participants respond to each other's behaviour and language and this is not laid down in advance. If participants do not contribute much to a discussion, do they agree with everything being said, disagree but don't know how to make their point, disagree but can't be bothered, or don't understand what is going on? Always ask why a group exercise is being used; often it is because there seems to be no other way of assessing performance in a group, and assessors enjoy watching them! Beware the group exercise that has a brief for the participant that is only a few lines long – it is unlikely to have been thought through or driven by the needs of the target job. We have developed a methodology that assesses group performance through simulation, using assessors meeting in pairs with participants. For example, a simulated project start-up meeting. Both participants and assessors say that they find it stretching – but participants feel they have been able to show what they can do and assessors believe they have high-quality data on how the participant deals with colleagues.
- Written – in-trays, analysis exercises and written aspects of other exercises (such as writing up a simulated meeting with a customer). Written exercises can be a good source of data, although there should be clear guidelines that participants are asked to follow, so that the right kind of evidence is elicited, for example, in an in-tray telling the participant that they should tackle the most urgent and critical issues themselves rather than delegating them.

The criteria – multi-trait

Assessment centres need a set of defined criteria against which judgements about participants are made. Most organizations that employ the

AC method use a set of competencies as the criteria. What is a competency? Wood and Payne (1998) attribute the first use of the term competencies to Boyatzis in 1982. However, as Schippmann et al. (2000) point out, part of the confusion felt by practitioners around the term competency arises from the wide-ranging use across fields including law and clinical psychology.

There have been many different definitions of competency, for example:

- 'An underlying characteristic of a person which results in effective and/or superior performance in a job' (Klemp, 1980).
- 'A mixture of knowledge, skills, abilities, motivation, beliefs, values and interests' (Fleishman et al., 1995).
- 'A knowledge, skill, ability, or characteristic associated with high performance on a job' (Mirabile, 1997).
- 'A written description of measurable work habits and personal skills used to achieve work objectives' (Green, 1999).
- 'The collective learning in the organization' (Prahalad and Hamel, 1990).

Part of the confusion has been generated by the use of the terms *competencies* alongside *competences*. Competencies are seen as personal characteristics that identify superior performers, whereas competences are descriptions of tasks that identify minimum standards.

A good competency framework is based on an analysis of what makes people successful in the organization, as well as a review of the business strategy and implications for management behaviour. Nearly all competencies are, as a minimum, defined in terms of high performance (or positive indicators). Some organizations have realized that this does not give enough depth to the definition and have gone one step further by adding low-end (or negative) indicators. We have found that whilst this is better than only having high-end descriptors of performance, there is still room for improvement. We do this by adding a middle 'on par' description of acceptable performance. So, in practice, we end up with one of the indicators for 'commercial nous' being shown in Table 14.3 – we would typically expect to identify between eight and 12 of these per competency.

Table 14.3 Example competency indicator for 'commercial nous'

High performance	Benchmark performance	Needs development
Systematically uses financial analysis to evaluate the potential costs and benefits when making decisions	Takes broad financial implications into account when making decisions	Does not take financial information into account when formulating his/her ideas

Clients with whom we work to design competency frameworks say that having the three descriptors for high, on-par and low performance allows a much more thorough application of the framework across all of the human resources processes – appraisal, assessment, and so forth. Assessors like it because it provides a clear definition of where, on the continuum between high and low performance, the acceptable level really is.

Guidelines on using and investing in ACs – graduate, middle manager, executive

Here we look at what it is appropriate to include at different organizational levels, for graduates, middle manager and executive populations, the types of exercises, issues to consider and likely costs. We also provide some pointers on choosing a supplier/partner to work with on an AC project.

Graduate assessment centres

There are many variations on the graduate AC theme and this is probably the single biggest application of the AC method today. A typical graduate AC comprises:

- A competency-based interview.
- Numerical and verbal reasoning tests – sometimes undertaken prior to the centre and these may be used as part of a sifting process to reduce the numbers attending the final centre.
- Presentation – either prepared prior to the centre or after, typically, a brief analysis of a business case.
- Group exercise – this can be one of the many types outlined above and suffers from the same problems. However, graduate ACs are the one area in which organizations seem unlikely to move away from group exercises. The reason for this is mixed but usually a balance across four points – it is what the business assessors expect, it is what the business has always done, it is what the business' competitors do to recruit graduates and it is what the graduates themselves expect.

Given the widespread use of ACs at this level, surprisingly few organizations actually undertake validity studies of them. From discussions with practitioners, graduate recruitment managers and line managers within business the authors believe that there is a key reason for this: the success of graduate ACs is judged on getting graduates into the business who are reasonably intelligent and socially skilled. Generally, graduates have little, if any, work experience that is directly related to the role they will take on within an organization. So the issue for the AC is to identify those who

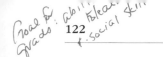
have the ability to come into the business, learn how to perform a role and be pleasant while doing so.

Key challenges for graduate ACs

- The sheer volume of applicants for graduate roles makes paper/Internet sifting difficult. Graduates as a group are hard to differentiate from each other, certainly on paper. So sifting becomes heavily driven by educational qualifications and, often, aptitude test results.
- Graduates become 'professional' AC candidates because they apply to so many different organizations. This is compounded by many organizations using 'off-the-shelf' ACs at this level and candidates can be exposed to the same exercises in different organizations.
- Graduates, possibly more than any other applicant group, have a higher expectation of themselves and their ability to contribute to the organization they are seeking to join. Stereotypically, in the last few years they say they want to work on 'strategic' issues within the business and when challenged cannot give a coherent view of what this actually means. The reality may be that they are going to spend the first 12 months serving customers in a bank branch. However, to give realistic job previews to these graduates is seen as having a detrimental effect on the organization's ability to attract them and they may not be so keen to join if they fully understand what their role will be.

Likely costs

As with ACs at other levels, the absolute cost is high when compared to selection methods such as interviews or testing. However, the high numbers of candidates that are assessed each year in large organizations – hundreds in many and thousands in some – mean that the cost per candidate is reasonable as most of the costs are front-loaded in the design and assessor training phases of AC implementation.

From our experience and after discussion with a selection of graduate recruitment specialists in organizations, we believe that the range for the design and implementation of a one-day graduate AC should be £25,000 to £40,000.

This cost includes training assessors, and perhaps training the trainers, so that organizations can become self-sufficient in the management and running of the graduate AC. So when this is spread across even a few hundred graduates over two to three years, the cost per person is reasonable. Note, however, that this does not include the organizational costs of assessor and administrator time, venue, and so forth.

Getting the most for your money

(handwritten: Don't outsource)

There are a few key points to bear in mind for graduate ACs:

- Buyers of recruitment processes and advice should always take these ACs into their business rather than rely on an external supplier/partner to deliver them on their behalf. The reasons for this include that buy-in to the recruitment decisions will be much higher if the managers have been involved in those decisions and understand the assessment process. Beware of any supplier/partner who tries to introduce ongoing dependency for running these.
- Assessors must be thoroughly trained – not only to increase the validity of your AC, but because untrained assessors can leave behind a very poor impression of your business with candidates.
- Run a pilot AC wherever possible to test the exercises, give the assessors a dry run and allow for final tweaks before a launch (this may have implications for the costs outlined above).
- Given the speed of change within the business world, the AC is likely to need changing, or perhaps a total rewrite after around 3 years. So building a partnership with a supplier who can get to know your business will benefit you over time.

Middle-manager assessment centres

(handwritten: Exercises need Hb completely focused on biz issues.)

Middle-manager ACs should differ from graduate ACs, in that the exercises need to be completely focused on business issues. This is where the AC begins to come into its own; when properly designed, it can tap into the interpersonal, organizational and commercial skills and abilities of a manager.

A good middle-manager AC lets participants feel that they are immersed in a real job by presenting them with (and assessing them against) a much more complex set of exercises. This means that the AC must be themed around a single business case and we recommend that this is not within their own sector, so a manager within financial services will be faced with a business simulation based in, for example, a travel company. This allows the participant's skills to be assessed free from their personal experience of the industry and provides a level playing field for all participants, irrespective of background. The industry knowledge and experience is typically assessed at other parts of the selection process, most often at first and last interview stages. *(handwritten: industry knowl tested commonly @ init.)*

Examples of the components of a strong AC at this level are:

- A business case simulation comprising:
  - a paper-based review of the business case: the participant is asked to prioritize key short- and long-term challenges for the business;

- a strategic interactive boss presentation: the participant has to present a high-level analysis of the business described;
- an interactive direct report coaching meeting: the participant has to coach and mentor a difficult team member as well as deal with a pressing commercial issue.

- A biographical/competency-based interview, in which the assessor looks for evidence of the participant's ability in key competency areas. Career aspirations are also explored to understand what drives the candidate.
- A verbal reasoning test to measure overall learning ability – if the business simulation is at the right level, numerical skills will be tested through the understanding of the business commercial issues in the other exercises.

Note: we have not included a group exercise for the reasons outlined elsewhere in this chapter.

Key challenges for middle-manager ACs

- Two issues centre around the exposure middle managers have had to ACs:
  - Middle managers who have had a good deal of exposure to ACs – either as participants or assessors – will have a slight advantage, similar to the 'practice effect' in aptitude testing. In brief, they will be less anxious about the AC situation itself and therefore be better able to show their full range of competency. However, there is a danger that these managers second guess what each exercise is looking for – and get it wrong, which then underrepresents their abilities.
  - Middle managers who have not had previous exposure to ACs might suffer from higher anxiety about the assessment for a variety of reasons. For example, simply not knowing what will happen, not understanding what the AC is trying to assess or not agreeing with the use of ACs as a selection method (this often results in participants not giving of themselves fully in the AC and so having a poor result). Most of these issues can be addressed, to a greater or lesser extent, by providing good-quality, paper-based briefings to participants prior to the centre, and offering the opportunity for a conversation with a human resources specialist.

- Dealing with internal participants after the centre:
  - Within a selection context the main challenge is dealing with a group of participants who have been unsuccessful in gaining a new role/promotion. It is more complex when an AC has been used over a simple interview process because the participants have had to

[handwritten margin notes:] practice effect + b/b less tense + may know wrongly – anticipate it's after. those not familiar won't try as hard if don't agree may not know what to do

commit so much more of their time and energy in being assessed and it is much harder as a participant to believe that you were not given the role because the interviewing manager does not like you.

– Within a development context, all of the participants will need full debriefing and development plans put in place. There may be some issues to deal with if the AC is being used to identify high-potential managers or place people into a succession plan because not all participants will have had the outcome that they were hoping for.

• Other issues to consider include confidentiality with external candidates (this is discussed more fully under executive ACs) and the cost for the organization in terms of the time participants and internal assessors spend away from their 'day jobs'.

Likely costs

From our experience, and after discussion with a selection of resourcing managers and talent management specialists in organizations, we believe that the range for the design and implementation of a middle-manager AC should be: £35,000 to £50,000.

Clearly, this cost cannot be spread across a high number of applicants as with graduates. However, there is scope to use a middle-manager AC for both recruitment (of external managers) and development or promotion, which reduces the cost per head. Note, however, that as with the figure for graduate ACs this cost does not include the organizational costs of assessor and administrator time, venue, and so forth.

Getting the most for your money

There are a few key points to bear in mind for middle-manager ACs. The decision about whether or not to take middle-manager ACs in-house is often much harder for organizations: *best if in partnership.*

• There are clear cost issues to keeping external specialists involved in the process and we believe that organizations should take ownership of the AC. At most, the AC should be run in partnership with external specialists, for example, by having internal and external assessors work in pairs.

• There may be other advantages that organizations value such as

– the views that an external assessor can provide about similar participants in other organizations;

– taking away some of the administration (for example, report writing, which can take up a good deal of senior assessors' time);

– 'coaching' less able/experienced internal assessors; or running more challenging sessions such as the wash up.

- As with graduate ACs, because of the fast-paced change in business, the AC is likely to need updating, or perhaps a total rewrite after around 3 years. So building a partnership with a supplier who can get to know your business will benefit you over time.

Executive assessment

When assessing senior managers, it is important to design the AC to run effectively with *only one participant at a time.* There are a number of reasons for this:

- Applicants to senior posts nearly always go through a sifting process (most often by head hunters or senior HR managers, or both) before being assessed and therefore the numbers involved are significantly reduced. It is common for us to be asked to assess a single applicant for a senior post within a client organization.
- Senior managers are more likely to know each other, or at least know of each other, because the pool is limited within a particular sector and high-performing managers can often build a reputation across the whole sector. Again, we occasionally have to assess on different days for the same role, so that word does not get around about who is on the job market in a particular sector.
- The final reason is one of competition – when participants are required to interact in an assessment exercise, for example, a group discussion, despite being told about the need to work collaboratively to do well they know that they are in competition with each other. If the exercises are designed such that the participants do not interact with each other, this element is reduced and a much 'cleaner' observation of their performance can be made. This issue of competition is particularly worth considering in the following circumstances:
  - benchmarking groups of managers for succession planning or development needs identification;
  - when there are internal and external participants being assessed simultaneously – the issue here is often one of perceived fairness;
  - where participants work with each other, or just know each other, for example, when ACs are being used in an internal restructuring.

Typically, the range of exercises used in an executive-level AC is the same as at middle-manager level. However, the complexity of the business case, as well as the benchmark performance, will be at a higher level.

Key challenges for executive ACs

- The use of ACs at executive level causes debate in some organizations.

As described earlier, senior managers and executives are often seen (not least by themselves) as being above this type of thing – they have track records that show what they can do. However, from an organization perspective, these are the most critical people to future success and if they do not perform it will be difficult for the business to perform. It is essential to gain a good understanding of them via an assessment.

- There is a school of thought that says that a battery of personality and aptitude tests plus an in-depth interview is the best way to assess the most senior people. However, given what we know about faking, particularly in light of the issues around over-exposure to certain methods of assessment, we believe that putting executives through an AC is much more appropriate – we are interested in what they can do and how they do it, not what they can tell us they would do or have done. Given the point above, our experience suggests that the interview-plus-test route is more comfortable for executives because everything happens beneath the surface and it is assumed that the practitioner (usually a psychologist) has access to a range of deep insights which are unavailable to 'normal' people.
- One of the key challenges for an executive AC is getting the level of the business simulation right. It can be difficult to pitch the complexity of commercial and strategic issues at the right level and to demand a sophisticated interpersonal response from participants. It is essential that anyone designing an executive AC tests out the simulation and component exercises whenever possible.
- To outsource or take in-house? Most leading organizations now use external specialists to assess the final candidates for an executive position. This happens for two main reasons: firstly, at this level, organizations want to know how well participants stack up against similar level executives in the market in general; secondly, there are often not enough senior internal assessors who can take part in these ACs – and organizations are rightly reluctant to delegate this to more junior assessors.

Likely costs

As executives are typically assessed individually we have given a cost range for a one-to-one assessment. This number varies depending on how many people will be assessed – for example, as part of a benchmarking exercise, or change programme, and so forth, as well as the amount and type of feedback/development activity (for example, coaching) that follows on from the AC. From our experience and after discussion with a selection of HR directors we believe that the range should be £3,000 to £5,000 per person.

Getting the most for your money

The main points to bear in mind about executive ACs are:

- Dovetailing the AC process with the headhunter activity. Ensuring that the headhunter fully understands the rationale for using an AC as one of the final steps in the process and giving them the language and knowledge to be able to sell this as a benefit to the participants. This is particularly important when working with an external partner for the assessment.
- As mentioned earlier, it is absolutely critical that the participants regard the AC as a stretch in both the commercial and interpersonal terms. Failure to ratchet the AC to a high enough level of complexity will result in the AC losing credibility in the eyes of the participants, and most likely the HR function and organization itself.
- Benchmarking the participants – how is this going to be done against an external norm? This can be difficult to address when an internally developed AC is used with internal assessors and is a key reason for many top organizations outsourcing this level of AC.
- Partnering with an external specialist to run the AC on the organization's behalf can add significant value at the executive level: to provide increased objectivity, benchmarking data and advice on process. Key questions to consider (and actually ask) are:

  - What will be the content of the AC?
  - What information is available on the performance of executives in other organizations on this AC?
  - Has the supplier undertaken a validation study on the AC and what were the results?
  - How adaptable are they to the issues and drivers in your organization?
  - What are the typical issues they have had to face at this level and how have they overcome them?
  - How well do they know your sector?
  - How well do they fit with the organization culture?

Ethics in AC use

The ethical treatment of candidates is important in its own right. However, there are also practical reasons for considering ethical issues. Assessment centres can provoke a degree of apprehension in even the most experienced of managers and the ethical treatment of candidates may go some way to ensuring that they are allowed to perform to the best of their ability, so that there is good predictive validity from the AC.

The following guidelines represent an amalgamation of a variety of sources such as BPS, CIPD and APA guidelines on ethical treatment of clients and experimental subjects – as well as practical insights that we have gleaned from our work here at Kiddy & Partners.

There are broadly five areas of ethics that must be considered in the design and use of ACs:

- informed consent;
- assessor competence and professionalism;
- maintenance of candidate esteem;
- appropriate confidentiality;
- debriefing.

Informed consent

Potential candidates must be told about what the assessment process involves before they decide whether to take part or not. In practice, this should take the form of written notification rather than a briefing over the telephone. Such notification should explain:

- the purpose of an AC and how it relates to other steps in any assessment process;
- the exercises or activities that would be involved in the AC;
- the time, date, duration and location of the assessment;
- who candidates should approach if they have questions about the nature of the AC.

In addition, assessors should aim to be fair in running the assessment. For example, if the assessors intend to spring surprises on candidates, such as presenting them with additional, unexpected information or giving them less time to complete an exercise than had been explained, then it is only fair to provide some warning that these situations could arise at some point during the assessment.

Assessor competence and professionalism

The organization should take steps to ensure that all assessors have minimum (high) professional technical standards. Firstly, the organization should train as assessors only individuals who are recognized for their ability to collect evidence and make decisions about other people on the basis of evidence as opposed to prior opinions, hearsay or 'feelings'. Secondly, the organization must take steps to train the assessors to ensure that they become familiar with the administration of assessment materials. In addition, this training should be used to check inter-assessor reliability – in practice, helping different assessors to 'calibrate' in terms of using the same data to make consistent decisions about candidates.

If an AC is to be used on an ongoing basis, then it behoves the organization to ensure that assessors continue to maintain their standards. For example, this could mean giving each assessor sufficient numbers of ACs to run that his or her ability to assess does not atrophy.

Maintenance of candidate esteem

It *almost* goes without saying that an AC should be constructed with regard for the personal needs of candidates. However, overenthusiastic assessors can easily design ACs that do not allow sufficient rest breaks or think about food, travel and overnight accommodation needs for candidates who may have to journey some distance to attend.

The more important point, though, is that candidates should never at any stage be made to feel uncomfortable, humiliated or degraded. Assessment exercises should be designed to be testing but should never make candidates feel embarrassed. Moreover, candidates should be able to receive feedback about the results of the assessment before that information becomes common knowledge across the rest of the organization.

Appropriate confidentiality

The results of an AC are obviously intended for use in making some sort of decision about a candidate, so the results can never be entirely confidential. However, the organization must think through how it will control access to and circulation of the results of the report. The detailed nature of assessment reports could otherwise, for example, be used to make detrimental decisions about a candidate if taken out of context.

Typically, reports should only be made available to people who are directly involved in making a decision about the candidate. If an AC is being used to identify managers for a new business unit, it may be the case that even the current line manager of a candidate does not need to see the report. In such a situation the organization could advise candidates to share an AC report with their line managers, so that they could work together on a development plan.

Debriefing

It is reasonable to expect that AC candidates should be given some form of feedback on their performance. The feedback need not be so detailed that it encourages a candidate to debate the validity of the results. At a minimum, however, candidates should be told of their overall performance in terms of areas of strength and development much in the same way that users of psychometric instruments are expected to provide feedback after testing.

Where next for ACs?

Looking back at AC use since the mid-1980s, the academic literature seems to be discussing more-or-less the same general areas: whether assessors rate by competency or exercise (the exercise effect), candidate reactions to being tested or assessed, and what constructs are really measured in ACs. On the practitioner side, organizations have become more sophisticated in their use of ACs and many more managers have been through the AC experience either as participants or assessors.

Challenges to researchers

We see a number of key questions for researchers to address that we believe would directly benefit the practitioner in ACs:

- What do organizations actually do with the information generated by ACs? This is intrinsically linked to the question of what line and HR managers see as the benefits of ACs. Some preliminary research by one of the authors (Brittain, 2002) suggests that there is limited understanding of validity in these communities and that this is linked to the likelihood of managers using AC data to influence decisions or development activity. The research concludes that strategies need to be developed further to develop a shared language for ACs within organizations.
- How do different exercises contribute to the overall validity of the AC? This is not asking about the exercise effect; rather, it is asking about which exercises predict job performance best and why.
- Look at other things to measure than just competencies – examine how goal achievement, alignment with organization values and fit with culture predict success (Brittain and Ryder, 1999).
- Our final plea is for researchers to devote some energy to looking at actual ACs with real people as participants – not students, whether undergraduates or postgraduates. This echoes a request made by Herriot and Anderson (1997), but which seems to have been ignored by researchers.
- There is a particular paucity of research that deals with executive-level ACs and this can potentially have the biggest single impact on an organization in people terms.

Challenges for practitioners

There are a number of challenges that we see emerging within our clients that will become more prominent over the coming years:

- Assessment centres will continue to become more sophisticated – the age of the two tests, an interview and an unstructured group discussion being regarded as an AC will pass. Assessment centres will focus on becoming simulations of complex businesses and they will continue to evolve as the business world develops and changes. One of the challenges for practitioners in this respect will be keeping their understanding and knowledge of how large organizations work up to date, so that they can design high-fidelity simulations.

- There will be an increasing demand from clients for practitioners to understand the commercial world. It will no longer be sufficient for practitioners to be 'experts in people' – they will need to be able to show that they understand the realities of life in organizations and the demands that this places on the participants they are being asked to assess.

- The focus for measurement in ACs will begin to shift. In simple terms, ACs at present assess EQ and IQ but we believe that organizations will necessarily become more concerned with two areas:

  - Strategic change capability. The closest that most ACs seem to get at the moment is the ability to lead or manage change, or work in a changing environment. The move will be towards identifying individuals who can define the future for organizations and then lead the organization to that point.

  - Leading the new generation – most models of leadership are based on leading teams and organizations that are populated primarily by people who regard work as a main part of the life. With the rise of Generation X and Y, there is an increasing and significant proportion of employees who see work as a necessary evil and who demand more flexibility from their employer regarding career breaks, working patterns, and so forth. We are beginning to see senior executives in some of our medium-sized clients being faced with these issues and it is a real paradigm shift for them.

- Talent management will become much more important over the coming years. This is not about how hipos are managed, but about how the organization deals with all of the talent. Assessment-centre practitioners are going to be asked to work within a much broader framework of people strategies and processes and the challenge will be to make the links with these more effective and impactful.

In conclusion, ACs are here to stay. They are reasonably valid, more fair than many other assessment methods and they are one of the best ways of gauging fit between the participant and the organization. For these reasons, among others, they have become an integral and rightly valued tool in the evaluation and development of people in many organizations.

CHAPTER 15

Technology and large-volume assessment

JAMES BYWATER, HELEN BARON, HOWARD GROSVENOR

Large-scale assessment, like the smallest selection procedure, should start from a clear understanding of the job requirements and move on through the use of appropriate tools to generate interpretable information about each individual that can form the basis for objective decision-making. The aim is to provide the best information possible to allow effective decisions to be made. However, where large numbers are involved in the assessment process, the impact of less than optimal practice can be far greater.

Introduction

Large-scale assessments tend to occur in three main situations:

- recruiting significant numbers in one batch – for example, business startups;
- a large number of roles to be filled on an ongoing basis – for example, recruitment by famous organizational 'names';
- many applicants who are able and willing to perform the role – for example, graduate milkrounds.

Large-scale assessment differs from more modest recruitment processes in a number of ways:

- The large number of people being processed allows more detailed statistical monitoring and evaluation of the process to be undertaken. It is thus easier to show that a process is or is not fair and valid.
- The large number of applicants tends to create a 'multiplying' effect – if the process is 'wrong' in some way, a minor error will be compounded into a more serious problem because of the sheer weight of numbers. For example, posting a badly phrased advert or wrongly quoted salary range on the Internet could 'swamp' a recruitment department overnight.

- Where large numbers of applicants being assessed could in fact perform the role competently, the efficiency of the process starts to become almost as important as the quality of the assessment.
- The significant, high-profile nature of the process may make it more controversial and thus likely to be investigated by external agencies (such as the Commission for Racial Equality, Equal Opportunities Commission).

Technology in large-scale assessment

Modern large-scale assessment is, inevitably, technology driven. Most organizations will use technology at some, if not all, stages of their large-scale assessment processes. This may take the form of attracting potential candidates through a corporate website, gathering applicant information through an online application form, processing candidates using a recruitment database, or even testing candidates using psychometric tools online. The use of IT carries with it many advantages, as well as some potential hazards.

Generally, technology is used in assessment processes either to:

- provide additional information that would be unavailable without it; or
- provide users with the same information as before but faster and with improved quality.

This is an important distinction to make. The nature and extent of the IT involvement depends on the organization's willingness to make some procedural changes to accommodate the technology. It is better to use technology in a thoughtful way rather than merely trying to re-create a paper-based system in an electronic medium, as this under-utilizes the strengths of IT systems. A good business psychologist will take the time to debate the advantages and disadvantages of various strategies as part of a wider needs analysis.

Some advantages of technology in large-scale assessment, in particular, the use of the Internet, include:

- cheap and immediate international communication via the Internet, 24 hours per day and 7 days per week – excellent for liaison with candidates;
- cheap, interactive web content – good for giving candidates a clear idea about the job and the organization;
- direct access to database information – good for tracking, sifting and sorting candidates;

- big savings for the organization in advertising fees, travel/postage expenses and reduced administration.

Some of the potential issues to be managed include:

- access of applicants to technology and comfort of using this medium;
- adequate helpdesk support for candidates using your assessment system;
- candidate identity and the security of any Internet systems and the information that is transmitted to or by them;
- adherence to best-practice guidelines when asking candidates to complete assessments in unsupervised settings.

The process of technology-driven large-scale assessment

The principles of using technology in assessment processes are not so very different from more manual, paper-based approaches. Indeed the sophistication of the computerized technology should not be allowed to distract the user from the function that it is performing. The steps of job analysis, design, implementation and monitoring are equally relevant.

Step one – job analysis

Job analysis aims to focus on the job, identify the essential and desirable skills that are necessary for its successful performance, make these explicit to all parties in the selection process and provide a clear 'audit trail' in case of dispute.

Before embarking on the design of the process, it is important to focus on the job that is being performed. This preliminary groundwork or 'job analysis' is a significant first stage in the process because:

- It encourages designers to focus on the role being targeted and to identify the essential and desirable skills that are necessary for its successful performance.
- It encourages designers to make the role requirements explicit to all parties in the selection process. These data can be used to manage expectations on both sides. The negative parts of the role can be communicated alongside the positive parts to encourage accurate self-selection (sometimes known as 'realistic job previews').
- The data can be used in tribunal settings to explain and justify the relevance of the selection process, if required. A clear 'audit trail' should be created.

Step two – design of the assessment process

Flowing from the job analysis stage, this is especially relevant for large-scale processes because relatively small increases in the validity of the tools chosen will have surprisingly large impact in organizational terms. (Validity relates to utility in a more or less linear fashion.) If 10 call-centre operators are 'worth' £500,000 of sales to an organization, then 100 will be worth £5 million! The potential payoff should be balanced, however, with the decreasing margin of return that is experienced when adding successively more assessment tools to the process. The only way to balance these essentially conflicting requirements of quality and efficiency is to base the process as closely as possible upon the job requirements.

Recruitment processes with multiple stages are a means of narrowing down the applicant pool. Typically, the shortest stage comes first. This methodology has the advantage of saving the most resource-intensive and time-consuming stages until last (see Figure 15.1).

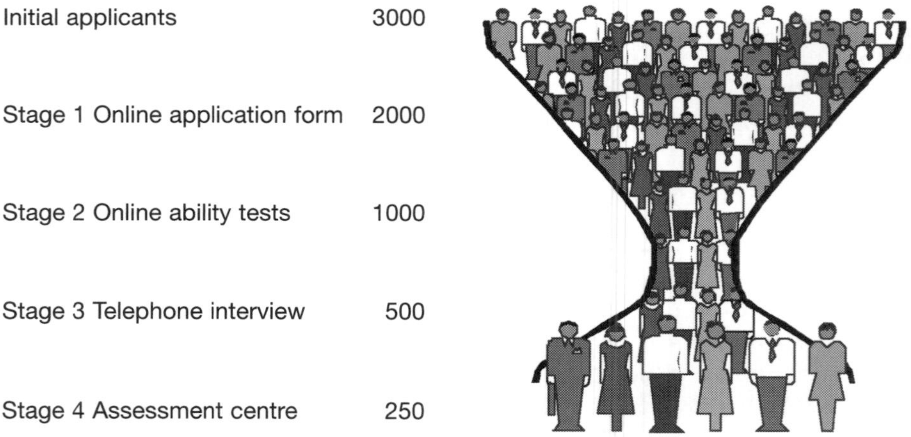

Initial applicants	3000	
Stage 1 Online application form	2000	
Stage 2 Online ability tests	1000	
Stage 3 Telephone interview	500	
Stage 4 Assessment centre	250	

Figure 15.1 A recruitment process with the shortest stage coming first and the more resource-intensive stages later.

However, the following points should be borne in mind:

- The first sifting stage must be of good quality. A consistent and objective scoreable application form is a much better tool than a potentially poor sift of CVs, for example.
- When designing these processes, it is easy to keep adding stages (such as 'final' interviews) until the process starts to lose its edge. Not only does this postpone the final decision unnecessarily, but it is likely to put candidates off altogether.

- The stages should be balanced to assess the different aspects of the role in appropriate measure, and not be allowed to overplay the importance of some skills. For example, applying psychometric tests with unrealistically high cutoffs can have the effect of supplying a shortlist of very bright candidates who do not possess sufficient interpersonal skills for the role.

Step 3 – implementing the process

At this stage it is essential to gain the buy-in of all relevant stakeholders both from human resources and information technology areas of the organization. Typically this involves using mockups to show the likely content of the system and its functionality. Even then there can be some expectation 'gaps' when the process is finally delivered, especially if the provider over-promises and under-delivers at this and later stages. The acceptance of the recruiting business area is also critical. The implementation of technology-driven large-scale assessment processes typically takes longer than other assessment processes because of this, and the fact that it is important to get things right first time. Once a system is 'live' to candidates, making *ad hoc* changes is difficult as repeated trialling is fundamental to the success of the project.

Step 4 – monitoring

Monitoring is carried out to evaluate the effectiveness and fairness of the procedure. This becomes imperative with a large-scale process, where even a small degree of unfairness can affect a substantial number of people.

Things to think about in respect of monitoring include:

- Are you collecting data about how the different stages of your process are working? Does your ethnic classification comply with best practice? (See: http://www.cre.gov.uk/.)
- Are you reviewing these data periodically having collected them?
- Are different groups of people (for example, men and women, younger and older candidates) equally likely to succeed in the selection process? It is quite common to find that different stages in the process will have different effects upon the applicant pool. A good business psychologist will ensure that overall these effects get balanced, neutralized and reduced so far as is possible given the role.

Each of these issues should be addressed from both a qualitative and a quantitative perspective. It is important that the line managers and trainers of those appointed through the process are satisfied with the new appointments but you should also check the statistical evidence that the system is identifying the best performers by looking at the relationship between performance on the different selection exercises and later on the job. This can show whether all elements of the selection procedure are useful and effective.

Potential issues

Remembering your candidates

Assessment processes are designed to meet organizational needs. The organization designs and pays for the assessment – and also pays the price if the wrong person is appointed. It is easy, but dangerous, to forget the needs of the individual candidate within this process. There are a number of reasons why it is important to consider how the process will feel from the candidate's perspective:

- The best candidates are likely to be sought by many employers. They will reject the job, even if offered, if their impression of the organization gained during the selection process is negative.
- Rejected candidates may well be future customers – so a positive impression is desirable – and you may want the best of the rejected people to apply for another position. Unhappy candidates will not apply again and are unlikely to persuade their friends to do so.
- There is a moral obligation to treat candidates with respect.
- Unhappy or ill-informed candidates are more likely to contact you with queries – and this can be a drain on resources.
- A disgruntled candidate is more likely to take a claim of unfair process to tribunal. Even if there is no case to answer, the management and professional time required to deal with this type of case is considerable. The negative PR involved in such situations is also undesirable.

Resourcing the process

It is likely that meeting all of these requirements may take some advance planning – for example, designing the literature which is sent out at later stages in the process and making sure the resources are available to provide feedback where promised. However, this initial investment will bear fruit in ensuring that the process runs smoothly as well as meeting candidates' needs.

Providing feedback for many candidates is a difficulty with large-scale assessment because of the resources required. Where psychometric instruments are used this should be provided wherever possible, and is often done by telephone upon request by candidates. Unlike more straightforward procedures such as the interview, it is difficult for candidates to know how well they have done or what their answers signify. The use of feedback can help candidates to see that the information they supplied was fully considered and that there are clear reasons why their application was, or was not, progressed.

The Data Protection Act (1998) (www.psychtesting.org.uk) places a requirement to provide, upon request, written information on any data held on a candidate in a searchable database (computer based or otherwise). It is thus important that you should build in some way of dealing with such requests. One way of dealing with the issue of feedback where computer-based assessment is used, is to design in 'expert systems' that can provide a report directly to candidates explaining their results in an appropriate manner. This should be supported with a helpline, but a well-written report alone will suffice for many candidates and they may well appreciate the personal learning it allows from the selection process.

Data protection

The aim of the Data Protection Act is to safeguard the individual against the misuse of information held in computer or other databases. In the assessment context, this means that files on individuals, whether electronic or paper, should be:

- Securely stored. Access to paper records should be restricted to those involved in the recruitment process. Data should be locked away or otherwise secured. Computer files should be password protected.
- Only used for the intended purpose. Candidates should be asked to agree to the storage and use of their data for selection purposes. They should be informed of any other uses to be made of the information they supply and for how long it will be kept.
- Accessible to the individual. Under the Act individuals can request a written report of any data pertaining to them that is held. They have the right to request corrections of any inaccuracies. Even if you dispute the inaccuracy, you should make a note on the file that the candidate does not agree with the original statement. Such requests should be complied with within 40 days.

Dealing with special cases

Where a system is in large-scale operation, the frequency of 'special' cases should be anticipated and provision made to deal with them. Typically this is less than 5% of cases. They include:

- requests for accommodations by candidates with disabilities;
- appropriate procedures for candidates who miss deadlines due to illness or other circumstances;
- policy on requests for retesting, missed assessments, and so forth.

It is important that all those involved with the system understand the process for dealing with special cases and follow consistent procedures. These can involve special treatment (for example, extended timing), or exemptions from the process among others, depending on the severity of the disability.

Need for policy and training

Large-scale assessment processes will almost certainly be administered by a number of different users. The pool of users is likely to change to some extent over time and different users may be operating in different locations simultaneously. It is important therefore that these individuals have some way of checking that their activities are compatible with each other. A policy for designing and administering an assessment process is thus strongly recommended as a template against which system users can operate. Training is vital in the implementation of this policy. If training can be conducted face to face, thus giving the users the chance to meet and share experiences, then this is preferable. Examples of policies and the key steps to produce them can be found published by the CIPD and major test publishers such as SHL.

Summary

The use of technology in assessment is a necessity for any large-scale process to succeed. The need for careful design of the process and consideration of potential issues associated both with the technology and with the candidates cannot be overemphasized. Through this, the many benefits of technology-based assessment can be realized. These benefits are made greater by the utility of assessing candidates on a large scale.

Case study – changing the face of Internet recruitment at Abbey

Business issue/objectives

Economic conditions over the past few years have forced banks to re-examine their recruitment processes and identify ways to reduce early staff turnover and respond to talented applicants in a more effective and efficient manner.

In order to manage the costs involved with the hiring process, Abbey used its own website and introduced online psychometric sifting to improve its hiring methods and reduce the number of unsuccessful hires.

The overall objective of the programme was to implement an IT-based application process into Abbey's existing systems to help them deliver pooled recruitment.

Solution

The solution was to extend the boundaries of Internet sifting. There has been an assumption that Internet sifting and shortlisting systems are really only appropriate at graduate level. However, Abbey and SHL have challenged this position in the form of their new website – http://www.jobsatabbeynational.co.uk. This site is aimed at all jobs within Abbey. Technology-based sifting processes have so far been introduced for the roles of Financial Adviser and Call Centre Adviser.

These processes are innovative because:

• Applicants are given a realistic expectation of the roles using a series of job 'previews' on the site itself – if they do not like what they see, then they do not have to waste their time applying (see Figure 15.2). This has been designed to reduce early staff turnover and be compatible with Abbey's brand value of making life simpler for its customers. Inevitably, this design process involved making compromises – only a limited number of scenarios could be produced so the best ones needed to be selected over others. Equally there is often a compromise that

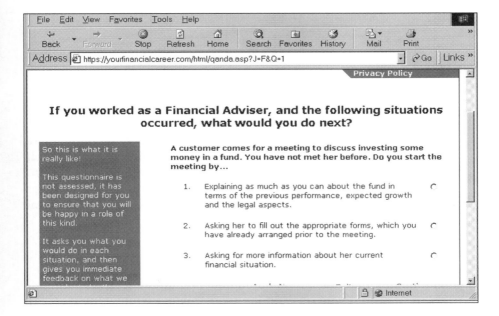

Figure 15.2 Job preview.

needs to be struck between painting a 'realistic' picture of the job and coming across as overly negative to potential customers of the future.

- A range of useful data (work experience, qualifications, and so forth) are collected about the applicants, so that the first sift can be conducted as effectively as possible (see Figure 15.3).

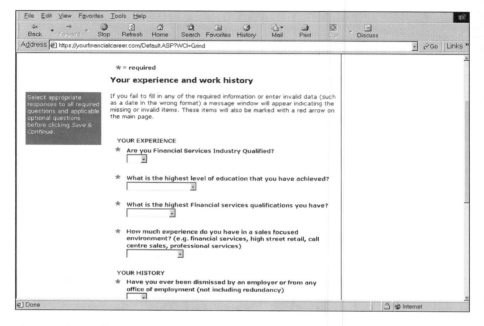

Figure 15.3 Collection of data about the applicant.

- A measure of 'fit' against the core competencies required for the role is collected using a short online questionnaire. This questionnaire was based upon some well-researched psychometric principles (SHL, 1999). These show that, even in an Internet domain, answers to self-assessment questions can yield reliable and valid information about a candidate, especially when they are presented in this 'ipsative' (forced choice) format which limits the amount of social desirability and faking that can take place.
- Candidate data are exported into PeopleSoft to facilitate candidate management and metric production. This means that 'hot' applicants can be responded to as soon as they apply and 'kept warm' via targeted candidate care. This allows the Abbey recruitment function not only to focus resources on successful versus unsuccessful applicants, but also release resources to support line managers.

Figure 15.4 Ipsative format questions.

Vannessa Green, recruitment manager at Abbey says:

Introducing a system like this has a huge impact on the traditional recruitment and selection cycle. We are only now just beginning to come to terms with the necessary alterations in both process and culture. Many of the biggest challenges have come not from the IT *per se* but from the business process redesign that accompanied it. For example, our new process has moved into 'pooled recruitment'. This means that we are no longer recruiting for a single position but are seeking to have a pool of applicants 'on tap'. This has had some profound implications on us, not least in Northern Ireland where the fair employment legislation tends to be focused much more on single jobs. We have had to deal with issues such as this and stage our roll out as we come across them. However, we are already feeling the benefits of the system as we are able to respond to both applicants and line managers more quickly and professionally.

The idea of an IT based application process is to allow the recruitment consultant to spend less time sifting through piles of CVs, less time telephone interviewing every applicant and more time liaising with talented applicants. This will help them provide a more added-value consultancy service to their in-house clients.

Additional reading

http://www.onrec.com/content2/default.asp
http://ri6.co.uk/ri5/news_index.html
http://www.peoplemanagement.co.uk/default.asp
http://www.intestcom.org/
http://www.dataprotection.gov.uk/
http://recruiter.totaljobs.com/recruiterzone/info_research/index.asp
http://www.ukrecruiter.co.uk/new.htm

CHAPTER 16

Practical issues in running international assessment and development centres

HELEN MARSH, PENNY MARKELL, ELLEN BARD,
MARK WILLIAMS, JAMES BYWATER

Introduction

Many multinational organizations are looking to structure themselves in increasingly innovative ways to meet the challenge of a 'global' service, whilst simultaneously retaining the capacity to respond to unique local requirements. Significant attention and resources are being given to the coordination of talent across these international organizations in order to increase their effectiveness (Bartram, 2002). Reviews of the selection methods most often used both within and across different countries reveal a broad spectrum of techniques, ranging from application forms and interviews to psychometric tests and assessment centres, graphology and medical examinations (Shackleton and Newell, 1991; Nyfield, Gibbons and MacIver, 1993; Ryan, McFarland, Baron and Page, 1999; Bartram, 2002). Whilst practices are continually evolving, at present selection tools tend to vary across countries as a result of different political, legal and regulatory factors (Briscoe, 1997). The use of assessment centres, historically an Anglo-American approach, is steadily becoming more widespread as greater emphasis is placed on the identification of specific competencies, discrete sets of knowledge, skills and attributes, that are required for effective performance (Nyfield, 1998), and as international organizations seek to adopt common recruitment and selection practices across different countries (Bartram, 2002).

Inherent within this global shift towards more objective assessment and development is the need to identify methods of selection that are effective but also acceptable (Nyfield, 1998) within the cultural boundaries of different belief and value systems. If managed sensitively, the implementation of international assessment and development centres may be a significant contributor to the management of talent within organizations. The following outlines the practitioner perspective on the concepts and issues arising in the international arena for occupational selection and development, and considers a range of practical considerations and possible future directions for international assessment and development.

An overview of international assessment and development centres

Appelbaum, Harel and Shapiro (1998) define assessment centres as:

> A process in which individuals participate in a series of work samples or simulations that resemble what they might be called on to do in an actual job, and their performance is evaluated by trained evaluators (assessors) . . . All centres aim to give information about the participants' current or potential competence.

Assessment and development centres focus on the systematic and objective identification of an individual's behaviours for the purposes of selection, placement, promotion, development, career management, training and, if managed sensitively, organizational restructure programmes. In the UK a survey by Roffey Park Management Institute (www.roffeypark.com) reports assessment centre usage by 62% of its sample of employers and development centres by 43%. The assessment and development centre method has historically been regarded as one of the most accurate and valid assessment procedures available, in as much as it combines the benefits of the range of assessment methods and provides a more holistic and detailed picture of the individual's potential job-relevant strengths and development needs. More recent research has questioned the precise level of validity that they deliver (Robertson and Smith, 2001), which has been found to be dependent in part on the definition and content of assessment centres (for example, ensuring construct definitions are job related), and the criteria of success (promotion or wider job performance measures) being used, ensuring that the constructs against which participants are to be rated are limited and discretely defined. Factors that improve the validity of an assessment or development centre include using psychologist assessors in addition to other trained assessors, number of exercises, inclusion of peer evaluations, and using cross-exercise assessment (Hough and Oswald, 2000; Gaugler, Rosenthal, Thornton and Bentson, 1987). Best practice assessment centres may also be used to enhance equal opportunities for different ethnic and gender groups, although the data to support this supposition are relatively limited (Baron and Janman, 1996).

Best practice in the field of assessment and development centres is reasonably well documented (International Taskforce on Assessment Centre Guidelines, 2000; SHL Guidelines for Best Practice, 2002 and www.psychtesting.org.uk) and a number of practical handbooks are available (Woodruffe, 1993). These documents emphasize that it is important to recognize and manage any potential negative impact that assessment centres may have, by minimizing the feelings of uncertainty that they instil in participants (Iles, Robertson and Rout, 1989; Noe and Steffy, 1987). Overall participants in such processes tend ultimately to view them positively, however, research also shows that those who did less well perceive the method to be less fair and to possess fewer career benefits (Teel and DuBois, 1983). The benefits to organizations have included reduced turnover, identification of potential 'high fliers', and opportunities to address both individual development needs and any wider 'skills gaps' within the organization. Assessment and development centres not only provide a comprehensive evaluation of a candidate's potential strengths and development needs for a specific role, but also afford participants opportunities to experience higher-level work and to make judgements themselves of their own suitability (Dulewicz, 1991).

The specific aims of an international assessment centre will vary, so in each case it is important to clarify the unique purpose for which an organization is approaching personnel selection or development. Historically, the aim of many assessment centres has been to identify local potential for local job vacancies. Increasingly, organizations are looking to recruit either local or international potential for both local and international postings.

Cultural differences

There is a growing body of research recognizing that management behaviour has distinct similarities (around charismatic, team, humane and participative leadership styles) and differences (around self-protective and autonomous leadership styles) across different cultural and national groupings (House et al., 1999; House, Javidan and Dorfman, 2001). For example, Lawrence (1994) studied management practices in different countries, and found that, whereas in Britain management is about leadership and social relations, in Japan management is more about hierarchy and solidarity. Many managers within multinational organizations are required to operate in environments where more than one culture is present (Hofstede, 1992). In its simplest form, culture refers to the attitudes and beliefs that a group of people hold that determine what they consider to be right or wrong, their 'norms' of behaviour. There are two implications for this:

- Different work behaviours such as persuasive skills, degree of cooperation, assertiveness and friendliness will have varying degrees of cultural acceptance, and this will have consequences for their evaluation. Cultural factors should be considered throughout the design, implementation, assessment and feedback stages in an international assessment process. For example, when designing within the UK in English and translating into other languages, exercise designers will need to avoid using local colloquialisms and 'turns of phrase' that will not easily translate into other languages. This may mean asking people in relevant local countries to review exercises once translated.
- International cultures may differ in their acceptance of standardized selection processes, and thus organizations need to be aware that the idea of rolling out a programme of identical assessments across the globe might appeal to practitioners in one country but not in all. The alternative is to set quality standards and allow each country to specify the recruitment and selection methods by which they intend to meet these standards (Bartram, 2002).

International process or 'international manager'

A distinction must be drawn between two reasons for which an international assessment or development centre may be used:

- to introduce common assessment of local management capability across international offices;
- to select 'international managers' who will be expected to work in many different countries and be sensitive to many different cultures.

This distinction is important because the latter of these is much more difficult to accomplish, involving the assessment of people from different cultures side by side:

> The international manager works with people of diverse cultures and mother tongues. He or she manages across large geographical distances and often across different time zones and works in more complex international organizational settings. (Barham and Willis, 1993)

Working with over 100 international managers, collecting data through repertory grid interviews, SHL identified the following nine competencies for critical success in an international arena, including:

- flexibility, open-mindedness, adaptability;
- interpersonal sensitivity, sociability, cultural sensitivity;
- strategic thinking, vision;
- leadership qualities, non-authoritarian control;
- energy, drive, determination;
- intellectual capability;
- family support;
- resilience;
- political awareness, commercial orientation, credibility, overseas experience.

Interestingly, most of the characteristics identified were not dependent on overseas experience, suggesting that it should be possible to select people who have higher chance of success from a variety of local countries (Nyfield, 1998).

Other researchers have also found a range of skills are needed to be effective across cultures, including an ability to provide clear guidance to staff, to build multinational teams and to understand the pressures of local management whilst also managing their own work–life balance (Barham and Willis, 1993).

Case study of an international development centre in a consumer electronics organization

SHL worked with a large international electronics organization to identify and develop managers with the potential to be the next generation of international business leaders. A two-day development centre based around international competencies was recommended. A global competency framework was designed after a thorough job analysis, and appropriate SHL exercises were then selected. The group exercise and in-tray were 'internationalized' to ensure that these were both culturally sensitive and neutral. For the group exercise and presentation, written instructions were provided in the candidate's native language; however, the responses and interactions were requested in English as this reflected the requirements of the role. The personality questionnaire, motivation questionnaire and 360-degree evaluation were completed in the candidates' native languages in advance of the centre. One-day assessor training was provided for appropriate line managers, a briefing that focused on the specific exercises of the centre and on raising cultural awareness.

The exercises were trialled, and the process was rolled out to the rest of the target population. Figure 16.1 represents the overall process followed when designing this international development centre, and the impact of international considerations.

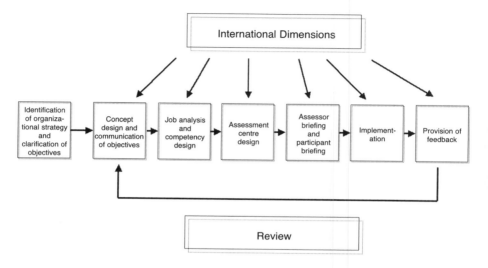

Figure 16.1 The process of international assessment and development centre implementation.

Practical considerations for international assessment and development centres

From our experience working with client organizations, to identify international managers it is essential that cultural sensitivity and fairness is a key focus in the design of the centre and the evaluation of participant behaviour. The issues to be addressed are concerned with:

- identification of global competencies and standards;
- desirable behaviours for international managers across different cultural settings;
- selection and preparation of both assessors and participants;
- validity and cultural acceptance of different selection techniques;
- subsequent validation and review of the overall selection process.

Clarifying the purpose

In order for any international project to be successful the organization needs to understand what, how and why the process is to be implemented.

- Involve all international offices in identifying the organizational need. Clarify and fully communicate the objectives to all employees.
- Define a policy outlining the process, including: selection of participants and assessors; methods of assessment; feedback procedures; and how to review the process.

Defining the competencies

Any successful assessment or development centre must be based on job-relevant competencies and this is even more important for international projects.

- Conduct a job analysis of current international managers to identify key behaviours and skills for successful performance, ensuring all international offices are represented.
- From this information design a global competency framework, with both positive and negative behavioural indicators.

Recognizing cultural differences

One of the most significant issues to be addressed is that of different 'norms of behaviour'. For example, verbal fluency and assertiveness or 'willingness to speak out' may be more socially acceptable in some cultures than others. These differences may be apparent in participants' responses to ability tests, work simulation exercises and personality questionnaires.

Group exercises can be more complex when run in an international setting due to differing cultural expectations of how to behave in groups. Their inclusion may be minimized in the design of the centre, or heightened awareness of the sensitivities achieved through the assessor training.

Identifying language issues

Failure to clarify language issues is one of the most common causes of problems that might arise for both participants and assessors.

- If international managers are required to complete all work in English as the global business language, then it may be justified to conduct all assessments in English. If managers typically receive information in their native languages but hold meetings in the common business language, this can be mirrored in the process. (See International Tests Commission Guidelines on Test Adaptation: www.intestcom.org.)

- For personality, motivation and 360-degree feedback, where possible participants should have the opportunity to complete and receive feedback on the questionnaire in their first language.
- In order to ensure fair assessment and cultural sensitivity it may be helpful to conduct the interview in the participant's native language.

Depending on the skill being measured, a dictionary or an interpreter may be made available for those working in a second language.

Exercise selection and design

In an international context it is important to select or design appropriate and valid exercises that are acceptable to all participants and assessors.

- It is vital that ability tests and personality questionnaires originally written in one language are appropriately translated and validated for the languages and cultures of all participants. Some items may be inappropriate or culturally specific, and these need to be identified and either removed or replaced. This is likely to mean that each translated test will need validating on an appropriate group of participants, thus creating new appropriate norm tables.
- Simulation exercises should reflect the international nature of the assessment or development centre. This can mean either customizing existing exercises or designing new ones. One example of customization would be inventing fictional countries, so that the exercise content is geographically and culturally 'neutral', avoiding cultural stereotypes.
- Exercises in an international context should also be designed to explore participants' knowledge of and sensitivity to cultural issues.

Logistical issues

Any assessment or development centre requires a great deal of planning and organizing and this is even more important for an international project.

- Consider process issues such as time keeping, forms of address, dress code and timetabling, as these can all be affected by different cultural or religious expectations.
- Ensure that relevant laws have been taken into account: data protection; storage of materials; availability of feedback; need for content validity.

Selection and preparation of candidates

Candidates from different countries are likely to come to the centre with varying degrees of familiarity and experience with objective assessment procedures.

- Selection of candidates must be conducted carefully, where possible seeking balanced representation of different cultural groups within a particular centre.
- Prior to the centre, participants should be thoroughly briefed about the process, particularly by providing information regarding: what exercises and tests will be used; what the focus of assessment will be at a behavioural level; what feedback may be expected.
- Preparation materials such as practice leaflets for ability tests and other activities, where available, should be provided to all candidates.

Selection and preparation of assessors

Assessors require many skills in order to be effective. The assessors must be made aware of appropriate benchmarks for the evaluation of behaviour and of the potential biases against different cultural styles. The aim of this is to avoid certain behaviours being interpreted in different ways by assessors with different cultural expectations, which may lead to 'poor evaluations of exhibitions of cultural idiosyncrasies evaluated by an outsider' (Cook and Herche, 1992).

- All assessors should be trained in behavioural assessment, in how to assess each of the exercises and in how to provide effective feedback. It is also important to address issues of cross-cultural sensitivity and understanding. Raising awareness of the possibility of bias is essential in an international environment.
- Assessors representing the participants' countries, both in terms of language and culture, should be involved at all stages. This is particularly important at the interview, data integration and provision of feedback stages in order to ensure understanding of cultural influences and expectations relating to behavioural performance.

Provision of feedback

Feedback is a vital part of any assessment or development centre, and is best conducted face to face in a style in keeping with cultural expectations. When designing the centre and choosing assessors, this requirement must be taken into account.

It is most beneficial for the participants to receive feedback from someone of the same cultural background. This has advantages in terms of understanding of behavioural norms, providing feedback in their native language, and awareness of cultural differences. If this is not possible, time must be allowed for the challenges candidates face when receiving feedback in a second language.

Reviewing the process

A review against the original objectives should be conducted for all assessment and development centres in order to understand whether or not the process has been successful.

In an international project it is even more essential to monitor for equal opportunities. Any adverse impact on different cultural groups should be considered when designing or redesigning future centres and 'positive action' may be taken in advance of the centre in order to attract or prepare such groups of individuals.

Future directions within international assessment and development

There are two main changes that practitioners and researchers are predicting for assessment and development centres. One focuses on the introduction and use of technology in the running of centres, and the other focuses on how development centres will be further enhanced.

Applications of technology

Technological solutions are already becoming more common for recruitment, job analysis and competency profiling, administration and scoring of questionnaires, design of assessment centres and use of IT to deliver in-tray analysis and presentation exercises. This has advantages in terms of enhanced fidelity (looks more realistic), better-quality data capture (improved legibility), and with Internet delivery it also removes the need for international managers to be away from their offices for the duration of the centre.

New approaches in development centres

Much of the discussion of changes to development centres focuses on more integral involvement of participants in decision-making and development planning (Griffiths and Goodge, 1994). Constable (1999, cited in Lee, 2000) designed a 'peer centre' or 'development workshop', emphasizing the importance of peer feedback and coaching, practical and realistic development planning, senior management support and use of external consultants. There are some issues that may arise specifically in the international context. These include the question of cultural acceptance of peer review, and attitudes to the concept of lifelong learning.

Conclusions

The advantages of international centres are clear. As Cook and Herche (1992) write: 'Not only can top notch talent be identified for the future success of the organization, but these individuals can also be provided with a unique opportunity for continuing personal growth and development in a complex, often intimidating, multinational environment.'

It is also clear that devising and running an international assessment or development centre can be a complicated procedure. As Nyfield et al. (1993) advise: 'For the HR practitioner involved in assessing managers for international work, the recommendation must be to approach the task cautiously, and to be aware of the difficulties of comparing managers from different cultures.'

Our review of current research and practice has shown that the organizational, cultural, linguistic and ethical implications of international assessment and development centres are only now beginning to be understood. Practitioners are encouraged to continue to monitor the process, gather and publish case studies and raise awareness of cultural sensitivities and best practice implications for international assessment and development.

CHAPTER 17

High-potential talent assessment

MARIA YAPP

The talent director of a global fast-moving consumer goods (FMCG) organization proudly described a comprehensive management talent audit of over 150 of the company's senior managers. Rigorous behavioural interviews were systematically scored against competency behaviours to arrive at a rating of each manager's performance in his or her current role. So far, so good. In addition, each manager was given a rating of 'potential' – either high, medium or low. However, given that the assessment was based on *past* performance data (the interview) and a set of *current* performance standards (the competencies), how the assessors were in a position to judge the managers' potential (and by the way, potential for *what?*) is mystifying. The director assured me that the ratings were down to the expertise of the assessors – in this case a firm of global search consultants – but was this confidence justified?

This chapter addresses issues relating to high-potential talent assessment and the early identification of leadership potential in the business context. How do organizations identify their high flyers or high potentials – those capable of pursuing a 'fast track' to business leadership? How is it possible to tell, at a relatively early career stage, someone's longer-term potential for succeeding in the business? Why do some people achieve outstanding success and rapid career progression to the top of their organization while others (the 'solid performers') follow a more conservative path? How can organizations identify the future pipeline of business leadership talent?

The relative merits or demerits of fast-track, high-potential or high-flyer schemes have been discussed extensively elsewhere (Baruch and Peiperl, 1997; Wood, 1998). The necessary elements of development *experience* that are essential to transform raw talent into finely moulded business leadership capability have also been addressed comprehensively by, for instance, McCall (1998), Carey and Ogden (2000), and McCall and Hollenbech (2002).

There are a number of myths associated with predicting potential, with the result that businesses often focus on the wrong criteria when they assess for 'potential' – but neglect stronger predictors.

Pitfalls when assessing potential

Current performance is *not* the same as future potential

[handwritten marginalia: strong perf in a speci function can delay progression ... of narrow functional focus.]

Judgements of potential become flawed when the assessor confuses indicators of *current performance effectiveness* with predictors of *longer-term potential*.

The problem is that the skills needed to be effective *now* are not the same as those needed to progress in the longer term. In a study of 457 managers, for instance, Luthans et al. (1988) found that *successful* managers (as measured by the speed of their career progression) were not always the most *effective* (as measured by their unit performance). As we shall discuss later, when roles progress upwards in the organization hierarchy they require qualitatively different skills and approaches. Therefore potential for more senior roles cannot always be gauged on the basis of an individual's current or recent performance. McCall (1998) also observes that managers with strong track records in a specific function can actually experience *delayed* career progression as their ability can be restricted by a narrow functional focus, whereas for rapid advancement to seniority a more broad-ranging skill set and a view of the bigger picture is necessary.

Line managers can make mistakes *[handwritten: ✓ subjective]*

A recent UK study of 279 FT500 companies (HRM Software, 2000) revealed that 80% report using supervisor or line manager ratings to identify high potentials. However, managers' assessments can be highly subjective and are often based on erroneous criteria. For instance, longitudinal studies by Dulewicz (1994) found that competencies rated by bosses as 'vital' or 'important' for jobs likely to be held in five years' time subsequently failed to distinguish those managers who actually progressed most rapidly.

The brightest are not always the best

Measures of cognitive ability, or 'IQ', generally correlate well with measures of *current* job performance – for a review see Robertson and Smith (2001). However, research on the ability of traditional IQ measures

IQ Clos to
not suff
predict
long .success

to predict longer-term career potential is rather less encouraging. Goleman (1996) quotes evidence to indicate that IQ at best contributes about 20% of the factors that determine success in life. In the organizational context, Bahn (1979) found that leaders tended to be more intelligent than the average organization members but not the most intelligent. The findings on IQ research generally suggest that there is a minimum level of IQ that is *necessary* for progression to the top, but that IQ alone is not sufficient as a predictor of business leadership potential.

Leadership competencies are not the answer

The argument for leadership competencies is that by expressing the requirements for effective leadership in objective behavioural terms, assessments of high potentials will be accurate. However, the most that leadership competencies can ever do is indicate the gaps between managers' current and desired levels of performance.

Leadership competencies typically describe the *end-state* for business leadership talent – developed over time and experience – in other words, what business leaders will look like when they have finally 'arrived'. What they do *not* describe are the prerequisites for a successful journey. Wood (1998) entertainingly describes the 'Russian Doll Syndrome': 'We analyse successful performance now, call the ingredients X and then look for X in others. Not X exactly, but a scaled down version of X, fully expecting that with the passage of time little X will become big X.'

There is a very big (but often underestimated) difference between end-state leadership competencies and true *high potential indicators*. McCall (1998) describes them respectively as 'performance orientated' and 'learning orientated'. For instance, a senior manager may be able to demonstrate 'visionary leadership' while the inexperienced high flyer is more likely to demonstrate the building blocks of this competency – for instance, the ability to win others over, to inspire them to a course of action (in the absence of formal leadership authority).

So how should it be done?

The model for high-potential assessment presented here is based on both research and experience. While not an exhaustive list of all the factors that predict potential, it highlights the key areas of focus for effective talent prediction in the business context and discourages a focus on areas that are perhaps less helpful.

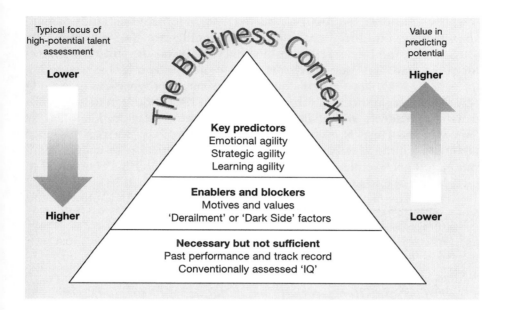

Figure 17.1 High-potential talent prediction.

Key predictors

Key predictors are the factors that most strongly predict future career progression. They are *not* an exhaustive set, but they emerge consistently and any 'potential' assessment that does not address these issues is likely to be deficient. We have identified three areas of agility: emotional, learning and strategic.

Emotional agility

This area is derived from work on emotional intelligence, or 'EQ', which is the ability to:

- be aware of one's own feelings and have the capacity to handle them;
- motivate oneself and perform at one's peak;
- sense what others are feeling and handle relationships effectively (Goleman, 1996).

Much has been written about EQ and its relation to effective performance in the business context. More recently it has been established that emotional intelligence has implications for identifying *potential* too.

EQ stronger predictor of success than IQ [handwritten margin note]

Dulewicz and Higgs (2000) conducted a 7-year longitudinal study of managers' career advancement. Emotional intelligence (as measured by self-assessed and boss-assessed competency data) was the strongest predictor of the managers' rate of advancement in their organizations, accounting for 36% of the variance in explaining speed of career progression. In fact, EQ was a stronger predictor of career success than IQ. In addition to 'soft' skills (such as sensitivity and ability to influence), the EQ factors identified by Dulewicz and Higgs also covered 'harder' characteristics such as resilience (ability to handle stress or difficulties) and aspects relating to energy, motivation and achievement orientation, which have previously been linked to high potential (McClelland, 1985; O'Reilly and Chatman, 1994).

The dimensions of emotional intelligence identified by Dulewicz and Higgs are:

Predictors if measured can see potential [handwritten margin note]

- Self-awareness
  Aware of own feelings and able to control them

- Emotional resilience
  Adjusts readily to new situations, maintains a focus on delivery

- Motivation
  Focuses on results and effective completion – sets and achieves challenging goals

- Interpersonal sensitivity
  Takes into account the needs and perceptions of others; explains and listens well

- Influence
  Wins others over to a viewpoint; influences their views on a problem or issue

- Decisiveness
  Makes decisions in difficult situations; sees need for action over precise or complete information

- Conscientiousness and integrity
  Consistent words and actions, doesn't always believe 'end justifies the means'

Other studies support the emotional intelligence connection. In a UK study, Andrews Munro (2002) found that managers who advance rapidly in their careers are more aware of political management, deal quickly and proactively with difficult issues and work well with others to delegate effectively and manage conflict. Other studies similarly attest to the superior predictive ability of interpersonal skills relative to intellectual ability or academic achievement in predicting career success (Thompson et al., 1996; Martinez, 1997). The particular power of Dulewicz and Higgs's work is the predictive and longitudinal nature of their study, which enabled them to identify EQ as something that *predicts* career success, not merely a factor that is correlated with it.

Need to obs behaviour, → interview similar work

Assessing emotional agility

A number of proprietary questionnaires measure emotional intelligence. In general, though, these questionnaires (for instance, ASE's 'EIQ') are more useful in the context of a *development* discussion about EQ and are less valid or robust as predictors. Also, established measures of personality (such as SHL's Occupational Personality Questionnaire – OPQ) can yield dimensions that measure characteristics linked to EQ criteria.

Dulewicz and Higgs observed that behavioural competency data about EQ were highly predictive of career progression whereas EQ data derived from personality questionnaires (including the OPQ and 16PF) were not a significant predictor. They therefore advocate *behavioural* measurement of EQ constructs. This can include rigorous interviewing that examines patterns in individuals' responses to a variety of situations, the choices they have made in life and work, and so on. Work simulation exercises in the context of an assessment or development centre could also be developed – for instance, interpersonal exercises that require key EQ constructs to be demonstrated in a live and dynamic setting.

Learning agility

The ability to learn – to search out challenging experiences, to seek and respond to feedback, to relate the lessons learned to practical experience and to improve as a result – is another factor consistently associated with rapid career advancement. McCall (1998) argues that 'the focal point in early (talent) identification is the assessment of learning ability'.

McCall et al. (1994) conducted an extensive study of 838 managers in countries that spanned the US, Europe, Australia and New Zealand. They identified 11 characteristics that distinguished fast trackers from those who progressed through the business at a slower pace. These dimensions are:

LA = Long Agility EQ.

LA 1. Seeks opportunities to learn
   Consistent pattern of learning over time; seeks out experiences to change perspectives and opportunities to do new things.

2. Acts with integrity
   Tells the truth and is described by others as honest; takes responsibility for own actions.

3. Adapts to cultural differences
   Enjoys experiencing different cultures; sensitive to cultural differences; changes behaviour in response to them.

EQ 4. Committed to making a difference
       Strong commitment to success of the organization; makes personal
       sacrifices to contribute to success; strong drive for results.

LA 5. Seeks broad business knowledge
       Understands business beyond own limited area and how different
       parts of the business fit together.

EQ 6. Brings out the best in people
       Pulls people together into highly effective teams; works well with a
       wide variety of people.

LA 7. Insightful – sees things from new angles
       Asks insightful questions; able to see things from different perspec-
       tives; to identify the most important parts of problems/issues.

EQ 8. Has the courage to take risks
       Takes a stand when others disagree; goes against the status quo; takes
       personal and business risks.

EQ 9. Seeks and uses feedback
       Pursues, responds to and uses feedback – and changes as a result.

LA 10. Learns from mistakes
        Changes direction when current path isn't working; responds without
        getting defensive; starts over after setbacks.

LA 11. Open to criticism
        Does not act threatened or defensively when others are critical.

Six of these dimensions related to learning ability: 'seeks opportunities
to learn'; 'seeks broad business knowledge'; 'sees things from new
angles'; 'seeks and uses feedback'; 'learns from mistakes'; 'open to
criticism'.

The remaining five ('acts with integrity'; 'adapts to cultural differences';
'committed to making a difference'; 'brings out the best in people'; 'has
the courage to take risks') relate very strongly to the EQ predictors identified by Dulewicz and Higgs.

Comps   McCall et al. concluded that competencies relating to the ability to learn
rel. to – and to develop as a result of that learning – are strong predictors of high
lrng ability potential. Bennis and Nanus (1985) conducted in-depth case studies of 90
strong   leaders from a variety of disciplines. They identified 'development of self'
link to as a key dimension associated with successful leaders: 'nearly all leaders
potential are highly proficient in learning from experience.' The leaders they
researched constantly sought out feedback and developed specific strategies to compensate for their weaknesses.

Assessing learning agility

McCall's dimensions contain clear, specific behaviours that can be used to assess learning agility via behavioural methods. A well-constructed behavioural interview can specifically probe achievements and experiences in relation to most of the learning dimensions – for instance:

- 'Describe an occasion when you felt that others were unfairly critical of you . . .'
- 'How have you ultimately changed as a result of a learning experience?'
- 'Describe a time when you had to work outside your comfort zone.'

Learning agility also lends itself well to assessment by *dynamic* work simulation or assessment-centre exercises, particularly when using a 'test, train, retest' model. These require an individual to demonstrate various learning abilities in a relatively realistic context – for example, to ask questions and gain new insight on issues; to seek and respond to feedback or criticism; and so on. In the psychometric context, cognitive process profiling (see below) provides a measure of an individual's capacity and potential for learning, particularly when operating in novel environments with limited cues to action.

Strategic agility

Conventional measures of IQ do not particularly distinguish high potentials but alternative measures of cognitive ability have a stronger bearing. A key predictor of potential for future seniority relates to strategic or complex thinking ability. This means being able to work deftly with complex, dynamic ideas, to entertain 'step' change and discontinuity and to take a strategic or 'big-picture' view when considering business issues.

Senior roles are associated with longer time frames of responsibility, and consequently, more complex and strategic decisions. Elliot Jaques's (1989) theory of stratified systems identifies eight different levels at which decisions become successively more complex and strategic (see Table 17.1). Approaches to measuring cognitive complexity (and by extension the capacity for strategic thought) claim to predict the 'ceiling' of a manager's potential career advancement. This idea is supported by other empirical research which reveals that while IQ is not a strong indicator of potential, the ability to think strategically and take a 'whole business' view predicts rapid career advancement to more senior levels rather more strongly (McCall et al., 1994; Dulewicz and Higgs, 2000).

The two most well-known measures of cognitive complexity are career path appreciation (CPA) (Jaques and Stamp, 1993) and cognitive process

Table 17.1 Elliot Jaques's organizational levels (Jaques, 1989)

Jaques level	Time span	Typical role	Focus of role
VIII	50+ years	Super corporation CEO	
VII	20+ years	Corporation CEOs and COOs	Strategic corporate
VI	10–20 years	Strategic business unit VPs	
V	5–10 years	Business unit presidents	General
IV	2–5 years	Specialist general managers	
III	1–2 years	Unit/department managers	Operational
II	3 months–1 year	First-line managers	
I	1 day–3 months	Operators	Shop/office floor

profiling (CPP) (Prinsloo, 1992). Both aim to assess the levels of complexity associated with Jaques's (1989) stratification. While each measure uses different methods (CPA uses a card sort and interview, CPP is based on a computer-based problem-solving exercise), the principle behind them is broadly equivalent. They measure the *process* of problem solving and, in particular, how individuals structure and deal with ambiguous or 'fuzzy' information. CPP additionally captures *learning potential* by the incorporation of a 'test–train–test' paradigm in the computer exercise.

Measures of cognitive complexity are distinct from conventional psychometric tests, where the focus is on the *output* of problem solving rather than the process. Cognitive complexity measures are correlated with IQ but not perfectly. They therefore appear to tap a different construct. In particular, high scores reflect the ability to think fluidly, operate on long-term time frames and make strategic connections.

The rationale behind the cognitive complexity approach is that there is an upper limit on each person's capacity for complexity and this limit determines the highest organizational level at which he or she will optimally perform. It is also possible for an individual to demonstrate *potential* for working at levels of cognitive complexity far higher than those at which he or she has so far operated. Therefore, a young manager currently working at Level II (first-line management) can demonstrate the *potential* to operate at Level V (business unit president or MD) for instance.

Cognitive capacity measures are an exciting innovation in high potential assessment and a useful complement to the existing methodology repertoire. However, it is critical that their results are interpreted in the context of other information about the individual. High levels of cognitive potential alone do not predict career success unless they are accompanied by the required interpersonal and technical skills and the requisite levels of motivation.

Enablers and blockers

Enablers and blockers are factors that can exert significant influence either to accelerate or prevent career advancement. They require early attention and constant follow-up, so that with appropriate coaching and support, they can enhance rather than blight the career progression of individuals with high potential.

[handwritten annotation: Motivation : energy, drive, achievement]
[handwritten annotation: Motives: Values, prefs, aspirations]

Motives, values and aspirations

Motives are distinct from motivation. While *motivation* refers to an individual's overall levels of energy, drive and achievement orientation, *motives* reflect values, preferences and aspirations. Clearly establishing motives is essential, as they *direct* energy and effort towards particular outcomes. The personal motives and values of high potentials can critically block or accelerate career progression. While some managers value a fast-track route to general management very highly, others report alternative motives – for instance, to increase satisfaction or enjoyment at work (Andrew Munro Ltd, 2002) or to pursue a specialist functional path (Tarleton, 2002).

Managers who value and are motivated by the prospect of rapid progress to senior roles employ specific 'career tactics' and behave very differently from those who are not. They focus on projects that make the maximum contribution and have maximum visibility in the business. They also play to their strengths and use controlled delegation to focus on what they do best. Furthermore, managers who prioritize such career tactics actually progress more rapidly than those who do not (Andrew Munro, 2002).

It is therefore surprising how many organizations still assign managers to the 'fast track' without prior discussion or exploration of their values, motives and aspirations. There remains an implicit assumption in many businesses that everyone wants to succeed to the top. Tarleton observes that many large organizations fail because their high flyers are in the wrong jobs. This is often because the focus is on assessing high flyers' *competence* – what they 'can' do (or what they are good at) but not their *motives* – what they 'will' do (or what they want to do).

[handwritten annotation: need to focus on what as well as ability]

In conclusion, motives and values consistent with rapid progress to seniority are an essential enabler for any high flyer. A number of questionnaires exist to establish managers' motives, for example, SHL's Motivation Questionnaire or MQ, Hogan's MPI and the Motivational Styles Questionnaire (MSQ). In themselves, these questionnaires are not valid predictors of future potential and would not be recommended as an element of the assessment approach. They do, however, provide a useful platform for beginning the process of self-examination, coaching and dialogue that is essential in helping high potentials to clarify their goals and ensure that the fast track programme is a place they really want to be.

Potential blockers – the 'dark side' and derailment

Research on the 'dark side' of personality (Hogan and Hogan, 1997) investigates how certain characteristics that can often be strengths can under some situations become liabilities. McCall and Lombardo (1983) coined the term 'career derailment' to describe the phenomenon of highly talented managers with strong track records who nevertheless fail spectacularly in their careers. They found that derailed managers have many characteristics in common with high potentials but that invariably the very strengths that propelled these managers to the top became their undoing.

Hogan has identified that the 'dark side' of personality is most likely to emerge and to derail performance in highly stressful or unfamiliar situations where managers are pushed beyond their level of competence. The 'dark side' can also emerge when individuals are otherwise caught 'off guard' and are therefore not managing their behaviour as effectively as they might (for instance, in situations where they have become overconfident in their position). In the context of high flyers, the 'dark side' is particularly likely to arise when an individual is promoted or exposed to areas beyond their existing range of experience.

The emergence of 'dark side' characteristics can never be predicted with complete confidence. Firstly, it is impossible to foresee all the situations or difficulties a manager could potentially encounter over the course of his or her career. Secondly, by definition, dark-side characteristics only emerge under extreme conditions so are unlikely to be visible under conventional assessment situations.

Hogan's Development Survey (HDS), although it is not an infallible predictor of derailment, does identify those areas of the 'dark side' *most* likely to emerge for an individual given the right (or should we say wrong?) circumstances. Used at an early stage in high potential identification it can begin the process of coaching and preparation for career progression, so that the manager can identify his or her potential dark side characteristics and develop in advance the necessary coping strategies to recognize and deal with them. Ongoing coaching throughout the individual's career is also vital in ensuring that their strengths continue to be appropriately directed.

Table 17.2 Strengths and their dark sides (Hogan and Hogan, 1997)

STRENGTH	DARK SIDE
Enthusiastic Develop strong enthusiasm for people and projects; enjoy pace, change and variety	*Volatile* Easily annoyed, let little things bother them – can be irritable and hard to please
Shrewd Alert and shrewd; well tuned-in to politics, difficult to take advantage of	*Mistrustful* Suspicious; cynical; mistrust colleagues; find fault easily
Careful Maintain order and predictability; good corporate citizens; gracious and obliging	*Cautious* Over-cautious; can shy away from issues; resist innovation and challenge
Independent Concentrate on the job; self-sufficient and can work independently; forthright and able to speak out	*Detached* May be selfish with own time; seem preoc-cupied; appear detached, indifferent and difficult to get close to
Focused Stick to own agenda – not swayed by others' comments; good at maintaining a social façade	*Passive-aggressive* Dig their heels in; procrastinate or ignore others' needs; blame others for difficulties
Confident Socially confident, self-assured, energetic, pleased to take the lead	*Arrogant* Overbearing; annoy others with self-aggrandising behaviour; overestimate own talents and ignore criticism
Charming Charming, persuasive and self-assured; remain composed; don't dwell on past mistakes	*Manipulative* Use social skills to manipulate others; may lack regret or guilt about things they do
Vivacious A talent for impressing others; enjoy sell-ing their vision; perform well in public and in 'sales' situations	*Dramatic* Can be seen as self-absorbed and superfi-cial; may lack genuine interest in/empathy for others
Imaginative Have insight, creativity and unusual mental capacities; entertaining and visible	*Eccentric* Can be impulsive and eccentric; may go off at a tangent; display inappropriate behaviour
Diligent Work hard and diligently; detail conscious and conscientious, organized and have high standards	*Perfectionistic* May be too perfectionistic; possessive about workload; excessively fussy and critical
Dutiful Keen to please others; affable, courteous and friendly; good team members	*Dependent* Find it difficult to say 'no'; promise more than they can deliver; have difficulty taking decisions unaided

The business context and high-potential competencies

We discussed earlier the problem of using leadership competencies to assess high potentials. They may reflect key aspects of strategy but these competencies express the 'end state' for business leadership and are therefore not wholly suitable for assessing potential.

Competencies for high potentials must identify those who will be able to lead a particular business at a future point in time. They are a way of grounding the definition of 'talent' or 'potential' firmly in the organization's chosen strategic direction. They also need to indicate those individuals most likely to close the gap between their current performance and what is required in the future. To do this successfully they need to:

* express the management behaviours and abilities needed for business to be successful on a specified time frame; and
* focus on assessing *potential to develop* rather than end-state characteristics of successful business managers.

In recent years, competencies have more closely reflected the organization's strategy and values instead of focusing only on job- or person-specific characteristics (Cohen, 2001; Robertson and Smith, 2001). It is also the case that succession planning and high-potential identification is becoming more people driven than position driven, with the emphasis on identifying generic leadership talent, rather than task- or role-specific skills (HRM Software, 2000). There is therefore a strong case for the competency-based approach, with a focus on *high-potential indicators* rather than end-state competencies. These indicators must be strongly linked to business strategy and values.

Case study – high-potential competencies for a major UK retailer

The company's board had set a priority for the human resources function to secure the business's future pipeline of leadership talent. The High Potential Young Managers programme was one of the elements in a comprehensive human resources strategy aimed at consolidating the business's performance and securing its long-term future in a highly competitive market-place. As business psychologists our brief was to develop an assessment approach that would enable the business to select onto an accelerated development programme, young managers with the capability to reach senior business leadership positions on a time frame of around 3 to 5 years.

We developed high-potential indicators for our client by:

- establishing the future direction and strategy of the business on a 3- to 5-year time frame through 'scenario planning' discussions with the CEO and directors;
- developing future-oriented competencies to describe the end-state for senior managers on the basis of these predictions;
- translating end-state competencies into *high-potential indicators* that distinguish young managers with the greatest potential to achieve the end-state competencies.

The high-potential indicators were subsequently used to underpin the full range of assessment and development activities for high potential young managers. The key value to the business was that assessments based on these competencies have enabled them to target, at a very early stage in their careers, those high flyers who are most likely to benefit from participation on the fast track programme and who are most likely to supply the business's pipeline of future leadership talent.

Table 17.3 Best practice guidelines

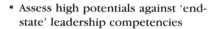

Do	Don't
• Assess your high potentials against high-potential indicators	• Assess high potentials against 'end-state' leadership competencies
• Base high-potential indicators on analysis of long-term business drivers and cultural priorities	• Confuse current effectiveness or past track record with future potential
• Use dynamic assessment activities – (business simulations, role plays) – to gauge emotional intelligence and learning agility	• Use only 'paper-and-pencil' measures of intellect or business knowledge
• Assess capacity for strategic and complex thinking	• Assume that high IQ equals high potential
• Coach high potentials to identify 'blockers' before they become a problem	• Leave high potentials to get on with it
• Encourage high potentials to explore their motives and values	• Assume that everyone aspires to be a high flyer

Conclusion

Having challenged some of the common myths and pitfalls associated with the early identification of high potential, we argue that it is not possible simply to translate current performance effectiveness into a judgement about longer-term career potential. Instead, the proposed model for high potential talent assessment aims to refocus organizations' thinking when identifying and implementing high potential talent assessment approaches. Table 17.3 summarizes some best practice guidelines.

Don't assess against end state competence but against high potential indicators that will get to end state

CHAPTER 18

Assessment in organizations at the crossroads

MALCOLM HATFIELD

The challenge for business psychology is to develop its unique and separate contribution, a paradigm fully grounded in psychology and orientated to business. This chapter is a critique of the way psychology-based assessment takes place in organizations and the way different interest groups (including academic psychologists, management consultants, the British Psychological Society and test publishers) may not be helping to add value to organizations or, for that matter, to the profession of business psychology. The argument is derived from the author's specific experience after many years' practice as a business psychologist.

Introduction

Assessment is an aspect of the domain of the business psychologist that parallels the contribution made in business by other professionals such as lawyers or tax specialists. I will illustrate this by presenting a number of scenarios directly taken from experience followed by an analysis and definition of the assessment process.

Much of the discussion about assessment methodology that has been ongoing for years misses the point. This includes the focus on fine tuning assessment methodology, the process of so-called validation and how it is taught to non-psychologists, and the continual search for the Holy Grail of new assessment descriptive techniques, such as the 'big five' theory or emotional intelligence. They miss the point because few of the psychologists concerned have been fully involved in assessment processes within a business organization and so have little idea of the range of issues and the real priorities involved from a business perspective. A great deal of resources and intellectual energy have been expended leading to inappropriate public visibility. As business psychologists, we need to re-examine the overall paradigm of the assessment process and focus our attention on making improvements in areas of greater priority.

The following practical scenarios, drawn from experience and covering a range of assessment situations within business, provide our context for the subsequent discussion.

Scenario 1: validity and application of HJ5

The HJ5 is a short questionnaire designed to help select customer-facing staff in a sales or customer service role. A criterion validity study was undertaken for a well-known national UK retailer of electrical goods, which was able to validate it concurrently against actual sales value of each salesperson through the till. The sample yielded a multiple correlation of 0.53. Notionally this looks to be a conventional success story: a structured psychological instrument, professionally validated to agreed technical standards against an objective and technically reliable criterion, which was seen as important by the organization. A real glow in the mind of a commercial test publisher!

However, when implemented it was a failure. The questionnaire was extremely successful in selecting the kind of person who could sell high volumes through this particular organization's stores. The personality profile was of an assertive (but not excessively), highly shrewd, individualistic, unscrupulous, tough-minded individual. No other criterion was considered. The reality was that the test was in some senses too effective at predicting an individual's sales. However, they were likely to be gained at the expense of the performance of colleagues in the store. The simplistic implementation of these results, by management entirely focused on sales volume, created a large backlash – particularly when more than one of these people was in place in the same store, resulting in even less teamwork than was otherwise the case!

Scenario 2: audit via assessment of the top 40 senior managers

The company is a well-known British manufacturer of household products and our client was the MD. After a great deal of work and discussion about the detailed characteristics of each person, their potential in general terms and how their performance in their current jobs might be improved, this particular MD suddenly faced the writer with his ultimate question. Paraphrased and rather less directly expressed, the question was: 'Right, Malcolm. Interesting discussion. But which one of them can run a company?'

The immediate reaction to this was that it was a simplistic question. Had the MD understood any of the subtlety of the preceding discussion? With so many different variables to include could a direct judgement such as this be made, and indeed would it ever be appropriate to make such a judgement?

The eventual outcome was a more productive discussion, which developed as the writer took on an orientation more aligned to business and the MD's perspective than a purely academic psychological one.

Scenario 3: a new CEO

The writer was working as a business psychologist within an organization that assessed all its senior managers and used the input very systematically. The CEO, for whom all the directors and senior managers had been assessed, was suddenly removed. The first person that the new CEO asked to see was me and, on arrival in his new office behind his new large desk, I found open in front of him my objectively critical review of him and his colleagues. He opened the discussion . . . 'So I see here that you think I am . . .' In this situation superior competence in psychometric statistics is not going to sustain continuing employment!

Scenario 4: management selection in turbulent environment

The client in this case was an expanding, highly commercial energy business. It was clear that there was a need to find the right people to work in the organization, where the situation was very demanding, highly unpredictable and with a high casualty rate. On each occasion that I worked for this organization I attempted to define the requirements of the job, but by the time a new person joined, the organization had changed so significantly that it was quite common for the job to be different from the one they were recruited for. The ownership, shape of the business, and the culture within it was in a state of continuous change. The complex competency structure put in place by a well-known management consultancy 3 years previously did not, in my view, reflect the current organizational requirement or culture. On what basis could I make assessment judgements in this situation?

This is not a blanket criticism of competency frameworks, but these potent tools can be used both to advantage and to detriment. A business psychologist responsible for high-level assessment may have to look beyond the obvious criteria and try to engage with the most relevant one at the time to meet the business need. How do we select and develop our professionals to be able to do this?

Scenario 5: assess approximately 100 people in a weekend with very limited resources

A national retail organization, in a parlous financial state with the banks, was owed very significant amounts of money. It demanded instant, wholesale, corporate restructuring to remove approximately 30% of the managerial overheads, with plans to be put in place within a week. We were asked to devise some form of assessment-centre process in one-and-a-half days. Taken at face value it is impossible to do a proper job in the time; there was a view from some colleagues that as 'professionals' we should walk away.

A judgement had to be made. Managers in the organization had no choice. Business decisions have to be made and will be made, one way or another in a time scale defined by the business and the market-place, not by any psychologist. The organization requests that you contribute. It is my view that this should be seen as a challenge to use experience and innovation to do the best you can. A good business psychologist will educate the client to understand appropriate ways of doing things well, such that everyone knows when risks have to be taken. Again, this raises the question of how the business psychologist can develop these levels of expertise and judgement.

Scenario 6: selection for the Oman Navy

We were responsible for devising a selection system in Arabic for relatively uneducated young men from desert villages to train as officers in the modern and sophisticated Navy in Oman. Selection had previously been on the basis of tribe, status, and other culturally defined factors. A cousin of the Sultan asked to see me to point out that one cannot ever hope to learn and obtain the real political grasp of the highly complex tribal and other power interrelationships in the ruling caste of the country. Furthermore, it is to an extent counter to the culture to make ratings or judgements about individuals. So, how could we contribute to the running of the Navy?

Perhaps surprisingly, conventional methods of test development worked well in this context, but a level of flexibility and innovation was needed in validation, test administration and training, in addition to a subtle discussion about what was possible and what should be left well alone.

Scenario 7: management selection in a growing company

An organization in the finance sector had been started virtually from nothing, and grown quickly by the clear vision of the founder. An assessment process brought in people whose personality, style, way of working and values fitted the clearly identified culture, and helped to differentiate it from competitors. However, the organization had reached a size where it required, or appeared to require, an IT director to bring a greater sense of balance, a wider range of experience and functional expertise to this rather individualistic and commercially oriented management culture. The assessment process helped the organization to identify someone who was widely experienced, interested in contributing to the progression of the business, and who had the potential to bring a measure of consistency and stability to decision making. Was this a successful recruitment?

This was not a successful recruitment, although the assessment process itself worked well as far as it went. The individual concerned behaved very much in the manner predicted but in practice the appointment did not work out. The organization obtained the person that it said it wanted, and indeed the person that it actually needed, but because of their own entrenched culture they were unable to use her effectively and the problems of growing and developing the organization continued. Interestingly, the organization went rather spectacularly bust in 2001!

These examples are all 'real' and they will be typical of the experience of any practising business psychologist. I would suggest that the formal assessment methodology involved is the least of the concerns that business psychologists would have in ensuring that they are able to make an effective contribution. For example, in the case of the validity of the small selection test for customer service staff, the issue was the overly specific and simplistic nature of the criterion and the failure to understand that effective performance in a store was much more subtle and widely based than simple profit. In the example of the retail company experiencing an emergency, the ideal had to be abandoned and something creative had to be designed in order to do what was possible.

The crunch issue here is that businesses have to make decisions about people, whether or not a business psychologist is involved. There is no point in businesses employing or using business psychologists unless their decisions will be improved as a result – which will lead to some improvement in performance. The MD who asked apparently simplistic questions was seeking an opinion. He valued the opinion – people like him do not waste time on charity! The task of business psychologists is to remove themselves from the academic psychological paradigm and to operate in the business context without losing their essence as psychologists. How is this capacity to be acquired?

So what is assessment?

When consulting dictionaries for the word 'assessment' or 'assessor', one finds a variety of definitions that encompass 'giving a considered opinion', 'to appraise critically', and 'to estimate the importance, value or worth of something in relation to something else'. Looking at the meanings of 'estimate' and 'judgement' we find 'the formation of an opinion concerning something by exercising the mind on it'.

The important thing in these definitions for me is that there is both an element of both knowledge and experience, but also of evaluation against some form of criterion. There is an implied human input into this process, which seems to consist of:

* gathering information;
* coming to a view; then
* evaluating what has been found against a concept of value and worth.

The implication is that assessment involves both developing an understanding of who or what it is you are assessing and then, in some way, relating it to the context within which it is being assessed.

To illustrate this point further I will use the analogy of antiques valuation. Assessors in the antiques field tend to be specialists who know a lot about their subject. When presented with a given antique item assessors would be able to judge, for example, that it was made between 1810 and 1830 by a good maker and is of a particular level of quality. They would also be able to say why they took this view about quality, and what evidence they had for placing a given date.

The identification of date and type is a description, and effective description requires knowledge. The view that it is of a particular quality is something else. This is, I suggest, a judgement. It is based on knowledge, but also on a level of comparison and experience. So, for example, the assessor might use past experience of other similar items to say that this 1820 item is better than this other one because of certain features. This judgement might represent a high level of skill and expertise, so not everyone can do this. It is clearly possible that there is a subjective element. But it is still based on a description. In my view this is not yet an assessment because there is, as yet, no opinion about value, worth or goodness of fit. There has been an identification of type and a comparison, but no choices, no evaluations, no decisions.

Continuing the analogy, the expert might say: 'This first item is a good 1820 piece and, at £500, it represents good value. This other is better.' But we still do not know whether, at £750, the second is good value. The choices depend now upon both judgement and an understanding of the context; these together, in my view, enable a value judgement to be made. Are your requirements for a sound, good value 1820 piece? If so, then take the first. But if you want the best 1820 piece you can get, do you take the second? Or is it not quite good enough? Or might you be able to obtain one of this quality for £650?

There are, I hope, clear parallels with assessment in business. These examples are, in my view, 'assessment' judgements in the true sense. They are appraising value.

- they require *knowledge* in order to give an effective description;
- they require *experience* to give a comparison;
- they require *understanding of the context* and the requirement in order to make a *judgement of value*.

Transferring the analogy to assessment in business psychology, psychologists have expended an enormous amount of time and effort over the years to produce a methodology that effectively and reliably describes what people are like and to compare one with another. People are complex, subtle and different. This description is supplemented by the specific knowledge and experience of the psychologist making the assessment concerned. In the scenarios above, the descriptions of people were accurate enough. However, the result of all of these methods, a good description, is not yet an assessment.

The importance of context

In the scenarios above I tried to illustrate the variety and subtlety of the contexts in which business psychologists become involved and the situations in which they are required to make an assessment. These are often not what they seem, and if we misunderstand the context, then the assessment is flawed, however accurate the initial description. This understanding seems to require a real appreciation of business, the environment in which business operates, the organization strategies and how they place demands on people.

But a full assessment process requires judgements as well as understanding. The measurements of the people concerned and of the contexts in which the decision is embedded are not sufficiently clearly and objectively defined to enable a purely logical decision. A judgement leading to a decision in this context is a process. Interestingly, most of the standard business psychology texts are of little help in this crucial area. Surely business psychology should have a great deal to say about the process of decision making in complex situations such as this, but it seems more important to teach HR managers about correlation statistics and standard error of measurement . . .

To summarize the discussion so far:

- an assessment process implies a level of professional knowledge and experience leading to an effective description of the subject matter involved;
- this then has to be integrated into an understanding of the context both in the present and in the future;

- and then finally a judgement, which represents the mapping of the description of the individual into the context in which they are placed.

These activities involve the challenging combination of the application of functional expertise and judgement, looking to the future and the courage of convictions in coming to a view. The outcome impacts upon the performance of the business and the lives of individuals. This encompasses all the background psychological knowledge that might be applied but also implies innovation, risk, living with uncertainty, being prepared to be faced with the consequences of your judgements, and going beyond academic training. It is forward looking, proactive, engaging with the unpredictable future using knowledge, experience and innovation. This is what being a business psychologist should be about!

Business psychologists as professional advisers

We are similar to a variety of other professional advisers used by business who also make assessments in their specific fields of expertise. For example, business strategists make assessments of the likely impact of new strategies in a particular market. Advertising managers make assessments of the impact of a given spend in different advertising media. These activities involve some assessment of knowledge and experience, clear descriptions of what is being examined, an understanding of the context, and a judgement of the relative value and worth of the likely outcomes. The common characteristic of a wide range of really strong functional specialist contributors within businesses is that they add value by good judgements in their own field of expertise, which are aligned with the company's objectives and support the business. This applies to tax managers, treasurers, lawyers, accountants, marketeers, finance people or indeed psychologists.

Functional experts who are less influential are people who might be described as the technical specialists. They are the tax experts who happen to be in the business, the auditor who only counts figures and assembles reports, the marketeer who writes copy to a format given to them; and . . . the psychologist who gives tests and describes what the tests say.

The efforts of psychologists recently to demonstrate improvement in testing technology, the technical debates (for example, normative versus ipsative tests) and the issues about validity are mostly irrelevant. This is because most of this effort is only directed towards bettering the description stage of the process, probably the least important area that we should be investigating. The major issue in an assessment context is how, as a business psychologist, it is possible to make an effective assessment that parallels the contribution made by other functional specialists. Only by doing this can we raise the profile and contribution of psychology in business.

The roots of the dilemma

There are, in my view, a number of reasons for having focused on the wrong things. Some of these are to do with the psychology of the psychologists themselves. Others are to do with the legitimate but different aims of groups that are in conflict with the need to develop assessment as described.

- *Altruism.* It has been suggested that psychology gave away market research in the 1950s because the ethical issues were too muddy to deal with; it could also be said that psychology gave away psychological testing in the 1980s. These decisions may have been made by psychologists from an academic background with no interest in being business psychologists. Perhaps they did not understand what was involved or the implications of their actions because they had little experience of it. This is not to criticize them. Indeed, their response was very appropriate within the context in which they were operating. The outcome is a fact rather than a value judgement.

- *Commercial interest:*
  - Of test publishers. One result of giving away testing is that there are potentially far more purchasers than there were ever psychologists as test users. These massive commercial opportunities have naturally been seized upon by some psychologists and businessmen. So, issues like improving the quality of training of non-psychologists and minimizing the impact of the experience and judgement elements that would need a high-level business psychology input would obviously be an element of business strategy of any test-publishing house. Progressive automation and expert system reporting are examples of apparent deskilling that will enhance test sales. As test publishing becomes a more effective business, one can hardly blame the test publishers for promoting their own commercial interests.
  - Of other non-psychological consulting operations, such as market research, surveying, advertising, or public relations. They happily cherry pick and tap into the more obviously applicable outcomes of psychological research without being interested in developing a rigorous psychological underpinning of what they do. As before, their commercial interests and objectives are quite straightforward and very clear.

- *The psychology of the psychologists.* In the mid-1980s there was a strong move within the BPS to give psychology away and encourage use of psychological techniques by a wide range of people. This laudable value might not have had the results in practical terms that were envisaged. The most obvious things to 'give away' are psychological tests and questionnaires. The attendant significant visibility of this has had the consequences that the general perception of psychology within business is now equated with psychometric testing. This perception is increased in people at large by the public debates about the validity of tests and discussion about which test or other is best to use.

Nonetheless there have also been some advantages of the foregoing for psychologists working within business: the fact that one is now able to talk in jargon that few other people understand; the fact that one can gain mutual support from a group of psychometricians; the fact that this whole activity is identifying something that is definitely 'psychological' and not appropriate for discussion by non-psychologists. All this helps some psychologists gain a sense of identity and control. However, this benefit has been at the cost of a resultant restricted perception of what psychology can potentially contribute. From this viewpoint, psychologists have opportunistically hidden behind specific techniques. Not enough business psychologists have been interested in wider business activity and aims, and thinking through the issues about how they would most effectively contribute in the wider arena. Assessment is perhaps the most obvious, but is not the only contribution that could be made.

In this discussion it is not intended to belittle the great advances that have been made in assessment technology. Assessment tests are a great deal better than they were in the 1970s. For example, they are less discriminatory, which is extremely important both because of their more widespread use and also for their continuing commercial production; they are presented in a more user-friendly format and so are more acceptable. They are certainly more expensive but in the context of the costs involved this is probably acceptable.

Assessment techniques have been proved to work many times over a huge variety of situations. They yield a better and more consistent result in most decision-making situations than if you do not use them. The issue is that allowing ourselves to get stuck in discussions that businesses (our clients) see as irrelevant, whilst it may make some of us feel 'scientific', does not make us better or more effective psychologists within business. From this perspective of the BPS work on Level A, Level B can be seen as a distraction to the development of business psychology as a real profession that contributes to business.

This argument also applies to other issues, which can be seen as a distraction in terms of the overall process of improving assessment. For example, consider popular concepts such as 'emotional intelligence'. Has it got us further forward in terms of producing overall more effective assessments in business? We cannot really blame test publishers for developing tests of EQ (which has been promoted more to managers than to business psychologists – a clear indicator of who is seen as more important). On one side we have an academic debate pro or contra, which may have a level of interest but has little practical relevance. On the other side we have clients who ask why we don't use this wonderful new tool or, because it is available to all, they decide they can do without their professional adviser.

The future for business psychology

The business world moves on. All the examples quoted show the importance of achieving a balance across the four elements of the assessment process: *knowledge, experience, understanding the context* and *judgement.* As business psychologists we need to develop our breadth of competence across these four areas. We need to promote this competence and, in so doing, recognize that our aims are not the same as academic psychologists, academic occupational psychology, test publishers or generalist consultancy firms. The business psychologist must possess an understanding and empathy with business, market-place, performance issues, strategy, capability and resource availability, corporate history and collective memory.

Maybe I am asking a lot of individual business psychologists, but I believe that this is what it should be all about. To go back to an earlier point, the really good functional specialists are those who can think company-wide in a strategic manner and marry their own discipline and its standards to the company need to impact across the business with its wide range of people. As an assessor, frequently involved in selection, I often find a clear divide between those who can develop a real breadth of creative contribution in the business and those who are unable to make the leap from a focus on functional speciality. There are many organizational tax advisers but rather fewer effective corporate tax directors. There are too few business psychologists with real influence at strategic level but there are huge numbers of Level A trained testers . . .

So to summarize

Assessment, as part of the role of business psychology, is a complex and sophisticated process requiring a level of breadth and judgement that is challenging but also has parallels with other professions working in business.

Assessment is much more than measurement using specific tools. Developing some understanding of the breadth and subtlety of the assessment process yields insight that helps us to see the range and type of contribution the business psychologist is potentially able to make.

Assessment tools can always be improved but are of sufficient potency to add value as they are. Specific discussion about methodology is of relevance in a purely psychological context but mostly a distraction for business psychology. Much more helpful areas of research can be identified such as decision-making processes in practical situations.

The goals, values and actions of academic psychologists, test publishers, management consultants, and the BPS are all valid for those organizations but are not necessarily congruent with business psychology.

Being a psychologist in business can therefore be difficult or lonely because it is possible to be alienated from both academic psychology and from business people – neither fish nor fowl. We are just as liable as others to retreat to our comfort zones at the expense of what we might be trying to achieve.

A common theme of the examples given is the need for the psychologist to contribute to understanding of the context and clarification of the criteria against which judgements are made. If business psychologists do not address the issues raised, there is a danger of becoming sidelined as administrators of techniques developed elsewhere and evaluated by others. No one will tackle this other than business psychologists because it is in no one else's interest.

For the twenty-first century we need a model and understanding of our contribution and our own defined agenda, qualifications and training. Otherwise twenty-first century assessment processes will remain determined by theory developed in the first half of the twentieth century and practice developed in the second half. As business psychologists we have the potential to contribute in the front line if we grasp the opportunity, have the courage of our convictions and show confidence in our unique contribution and ourselves.

PART 4
RELEASING TALENT

CHAPTER 19
Introduction

SARAH LEWIS

> . . . for the first time ever it is possible to state with confidence that how organisations manage people has a powerful – perhaps the most powerful – effect on overall performance, including the bottom line.
>
> (Chartered Institute of Personnel and Development, 2001)

This bold statement from the Chartered Institute of Personnel and Development (CIPD) reflects the culmination of many years of effort to demonstrate the impact on organizations of effective people management. 'Our people are our greatest asset' has become a management cliché. Research, however, confirms the suspicion that as a sentiment it is more honoured in the breach than in the observance. For instance, the 1998 Workplace Employment Relations Survey reveals that while two-thirds of UK organizations surveyed relied strongly on people for competitive advantage, only one-tenth prioritized people issues over marketing and finance issues (Guest et al., 2000).

West and colleagues found that, amongst the manufacturing businesses they researched, 18% of variation in production and 19% of variation in profitability could be attributed to people-management practices, these representing the largest impact of the variables investigated. By contrast, research and development accounted for 8% whereas perennial favourites quality, new technology and competitive strategy only accounted for approximately 1% each (West and Patterson, 1998). Similarly, Caulkin's examination of 30 organizational performance studies in the UK and US since 1990 notes that the results leave 'no room to doubt that there is a correlation between people management and business performance, that the relationship is positive, and that it is cumulative' (Chartered Institute of Personnel and Development, 2001).

These findings suggest that good people management policies and procedures are at the heart of profitable businesses. However, policies and practices are necessary but not sufficient for good results. It is how they are enacted that counts. For example, employees, if asked about the appraisal process, will refer to their own experiences with their managers, not to the elegance of the written policy (Chartered Institute of Personnel and Development, 2002). Following this observation, a number of researchers have recently investigated the connection between good human resources strategy and good business outcomes in more detail, to examine more closely how these inputs and outputs are actually linked. Early results suggest a number of points of interest to business psychologists.

For example, is it apparent that good human resources practice can provide a source of competitive advantage by enhancing skills, promoting positive attitudes and giving people more responsibility, so they can make the fullest use of their skills (West and Patterson, 1998). These findings are supported by Stern and Sommerdale (1999) who note that 'practices that encourage workers to think and interact to improve the production process are strongly linked to increased productivity'. The work of West and Patterson (1998) indicated that two specific HR practices are related to improvements in profitability and performance: acquisition and development of skill, and job design. These suggested linear chains of causality are of great use to psychologists working to improve organizational effectiveness. At the same time, findings of large research studies point to the importance of system-wide influences on organizational performance.

West and Patterson (1998) note that an interesting and unexpected finding of their research with manufacturing organizations was a positive predictive correlation between the global organizational measure of employee satisfaction and positive organizational outcomes. 'One of the most exciting results from the study is that the satisfaction of the workforce is such an important predictor of future productivity', they write, concluding 'that good people management is not simply about selection, appraisal and so on. It is about the development of whole communities in which people feel socially included rather than alienated, by the experience of work.' Meanwhile John Purcell and his research team at the Work and Employment Research Centre at the University of Bath have been examining employee 'discretionary behaviour' as a possible link between human resources practices and performance. Their research is starting to suggest that the degree to which such behaviour is exhibited is a function of ability, motivation, and opportunity (Chartered Institute of Personnel and Development, 2002) – in other words, the relationship between the individual and the possibilities offered by the organization.

Caulkin adds another perspective. Having examined how practice affects performance he suggests that 'capacity determines what strategic intent can be' – that organizational strategy follows development rather than vice versa, which suggests a much more circular causality of organizational performance than that which underpins the typical top-down strategy development models (Chartered Institute of Personnel and Development, 2001).

So good people management is good for the organization, and ultimately, it can be assumed, for the shareholders, but is it good for the employees? Research into the area of 'what makes a good life' notes that people are more likely to consider themselves happy when (amongst other things) they experience periods of 'flow', a sense of being happily engaged in a challenging task, and when they consider themselves working towards or for something bigger than themselves (Seligman, 2003). These conditions can be met in a workplace following best practice.

Often psychologists interviewing candidates for jobs hear them express their work motivation in terms of 'wanting to make a difference'. But such an outcome is not inevitable as many organizations still ignore individuals' needs for group affiliation and personal achievement. For instance, research suggests that most firms concentrate only on developing those skills that are targeted at broadening the scope of the individual while ignoring those focused on developing quality and group-based skill (Stevens and Ashton, 1999). In other words, managers tend to think of high performance as getting individuals to work harder individually, not smarter together.

This section demonstrates different ways that business psychologists add value to good human resources practices by releasing organizational talent. Throughout, the authors demonstrate an awareness of their responsibility to individual employees as well as to the hiring organization. In addition, the psychologists each take careful note of the specific organizational context into which they have been invited, demonstrating an awareness that 'one size does not fit all, a degree of fit with the company's environment, with its business strategy and with its other people management policies and with its own history' is needed (Chartered Institute of Personnel and Development, 2001). Business psychologists are well placed to create a phenomenon known as 'learning in context' – that is, learning relevant to the individuals involved, the situation and the business environment. Our various authors introduce us to interventions at the organizational, team and individual levels that release and develop the talent within the organization by focusing not just on the individuals, but also on the connections and relationships between individuals. There is a strong emphasis upon organizational and social context throughout.

All of the authors in this section are writing from and about personal professional experience and, where appropriate, the theory that supports their particular choice of practice. They share with us what it is really like attempting to apply organizational, team or individual theory to live organizations concerned with issues of profitability, competitiveness, service quality and change. Their writing styles vary considerably but, through their contributions, these experienced practitioners reveal some of the thinking behind their way of working, their 'mental models' (Senge, 1994). They provide a fascinating insight into the working lives of consultants active in this field.

CHAPTER 20

Releasing talent across an organization

KATE OLIVER, SHANE PRESSEY

Introduction

Increasingly, when talking with human resources professionals and leaders, we are finding that the area of talent is a key concern for organizations. It seems helpful at this point to define what we mean by 'talent'. Talent in its most general sense can be said to be the sum of people's abilities – their skills, knowledge, experience, intelligence, judgement and personality. It also includes their ability to learn and grow to realize their full potential. It is unsurprising therefore that the way that talent is managed is seen as key to an organization's success.

This focus on talent also emerged in two recent surveys undertaken by our organization (Human Qualities, 2001, 2002). In their responses organizations identified attracting, leveraging and retaining talent as key challenges facing their businesses. The response to these challenges is commonly labelled 'talent management'. It is apparent both from research and our experience that there is a number of forces fuelling this quest to effectively manage talent. These include:

- the intensifying demand for high-calibre leaders (McKinsey & Co., 2000);
- the growing propensity for people to switch from one company to another (Capelli, 1999);
- the increasing importance of knowledge in the Information Age (Butler et al., 1997).

As such, talent is now a critical driver of organizational performance and a company's ability to attract, develop and retain talent will be a major competitive advantage, now and into the future.

The role of managers

Given this growing awareness of the need to manage talent effectively, we might ask where in the organization such responsibility should lie? Many large organizations will have a specialized HR or development department – some may even have renamed this department 'talent management'. This department's contribution to releasing talent will vary from company to company. However, typically it might include setting standards, putting in place processes to support talent management and providing support for skills development.

It is our belief that it is not the human resources department that is really responsible for releasing talent; it is leaders and managers within the business. It is the mindset of leaders that makes the difference. This is because releasing talent is about what happens to individuals on a day-to-day basis – how they are led, what they are encouraged to do, how their behaviours are reinforced. This is the essence of the role of the manager.

This belief is backed up by recent research showing that top-performing organizations managed talent differently from average-performing companies – and that they did so in terms of their managers' beliefs and actions rather than their human resources processes (McKinsey and Company, 2000). Thus, we assert that it is leaders and managers who are really key to the releasing of talent, as outlined in Figure 20.1.

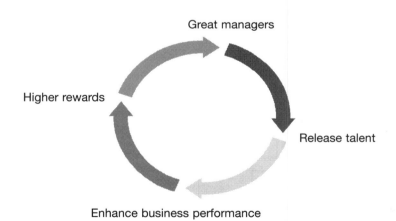

Figure 20.1 The virtuous circle of talent.

The process of releasing talent

So what does the process of releasing talent actually involve? There are many ways, some complex, to answer this question. On a practical level, a simple model that we have found useful in our work with leaders and managers is given in Table 20.1. This model portrays releasing talent as a four-stage process.

Table 20.1 Releasing talent – a process

Stage	Activity
1	Understand business context • Strategy • Vision • Culture and values
2	Understand yourself • Strengths • Development needs • Impact on others
3	Understand your people • Performance – *What underlies performance* • Abilities • Motivation
4	Take action • Objective setting • Feedback • Coaching

Great Process!

Initially, managers need to understand the context in which they are operating – the business strategy, goals and culture. Once that is in place then the process of self-insight comes into play. Managers need to know themselves and to understand the impact they have on others. In other words, they need to understand how to release the talent within themselves before they are able to release talent in others. This then leads onto the need to understand their team members, not just in terms of their current level of performance, but also in gaining a deeper appreciation of what underlies this in terms of abilities, style, motivation, and so on. Having gained this understanding a manager is well placed to know what action to take in order to release talent – to direct, motivate, empower, guide and coach their people to fulfil their potential.

The role of psychology

How can we, as business psychologists, help managers to release talent?

3 main thing
4's bring of techniques
1) tools 2) people insight 3) theory & research

When we asked ourselves this question, we started to think about the different contributions that we bring to our work with managers in organizations. Based on our experience, we believe that our contribution can be divided into three main areas: tools and techniques, insight into people, and theory and research.

Tools and techniques

Firstly, we believe that as psychologists we possess analytical problem solving skills, rooted in our knowledge of experimental techniques. These skills give us a framework within which to operate and a language with which to diagnose and understand situations. This helps us to structure our thought processes and to communicate these in a meaningful way to our clients. We also find that these are skills that managers can benefit from developing for themselves. Thus, in much of our work with managers we aim to share these tools and techniques, transferring some of the underlying skills to enable them to use these to release talent within their teams.

Insight into people

Our background and training leaves us well equipped with the skills required to gain insight into people, appreciate difference and demonstrate empathy. This does not mean that we believe all psychologists are experts in emotional intelligence (Goleman, 1998)! However, we do believe that our training has helped us to look at people in a different way, and to understand the complexities of interpersonal relationships to a more sophisticated level than the untutored. In fact, when working alongside non-psychologists, we find that they often give us feedback confirming this. We also believe that these are fundamental skills in facilitating managers to develop their skills in releasing talent.

Theory and research

From a practitioner's point of view, we find that we spend most of our time using our knowledge of tools and techniques and insight into people, in helping managers to release talent. Occasionally, theory in its own right will be highly relevant. For example, when exploring the various factors that motivate individuals, we frequently share with managers a number of theories of motivation. More often, we see that theory will have informed our tools, techniques and insight. One example of this would be the underpinning use of Skinner's reinforcement theory (Skinner, 1938, 1953, 1969) in much of the training and coaching we conduct with managers.

Releasing talent – a case study

To demonstrate how all this comes together in practice, a case study, taken from our work with leaders and managers in one organization, will be used throughout the chapter. This case study characterizes the added value that psychology can bring to the area of releasing talent. It also demonstrates the pressure on the practitioner to interpret what psychology has to offer in a pragmatic and user-friendly form, for the busy and impatient senior manager.

Background to the intervention

A technology department within a leading international organization was undergoing a major change initiative to realize a stretching 5-year vision, aimed at increasing efficiency and productivity. To achieve this it recognized that their managers would require greater leadership and performance management skills, to be able to release the talent within their teams. It was with this aspect of the initiative that we were asked to help.

Design of the intervention

The objectives of the specific project with which we were involved were for managers to:

- understand their role as a leader/manager and feel confident in fulfilling this;
- recognize the value of people management as a driver of individual and business success;
- grow the capability of individuals and their teams.

The time constraints within which we were asked to work called for a step change – a fundamental and rapid shift in these behaviours across the department.

There is a huge body of psychological evidence around the ways in which group dynamics impact on individual behaviour through social processes such as the development of group norms and the phenomenon of conformity, which suggests that any individual will behave in a way that fits in with the majority. So for a behaviour change, such as our project aspired to achieve, it would be important for a critical momentum to be built up – if only a few individuals were targeted, the required change would not be achieved. Moreover, it would be important that senior managers' role modelled and reinforced the new behaviours – experience shows that leaders within a business are watched more than anyone else and hence will have the biggest impact on others' behaviour.

snr mgrs need to role model + reinforce new beh's

This led us to believe that the success of the intervention would require the involvement of all managers in the department. To achieve this involved a tiered process, beginning with the director and his executive team, and cascading down through the three management levels. The design centred around the use of an embedded learning process (a series of integrated learning interventions), that aimed to tackle both group and individual learning needs. This learning process involved a variety of elements, including pre-reading, diagnostic questionnaires, two workshop modules, experiential learning, action learning, peer feedback and coaching.

This process draws on learning theory, such as Kolb's learning cycle (see Figure 20.2 below) (Kolb, 1984). This describes the stages that an individual needs to go through to learn most effectively. In reality, different people will tend to focus on one or two of these stages, rather than working through the entire process. An effective learning intervention therefore needs to help individuals to stretch into the zones of the process with which they are less comfortable in order to release their full talent.

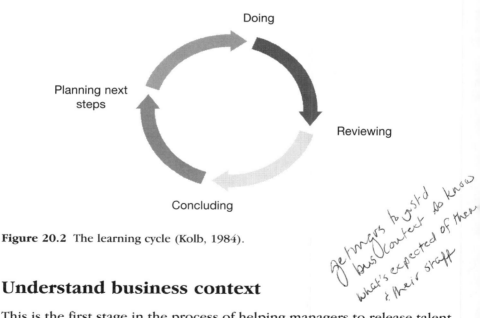

Figure 20.2 The learning cycle (Kolb, 1984).

Understand business context

This is the first stage in the process of helping managers to release talent. It focuses on helping them understand the business context they are operating in and shaping this for the future. In this case, the managers had historically dedicated little time to understanding their wider business context. So this stage was about helping them to look up and around themselves, rather than just down at their immediate work.

There are numerous reasons why this is important from a business perspective – fundamentally because managers need to understand the business context to know what is expected from them and their people and thus the ways in which the talent in their teams can best contribute to business success. From a social psychological perspective, there is an additional compelling driver. This comes from research in the area of social identity theory – how one gets one's own sense of worth and identity from identifying with a group (Mead, 1934). In this case, this was about enabling the managers to find a shared sense of identity with each other and their area of the business.

As a first step in achieving this, the organization had undertaken work to review its existing culture and to define where it would like to be in the future. The desired change, it transpired, would require a shift from a culture where individuals tended to control, compete and find fault (and thus where people were unwilling to take risks to fulfil their potential) to one where they would be achievement focused, encouraging, cooperative and focused on learning and development.

Our chosen approach drew on social psychology theory and research in the area of norms. This tells us that changing group norms (which is the essence of organizational culture change) will be most effective if those impacted by the change are involved in making the decisions needed to effect it (Coch and French, 1948).

So what was needed was something to help the managers really relate to and understand how the cultural shifts could help them in releasing talent. A key step in doing this was to help the managers create a vision and values set for their department, linked to the strategy, to enable them to say 'This is who we are and this is what we stand for'. By each playing a part in shaping this, the managers were able to emerge with a vision that they could buy into and believe in.

Understand yourself

The second stage in the process of helping managers to release talent is to help them to gain enhanced self-insight. We have repeatedly found that this process of 'holding up the mirror' is essential to enabling managers to release the talent in themselves – which they need to do to be in the best position to release the talent in others.

The importance of understanding oneself is reflected in recent work by Goleman (1998), in the area of emotional intelligence. One of the core competencies in this model is that of self-awareness, which is defined as 'Knowing one's inner states, preferences, resources and intuitions'. Supporting the importance of this aspect of a manager's behaviour, there exists a body of research demonstrating that managers with higher levels of self-awareness are superior performers (for example, Boyatzis, 1982; Nilsen and Campbell, 1993).

From the preliminary meetings held with managers, it was apparent that, whilst some had reasonable levels of self-awareness, self-knowledge was generally limited. We therefore introduced a range of mechanisms as part of the embedded learning process, to facilitate increasing levels of self-insight in this population. In all cases, self-insight was related closely to the new culture, vision and values. Techniques used to facilitate this included a pre-workshop self-review questionnaire focused on management attitudes, beliefs and actions. This was particularly illuminating for many managers who found that they had an appropriate belief set to release talent but weren't actually carrying out the actions required to do this. In facilitating discussions around this challenge, we were able to draw on research into the link between attitudes, beliefs and behaviours, such as the theory of planned behaviour (Ajzen and Madden, 1986). This suggests that perceived control over one's own behaviour influences behaviour directly, and also indirectly through intentions, thus explaining why managers may believe in something (have the 'attitude') but not actually do it (the 'behaviour'). This bears similarities to Bandura's (1986) concept of self-efficacy, which will be discussed later in this chapter.

Resolution of this issue was also helped through use of a simple model of leadership activity – action-centred leadership (Adair, 1975). This model suggests that managers have three responsibilities – focusing on the task, the individuals and the team – and that they need to balance time and activity across these three areas to release talent. Reflection around this model helped the managers to think about the balance of how they were spending their time and how this might need to be redressed.

To facilitate self-insight around personal behaviours and impact, relating to the new culture and values, a specific technique used was experiential learning, which involves active experimentation with immediate feedback. This technique uses unusual projects in unfamiliar settings, with the spotlight on the process rather than the task. We find it is a key way to build emotional competence through enabling reflection on personal impact and consequent fine tuning of behaviour. Managers were also encouraged to add to each other's levels of self-awareness, through providing peer feedback on an ongoing basis through the programme. This included targeted activities where managers worked together in buddy pairs to observe each other in the workplace and then provide feedback on behaviours that they perceived to reinforce, either positively or negatively, the new culture and values.

The facilitator's skill throughout these interventions was to create a climate to enable learning – where participants felt able to discuss emotions,

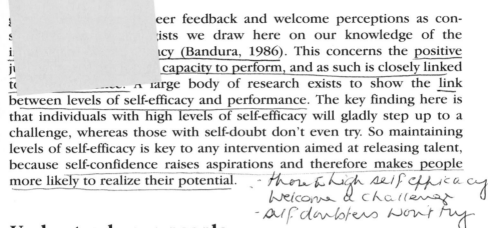

eer feedback and welcome perceptions as con-
ists we draw here on our knowledge of the
cy (Bandura, 1986). This concerns the positive
capacity to perform, and as such is closely linked
A large body of research exists to show the link
between levels of self-efficacy and performance. The key finding here is
that individuals with high levels of self-efficacy will gladly step up to a
challenge, whereas those with self-doubt don't even try. So maintaining
levels of self-efficacy is key to any intervention aimed at releasing talent,
because self-confidence raises aspirations and therefore makes people
more likely to realize their potential.

- those to high self efficacy welcome a challenge
- self doubters won't try

Understand your people

The third stage in the process of helping managers to release talent involves
enabling them to gain an understanding of the people working for them.
This understanding will form the basis for deciding what action can be taken
to further release talent. It requires psychologists to draw on their own
insight into people and behaviour, and to share this with managers. Often a
manager will be aware that an individual in their team is under-performing
in relation to their full potential, but will be stuck as to how to effect any difference. On a practical level we find that this often means challenging
managers to ask 'why?' – in other words, to reflect at a deeper level on what
contributes to the current performance level of their team members.

A simple model that we have found to be useful in helping managers
to do this is outlined in Figure 20.3. This model is effective because it
gives a framework for thinking about what holds an individual back from
behaving in a different way.

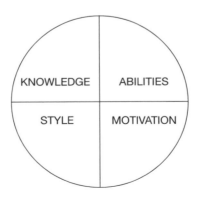

Figure 20.3 What determines behaviour?

There are of course many occupational psychology tools and models available to help diagnose the performance of individuals in terms of their abilities, style and motivation – this is what psychometric testing is founded upon. Two that we found particularly useful in this context are discussed here.

The first of these focused on the area of style, and was a simple questionnaire and model, concentrating on conflict handling. It was particularly relevant because the way in which conflict was typically managed required change to achieve the new cultural vision. This enabled managers to gain insight into their own style when faced with conflict and those of their people.

The second area of emphasis was that of motivation. This is an area of extensive research, dating back to the 1940s (Maslow, 1943). A number of theories of motivation were shared and discussed with the managers, giving them insight into the various factors that can motivate and demotivate individuals and the importance of appreciating individual differences.

Take action

This final stage in the process of releasing talent focuses on equipping managers with a range of tools and techniques they can use to make an appropriate intervention with an individual. In this instance it was also about helping them to realize that there was a commercial imperative to growing talent – that taking action to release talent would benefit themselves, the individual and the organization.

Our work focused on developing skills in a number of areas, and exploring the potential barriers to and benefits of applying these in the workplace. This required judgement over the appropriate mode of facilitation to use at various points. On several occasions, a challenging style of facilitation was needed to help managers explore possibilities and overcome limiting beliefs.

The first of these areas was that of objective setting. Probably the most consistently supported theory in occupational psychology is goal-setting theory (Locke and Latham, 1990), which proposes that specific, difficult goals, when they are accepted by the individual, will lead to effective performance. In management applications, this has been translated into pragmatic mnemonics, such as SMART: effective objectives need to be specific, measurable, agreed, realistic and time bound.

Goal-setting theory also states that feedback on goal attainment is necessary for goal setting to be maximally effective. This ties in with other classic behaviourist theories around feedback, such as reinforcement (Skinner, 1938, 1953, 1969). The area of feedback was one of significant focus in this intervention because, for behaviour change to occur, managers would need to reinforce more and less conducive behaviours appropriately, both positively and negatively, on an ongoing basis. This was achieved through the use of various mechanisms – input on models of feedback, practice delivering peer feedback both during the workshop and as part of action learning assignments, and via facilitator feedback on the effectiveness of the feedback provided.

A third area of focus was that of coaching. Coaching is an approach that is currently very much 'in vogue' in organizational life and is discussed later in this section. It is a powerful mechanism for releasing talent. We find that much of the current thinking on effective coaching draws on work in the area of psychology (such as self-efficacy and goal setting, as described previously in this chapter). As such it emphasizes the need for involvement of the coachee in defining goals and agreeing solutions – a far cry from more traditional methods of 'instructing', where managers would tell their employees what to do and how to do it.

In this application, a coaching approach also closely mirrored the desired cultural changes – another compelling driver for its usage. Managers learned the skills of coaching and practised these during the workshops. Significantly, the workshops were followed by a 3 month period of workplace coaching, where the executive team were coached by one of the occupational psychology facilitators; they then coached their middle managers, the middle managers coached their team leaders, and so on. This cascaded period of coaching enabled these behaviours to become embedded in the department, and encouraged their ongoing usage.

Case-study conclusions

So what did we learn from this intervention? The major thing it reinforced in our minds was the number of levels on which a behaviour change intervention needs to operate in order to really enable the releasing of talent. This is illustrated by the model in Figure 20.4.

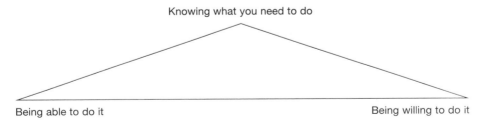

Figure 20.4 Releasing talent – changing behaviour.

In essence this model says that for individuals to change their behaviour they need to:

- know what is needed;
- have the skills to do this;
- be motivated to do this.

Business psychology, with its unique contribution in terms of tools and techniques, insight into people, and theory and research, provides the rounded approach necessary to enable this.

In this particular instance, an evaluation questionnaire used before and after the programme showed that managers are dedicating more time to leadership and people management and value these behaviours more highly than prior to the intervention. Moreover, several months after completing the assignment another department in the business approached us to conduct a similar intervention, based on perceptions of the changes witnessed in these managers. The impression was that these managers appeared to have a sense of unity and identity and were working together better as a team as a result of the intervention. In other words, the process had had a positive impact in terms of releasing talent within this management population.

CHAPTER 21

Teams: systems within systems

GEORGE KARSERAS

Team building is not going on corporate jolly!

A client recently expressed an interest in an off-site team-development event for his management team. When I asked him what kind of event he had in mind, his response was a day at Brands Hatch racing single-seater sports cars! Most commentators recognize the organizational significance of effective team working (see, for example, Nadler and Tushman, 1999). Unfortunately, this particular leader assumed the route to team effectiveness was to build social cohesion. Task and social cohesion are certainly worthwhile goals (Carron, 1982) as long as they do not lead to groupthink (Janis and Mann, 1977). But it is a dangerous assumption to think that social cohesion alone is the answer to a team's problem.

Team building is not about putting a team in a box

Besides the misconception that team building is the same as a corporate jolly, there is also, in my opinion, an over-developed tendency for teams to spend too much time analysing whether they are forming, norming, storming or performing. These well-known stages of Tuckman's have received much publicity over the years (Argyle, 1969; Bateman and Wilson, 2002). Whilst his theory is quite impressive because all his stages end in '-orming', I have found little evidence, especially for the teams of today, of its utility in actually improving team performance. Today's team is very different to that observed by Tuckman 30 years ago. It is likely to be partly or wholly virtual, be made up of cross-functional members, to be continuously changing in its membership, to be subjected to greater environmental influence and change, and to be operating under more pressurized time and resource conditions. Furthermore, the current trend is for alliancing and for forming joint project teams across organizations

(Mozenter, 2002). Typically these teams have a high turnover of staff joining and leaving projects at various times. Consequently, today's teams are
unlikely to move through a series of stages in sequential order (I have
worked with several teams who have performed before storming), nor are
they likely to occupy one stage at a single moment in time; they are more
likely to occupy a combination of stages at one time.

Instead of investing valuable team time on generalizing themselves into
a predetermined psychological stage, racing cars, building bridges across
rivers or getting drunk together in a bar, teams would be wiser to pay attention to their actual internal functioning and to discover ways to improve it.
Helping teams view themselves as a system can be a useful starting point.

First view the team as a system

A system can be defined as a group whose parts interrelate and who perform a shared task (Syer and Connolly, 1996). A team, too, can be viewed
as a system, as a team is commonly defined as a group of people who
interrelate and who share a common goal (Syer and Connolly, 1996). The
team receives *inputs*: objectives, information, materials and tasks.
Through the application of team *structures* – the skills and qualities of its
membership, their roles and responsibilities – and together with its
processes of communication and leadership norms, these inputs are con-
verted into *outputs*: results, decisions, actions and products.
Environmental factors, such as external demands and organizational culture will influence both processes and structure. *Feedback* loops operate
throughout the system, enhancing reflexivity – the team's ability to moderate and sustain performance. Reflexivity has been found to be one of
the most important predictors of team performance (Carter and West,
1998) and improving the ability of a team to regulate its own system is
always a worthwhile goal for the team developer.

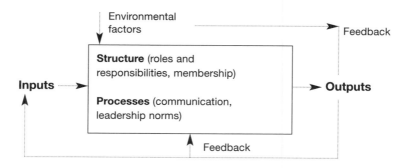

Figure 21.1 The team viewed as a system.

Teams are not static. They are a complex array of interrelationships, and when seen as such it is inappropriate to view cause and effects throughout the system linearly. To do so can lead to inappropriate attribution of cause. For example, during a recent assignment, I was told by Peter, a project manager, that he was unhappy with the performance of Brian whom he believed was compromising project deadlines by failing to manage his relationship with his marketing colleague, Anne. Brian was not getting along with Anne because Anne was not giving Brian the timely information he needed. Anne was unable to do this because she was not getting timely information herself from Julie in finance. In turn, Julie was not able to access the information she needed for Anne because her software was failing her. Julie's software was not functioning because Gary in data support was managing two people's workloads because his colleague, Harry, was working on a project seconded by none other than Brian in marketing. Brian was under pressure from the project manager to accept this additional piece of work for political reasons.

The project manager was convinced that if Brian were to better manage his relationship with Anne, the team deadline problem would be eased. He was applying linear causality when circular causality would have been more appropriate. In his opinion, Brian's performance was affecting the overall team performance. In fact, Brian was part of a larger system of which the project manager himself was a part. The project manager looked first at the overall team and attributed the problem to Brian, a constituent part of the team. Circular causality would have highlighted the reality of the situation – that the overall team was affecting Brian at the same time as Brian's performance was affecting the whole team.

When system thinking is applied to the team context, it opens the door to a variety of different interventions aimed at various components of the system and the system as a whole. These interventions include process improvements (how the team communicates and makes decisions), structural improvements (the distribution of roles and responsibilities), and interface improvements (the support the team is getting from management or its customers). Useful interventions cannot be made without a proper analysis and interpretation of the team system. Team development is therefore a process that passes through several distinct phases and is not simply a one-day, one-off, off-site event as some leaders and many team builders might like to believe. The first step in the process is data collection.

Stage 1 – data collection

Understanding the whole team system means collecting information from the whole team. This can be achieved by observing behaviours at team meetings, studying historical data, giving out questionnaires or by asking the right questions in the right way. Face-to-face interviews are an ideal data collection method because, conducted well, they help to foster good consultant-team member relationships. An underestimated determinant of facilitating behavioural change in others is the 'contact' or rapport the facilitator makes with these 'others':

> our deepest, most profound stirrings of self-appreciation . . . self knowledge surface in the presence of the person whom we experience as totally accepting. (Zinker, 1994)

Useful questions to ask the team members are those that explore the structure of the team, goals, roles and responsibilities, norms, leadership, current levels of motivation and well being, current and future issues and challenges, where the team has come from and where it is going, the external pressures and meeting behaviours.

Open questions starting with 'how' and 'what' are useful because they increase team members' awareness of what they are or are not doing. Appreciative inquiry (Cooperrider et al., 2001) is a useful mechanism that increases awareness of what 'good looks like' and 'team strengths', although to do the full model justice may require a greater investment of time and budget than is feasible. At a very minimum, interviews need to include a good balance of 'what is wrong' and 'what is right' questions.

Leadership data can be collected via 360-degree feedback, historical appraisal data, behavioural observation (typically at team meetings) or through team interviews. Asking team leaders questions about their own leadership is a delicate issue but, done well, it opens the leader's thinking to new ways of working. As with team questions, useful questions are those that increase the leader's awareness of what they are currently doing and what they are not doing. For example:

'How do you inspire the team?'
'How do you create a climate that supports creativity and balanced risk taking?'
'How do the members of your team challenge each other, including you constructively – how do you support them in this?'

Stage 2 – understanding the system

We have to avoid the temptation to start offering solutions before we understand what we are actually fixing. Without adequate time spent understanding the whole team system, the decisions and interventions that follow may be totally inappropriate – as I have unfortunately experienced on more than one occasion.

A reliable content analysis is the most objective way of interpreting interview scripts – although the reality is that there is rarely the scope for such rigour. Extracting the salient points from a multitude of scripts is often the norm in the face of severe time constraints. Understanding the system, however, requires more than a summary of interview findings. It is through interpreting the data that the psychologist really adds value. Interpreting, making connections across the team system and coming up with hypotheses as to what is happening and why, is a skill, built on sound theoretical knowledge, that is developed with time and experience.

The subjective nature of data analysis and the fact that some team members are quite guarded in the information they provide, means that any conclusions drawn are to be treated with caution and an open mind. At one particular event, I witnessed whole sets of team issues emerge from nowhere during a team development event – issues that included a lack of communication coming from one of the two team leaders and several team members who didn't even know their role. The agenda was immediately changed to cater for these important issues, as without such changes the team would not have been able to move forward to tackle other salient issues, such as how to deal better with a project plan that kept on changing.

Stage 3 – collaboration

Here the consultant will present options and together with the team leader will decide on a solution. The challenge is to strike the right balance between exerting one's own views on what needs to happen and being told what to do by the team leader. Some team leaders have a preconceived idea of what they are looking for – usually based on past experiences. Their fixations have to be challenged, if in your opinion, there is a better route to achieving their objectives. I recall one manager who felt one exercise in particular I was proposing was too risky for her team. I had led this exercise literally hundreds of times and, although it is different, direct and quite challenging, I felt sure it was the right intervention. The key to managing our dialogue was to demonstrate to her that I had the confidence to make it work and that the outcomes from the exercise (increased trust and an emotional high on which to end the day's event) were exactly what she wanted. She relented and, ironically, she benefited from it more than anyone else.

Stage 4 – implementation

Some team progress will already have been achieved if the previous stages have succeeded in raising team member awareness of what they could be doing better, but it is during the implementation stage that the psychologist actually 'does something tangible' to move the team forward.

This tangibility is provided by interventions that target the component parts of the team system. It has been my experience that the most useful team interventions focus on structure and process. This is because it is the ability of a team to understand its roles, to manage its internal conflict, to communicate effectively and to trust each other's capability that most affect its performance (Spreitzer et al., 1997). Processes like how team members interact and make decisions actually determine structures like roles, meeting agendas and infrastructure (Syer and Connolly, 1996). Immediate gains can be made by the improvement of team structures. Longer-lasting gains, however, can be achieved by focusing on team processes such as leadership and followership skills and by developing relationships.

Developing leadership skills

The team leader is responsible for maintaining the team system and for interacting with the external environment to ensure that the team receives quality resource inputs and realistic output expectations. It is leaders' failure to address external issues that often causes internal problems. The team leader may have set up the system in the first instance. If the system is not functioning at its best, then the team leader has to bear some responsibility . . .

> We had to help lift them and they find the spirit of the team helps them. They have found comfort in the squad. 30 or 40% comes from their teammates at the club – the rest is down to me. (Arsene Wenger, *Evening Standard*, 18 November 2002)

An unfortunate observation, gained over the years, is that managers and team members do not spend enough time attending to the formation of quality relationships across the team system – particularly, those that facilitate effective conflict resolution. It is not that managers don't have the time: they choose not to prioritize the time. Sometimes they are not aware of the potential benefits of attending to relationship issues; sometimes they are aware of the benefits but they don't have the skills, and sometimes they have the awareness and the skills but lack the necessary motivation. Successful team development is underpinned by developing relationship building skills and by understanding why relationships are not working and then applying interventions to make them work.

In a typical project team there will be several leaders. Teams that share the leadership are more successful than those that don't (Pearce, 2002). Leaders who include team members in decision making lead more effective teams (Phillips, 2001; Doorewaard et al., 2002). A successful team-development intervention will need to include the development of the leadership within and not just of the team. The best team leaders are effective task managers *and* great leaders of people. The majority of my work is developing people leadership skills for managers, most of whom have risen into their positions more through their technical expertise than via their expertise in human relations.

Through 360-degree feedback, coaching, behavioural observation and feedback, the psychologist needs to ensure that the leader has set up and is managing effectively all the team processes and structures. In a project team of 20 there are exactly 190 possible different relationships: $[20 \times 19]/2$. Assuming all team members interact with each other, the success of the project will depend on the quality of all these relationships. Typically the project team has an overall project leader, team leaders reporting to the project manager and team members reporting to their team leaders. Key interactions occur between leaders and team members, team leader and team leader, team members within each of the teams and team members across teams. Clearly leaders dominate these interactions. Leadership development is designed to focus on transformational type leadership behaviours such as coaching, creativity, role modelling, visioning, challenging the status quo, personal presence and balanced risk taking (Bass, 1985). It also needs to include a healthy portion of emotional intelligence as this has been found to enhance team effectiveness (Huy, 2002). One area that has not been researched, but which I have found to be particularly fruitful, is to develop leaders' ability to facilitate dialogue between their team members as a means of improving working relationships.

Developing relationships

The best team-development interventions are specifically designed to improve working relationships. I will focus here on one commonly used technique – psychometric profiling and an alternative that I have found to be far more rewarding.

Psychometric profiling

Psychometric testing is commonly used to achieve a balance of personalities and skills throughout a team in the hope of maximizing team effectiveness. Unfortunately, research tells us little about what is the best combination, except that a variety of skills and personality types is preferable (Prichard and Stanton, 1999). Belbin's (1972) team profiles, which have been much used, have failed to demonstrate predictive validity (Jackson, 2002). Furthermore, most teams that undergo profiling do so when they are already up and running, and any profiles produced are rarely used to redesign the team structure. However, increasing the awareness of a team member's thinking or behavioural style is usually a useful platform from which to create behavioural change. Psychometric profiling is one way of increasing this awareness and has been successfully used as an intervention to enhance team effectiveness (Dubey et al., 2001). Despite this there are two major disadvantages for the organizational psychologist to consider:

- First, psychometric feedback propagates the risk of creating limiting self-fulfilling prophecies. The danger of categorizing a team member based on Myers Briggs profiling as an 'ENTJ' or a 'sensing thinker' is that it may reinforce that behaviour pattern and others' expectation of that pattern. Too many people I have worked with have gone through profiling and been put in a 'pigeon hole' with plenty of time dedicated to explaining what the pigeon hole is and why they have been put there but insufficient time spent in the exploration of and development of their full range of behavioural options. Unfortunately, I spend valuable team development time challenging the resulting self-limiting beliefs of team members such as 'well I'm not a completer finisher and that's just the way it is'.
- Second, psychometrics also encourage the giving of poor-quality feedback. Psychometric feedback is often generated these days by expert system software and then fed back to an individual by a third party. It is also based on a number of statistical and psychological assumptions and is immersed in probability not reality. Team members need all the support they can get in giving good-quality feedback. Psychometric profiling can undermine such support and runs contrary to the great team adage 'talk to somebody, not about them'.

Facilitating dialogue

Peer feedback improves team effectiveness (Wolf, 1998). A skilled psychologist can facilitate meaningful feedback between team members by asking them to talk directly to each other and to communicate their experience of working with each other. Facilitation that precipitates the flow of information like

'what I really need from you is . . .'
'the impact of [that] on me is . . .'

'I want you to be aware of these constraints on me . . .'
'when you do this, that happens . . .'
'what I appreciate about you is . . .'
'I really like it when you do this because it means that . . .'

is far more meaningful and motivational than a 'psychological report' provided by a computer and then fed back by someone who sits outside of the team.

My work as a sports psychologist, particularly in football, has been characterized by the facilitation of dialogue between the players in each of the attacking, midfield and defensive playing units. Firstly, I get the players to sit in a small circle, as this shape generates group cohesion in itself, and I ask them to answer questions like

'James, tell Kevin what your specific role is on Saturday.'
'Kevin, tell James what you need from him to perform your role . . .'
'James, tell Kevin what you appreciate about the way he plays football . . .'

By talking directly to each other in this way, I found that players increased their levels of trust and played better together. When I run these sessions in the office for my organizational clients, the benefits are the same. I am currently working on an assignment in which the project team comprises over 160 people, arranged in six separate 'work streams', each led by a work stream leader who reports to one of two leaders, who in turn report to an overall project manager. My interventions to date have included the facilitation of dialogue between the leadership population, pairs of team leaders, all the members of several work stream teams, and between the work stream leader and one of their team members. Each of these interventions involves asking team members to look each other in the eye, use each other's name, and to make statements to each other like those above. When teammates talk to each other in this way, something happens that cannot be achieved by a report or a motivational speech. Facilitating the meaningful exchange of dialogue is the true essence of team development regardless of the team structure, nature, membership, domain or goals.

There are hundreds of different team-building games and exercises to chose from – in and out of the classroom. The key is first to match these exercises with the needs of the team and then to 'process' or talk about what happened afterwards. Team learning comes more from effective processing than from the exercise itself. Effective processing is all about helping the team to make links between its direct experience and what happens back in the office. Increasing awareness then paves the way for useful suggestions as to how things could be done differently in their working environment. It is important that these suggestions come from the team members themselves and not the business psychologist. It is also important for the facilitator to create an environment of fun and humour as this enhances the chances of team-building success (Terrior and Ashforth, 2002).

Developing follower skills

[T]he person who is truly effective has the humility and reverence to recognise his perceptual limitations and to appreciate the rich resources available through interaction with the hearts and minds of human beings. (Covey, 1989)

The development of follower skills is both underestimated and underutilized by team-development specialists. Great leaders often have great followers. Great followers are blessed with a great mix of skills and qualities. They go beyond their technical role and seek to influence their team system positively. They do this by challenging and supporting their peers and their managers. Developing high-performing follower skills requires a leader who is prepared to share leadership. Sometimes followers are held back because they do not have such a leader or the wider culture does not support or reward such behaviours. The responsibility for creating a high-performing mini culture in the face of this prevailing culture lies with, and requires substantial investment from, the team leader, who is more able than anyone else in the team to influence the team's external environment. Responsibility also falls to the team members themselves, who have to challenge, often through the aid of a third party, their own attitudes to their team membership.

Developing emotional intelligence

There is compelling evidence for developing emotional intelligence in team members as a primary team development intervention. Research suggests that great teams have team members who are both technically proficient and emotionally proficient (Goleman, 1996). Interaction style even predicts performance in virtual teams (Potter and Balthazard, 2002) and the ability of a team to manage its internal conflict, particularly its 'relationship conflict' rather than its 'task conflict', influences both team cohesiveness and performance (Jehn and Chatman, 2000). Effective conflict resolution skills are especially relevant for those teams high in cultural diversity (Voight and Callaghan, 2001). The characteristics of the contemporary team thus demand that emotional intelligence be developed as a means of building quality relationships.

Emotionally proficient team members see each other for who they really are and not for whom they imagine each other to be – as a result, misinterpretations are minimized. They are particularly empathic, are assertive, rather than aggressive or passive, speak unambiguously and directly to each other, actively listen and respond to, rather than react to, the needs of their teammates. They ask questions that efficiently provide them with the information they require, they regard themselves as colleagues, not adversaries, especially in conflict, and they engage in meaningful dialogue as opposed to defensive discussion. As Senge (1992) describes, they hold their positions 'gently' rather than being held firmly by their positions. Above all, they regard themselves as an interrelated part of their whole team system with control over their own destiny.

Stage 5 – evaluation

There are so many intervening variables that can affect a team's performance that providing reliable and valid evaluation before and after interventions is virtually impossible. Nevertheless, using team questionnaires is a readily available method, which despite often lacking in scientific rigour, can act as a motivational device for the team. If you can obtain more objective data such as productivity, turnover, absenteeism, revenue, cost or profitability improvements, then this is preferable. The best criteria are those chosen by the team itself. Ideally measurement that will be repeated will act to motivate team members to improve their functioning.

Summary

The intention of this chapter has been to share insights into building team capability and the subsequent release of talent. Viewing the team as a system, applying circular causality and attending to the processes of the team are likely to reap greater rewards for you than simply sending your teams on an outward-bound course, applying psychometrics or giving a motivational talk. You will have facilitated a productive team-building event if team members are resolved to do something different and useful on their return to the working environment. Rarely will such resolve be achieved without meaningful facilitation. By facilitating the meaningful exchange of dialogue between team members, you will avoid delivering an event which is, whilst lots of fun, not particularly beneficial, or one that causes the team to question why they have been taken away from their desks to be with you. You will also provide others and yourself with the opportunity to make a real contribution to enhancing the performance and the quality of working lives for other people.

CHAPTER 22

Unleashing leadership and learning within an international bank

ELLIE BOUGHTON, MICHAEL BURNETT, JAMES BYWATER, JOHN MAHONEY-PHILLIPS

Introduction

In order to place themselves in a strong competitive position for the future, today's organizations are seeking strategies to build the senior business leaders of tomorrow. It is not enough for people to be competent in a middle-level position. Instead future business leaders are those people who actively engage in behaviours that help them to continue to learn and develop. An effective way to highlight to managers their strengths and development needs is 360-degree feedback and, as such, it was chosen as the mechanism to instil a greater emphasis on leadership and learning within the talent pool of a leading global financial organization.

Introduction to case study

This case study relates to the development of a new 360-degree process designed to capitalize upon the latest research about the leadership competences required for middle managers to develop to more senior roles. It has been selected because it illustrates many of the common issues involved in such projects: developing the questionnaire, feedback report, piloting the questionnaire, and identifying the most effective way to administer the tool.

Background

The organization that commissioned the work wanted to forge a strong link between leadership (both people and thought leadership) and the importance of continued learning. This organization works on a global basis in the competitive banking sector. The bank embraces people from a diverse range of backgrounds with English and German being two of the main languages spoken. The bank was keen to develop its global leaders of the future and to use the latest research in 360-degree feedback to enable this to occur.

The 360-degree process was created to ensure that middle managers gained up-to-date feedback on their current strengths and development needs in relation to critical leadership behaviours. The client was clear in its expectation that all action plans must be created by participants on the basis of accurate feedback. It was also intended that the questionnaire, feedback and action planning all be associated with a subsequent increase in the extent to which these behaviours were demonstrated on-the-job (Fleenor, 1997).

The organization chose to use the Internet as the vehicle to administer the tool. This use of the Internet was intended to create a fundamentally more positive experience for the participants in the 360-degree process and to overcome problems of missing feedback and reports that had accompanied the previous use of a paper-based system. It was also expected to reduce the administrative workload of running a project of this size significantly.

The following describes in more detail the process of creating and successfully implementing this leadership and learning 360-degree feedback tool. This includes:

- research and development of the theoretical model;
- creation and trialling of the initial questionnaire;
- reviewing the 360-degree tool in the light of pilot study data;
- evaluation of the 360-degree process; and
- overall implications for business psychology.

Research and development of the leadership and learning model

In order to develop a model that encompassed the latest thoughts on leadership and learning, a literature review was undertaken of the latest academic research and the consultancy's previous research. Following this a business needs analysis was undertaken to understand how the organization wished to use the information gathered to support its business. The analysis revealed three key business needs:

- A need to increase understanding and regional agreement of what constituted an 'effective' executive in the organization. It was felt that this would help to ensure that people were developed who could actually meet organizational missions and goals.

- A need to improve organizational understanding of the behaviours that contributed to successful performance, so that the organization could target individual development with regard to these behaviours.
- The organization needed to assign individuals for future executive development programmes using criteria that were fair and job relevant in order to meet legislative requirements and to ensure that the best possible use was being made of the available human resources.

Literature review

From previous research jointly undertaken with the Institute of Management Foundation, the management consultancy understood the competencies required at the most senior levels within organizations (http://www.inst-mgt.org.uk). These included: guiding strategy direction, developing organizational culture, practising 'human' skills, and exercising executive control. The research suggested that in order for middle managers to develop these behaviours and knowledge, two requirements must be satisfied. Managers need:

- *inherent competence* in a range of cognitive, emotional, interpersonal and business skills; and
- the capacity *to develop competence* when working at higher levels in the organization where the challenges require adaptability and the ability to project individual behaviours in a way that helps foster organizational success.

Much of this working model was based upon the research by Spreitzer et al. (1997) into executive success. This research indicated that both 'end-state' competences (general intelligence, business knowledge, interpersonal skills, commitment and action orientation) and 'learning' competences (proactive approach, adaptability, use of feedback, acceptance of personal criticism) are necessary in order to perform successfully in the face of current and future challenges at a senior level.

This link between learning and successful business performance was further highlighted by Vandewalle, Cron and Slocum (2001) who showed that such 'learning goal orientation' is translated into success when it is combined with three things:

- a range of specific personal goals;
- a positive commitment to reach specific levels of work effort;
- the degree of planning put into specifying how objectives would be reached.

This brief review of the research literature suggested that a comprehensive framework for developing and assessing executive potential would require:

- Four main dimensions of leadership performance:
    - *thinking* – the capacity to acquire new skills and knowledge;
    - *emotional* – relates to seeking feedback for improved performance;
    - *interpersonal* – the capacity to work effectively with others;
    - *business* – the capacity to identify business improvements.
- Two aspects of competence:
    - *learning competence* – the behaviours that help people to continue to improve in their leadership;
    - *leadership competence* – which represents an assessment of current performance.

In total these yield eight leadership-related competences. They are shown in Table 22.1.

Table 22.1 Learning and leadership competences

Leadership dimensions	Learning competence	Leadership competence
Thinking	Seeks learning	Analytical effectiveness
Emotional	Emotional strength	Personal impact
Interpersonal	Improves organizational learning	Effective working relationships
Business	Breadth of vision	Breadth of impact

This model suggests that it is important to develop strengths in both learning and leadership competences. If there is a development need in one of the leadership competences, engaging in the related learning competence should help lead to an improvement. In addition, it is important to continue to engage in learning behaviours to help ensure leadership competence in the future. For example, people might currently demonstrate strong analytical effectiveness but they also need to be someone who seeks learning (to gain more skills) in order to keep up-to-date and to continue to be analytically effective.

Creating the questionnaire items

To design an instrument that was able to assess individuals against each part of the model, a large number of questionnaire items were drawn from SHL's item bank. Using the item bank meant that items had been through previous international trialling and were regarded as being unambiguous by raters. This was particularly important as the items needed to be clear when presented in both English and German to raters within the bank. After these items were compiled, human resources professionals within the bank reviewed the face validity and several items were removed or reworded.

A set of 100 items was identified for a live trial with 60 of the bank's executives. Item analysis techniques were used to refine the scales measuring each of the leadership and learning competences. A final set of 56 items was identified with seven questions per scale. The scales showed good levels of reliability (0.65 to 0.83). In addition, an exploratory factor analysis was conducted that showed a high degree of consistency with the research model. The factor structure recovered accounted for a total of 51% of the total variance. The business leadership and learning items both loaded on the first factor accounting for 18% of the variance. Items from each of the other scales (except personal impact) loaded on separate factors and accounted for between 4% and 7% of the variance each.

Rating scale

Choosing rating scales almost always prompts significant discussion about the number of scale points and descriptors and the development of this tool was no exception. In the initial item trialling a five-point, behavioural frequency rating scale was used which extended from 'rarely, if ever true' at one end to 'almost always true' at the other. A 'no-evidence' category was also used to reduce the distortion of results that can occur when raters are forced to judge each behaviour.

After initial trialling, it was felt that the questionnaire would add more value if the ratings were more evenly spread across the five-point scale. There was a suggestion in the research at the time that a comparative scale tended to possess good statistical properties (Fox, Caspy and Reisler, 1994). The scale was thus adapted to require raters to assess whether the person who was the focus of the feedback displayed the behaviours on the following scale:

Less than others				More than others

This new rating scale was used throughout the 6-month pilot.

Review of pilot study

The main learning point from the pilot study was that good statistical properties are not necessarily synonymous with an excellent feedback tool. Participants gained useful information from the tool when the comparative scale was used but it was felt that the rating scale created uncertainty about meaning and so barriers to accepting feedback. For this reason the final version returned to an original frequency rating scale and this has been found to be more effective during feedback and in helping participants to commit to change. This is compatible with recent approaches to 360-degree feedback where the buy-in of the respondent to the process and to form development actions is emphasized as being critical (Maurer et al., 2002).

Feedback report

In creating the 360-degree feedback report, the objective was to provide information against the competencies in the simplest format possible. The report was designed to summarize the various permutations of data in both graphic and verbal formats (see Figure 22.1).

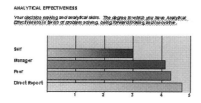

ANALYTICAL EFFECTIVENESS

Your decision making and analytical skills. *The degree to which you have Analytical Effectiveness in terms of problem solving, being forward looking and innovative.*

Behaviours	SELF	MANAGER	PEER	DIRECT REPORT	OTHERS AVERAGE
5. Gives constructive feedback to others	2	4	4.3	4.7	4.4
13. Shares access to personal network	2	4	4	4.3	4.1
21. Willing to learn from others in the organisation	3	4	4.3	4.2	4.2

SECTION 4   **HIGHEST AND LOWEST ITEMS**

This section lists the ten items, out of the total of 56 items, on which you have received your highest and lowest scores, based on the average of all the ratings excluding your own.

Top Ten Items

Item	Behaviour	Average Rating	Scale
3	Is effective in leading others	4.7	Effective Working Relationships
6	Evaluates information and identifies key issues	4.7	Analytical Effectiveness
7	Prepared to act on own account	4.7	Personal Impact
20	Stays motivated when put under pressure	4.7	Emotional Strength

Figure 22.1 The 360-degree format report uses graphic and verbal formats.

Investigation after the 6-month pilot showed that most of the participants felt that the report presented the data well. In particular, very positive feedback was given about the utility of the top 10 and bottom 10 rated items as a mechanism for quickly revealing strengths and development needs.

However, where the data were interpreted for participants (for example, using a two-by-two grid to show consistency and differences between manager and participant ratings) this was found to be less helpful. These elements were removed after the pilot, and a worksheet was created to enable the participants to engage with, and 'own', the data themselves during their preparation for a facilitated session.

Results of the intervention

Impact on participants

To date, the main information that can be used to evaluate the effectiveness of the intervention has been reaction sheet data. The data taken from a number of leadership programmes where this 360 tool is used have shown the following:

- 96% of participants rated this session as 'very relevant';
- the 360-degree feedback session exceeded expectations for the majority of participants;
- the feedback report also exceeded the expectations of the majority of participants; in particular, the development tips section was regarded as 'excellent'.

Impact of the Internet

One of the most useful aspects of using the Internet was the administrative benefits. This occurred in two ways:

- 92% of people had checked whether their raters had completed their ratings; this led to many participants encouraging others to provide ratings which reduced the amount of work that administrators were required to do;
- 98% of participants had reports at the scheduled feedback times, which was a significant improvement on the previous paper-based system (previously completion was between 50% and 70%) – much of this improvement was attributed to the ease of tracking completion rates, and the elimination of data 'lost in the post'.

Overall implications

The main learnings from a business psychology perspective are to always pilot a questionnaire and to listen carefully to the information gained. Ultimately for a 360-degree feedback process to be useful it needs to:

- Be accepted – the participants need to accept the feedback provided. If there is doubt about how the rating scale was interpreted, then it is very difficult for participants to use the feedback in order to discuss potential development needs. Thus, participant acceptability is ultimately more important than good distributions on rating scales.
- Be engaging – the feedback needs to be presented clearly, so that participants can access the data easily. However, the data should not be over-interpreted as participants prefer to work with the data themselves and identify their own strengths and development needs.
- Be efficient – we can use technology to our advantage to ensure that the emphasis is placed on feedback and development, rather than on 'Where are the outstanding 360-degree questionnaires?'.
- Emphasizing the importance of both current leadership competence and ongoing learning behaviours is beneficial in the continuing development of leaders.

CHAPTER 23

Releasing talent through coaching

SUE CLAYTON

Introduction

When we coach executives, managers, leaders – people in a position of power and responsibility – we have a duty to deliver to both the individual client and the client system. To focus on the development of clients without including the organizational systems in which they must work short-changes the client and can leave the best and most skilful psychologists feeling as if there is more that they could do. A sense of despondency can exist in the coaching room if you see the work of your clients dampened and undermined by a conflicting cultural environment in which they attempt to grow from their coaching. It's like repeatedly putting a cleaned, freshened and enthusiastic fish back into dirty water.

Doing more means thinking and working differently in our coaching practice. It means finding ways of viewing the organization and its subsystems through the eyes of the client, then understanding how the organizational system and subsystems impact the client, as well as how the client influences these systems. To do this, I use the analogy of different lenses to look into these systems and their subsystems. The systemic-lens view introduces a powerful ingredient into the coaching room for the business psychologist and their client, with potentially wide-ranging benefits for them and their business.

Looking through a systemic lens

Systemic work in coaching is based on the premise that people become who they are in their work through an intricately woven, ever-changing fabric of connections, relationships, organizational influences and social norms. They act in each moment according to their personal style *and* their circumstances. So if clients works in a 'blame' culture, the chances

221

are that they will feel less confident than if they worked in a 'trusting' culture. The systemic lenses help us to look from specific viewpoints and to assess the various influences that impact both the client and the various systems. It also encourages the client to think systemically in the way that they go about their work and brings into the coaching a rich field of data. A comprehensive work on systems and the challenge of complexity is offered by Ralph Stacey (2003).

The concentric layers of the system

All systems are made up of concentric layers – teams inside departments, inside divisions, inside the organization – all of which connect and impact on each other (Bentley and Clayton, 1998). These concentric layers help us to weave our coaching more powerfully: from individuals to their team to their organizational system, to the wider culture in which the business or organization exists – and so on. *Always* at the hub of the system are the coaching clients, whoever they are, wherever they operate in the organization.

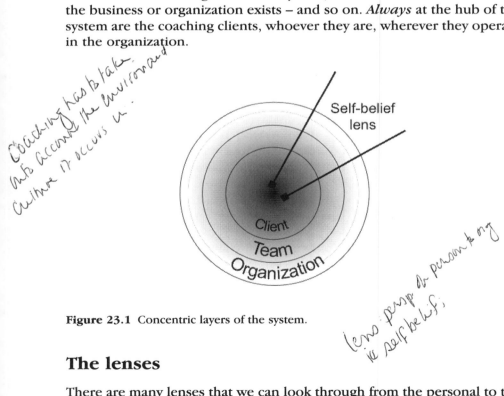

Figure 23.1 Concentric layers of the system.

The lenses

There are many lenses that we can look through from the personal to the organizational. Some examples of specific lenses are self-belief, self-support, diversity, leadership, business effectiveness, organizational values. In selecting lenses it is important that each lens 'begs a question' for each of the layers. For example, let's say my client is a woman in a senior role in a commercial business, with a team of four working with her. We could be addressing 'self-belief' so the questions might be:

- Does my client have belief in herself – as a person and in her role? To what extent does she bring her passion into her work?
- Does her team believe in 'itself' and have confidence to perform as a team in this organization? You will note here that I am not seeking to assess each individual member of the team, but to treat the team as a whole entity with 'team characteristics'. So I might ask my client: 'If your team were able to speak for itself what would IT say about ITS self-belief?'
- Does the organization believe in itself and its capacity to succeed in its competitive market? What is the interplay between the systems around self-belief? Where is the collusion that keeps things the same? How does this interplay impact my client?

Or in addressing *business effectiveness* I might ask:

- How does my client limit herself in her contribution to the business?
- How does her team limit its contribution to the business?
- How does the organization limit its business performance?

And what are the connections between these three?

Lenses can be combined, for example, personal human characteristics like *self-belief*, as well as organizational performance like *business effectiveness*. As long as meaningful and relevant questions can be asked in each system the systemic lens approach can be used.

Subdivisions of the lenses

Each lens can be further subdivided. For example, taking the *organizational values lens*, I might ask my client to break this down into specific values. If the values she generated were openness, fairness, diversity and trust, for example, I would invite her to take one of these values and look into each system, including herself, through this lens.

The coach–client relationship system

The coaching relationship is also a small system nested in a number of other systems – including those systems in which we as coaches and psychologists exist – our own business partnerships, the company that we are employed by, our self-employed systems, the professional bodies which dictate the ethics that we subscribe to. This may add extra complexity to the coaching work and for me it creates a number of realities:

- In our role as coach we become part of the system. However much we pay attention to keeping healthy boundaries, we cannot act as though we are separate entities even though we can see the system from an outsider's viewpoint.
- The coaching relationship is itself a system and we can at any time refer to 'how we are working together' as a system.
- The coaching relationship is interconnected with many different systems all of which may hold some relevance to the work – including those systems that are present in our own working environment.

This means that in our profession as psychologists we too need to check how well we work within the lenses being addressed, both personally and within the coaching relationship. We are not separate from the system – we are part of the system and affected by the many systems that exist. The questions I need to ask myself are 'do I have a strong self-belief?', 'to what extent do I bring my passion into my work?' and 'what does business effectiveness mean to me?'. I might also raise some questions in relation to my own business system.

There are many reasons for going through this process, not least to avoid any projections of unattended personal issues being transmitted on to the client. But most of all it can help us to 'stay present' in the coaching relationship.

Psychologists coaching in the business world

Working as coaches in the business world can produce a dilemma for psychologists. We come into our work with a well-grounded understanding of people and social psychology, but how much does a psychologist need to know about *business* in order to become an effective management or executive coach? Do we need more than an academic understanding of the economic and political world? Do we need first-hand experience of an industry in order to coach in it? Do we need to have been a director in order to work with directors? How much understanding do we need to be able to get a grasp of organizational dynamics?

There are two sides to this coin. On the one hand, we are not in this work as experts who are there to give advice. On the other hand, our clients expect us to be knowledgeable about organizational systems, business functioning, executive roles – and their industry.

The no knowledge/experience position

Coaching is generally much more about 'output learning' – helping clients discover for themselves what they need to learn – rather than 'input learning', which teaches the client to work in a way that the coach believes best. In this context, too much knowledge about *the business* can box us in and render us less effective, whereas *not knowing* allows us to step outside the box and inspire our clients through creative and metaphorical interventions. No knowledge also means that we are more likely to be vigilant in checking our assumptions, to raise awareness of hidden issues through innocent enquiry and to support a healthy power balance in the relationship through client ownership of their professional wisdom.

The knowledge/experience position

The other side of the coin comes from the need to be professionally attuned with our clients and their world of work, as well as attending to our own self-support in our coaching practice.

So what does being professionally attuned mean? Perhaps we can only assess this as we enter each client system. We can, however, keep ourselves informed with some up-to-date theory around organizational behaviour. Organizations are complex because of powerful tensions pushing and pulling within them – these tensions are necessary for a business to have energy and drive to succeed. No tensions mean a static business. This pushing and pulling is made up of organizational politics, power dynamics, tensions between formal and informal systems, management styles, the business structures, and so on. Tensions in a system can range from hugely creative to highly destructive. The ability of executives and managers to manage these tensions well is critical to business performance.

Business knowledge and experience is different, in that in some situations it can be useful, in others intrusive. For example, with a high level of knowledge of a client's business, good rapport can be established with them – you speak the same language, you can discuss key business and management issues in depth. Trust and openness can be established quickly, enabling early results through challenge and support. On the down side when we are knowledgeable in an area we make assumptions that go unchallenged. Many insights can be gained through simply checking out assumptions.

A good principle to follow is to learn how business operations and functions interconnect and affect each other. These points of impact are likely to be tension points in the system and offer a rich feeding ground for the client to learn the art of effective management and leadership.

Common examples of such tension points might be:

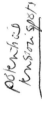

- human resources and key business areas (until recently human resources in general has not been given the respect it needs to perform a central role in 'the business');
- finance departments and business development;
- business operations and resourcing;
- staff and management.

It is then up to you to assess the extent to which you need to be informed about the business and the industry and your effectiveness as a coach to this particular client.

Summary

A high proportion of coaching skills and styles have been developed via 'one-to-one' training – client-centred counselling and coaching, clinical work, and psychotherapy. Taking the leap to a systems perspective is not easy, particularly when we feel confident in holding the personal view – but the rewards are worth it. Your individual client will feel like they are getting far more than they expected; the organizational client will gain benefit from the individual's learning that will also impact the immediate systems in which that person operates (for example, better leadership/ teamwork, improved relations with peers), *you* will feel a greater sense of satisfaction through genuinely releasing talent and your credibility will grow.

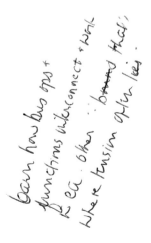

CHAPTER 24

Why chief executives hire coaches

JANEY HOWL

Introduction

The task of chief executive officers (CEOs) is to manage against major risk factors in order consistently to deliver acceptable total returns to shareholders. Like professional athletes, CEOs can expect relatively short, financially lucrative careers that continue only as long as they perform at exceptional levels. The current average tenure for a CEO in Europe is 6.5 years. With the turnover of CEOs increasing by 53% between 1995 and 2001, demands for accountability are growing, and are likely to continue to do so in the wake of Enron, Arthur Andersen, Worldcom, and other corporate scandals. The number of CEOs departing due to the company's poor financial performance rose by 130% over the same period (all data from Lucier, Spiegel and Schuyt, 2002). In an increasingly competitive market-place, CEOs look for top coaches who can help them to enhance their performance continually – performance that, in many cases, is already exceptional.

Successful CEOs are characterized by the ability to sustain beneficial change and to exceed market expectations consistently. They are motivated by winning the game, however the 'game' is defined. Sometimes it is about implementing an audacious vision, annihilating the competition, or simply achieving the impossible. They hire a coach to increase their competitive edge. As a coach, it is essential to establish what the CEO's real game is because the CEO demands results – big results.

Many CEOs are perfectionists, setting impossibly high standards for themselves, as well as for those around them. Their ascent to power has also often been facilitated by the development of a finely honed ability to detect fakes and falsehoods. The pressures of meeting the expectations of a variety of stakeholders and withstanding scrutiny from the media and the City are considerable. They are frequently characterized by high levels of energy, long working hours, and an ability to thrive on very little sleep. It is not surprising that many derive their identity from work and are

227

prone to feelings of guilt when taking time out. With this mindset, coaching can seem like an indulgence.

However, CEOs are intensely aware of the fact that flexibility and resilience are key to corporate survival. The coaching ethos of change, responsiveness and responsibility has huge value in a world of technological innovation, instant global communication, social instability, economic uncertainty, and increasing competition. Chief executives hire coaches because they want to increase performance and productivity, to improve creativity, to make better use of scarce resources – particularly, time and people, to develop staff, to enhance relationships, to become more responsive to change, to become better communicators, better leaders, and sometimes to become more fulfilled human beings.

Isolation is a constant concern for those at the top of organizations. The coach is often the only person to whom the CEO can talk honestly about problems and issues. Many CEOs have developed a myth of mastery by avoiding vulnerability. In exploring problems in a neutral way, they can access their own considerable wisdom. Learning is a continuous process and time is the scarcest resource of all, so coaching has immense value in accelerating the learning of the CEO.

What to coach with CEOs

In working with top leaders, coaches usually focus on three core areas: the organization, leadership skills and personal development. Rarely, if ever, does a CEO specifically seek coaching for personal development. This will be explored over time, as trust and confidence in the coaching relationship develop.

Organization

In seeking to create a climate of sustainable growth for the organization, the CEO will strive to communicate a clear and compelling vision. Coaching issues are likely to include: mapping the organization's strengths and weaknesses; spotting untapped talent, customers and resources; eliminating barriers between decision makers and customers; and identifying trends and future competitors. There may well be an emphasis on enhancing financial reserves, creating high and sustainable profitability, and maximizing shareholder value.

Leadership skills

Leadership in the twenty-first century is complex and multifaceted. The challenge is to optimize the production and delivery of goods and services in multidimensional, ever-changing circumstances. The CEO's survival depends upon continual innovation, evolution and learning in response to complex external forces. Globalization demands creativity in structuring project teams and joint ventures in flexible ways that integrate diverse cultures and political systems. Chief executive clients frequently bring their own leadership issues to coaching, and also the symptoms that indicate blind spots in some aspects of leadership.

Five key coaching transitions

The following five key coaching transitions are offered as typical examples of leadership shifts, based on many years of experience with CEOs and directors of international organizations. There are, of course, many other significant challenges.

From 'adapt' to 'innovate'

The emphasis here is on long-term solutions and better goals rather than on the linear, predictable, and frequently exhausting process of an exclusive focus on producing results. Creating a mission to become the very best, to become an industry leader, requires the continual implementation of innovative and profitable ideas that will ensure the long-term viability of both the organization and the CEO. This commitment to becoming a source of change, rather than a manager of change, is a defining moment for a CEO. As Peter Drucker famously observed: 'The best way to predict the future is to create it.'

Always refer to bad news [handwritten]

From 'optimism' to 'realism'

Organizations, as well as individuals, often show a bias towards good news. Frequently much time and effort is devoted to preventing the CEO from hearing bad news. Successful CEOs, however, understand that they cannot afford to miss bad news, which has a nasty habit of turning into even worse news. They tend to take the view that bad news is temporary and do not view failure as a problem. Instead, they measure it, learn from it and move forwards, learning to fix mistakes faster than they make them. When CEOs are ready to become totally realistic, they will benefit from nurturing front-line contacts around the business. It is essential that they resist the temptation to shoot the messenger and that they protect themselves by asking tough questions, by trusting their instincts, and by always *acting* in response to bad news. Just as the Catholic Church used to have a position of devil's advocate so are CEOs well served by assigning a worst-case scenario as part of every analysis.

From 'power' to 'empower'

Chief executives sometimes burn out because it is costing them too much to constantly motivate and monitor others. By creating a performance culture in which responsibility for motivation is delegated, the CEO becomes free to concentrate on strategic leadership. True leadership engages people's values and passions, as well as developing their capacities to contribute, resulting in a workforce that is dedicated to productivity and excellence.

From 'talk' to 'walk'

Chief executives, virtually without exception, talk a great talk. They are convincing and seductive communicators because persuading others in order to cause things to happen is part of the job description. If CEOs are to enjoy a long tenure, they have to start walking the talk. This leadership transition requires them to avoid hype, to promise only what they know they can deliver, and to sustain or exceed the standards that staff are expected to honour.

From 'communication skills' to 'advanced communication'

Chief executives are trained in presentation skills, in handling the media and in negotiation techniques. Most, however, benefit from the advanced communication modelling that executive coaching can provide. They welcome the development of aspects such as skills in phrasing, relating, evoking the best from others, listening to what is not said, and using silence effectively.

As enthusiastic communicators, CEOs are frequently accustomed to pitching their voices to create impact: using, for example, 'charge up' to convey optimism, energy, passion, and 'charge down' to deliver bad news or to signal negative emotions. The level pitch of 'charge neutral' creates no expectations of good or bad news, nor does it imply an anticipated response. Using 'charge neutral', the speaker can deliver messages, which are simply words with no judgements or emotions attached. There are many situations in which CEOs appreciate the power of 'charge neutral'.

Another important advanced communication skill is 'lasering'. Learning to laser, that is to deliver succinct messages without waffle, is a game that CEOs usually enjoy. As well as ensuring that their own output is concise and consistent, lasering enables them to cut through ambiguity in other people's communication. Chief executives who master advanced communication skills discover an ability to engage hearts and minds in an instant.

Personal development

The CEO's personal development agenda frequently includes life/work balance, enhancing self-care, raising standards, and extending boundaries. Other common areas for coaching include becoming adrenalin free, developing relationships and creating a life purpose other than running the organization. Innovating a game plan around financial independence is also something that many CEOs really enjoy.

Women CEOs

Women CEOs represent a tiny proportion of the CEO population. On the FTSE 100 list of companies, women hold around only 5% of directorships. Contrast this with the US, where 97% of Fortune 500 companies have a woman on the board. For the exceptional few who have transcended the glass ceiling many coaching issues are similar to those of their male counterparts. However, in coaching women at board level some additional themes emerge. *lack of role models.*

Typically, women at the top suffer from a lack of role models, and isolation from other professional and high-achieving women. Although they are *may be less defined by work as men* as dedicated to their work as their male colleagues, they are more reluctant to be defined by it and frequently struggle to make the compromises necessary to balance work and family. Unlike their male counterparts, they often understate their competence, contribution and achievements.

All directors display considerable tenacity and resilience. Senior women, however, tend to 'own' problems. Consequently, they may find it difficult to delegate effectively, to ask for help, or to learn from mistakes and to move on. In coaching, senior women often ask for support in learning to work with the informal culture of the organization and in improving their communication skills. They are all too aware of the fact that in this era of the sound bite, learning to keep messages succinct and memorable is an essential skill.

Kazerounian (2002) presents compelling evidence to show that business requirements in the twenty-first century demand skills held in abundance by women. They excel in juggling multiple priorities, seeing the big picture, and leading collaboratively. A recurring theme is the impatience of women executives to get things done. Their intolerance of unnecessary delays and bureaucracy results in adaptability and responsiveness to change as they subvert established procedures to find ways around barriers to progress. With more women actively building their career capital, it is likely that one day female CEOs will no longer constitute a minority.

The business psychologist as coach

Executive coaches, like CEOs and board directors themselves, come from diverse backgrounds. The core knowledge and skills of business psychology – including psychometrics, developing individuals and organizations, understanding how people learn – provide a strong foundation on which to build expertise in executive coaching. Working at board level requires considerable professional credibility and personal integrity. The following suggestions will support the experienced business psychologist in making the transition to top-level executive coach.

- Experience in organizational development, particularly across a variety of industry sectors, builds expertise.
- An understanding of how and why CEOs succeed and fail ensures a focus on outcomes.
- The ability to read financial statements develops personal credibility. In particular, it is helpful to understand something about key financial ratios: profitability, efficiency, leverage, liquidity, and market value.
- Constantly updating business knowledge is important if you are to understand trends and competitors and to identify the challenges facing corporations.
- Keeping up to date with the share price and media coverage of your CEO client's organization and industry sector is vital.
- Being connected to diverse networks significantly enhances your value as a resource to the CEO.
- Coaching at the top of organizations tends to be highly visible. Stay committed to outcomes because stakeholders expect a good return on their investment in executive coaching.
- Being able to model advanced communication skills enables CEOs to enhance their own communication skills considerably.
- A real commitment to ongoing personal and professional development is key. Chief executives learn very quickly, and executive coaches must keep ahead of the learning curve.
- Be courageous and truthful. Always perform and always deliver.
- Be self-assured, relaxed, on time and superbly presented – *always*.
- Charge what you are worth and continually add value.
- Be totally discreet.

Lord Sieff commented, 'Leaders must be seen to be up-front, up to date, up to their job and up early in the morning'. It is the same for executive coaches.

Finally, for anyone aiming to coach at the very top of organizations, perhaps the soundest investment in professional and personal growth that you can make is to have a coach of your own. The CEO frequently asks, 'if coaching is such a good idea, do you have a coach?'.

Coaching the CEO – 10 mistakes to avoid

- Thinking short term, even when profits are under pressure. Always think long term.
- Being dull, predictable or pedantic. Chief executives are quick witted and easily bored.
- Being overawed by their status, power, achievements or financial success. Appreciate their humanity.
- Taking the CEO's strengths and skills for granted. They may not be obvious to the CEO, so remember to endorse.
- Criticizing CEOs. Chief executives are self-critical enough and are subject to criticism and public scrutiny on a daily basis.
- Trying to persuade or convince. Simply state impressions and concerns clearly. If they are interested, they will ask for more.
- Talking in jargon and theories. Be pragmatic.
- Being attached to outcomes. It is their organization, their life and their decision.
- Telling them what they want to hear. Chief executives usually have enough people in their lives doing this.
- Saying less than the truth. More than any other client, the CEO always knows when something is being withheld.

Coaching the CEO – 10 winning strategies

- Listen carefully and look for patterns in everything you see and hear.
- Create momentum by targeting a few early wins. Nothing succeeds like success.
- Introduce appropriate psychometrics in order to accelerate and deepen the coaching relationship.
- Require the CEO to solve *big* problems, not small ones.
- Challenge mental models and assumptions.
- Be direct, provocative and evocative.
- Ask questions that go to the heart, rather than to the head.
- Give positive affirmations.
- Provide information, data, solutions and facts.
- Create a game in order to accomplish a task. Chief executives just love to win.

Coaching the CEO – 10 great questions

- What business opportunities are you not exploiting?
- What is your belief about leadership that may have to change?

- What would it take to double your value to (a) the organization, (b) the staff, (c) yourself?
- What is the dream you have given up on?
- How will you know how effective our coaching is?
- If you were to be fired, what would be the most likely reason?
- What false or outdated assumptions do people operate under at work?
- What horrendous blunder did you (or others in the organization) make in the past year? What did you learn from it?
- What if you are mistaken about this?
- And if you did know the answer?

CHAPTER 25

A case history of releasing talent through coaching

CHRISTOPHER C. RIDGEWAY

[handwritten annotations: motivation, power, achievement, self awareness, self perception]

Introduction

Helping top executives to optimize their organizational performance is a problematic matter. The initial problem is to be able to gain entry into their commercial world. Their motivational structure, power, independence, achievement drive, lack of openness about their limitations, and so forth, all tend to block their self-awareness and their willingness to seek help. However, the use of a number of methodologies or a change in circumstances can lead some to seek facilitation for professional or personal change.

The relatively recent growth in 360-degree feedback, particularly at board level, has led some to accept other's identification of their interpersonal limitations and thereby seek help in achieving major changes. Some have recognized how they influence others following feedback from behavioural observations of their interactions. An increasing number have identified the need to become more self-aware and change through redundancy. Downsizing, and mergers and acquisitions, have made top executives vulnerable. Those top executives who are made redundant will usually be supported by outplacement. It is during the outplacement process that many will, for the first time, or for the first time for a significant period, be given independent feedback on their motives and interpersonal behaviour and its possible effect on their colleagues, staff, and managers. It is within this scenario that the following case study is presented and analysed.

Case study

Background

Arnold was the CEO of a global business. In that position he was responsible for over 20,000 people and a turnover of several billion pounds. He

was 48 years old and had been in business since he finished his account-
ancy training, following a degree in economics. His one time out had
been when he had completed an MBA, which he had self-funded. He had
worked on two continents. In each overseas role he had been abroad for
around 3 to 5 years. He had made three lateral career transitions: finance
to marketing; marketing to HQ strategy; and then to commercial director.
His major achievements had been the launch of a major brand, closure of
an overseas operation and the leadership of a significant acquisition. He
had been with his recent employer for 4 years. His replacement was the
CEO of an acquired business.

He was married, and his wife was an accountant. They met whilst he
was doing his articles. He had two teenage children who attended a
boarding school. Following news of redundancy he was faced with an
uncertain future: portfolio career; non-executive directorships; charity
work; another CEO role; retirement; or something else? Possibly for the
first time in many years, he came face-to-face with himself and his relationships. For both areas of his life, it was possible for him to release more
of his talents.

Initial picture *based on psychics tests and dynamic orientated (interview)'*

The initial coaching session was based on data previously collected by a
combination of psychodynamically orientated interviews and psychometric data. From the perspective of the coach these suggested that Arnold
was very power centred and, as a consequence, he appeared to avoid
close, open and trusting relationships. His defence against possible failure seemed to be his ability to unconsciously provide a series of blame
stories. These stories attributed any failure to others, or to the system. His
fantasy was that he was omnipotent and, in most circumstances, perfect.
His very high need to be perfect appeared to produce an extremely high
level of control of others. This had led to him working very long hours
and, as a result, left little time for out of work activities, including family
pastimes. Arnold's home life appeared to have been initially formed by his
early experiences of his wife, Susan. She was more introverted and less
confident than he. She had developed a very dependent relationship over
a number of years.

From the coach's perspective his problems were therefore numerous.

- Would he recognize that his leadership and team style might make it
  difficult for others to select him because he might not match their
  desired organizational culture?
- Could he recognize that though his levels of control might be appropriate for maintenance and/or high cost control business strategies,

they would almost certainly clash with those where innovation and rapid change were the vision?

- With respect to his life–work balance, would he identify the limitations he imposed with his work-centred lifestyle and how his family style was restricting his wife's and possibly his children's growth?

It was surprising that when he was faced, in his initial session, with the question of his family relationships, he began to be very open about his early childhood. In this respect, it should be remembered that empathy, and the relationship with the client, had been developed during the data-gathering phase.

dev. empathy & rapport during data gathering

Coaching

He had, during the assessment process, been struck by his difficulty in remembering much about his father (an army officer), but his ease in remembering a great deal about his mother. Between sessions he had engaged, for the first time in many years, in introspection. He had recognized that his mother had always given him feedback that he was the best, and that others should approach him for advice, whilst he should ignore theirs. This was explored deeper, using gap analysis. Arnold was now encouraged to delve into how he saw himself and his personal relationships, and what were the gaps between what he perceived and what he wanted. He was at home more, so he had an opportunity to observe Susan during the time between sessions and he recognized that though he had developed intellectually and culturally, she had not, except perhaps for the fact that she usually agreed with him. She was almost totally dependent on him.

Further exploration focused on what resistance to change there may be in himself and Susan and what aspects of their relationship he felt most motivated to amend. It was suggested that he do some homework. The initial task was to further his self-perceptual evaluation and then, if he believed it appropriate, get Susan to do her own gap analysis:

- How did she perceive Arnold?
- What would she like to change?
- How would she want the change to occur?
- Additionally, if she felt motivated, how did she perceive herself, and what would she want to change?

At the next session, Arnold brought in considerable detail about his self-perception, his perception of Susan, and so forth. He wanted to help change Susan because he perceived he would be bored with continuing home-based time with her. He also said that she was considering psychotherapy as the 'trauma' of not being able to 'predict the future' was

becoming overpowering. He therefore asked for advice on possible ther-
apists. These were provided with the comment that it was good for her to
talk on the phone and then select the one that she felt might be appropriate to meet for an initial exploratory discussion. He was left with the
homework of visioning what his relationship might be in 10 years' time,
and to get there, what would his goals and action plan be? He was also
asked if Susan would take a similar suggestion to her therapist and, if she
and her therapist agreed, he could bring that to his next session. He was
told that, at some point it might be necessary to have, upon the agreement of her therapist, a session or sessions with himself and Susan.

Continuing the journey

Over a number of sessions, Arnold worked on his relationship with Susan.
This widened to his relationship with his mother (his father was dead)
and his children. In parallel, Susan was working with her therapist. The
outcome was an agreed action plan covering relationship(s) goals and a
vision of the future.

- He could visualize himself taking time off to watch the children's week-
  day and weekend sporting activities.
- He could see himself 'allowing' Susan to take the lead in deciding what
  activities they should jointly and individually follow.
- He was able to vision himself and Susan at social activities where he
  kept silent and, 'allowed' Susan to lead a conversation, and then support her.
- He was even able to inform his mother, now in her late 70s, that he had
  lost his job and it was, at least in a large part, his fault.

During this relationship exploration, Arnold had continued his examination of his career orientation. As with many coaching assignments, the
two had, in a complex way, crossed paths several times. He began to recognize that if he were to retain his perfectionist and controlling approach
at work it would be very difficult for him to achieve the change in his
home relationships. He would not have the time. This recognition of the
conflict was facilitated by the use of a homework assignment workbook,
which, in part, encourages the exploration of possibly conflicting goals.
    Many top executive roles, particularly global ones, require consider-
able time away from home and, even when based in the UK, due to the
influence of other time zones, they require long hours of work. In various
sessions, Arnold did return to his need to gain a sense of admiration, prestige and recognition from his place of work, although he gradually
decided that life consisted of more than power and that any future roles
he worked in should be UK based. It should be said that this was

influenced over the months by his acceptance that the market-place 'knew' he had not anticipated the need for radical organizational, strategic change and its associated culture change; this was the major reason the City and the chairman did not want him to stay. The market therefore, in part, made him recognize he probably would not get another large, global, CEO role. The market sentiment also made it unlikely that he would get any significant non-executive director roles.

Outcomes

Combining his relationship-change orientation with the market sentiment made him rethink, in a wider sense, what was important in his life. He was encouraged to explore what he had enjoyed as a child, but had not followed as an adult, and what he would like to improve, in his terms, in the wider world. This, again, was where his motivations and Susan's began to come together.

Susan had had an early life interest in horses. She had continued this by keeping one herself and one for each of her children. As she developed her confidence she had set herself the goal of developing a riding centre. Arnold recognized his business skills could help her, so it became a joint venture. As he freed himself from his need to control, he began to listen to those in the riding centre, and those associated with it. In association with a local entrepreneur, he began to develop related activities: an equestrian holiday centre with an associated hotel. A tack shop followed, as did – and this is where his international experience became relevant – a specialist vet centre for horses in less developed countries. Finally (at least to date), came a centre for mentally handicapped children, from the UK and developed countries, where the horses provide the therapy.

To finance this he had to downsize his former lifestyle but, in return, he improved his relationship with his family. His wife, with her therapist facilitation, has significantly become a person in her own right. His prestige and recognition comes from those who appreciate their tuition and equestrian achievements, thank him for his charitable work, and their horses' health. His power comes from the control of his own life. He is no longer dominated by the corporate timetable and airline schedules.

He has not had a complete transformation. Under high pressure, he may still respond in an authoritarian manner but Susan has learned how to give him feedback, so many now hear him say he is sorry. Their business is successful, so his talent as a businessman is not lost. Indeed he now takes considerable time to act as a mentor to his various business managers, his talents as a human being have been liberated.

A combination of psychodynamic-type therapy, relationship counselling, career orientation assessment and feedback, and time, would therefore seem to have produced a richer talent, which will probably serve Arnold well as he moves towards his next career transformation. What will he do with the later stages of his life? Write a book? Pursue academic disciplines he had last seriously thought about 30 years previously, like philosophy or history? Or even something completely new? He now knows how to self-evaluate, vision and adapt to change. Not everything may be possible, but much more is.

Dev. Ability to
self evaluate
vision to
adapt to Δ.

PART 5
BUSINESS PSYCHOLOGY
APPLIED TO SYSTEMS

CHAPTER 26

Introduction

PAULINE GRANT

Almost everything we do has some impact on something or someone else. Some impact is trivial but not all the non-trivial impacts are obvious. In the (real) example below, there was a failure to take account of key variables, because they were not in the project-monitoring schedule.

> A junior manager with an intuition that something was going wrong with a major project, but couldn't put his finger on it, started showing signs of stress. Because he had nothing concrete to take to his boss, and the metrics looked good, he just worried. His boss noticed that he was not his usual self, and in fact seemed to be drinking more heavily, but assumed there was a domestic issue that was personal, so did nothing. The junior manager was right, though. Something that wasn't being measured routinely *was* out of line, and several millions ended up being wasted. The senior manager responsible for delivering the project, someone who was deemed a rising star, nearly became a casualty, but for the intervention of a director who wanted to get to the bottom of it and see if there was a way of saving this person's career.

When Douglas McGregor (1960) launched his 'Theory X, Theory Y' descriptions of management approaches, a distinction that is still seen in many organizations, he drew attention to the drawbacks of treating people as if they were cogs to be wound up and set running. For him, the system encompassed how people felt and what motivated them, not just what they would do under instruction.

At YSC, we often encourage people who are trying to effect change to create an 'influencing map'. This transcends the formal structures that exist in the organization and maps the actual human system in which the proposed change would take place. As well as including the key decision-makers, stakeholders and potential blockers, we help them to think about the world from those perspectives. It often opens up discussion about connections that have yet to be made, benefits to others that have not been articulated, people who might have been left out, and wasteful

243

bureaucratic process that can be avoided. Understanding the real system allows effort to be targeted both more efficiently and more effectively.

In my first job after leaving university I felt the lack of intellectual stretch and so undertook an Open University technology module called Systems Behaviour. The case examples ranged from agricultural, industrial, biological as well as purely technical 'hard' systems. One that particularly sticks in my mind, even after all the intervening years, was air traffic control (Peters, 1978). This was of particular interest to psychologists because it highlighted the importance of applying psychological insight to interactions between people and their working environment. The simulation used to test a new air traffic control (hard) system threw out problems that would inevitably occur when it went live, but that had not been anticipated in the design. This highlights the point that systems have boundaries but we might not always know where to draw them. In fact, we define the boundaries of the system with reference to our reason for looking at them (to test a reaction, to deal with a problem, to automate a process). It takes lateral thinking, imagination as well as analytical logic to map out a system in a way that is going to be useful when taking the full range of interactions into account.

Systems thinking is the uniting theme in this section and, of course, the authors focus on the human element in their various examples. We see business psychology skills being targeted at particular areas of business endeavour that are, of course, subsystems of something larger, and sometimes it is this permeable boundary that forms the central thesis. Burton's analysis of performance management and the reasons it often fails to deliver desired outcomes helps us to recognize that, where initiatives are not joined up, their impact is diluted. She urges us to stretch the boundaries to encompass more than the rationally based process to give greater chance of success.

Henessey and Vincent go on to express surprise at how customer relationship management, perhaps against the tide of acknowledging the 'softer' people issues, is often seen as a hard technology, leaving scope for considerable benefits through adding the behavioural and emotional dimensions. By looking more systemically at how customers are viewed, talked about and regarded, they find opportunities to make a substantial difference to performance.

Duigan's chapter concentrates very specifically on the contribution of a business health psychologist, a nicely ambiguous term that I will refrain, as he does, from explaining; as the illustrative case study unfolds, the definition becomes clear. He comments on the legal and business rationale for concentrating on risk, and shows how the use of insight into people and interactions adds value to the more traditional approaches to managing risk. Finally, Share-Bernia looks at website design. She demonstrates how understanding of users' operating characteristics can be incorporated into design features to maximize effectiveness. This is a highly focused chapter but the themes within it have more general application.

Chapter 27

Best practice performance management in today's commercial reality

Nadine Burton

Introduction

Getting performance management just right so that it motivates individuals and focuses their efforts on supporting organizational goals is the Holy Grail of the human resources community. Organizational performance can be greatly affected by ensuring that people are aligned to common aims, are motivated and competent to do the job, and feel involved and committed to the organization. The opposite is true if people feel undervalued, demotivated or unclear about what they are doing. The answer to the key organizational issue of how to manage the people within the organization seems straightforward. Clear goals need to be set so that people know what they are doing, and these need to cascade from the strategic priorities of the organization so that everyone is pursuing consistent goals. Staff should be rewarded fairly for performing at a high level in pursuit of these goals and should be given training and development to equip them with the skills to do so. Yet, recent studies and surveys still show that the implementation of performance management is generally patchy and ineffectual. The highly attractive claims made for many performance-management and performance-related pay initiatives, such as increasing bottom-line performance and retaining key talent, often do not materialize in practice. So often the complaint from employees and managers alike is that the process is seen as an additional burden to their already busy working lives, a once-a-year form-filling exercise.

Performance management in various guises has been extensively researched, discussed and argued about over many decades. So why can't we get it right? This chapter seeks to answer this question by exploring the reasons why best practice and reality often don't match up in many organizations. It also provides some practical solutions for closing this gap.

What is best practice performance management?

In essence, a best practice model of performance management is a set of practices and procedures designed to enhance individual and group performance and focus it towards the achievement of strategic objectives, thereby improving organizational performance. In practice, performance management is implemented within organizations in many different ways. In 1992, the Institute of Personnel and Development carried out two extensive studies of the adoption of performance management in the UK (Bevan and Thompson, 1992; Fletcher and Williams, 1992), finding that there is a wide range of interpretations and schemes being used within the UK. This variability presents challenges to providing a clear definition, yet in a review of many research studies and surveys of performance management, Bevan and Thompson (1992: 5) state that most definitions of best practice performance management include the following:

- Communication of a vision of organizational objectives to all employees.
- Setting of departmental and individual performance targets related to wider organizational objectives.
- Conducting formal reviews of progress towards these targets.
- Using review processes to identify training, development and reward outcomes.
- Evaluating the effectiveness of the whole process to consider improvements.

Performance management as a set of practices has increased significantly since the 1980s. It has its origins in the US and has developed in the UK as a response to a number of environmental and organizational factors. The increase in international competition and growing concern with stakeholder value has led organizations to focus on departmental and individual performance. In the public sector, a drive towards increased accountability for public expenditure has led organizations to examine their effectiveness and efficiency, including setting and achieving targets. Making business units more responsible and accountable for their own performance has led to flatter, more decentralized organizational structures, which in turn have increased the need for practices and systems to make these structures work. There has also been a shift away from collective to individual employee relations with which the individualistic focus of performance management has a close fit. External standards, such as Investors In People, have also contributed to putting the need for more systematic and integrated performance management onto the business agenda.

The best practice performance management model seeks to integrate a range of human resources practices – appraisal, training and development, reward – with organizational processes, such as strategic and operational planning, budgeting and formal business measures such as key performance indicators and balanced scorecards. It aims to provide a consistent approach to cascading and setting goals across the organization, enabling individual and group performance to be compared fairly and equitably in all business units. It is this integrated approach that proponents of performance management state makes it unique from earlier approaches to managing performance within the business.

Challenges *en route* to the Holy Grail

In 1992, Bevan and Thompson conducted a survey of 1,863 organizations in private and public sectors in the UK, revealing that the uptake of performance management in organizations is patchy and incomplete 'with most organisations carrying out certain of the activities but none succeeding in integrating them all successfully'. This has also been the finding of case-study research by Fletcher and Williams in 26 organizations in the UK. Empirical evidence to support the view that strategic performance management approaches have a positive impact on organizational performance is equivocal.

There are a number of reasons why this might the case. Some relate to conceptual basis of performance management; others are more practical considerations. Both will be addressed here.

Conceptual challenges

Assumption of rationality in organizations

In its pure form, performance management assumes an objective and mechanistic model of management. Core elements include setting objectives, reviewing performance and revising objectives and plans. The effectiveness of these elements demands a level of rationality within organizations and tends not to allow for the complexity and messiness of organizational life. It is rarely the case that a simple model of setting objectives, reviewing progress, and making amendments, can be followed. Kanter (1989) states that the 'nature and extent of rationality within organizations and management is far from straightforward' and this serves to undermine a system of performance management that seeks to be overly rational in approach. Achieving consistency within the organization around common goals rests on the assumption that organizations are unitary, that clear organizational goals can be specified and that these will be shared with others across the organization. Moreover, the planning required to support performance management is often impossible. Systematically deciding on objectives and resources required is complicated by the fact that resources are interdependent and planning is often iterative and negotiated. Little allowance is made, therefore, for the fact that different people and business units may have their own interests and interpret organizational goals in different ways, or for the ambiguities and uncertainty of organizational realities. In many organizations, for instance, one of the biggest problems in implementing a performance management approach is that strategy is not clearly articulated or communicated and is constantly evolving throughout the year. The prescribed best practice models of performance management are typically too rigid for more fluid organizations.

This rationality often also underestimates the importance of the emotional side of organizational life (for example, the need to be liked, anger or conflict) and the ways in which these emotions can affect the relationship between the manager and individual. There is always constant implicit negotiation in role relationships, and successive understandings and misunderstandings about the nature of the relationship or the task.

Assumption of mutual benefits

Newton and Findlay (1996) point out that an underlying assumption of performance management is that employers and employees will share common interests and that performance management will benefit both equally. One of the biggest benefits, if it can be achieved, is the time that managers spend with their team members in constructive dialogue. In practice, however, employees' reaction to the process is often negative and suspicious as it can be perceived as an instrument of management control rather than an empowering tool. Too often the focus on short-term results and reward payments mean that the discussions centre instead on a negotiation of performance ratings. Managers themselves will often also dislike the approach, seeing it as overly prescriptive about how they should manage their staff.

Case study

This was clearly illustrated in a fund management company in which the human resources team introduced a complex performance-based reward system. The system relied on managers to make an objective assessment of an individual's performance against goals and competencies as a measure of both results (the 'what') and behaviour (the 'how'). The system had been introduced with considerable fanfare as a way of rewarding top performers as well as helping the company to achieve its strategic objectives through rewarding results and values – a system, therefore, that was equally beneficial to employees and the business. In practice, however, employees and managers perceived the system as an imposition of the company's view of good performance. To individual fund managers what really mattered to their career progression in the City was the performance of their fund. The performance management system sought to reward people not only for this, but also for management skills and teamwork. Often, however, the fund managers who received the highest rewards were not model company citizens in this respect, but all the same, were highly rated in the City. In this situation the performance management system did little to support a constructive dialogue about performance; rather managers and employees became frustrated with the system and sought to find ways to 'fiddle' the results to meet their particular needs.

Practical challenges

Speed of change required

Best practice performance management models are in reality often difficult to implement and result in incomplete or ineffective take up of the system across the organization. Far too often the focus is on filling in the forms rather than on the dialogue between manager and employee. One of the most frequent problems is the speed at which change is required in organizations. Performance management is repeatedly seen as a simple step in supporting strategic objectives or a new reward system. Implementation is then rushed and inadequate time given to developing the approach to match organizational realities or to piloting and training.

Lack of training

Investment in training is a critical element to effective implementation and is so often left out completely or given inadequate time to fully explore the complexities of the approach. For instance, many organizations seek to link reward decisions into the performance management discussions. This requires managers to set sensible and tangible goals, review these fairly and objectively with the individual and provide a rating of performance at the end of the year. Ensuring that this process is carried out consistently and fairly across the organization is critical to the perceived effectiveness of the whole performance management system. The time and input in getting this right, however, is often downplayed and left to the managers.

Time limitations

Another frequently reported practical challenge to effective implementation of the process is the time that managers and employees are able to give to the process. The expectation is often that managers should be carrying out ongoing review of performance with at least two more formal reviews per year. A common complaint is that this is almost impossible given the long hours people already work. The review process is seen as an extra burden that people could do without.

Linking performance to reward

Many organizations link some form of reward into their performance management system. However, the rewards on offer are often insufficient, not valued or inadequately related to performance to have the desired motivating effects. The link between effort, performance and reward is complex and often misunderstood by managers. Research has shown that what motivates people to perform well includes a range of elements such as enjoyment of the job, the sense of achievement people get from doing a good job, and recognition. Money usually comes in sixth or seventh place. Performance-related pay (PRP), as a form of reward, is often seen as a simple method for encouraging good individual performance by rewarding it with extra pay. There is significant evidence, however, that the effect of PRP on motivation and performance is minimal. Yet PRP continues to be seen as an important means of motivating better performers (Kohn, 1993). Human motivation is much more complex than many reward schemes allow for and, although they may produce temporary compliance and the retention of key staff in the short term, long-term motivation and commitment is often lacking.

The introduction of a link between performance and extrinsic rewards (such as pay or promotion) introduces a whole raft of issues into the performance management approach, which make its implementation particularly challenging. For example, the definition of 'effective' performance needs to be incredibly tight; managers need to have sophisticated skills in setting goals and reviewing performance; consistency needs to be achieved across the organization to ensure equity, and rewards need to be sufficient to act as a motivator.

Finding the best solution for the organization

As is clear from the preceding discussion, getting performance management to work effectively is a tricky problem. The effectiveness of the approach can, however, be enhanced in a number of ways.

Prioritizing dialogue, not form filling

In recent years, it has been recognized that people actively choose whether or not to apply their capability and creativity to help the company to succeed. Organizations that view people as simply another resource are unlikely to benefit fully from the talent within the business. Performance management plays a key role in leveraging this talent but can only do so by explicitly acknowledging that different people may have different interests and perceptions and that people have a choice about their actions. This means building into the process opportunities for proper *discussion* and *negotiation* between the manager and employee, so that aspirations, opinions, and perceptions can be aired and people feel that they are genuinely working with their manager to agree what is best for them and the organization.

One way that this can be achieved is by significantly reducing the bureaucracy required to implement the approach and focusing on giving time for dialogue. An overly rigid and mechanistic approach will stifle this. A number of organizations fail to recognize their good managers – those that create these opportunities for discussion and spend the majority of their time coaching and motivating teams. Instead they provide increasingly pressured targets to achieve, which distract them from their key role of managing their staff. Organizations therefore need to make a genuine commitment to giving managers time and recognition for doing this well.

Match the process to the reality of organizational life

Quite often the claimed benefits of the performance management approach outweigh the reality and this undermines the process. Avoiding the rhetoric and not overpromising is critical to stop this from happening. Discussing and designing the system in a way that speaks to business managers rather than human resources departments is vital. They need to know how it will help them manage their teams more effectively and deliver a commercial result, not that they have to complete lengthy and distracting forms just for perceived benefit of record keeping.

Good performance management is what effective business managers do naturally – for example, agreeing what needs to be done, coaching people to achieve and grow, giving constructive ongoing feedback, discussing and providing opportunities for development and career advancement.

Designing the approach to give managers maximum flexibility to decide how best to manage their own teams will lead to a higher-quality solution. This means, for example, giving managers the discretion to agree performance outputs that are appropriate for the role (for example, goals, targets, performance standards or key responsibilities) rather than imposing an approach such as SMART targets. This does, of course, rely on managers actually being effective at managing and this is where training comes in.

Train effective management

If performance management is seen as 'what good managers do naturally', then training becomes part of the core skills in management. Training and ongoing support to be an effective coach and leader will do more to support the performance management approach than simply briefing managers and staff how to use the system and what to write in each box on the form. Managers need to be skilled in *setting and managing goals*. There are many complexities within this goal-setting process that organizations simplify or overlook. Managers need to have a sophisticated understanding and capability to do this. For instance, managers need to know how to:

- Flex the goal-setting process throughout the year to match the degree of change that many companies experience, so that targets set at beginning of the year are still appropriate at the end.
- Set goals collaboratively rather than impose them on individuals.
- Manage the goal-setting dialogue in a context of restructuring and delayering.
- Measure the important things rather than simply those that are easily measurable. For instance, the less tangible but critical aspects to an individual's role can often be overlooked (such as creative output, relationship building and team working).

Give it time

Fletcher and Williams (1992) found, in their case-study research of 26 organizations in the UK, that the better ones took their time to implement a new approach, at around 2 years or more. Putting the basic steps in place initially is a sound place to start rather than attempting to introduce an overly complex approach in a short space of time, and this helps significantly in increasing the quality of the process.

Focus on fairness

Accuracy and fairness are critical to smooth implementation across the organization, which is difficult to achieve at the same time as giving managers discretion over the process. Longenecker and Ludwig (1995) found that most managers do not describe their ratings of staff as completely honest or accurate. Motives for this are often well intentioned (for example, to avoid harmful conflict, damaging someone's career or further demotivating a poor performer). This dilemma can be reduced by giving managers insight into their motives for giving inaccurate assessments and seeing the implications of doing so for the organization and its staff. Additionally, providing managers with the support to develop and communicate clear standards by which they will assess performance and provide constructive feedback against these standards will also increase the overall fairness of the approach.

Case study: the UK business of a large investment bank

Historically, the key challenge in one large bank that sought our help was that managers received very little training in how to carry out effective performance management. As a result, employees had limited faith in the system being able to deliver anything of value to their everyday working lives. There were pockets of highly motivated staff but this was a result of naturally good managers. A whole range of formats and methods had evolved over time in different business areas, which undermined the perceived fairness of the outcome. The decision was made to implement a new approach that combined a deliberately simple process with more sophisticated training. This provided consistency across the organization but encouraged a focus on the dialogue between managers rather than on form filling. The new format helped staff to agree performance outputs as a focus for an individual's activities and to discuss career, and training and development to support achievement of these. Training for all managers began with each manager collecting feedback from their staff about their performance management skills. Training input was then targeted to their specific needs and sought to uncover some of the blocks to managers' effectiveness. This avoided the all too frequent complaint of the 'sheep-dip' approach to training and made the training modules highly tailored to the specific needs of groups of managers. Employees were also involved – first to find out what they wanted from their managers and then in reviewing the effectiveness of the approach and revising the system accordingly. This meant that, for the first time, managers were given the tools and skills to use the performance management approach in ways that would work for their teams. Within the first year, feedback from employees was that the quality of the discussions was considerably higher than previously and involvement in the process rose to 99%.

Conclusions

It is clear that no one approach to performance management is going to magically solve the needs of all organizations. The best practice approaches to performance management assume a universal relevance that is unrealistic in practice. With increasingly global organizations, the systems have to be flexible around diverse cultures and countries, business units and teams as well as groups of staff. An effective system is designed to take account of and adapt to the particular context in which it operates. It also needs to emphasize the role of dialogue and negotiation of different stakeholder interests, balancing the needs of the organization for goals and targets to be achieved with the individual's personal motivations and aspirations. Performance management approaches cannot be imposed upon the organization and assumed to have equal benefits for all. Employees need to see that the system is fair and that it reflects and protects their interests rather than being just a system of control from management. Effective approaches depend on the employees having a stake in it as well as active involvement of line managers in improving their own capability to effectively manage their teams. Only by spending time to develop an approach that will meet the needs of managers and their teams will organizations move along their journey towards the Holy Grail.

CHAPTER **28**

The psychology of customer relationship management

JO HENNESSY, ROD VINCENT

Introduction and context

Customer relationship management (CRM) has had an enormous impact on business in recent years and, in particular, on the marketing and customer service functions. It is also a term that has a different meaning depending on whom you ask. Within the business world, it is commonly defined as: 'the process of acquiring, retaining and growing profitable customers. It requires a clear focus on the service attributes that represent value to the customer and create loyalty' (Brown, 2000). Another description is: 'CRM is about the management of technology, processes, information resources and people needed to create an environment that allows a business to take a 360-degree view of its customers' (Galbreath and Rogers, 1999).

As psychologists we can immediately see how we are able to contribute to this field. The mention of 'relationship' and 'loyalty' suggest fundamental features of human behaviour. However, the majority of CRM projects have concentrated on aspects such as the micro-segmentation of markets, and the technology needed to manage the mass of information that this generates. The psychological aspects of the *relationship* with customers have often been neglected.

When we first started working in this area, we were surprised to find that CRM is an organizational topic that has received little comment from our profession. This may be explained by the evolution that CRM has undergone over the last few years, taking on the guise of a technology solution, requiring high levels of corporate investment and being managed as an information technology project.

A technological approach to CRM promises to:

* gather customer data swiftly;
* identify the most valuable customers over time;

256

[handwritten margin notes: technological approaches about DATA / INFO]

- increase customer loyalty by providing customized products and services;
- reduce the cost of servicing these customers;
- make it easier to acquire similar customers down the road.

However, such promises have proved hard to deliver.

In a 2000 Gartner Group Survey cited in Kazimer-Shockley and Bergert (2001) it was found that for many of the thousands of firms attempting to implement CRM 'efforts are at best partly completed, and at worst unco-ordinated and fragmented'.

A major concern for businesses is the high failure rate of CRM IT projects. In a series of studies cited by Leverick et al. (1998) they quote from a survey of 400 British and Irish companies, which found that only 11% of IT projects had been successful. In another, it is claimed that three-quarters of IT projects were either not completed or not used when they were completed. However, from the IT managers' perspective this is more about management issues than IT failures. Leverick et al. quote these management issues as including:

- absence of strong sponsorship;
- a lack of cultural readiness;
- inadequate supporting budgets;
- absence of complementary customer management skills.

[handwritten margin notes: A c/b a big part of CRM initiatives · people need skill AND will to build cust. rel's.]

The introduction of CRM really does represent a significant change initia-tive for any organization: change in processes; change in technology; change in people; change in management styles. The management of change is another area where, as business psychologists, we have facilitat-ed the success of CRM projects, although this section will not cover the processes of change management. Customer relationship leadership (CRL) has been recommended by Galbreath and Rogers (1999) as the means to bridge the gap between a CRM vision and its reality. The deliberate and thorough application of leadership principles to CRM may well help to increase their success rate. Whilst it is possible to borrow from the sizeable leadership literature and applied leadership case studies, there is a need for further research and practical experimentation in how best to lead a CRM transformation with its incumbent culture and budget implications.

[handwritten margin notes: apply leadership principles to CRM]

Interestingly, there are parallel awakenings in the human resources profession (see Kiger, 2002). How can a company offer the customized services and products that CRM information can enable, if the employees do not have the skills or motivation to build customer relationships? Human resources have begun to step in here, seeing their role in recruit-ing customer-focused employees and filling customer service skills gaps through training. However, their role may go deeper than this.

258 (handwritten margin notes: Internal retention, Comp retention, Cost retention)

There have been some interesting findings in the retention research at Cornell University's Center for Advanced Human Resources Studies, showing that customer retention and employee retention may have more in common than we might have imagined (quoted in Kiger, 2002). Strong relationships between employees and customers can actually stop both from fleeing the company. As a practitioner, it has seemed to be common sense that happier employees will lead to happier customers. A Landmark 1999 analysis of 800 Sears Roebucks stores in the US (quoted in Kiger, 2002), can serve to illustrate this point: as for every 5% improvement in employee attitudes, customer satisfaction increased 1.3% and corporate revenue rose 0.5%.

We must guard against the danger of becoming too inwardly focused, and missing the most vital part in this equation, the customer. If the goal is to increase the loyalty of the most profitable customers, then surely we need to consider what makes customers want to stay loyal to a company or leave. Many have looked to data to demystify things, but as Table 28.1 shows, this does not always help.

Table 28.1 Why customers leave their suppliers

	%	
Complaints not handled	14	
Lured by competition	9	
Relocated	9	
No special reason	68	

Source: Rockerfeller Foundation Study (Griffin, 1995).

In a trawl of the business press, we have found a number of practical solutions offered. Businesses are told that 'the customer rules' and that they must get the right value proposition to offer to their customers. They are encouraged to explore the different notions of lock-in (when the cost, however defined, of moving keeps a customer from deserting) and lock-on (when the value gained from that organization keeps customers coming back for more). They are warned of the risks of stalking (rather than wooing) their customers and advised to understand 'the customer scenario' – how their products/services fit into the real lives of individuals.

As we have already mentioned, there is a tendency to ignore the psychological aspects of the *relationship*. The secret of success in customer retention may lie in the 'R' of CRM: achieving long-lasting relationships with customers. This concept of relationships, however, may have been suppressed by the seduction of customer management. A glance at the

CRM literature quickly shows that many have fallen into this pitfall. Much of the language used refers to attempts to manage customers as if they were employees with efforts to manage 'under-performers', 'improve their performance', 'develop' and even 'fire' them. However, is this really possible, and does it lead to an ethos of excellent customer service if staff view customers this way?

Much of the theoretical, empirical and applied work in the field of relationships emphasizes the need for different parties in a relationship to perceive equal rewards from the relationship. Psychologists have defined the informal rules of different kinds of relationships and the social skills required in forming effective relationships. Unsurprisingly, businesses are now beginning to realize that building close relationships demands that suppliers pay close attention to their customers. In order to achieve mutual trust and respect, the people involved need to interact over a period of time, to listen and respond to feedback and think of the value of that relationship. One of the surveys that bears this out was conducted in AT&T (Bhote, 1996). They found that sales wins and losses had the closest correlation with amount of time spent with each customer and the ensuing personal relationship of mutual trust and respect.

Relationships are two-way streets. This brings us back to the other essential part of the relationship, the employee. As we have already recognized, CRM often represents a culture change for organizations. We cannot predict the exact nature of this culture change as it will vary by situation. It may be that an increased customer focus will require more positive attitudes and behaviours from employees when interacting with customers. Conversely, it may mean giving less personal attention to some loyal customers who are deemed less profitable. Some employees may feel more empowered by increased freedom to develop relationships with their customers, whilst others may feel less empowered as they are required to log increasing volumes of customer relationship information for monitoring purposes. Thus relationships may be required to grow and flourish despite a backdrop of change and uncertainty.

Psychological understanding can help to unpick these problems and present a more holistic approach to customer relationship management. This chapter moves on to put the business case for CRM.

Market and business drivers: the business case

The rationale for CRM is based on the principle that mass media advertising is on the decline as a tool, and that CRM will be the best way to win, retain and increase business in an increasingly complex market and consumer environment.

Customer relationship marketing has its roots in relationship marketing, with seminal contributions from Reichheld and Sasser in 1990. They reported on the customer retention studies of Bain and Co., showing the business world that loyal customers are more profitable. This finding can be understood if one considers that customer acquisition costs may be high, so that customers may not become profitable unless they are retained for one or more years. Moreover, they found that customers often buy more over time and that as companies learn more about them, they can serve these customers more efficiently.

With the advent of increased information technology capacity, so the field has developed with further research showing that the profitability of customers can be analysed with even greater precision than degrees of loyalty. When profitability and loyalty are considered at the same time, it becomes clear that different customers need to be treated in different ways. This has led to more and more sophisticated segmentation of customers; one of the more straightforward segmentations models is shown in Table 28.2.

Table 28.2 Segmentation model from Reinartz and Kumar (2002)

High profit	**Butterflies** • Good fit between company's offerings and customers' needs • High profit potential *Actions* • Aim to achieve transactional satisfaction, not attitudinal loyalty • Milk the accounts only so long as they are active • Key challenge is to cease investing soon enough	**True friends** • Good fit between company's offerings and customers' needs • Highest profit potential *Actions* • Communicate consistently but not too often • Build both attitudinal and behavioural loyalty • Delight these customers to nurture, defend and retain them
Low profit	**Strangers** • Little fit between company's offerings and customers' needs • Lowest profit potential *Actions* • Make no investment in these relationships • Make profit on every transaction	**Barnacles** • Limited fit between company's offerings and customers' needs • Low profit potential *Actions* • Measure both the size and share of the wallet • If share of the wallet is low, focus on up- and cross-selling • If size of the wallet is small, impose strict cost controls
	Short-term customers	**Long-term customers**

In summary the advent of CRM has represented a significant shift in thinking, moving away from managing product lines/service offerings to managing customers, through recognition that profitability may be more easily managed this way. In organizations it is now commonly referred to as 'getting the right employees to focus on the right customers' and it is on this objective that we shall now focus our attention.

Relationships

What can social psychology tell us about building customer–employee relationships? Relationships are defined (see Argyle and Henderson, 1985) as regular social encounters with certain people over a period of time. It is clear how such relationships might have developed in the traditional family-run business, the kind of setup where the owner and his loyal staff typically knew their customers and could provide services on a personal basis. Larger organizations are now endeavouring to re-create this environment between dedicated account managers and their customers but, as one can imagine, this will only be offered to those more profitable customers – 'true friends'. Such long-term relationships can also be a useful feature of business to business interactions or professional service firms. These are the kind of customer relationships upon which we can shed most light in this section.

There has been considerable research into relationships within social psychology. It is a complex area to summarize as there are several prevailing theories and different conclusions have been drawn depending upon the nature of the relationship, be it marital, friendship, parent–child or work colleague. However, there are certain more general findings about relationships that may be usefully related to the field of customer relationships.

Forming a relationship

Berscheid and Walster (1978) argued that for a social relationship to be initiated it is useful for individuals to perceive that:

- they share similar attitudes, beliefs and interests, as this will ease early communication;
- there is mutual liking, for it is important that a relationship maintains and enhances self-esteem.

If one is to argue that customer relationships could and should share these features, it might be advisable for organizations to match employees more carefully with their valued customers, using all information available to get a good match in attitudes, beliefs and interests. Historically, customers may have been matched to employees on the basis of availability, location, size of account, and so on, when this tells us that relationships are more easily built if the individuals have things in common.

Whilst this deliberate pairing of individuals may help, we must also recognize that no amount of pre-planning can fully account for the resulting chemistry between two people – whether they like each other. Experienced and effective relationship managers will know when to step aside and introduce someone they think will fit better with the customer.

We find this as business psychologists when offering professional coaching to senior executives. This is an extreme example of where there needs to be chemistry between the client and the supplier, and where offering a variety of potential styles of coaches can increase the potential for success. It is also an example of where the staff member needs to know when to step down and let someone else develop the relationship.

Keeping relationships going

One theory that is useful here is 'exchange theory', which states that people will stay in a relationship if the balance of rewards minus costs is as good as they think they can get from the various alternatives open to them, making allowances for the costs of making the change. Interestingly this appears to underlie the phenomena of customer lock-in and customer lock-on (Vandermerwe, 2000).

Customer lock-in occurs when the customer has no choice but to stay with the supplier because there are no viable alternatives open to them. There may be one supplier with a monopoly for as long as its particular technology wave lasts. Alternatively, customers may have made an investment in one product and then find that the cost of changing suppliers is too high. They are locked in until an alternative comes along. Where this falls down is that a relationship has not been built up on the basis of trust and respect, but rather through necessity, and with such weak foundations this relationship can break down as soon as the situation changes. It will not lead to loyalty and voluntary retention and is not satisfying for either party.

Customer lock-on, in contrast, also makes use of exchange theory but in a much more enduring way. It concentrates on achieving a good reward to cost ratio for the customer, looking for ways to offer superior value at low perceived cost. This way the customers choose to maintain the relationship with the supplier, rather than being trapped or locked in. To implement this effectively, businesses will need to review the value they offer their customers.

Organizational perspective

A practical framework we have used with organizations to review their offering to customers is outlined in Figure 28.1.

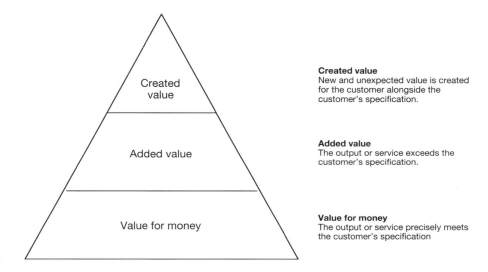

Created value
New and unexpected value is created for the customer alongside the customer's specification.

Added value
The output or service exceeds the customer's specification.

Value for money
The output or service precisely meets the customer's specification

Figure 28.1 The value triangle.

The value triangle suggests that there are three levels in meeting and then exceeding customer needs:

- the basic level entails ensuring that customers perceive that they have received value for money;
- at the next level customers perceive that they receive a little bit more than they expected through added value, be this delivering ahead of time, additional products, extra features or any other way that the benefits gained from the transaction are greater than those expected at the time of purchase;
- finally, businesses can work at the third level in creating value for their customers, suggesting innovative and tailored ways in which they can genuinely create new value for them.

We have found that working at the level of creating value is only possible where there is a strong relationship with the customer in which the supplier is able to anticipate needs that the customer has not yet identified and the customer trusts the supplier enough to be open to the possibilities of creating value.

Customer perspective

As we mentioned above, psychologists are able to assist organizations in understanding their individual customers better. Drawing on theories of personality, motivation and self-esteem, we have created a profile to outline the many different things that a customer may value to differing degrees in a customer–supplier relationship:

I want to buy . . .
Friendship
From people I like and can get on with. I want them to know me personally and show an interest in me beyond just wanting my business. I want to have a sociable relationship with people I buy from.

Professionalism
From people who are professional and credible. I want them to be businesslike rather than too informal.

Expertise
From people who are expert about what they are selling. I want them to know more about the product or service than I do. I want them to pass on knowledge and information to me.

Trust
From people who are genuine, sincere and honest with me. I want to feel confident that they will tell me about potential problems and that they will not try to exploit me.

Quality
The best possible goods and services available. It matters more to me to have the highest quality than to have the lowest price.

Aesthetics
Products that appeal to my sense of aesthetics. That may mean they are beautifully designed or visually pleasing products, or in the case of services they should be well presented by personable or attractive people.

Image
Things that make me look good in front of other people. That may mean buying from a prestigious supplier such as the market leader, or it may mean buying products that will impress those around me.

Value
Products and services that are good value for money. I want to be sure that
   I am buying things for the lowest cost possible.

Response
Products and services that will be delivered on time. I want my supplier
   to respond quickly to any queries I raise. I may be prepared to pay
   more for reliable service.

Practicality
Products that are easy to use and do exactly what they are supposed to do.
   Services that are easy to apply and that do not make things overly
   complicated.

Reliability
Products and services with a low level of risk associated. They should be
   safe to use and reliable.

Novelty
The latest technology and innovations. I like to use products and services
   that other people have not yet found out about.

Ethics
Things that fit in with my values. These might include buying environ-
   mentally friendly goods, or avoiding goods and services that exploit
   other people.

On an individual basis this structure enables a relationship manager to
understand the different things that may be important for any given customer, rather than assuming that the customer operates from the same
type of needs as they do, or that the customer simply wants to buy the
product. In reality the customer may have any number of additional needs
and these may prove the differentiator between suppliers. Practically this
model then serves as a guideline when picking up verbal cues and asking
questions to discover what matters to that person.

The rules and behaviours of customer relationships

Here, we draw on social psychology again as we review the rules and skills
that allow the development of relationships and give the tempo to social
interaction.

In their book *The Anatomy of Relationships*, Argyle and Henderson (1985) emphasized the importance of informal rules for understanding relationships and governing interaction in order to sustain a relationship. Their research, with over 900 participants from Britain and south-east Asia, revealed that there were four rules fundamental to all relationships ('universal relationship rules'):

• respect the other's privacy;
• look the other person in the eye during conversation;
• do not discuss that which is said in confidence;
• do not criticize the other person publicly.

Their research did not include employee–customer relationships, so how do the universal relationship rules apply to CRM?

The first two universal relationship rules appear to feed into CRM recruitment and training. It is easy to see how important it is to respect the customer's privacy when getting to know a new customer. However, employees may need guidance on getting the balance right between interested, empathic questioning and not appearing too probing. The second rule, concerning eye contact, seems to fit more generally into a whole raft of social skills required to form relationships in the cultures surveyed. It is well recognized that people differ in their skills here and some may need training to interact comfortably with others.

The second two rules are more akin to company values and culture. The research suggests that employees should endeavour to keep customer confidences. Some businesses manage this through establishing 'Chinese' walls to safeguard customer confidentiality, make promises not to disclose customer details outside of the firm, or work to professional codes of conduct. Interestingly some businesses pass customer details onto other organizations that then drench their loyal customers in junk mail, or else are quite lax about what they share around the office. A further challenge here is management of the CRM database; in sharing information in a customer file, do customers perceive a confidence to be broken or do they see this as joined-up service provision? For example, how do you feel when someone in a call centre knows how you have been using your money and makes suggestions about what you could do instead? There is a need for more research here to determine CRM relationship rules, as it is still relatively new in the world of relationships for one party to already know so much about the other even before they speak.

Finally, relationships suffer if one criticizes the other in public. How many businesses criticize their customers behind their backs, finding them a nuisance and a distraction? In working with account managers on CRM we have often heard the complaint 'this job would be so much easier if it weren't for the customers'. Here company culture and values can act to promote a positive customer attitude, requiring leaders and managers to establish standards of behaviour.

Customer relationship management competencies

As behavioural standards are required to ensure customer relationships are managed well, a competency framework can prove a useful tool. In our own work in the pharmaceutical industry, we have researched and defined a competency framework for CRM. The following is an abridged summary of this:

Building customer knowledge
Develops a thorough knowledge of their customers and the local market. Has close enough relationships with key customers to know what is going on for them and their work area.

Understanding needs
Focuses on the needs of customers rather than just on own agenda. Is skilled, attentive and patient when listening to customers. Facilitates customers in identifying their own needs.

Managing customer information
Keeps accurate customer information to enable the business to optimize the relationship and actively passes information to others. Maintains regular communication exchanges with customers.

Adding value
Provides help and solutions to meet customer needs. Uses a wide range of activities to work alongside customers. Links their understanding of the customer needs to relevant services or products.

Building trust
Has integrity and is trusted by their customers. Develops a track record of delivering what they promise and sorting out problems. They readily gain testimonials and referrals from existing customers.

This example of a CRM competency framework outlines the behaviours that were demonstrated by more successful customer relationship managers. It has been applied in practice as the basis for assessment centres with follow-up CRM best practice workshops, containing practical sessions to develop each CRM competency.

Conclusion

As with any technology-led change, many businesses underestimate the size of a CRM initiative and find themselves underprepared, as a workforce, to develop the customer relationships intrinsic to CRM. We have applied business psychology to this challenge, concentrating on how we can facilitate relationship development and enable improved customer understanding.

There is a real danger in leaving psychology out of CRM and a brief review such as this only allows us to touch the surface of the insights that psychology can bring. We might have made reference to the extensive research concerning the introduction of new technologies in organizations, looking for lessons to be applied in a CRM implementation. If we had taken a different tack still, we might have explored the concept of customer relationship leadership, relating this to more general leadership research and practice. There is a growing opportunity for business psychologists to take a more active part in all aspects of CRM initiatives, as organizations continue to search for effective interventions.

CHAPTER 29

Improving options for managing risks to business and employee health

KIERAN DUIGNAN

Introduction

The desire for a safe and healthy work environment is mounting the business agenda. In some sectors this is because the legal licence to operate depends on being able to show evidence of minimum standards of care for the safety and health of employees, customers and the public. More generally, it is because competitive advantage is served by managing risks to employee health and safety well. In this chapter, I outline how a business health psychologist can enable leaders to behave intelligently about both the health of their business and the wellbeing of people who work in it. A short true-to-life story illustrates how she may intervene in organizational life.

'Risk management' has entered the language commonly used about health in organizational contexts, especially in the light of the guidance of the Turnbull Committee and increasing pressures on accountability of directors (Power, 1997; Garratt, 2003). What I outline describes psychologists' contributions to risk management and three psychological traditions on which they can draw.

Facilitating change

The following story illustrates how business health psychologists can conduct a risk assessment about physical hazards in ways that enable them to facilitate organizational and management development, as well as improved control of these hazards.

The scenario

Eric, operations director of a systems refurbishment company in London, was very pleased with the way in which Ciara had provided redundancy support counselling to employees affected by the closure of the company's workshop in the north of England. When he considered who to ask for help with a sensitive problem at the root of recurrent musculo-skeletal injuries in the goods inwards section of the company's logistics department, she was the person he called on.

After arriving on time for her 9.15 a.m. appointment, Ciara waited for a few minutes in Eric's office before he breezed in. He explained in an upbeat style, using a computer presentation to illustrate, how he had been speaking to the whole workforce about the board's plans for change in the wake of the company's acquisition by a European-wide group. He indicated to her how their plans included the introduction of 'zero toler-ance' for unsafe practices, as a goal in the reconstructed company's commitment to 'world-class facilities' which now featured in its prospec-tus for customers. 'Let's see how you can contribute to the flywheel effect I'm working at to bring about lasting change!' he smiled.

The board's strategy for change included upgrading the logistics department in its London-based headquarters. Eric asked Ciara to come up with a business solution that combined automating processes of move-ment of the goods inwards section with reducing levels of staff absence and of reported musculo-skeletal injuries. Before Ciara got down to work, Eric sent a copy of her proposal to the secretary of the trade union rep-resenting employees in the firm, to keep him fully informed about the agreed scope and purposes.

Observations

Ciara spent some time observing the flow of consignments through this section, noting how goods were offloaded from trucks into check-in and then wheeled on trolleys into the unloading space. The staff responsible for this area estimated that about 75% of the incoming goods were 'small enough to handle' and about 15% were so awkward that they had to be dealt with separately. As part of the legacy from the pre-privatized history of the firm 15 years earlier, no data were available to confirm the figures.

In the goods inwards section, Ciara noted how staff used knives to cut open cardboard boxes, how they lifted goods out of them to inspect them and recorded details in the computer system before putting them back into trolleys again. She tested how it felt to use the available knives and noted the strains she experienced in her lower forearm as she cut through robust cardboard. She observed that, although the section leader in goods inwards – who had recently presented a letter from her doctor demand-ing alternative furniture for her to use – spoke the language of safe, 'kinetic' handling, she continued to consistently strain her arms and lower back by the postures she adopted as she lifted goods. Ciara also noted that all staff reported that they had been trained to handle goods safely, yet that they also suffered frequent pains in their arms and shoulders. They attributed the sources of their difficulties to lack of adjustability in the heights of trolleys, the lack of back support in the chairs available to them when entering data into the computer system, as well as to the sheer number of manual handling and repetitive keystrokes their work involved.

Ciara also observed the absence of any notices reminding staff about safe methods of handling goods, as well as major, recurrent discrepancies between the reported number of days absent due to 'sickness' and the nominal 'accident' book. She also spotted that there were no reports that staff in any other sections of the logistics department reported similar levels of injury or sickness absence and that they spent much less time in continual periods of routine manual handling and inputting data.

She listened to Ted, the logistics manager, outline his approach to management of his department. She noticed his relaxed style of interaction with section leaders and other staff, as well as the curt manner he adopted in turning down a proposal from Eric about an alternative method of dealing with goods mislaid.

Recalling Ted's repeated assertions that automation of the flow of goods through his department was simply 'not possible', Ciara felt perplexed when she discovered he had no method of recording the numbers of goods handled in the department and that he adjusted workflows simply on the basis of physical evidence of underload and overload.

In brief interviews with section heads, Ciara observed how they appreciated what they perceived as a 'hands-on' approach of Ted, as well as a reportedly down-to-earth direct but upbeat style of Eric. She also tested whether there was a business rationale for the existing structure of five sections that made up the logistics department.

Risk assessment

Ciara's report to management dwelt on two classes of risks: physical hazards and behavioural risks.

Physical hazards

Her recommendations relating to physical hazards were designed to safeguard employees from musculo-skeletal injuries and to automate the flow of 75% of consignment through the goods inwards section. As employees had already been complaining to managers about these, she concentrated on emphasizing the scale of the potential costs of these risks, the sources of hazards and how they could be controlled as reasonably as practicable. She suggested the introduction of colour coding in which red would distinguish 'high-hazard' loads likely to present manual handling hazards due to their mass, size, uneven distribution of weight or all three, from orange-coloured loads that required care but did not pose exceptional hazards in the normal course of events. She also proposed a feasibility study of changes to the structure of the department based on the hypothesis that the department might be more effectively organized in three sections: goods inwards, stores and goods outwards. Beyond that, she envisaged the introduction of automated movement of red-coded loads.

Behavioural risks

Ciara also reported on the behavioural risks concerned with performance. Observing indications of duelling between Eric and Ted, she formed the assessment that the critical risks concerned lack of coherent management strategies and indecision on Ted's part which threatened consistent implementation of Eric's plans for change.

She framed proposals for change on the hypothesis that an optimal method of facilitating change might lie in enlarging Ted's role in ways that could enhance the success factors inherent in his perceived strengths, namely his confidence about face-to-face communication and his acceptance by his team. In appreciation of Ted's apparent rapport with section heads she advocated the development of a coaching responsibility for the logistics manager. Ciara also recommended that a safety management role should be introduced and that it could be split amongst the redesigned section leader roles. She explained how these changes would probably require some investment in coaching, so that all the employees in enlarged roles felt able to engage pro-actively with uncertainties they were apt to face.

She recommended an economic study, in consultation with the trade union, on anticipated costs and benefits of the changes proposed, with the indication that restructuring of the department might be financed through arrangements that would involve redundancies.

The outcome

During the discussion, Ciara was pleased to see that Ted was much less wedded to the status quo than she had supposed. In fact, she discovered that the questions she had raised related to structures imposed under pressure from senior sales managers; as they had subsequently left, they were not in a position to oppose their dissolution. There would be costs involved in improving safety standards to match those of 'world-class' facilities, which would be offset by reorganization, leaving some positions redundant. This would have to be negotiated in detail with the trade union.

Ted's main concern arose about the proposed enlargement of his own role, which he recognized was unavoidable if the changes were to succeed. 'So, the change in goods inwards simply means rollers and conveyors, then?' he said. And he added, 'I'm going to need coaching myself before I can coach the section leaders, especially about safety matters.'

Before the meeting ended, Ted and Ciara organized their notes into two clusters like this:

The earlier situation

- Complaints by goods inwards staff about musculo-skeletal disorders and stress were not recorded in the company accident book.
- There was a lack of regard for repeated expressions of frustration by goods inwards staff.
- Eric's vision of 'world-class facilities' was not linked to Ted's communications with staff in the logistics department.
- There were five sections in the logistics department.
- No systematic planning was apparent in the logistics department.
- Attention to employee health and safety was haphazard.
- Boredom appeared to be the only thing staff shared with management.

Looking ahead

- Sources of risks of musculo-skeletal disorders and stress were agreed in principle.
- Key points of a phased ergonomic plan for controlling safety and health were agreed.
- A feasibility plan for automation for the goods inward section was to be developed, which would include the possibilities of automating 70% to 75% of incoming goods and of reducing the number of sections in the logistics department from five to three.
- The feasibility plan for automation, including possible redundancies, was to be tabled for negotiation with the union.
- Section heads were to receive training in management of health and safety.
- The company accident book would be used to record information about incidents of musculo-skeletal disorders and related levels of absence.
- A brief survey would be used to monitor levels of occupational stress and related levels of absence, every quarter.
- A statistical model would be introduced with Ciara's help to explore links between absence, linked with levels of stress and musculo-skeletal problems, and categories of management behaviour and organizational change.

- After 18 months, an audit would be carried out, with trade union support about management of stress, musculo-skeletal problems, slips, trips and falls.
- The logistics manager would receive training and development in performance coaching.

As they read through these summary notes, Ted remarked, 'It's quite a relief, really. I no longer feel so bogged down now!'.

Engaging with risks at work

Risk, according to Rosa (1998), is 'a situation or event in which something of human value (including humans themselves) has been put at stake and where the outcome is uncertain'. In the story involving Ciara, the 'something of human value' embraces the business vision of the board being advanced by Eric, the quality of work performance of employees at all levels and their safety and health.

Rosa's view incorporates the statistical concept of risk, namely the probability of an occurrence or event multiplied by the value of the outcome of that event. It also reflects the fact that uncertain environments at work may include physical settings, human artefacts and human behaviour.

Business health psychologists can help with the following classes of pure risks:

- occupational stress;
- harassment and indignity;
- musculo-skeletal disorders;
- voice problems;
- slips, trips and falls;
- substance misuse;
- workplace violence;
- occupational driving and road safety;
- safety at public events;
- fire prevention and response management.

As a business health psychologist, Ciara can contribute to the calibration and management of pure risks associated with behaviour at work and to improving an employer's system for managing these risks. She can help to identify and assess the areas of risk listed above; she can provide the tools and guidance managers need to weigh up the level of resources required to manage the risks posed by each of these hazards in their situation. This level depends on the estimated likelihood of injury, illness or other kind of loss, on the one hand, and on the severity of harm anticipated should an incident occur, on the other. She guides managers in their choices and decisions regarding the extent to which they protect employees from injury, illness or death.

In practice, to influence managers and other employees about protection from physical and psychological risks requires one to understand the hazards well enough to control the level of risks through training and other kinds of intervention. So, a business health psychologist's interventions are most convincing where they help management to carry out well-informed evaluations of the balance between economic costs and benefits associated with risks of injury and illness related to work. Most experienced health/safety practitioners, who are also competent in ergonomics and relevant law, may be able to do a good job assessing some of the classes of risk listed above and offering guidance on their management, including cost analyses. What the business health psychologist is comparatively well equipped to do is to help in sensitive situations, such as that illustrated with Ciara. Here what makes a difference in how managers and staff behave may often not be clearly specified in the brief to a consultant. Indeed, shortcomings in management of employee health and safety may not be something that managers feel sufficiently knowledgeable about, or comfortable with, to put into words at the start.

Influencing management with regard to risks of stagnation and underperformance

Business risks invariably involve some underperformance and these areas of risk to the business are listed below:

* lack of coherent management strategies;
* apparent management indecision;
* inconsistent implementation of plans for change;
* rifts between managers or within a team;
* lack of employee 'buy in' to management thinking;
* recurrent failure to deliver as anticipated;
* loss of valued staff;
* relative lack of quality of customer service;
* recurrent difficulties with implementing service and product innovation;
* recurrent failures in IT systems;
* access and inclusion of people with disabilities;
* indirect and direct discrimination, which is not fair and legal.

The business health psychologist can also help to identify and assess these performance risks and offer guidance in addressing them.

To contribute to successful performance management, the business health psychologist guides managers in their choices and decisions about enabling employees in the domain of successful performance in organizational life. Ciara, for example, did not simply advocate an ergonomic plan and automation to control risks to employee safety and health, but also suggested role changes and competency development for Ted and the section heads, to contribute to business gains. In this sense, the psychologist also intervenes in the domain of employee development.

The approach to managing risks associated with employee development and performance effectively depends on the likelihood of estimated levels of gain or loss and on the scale of the impact. Where possible, the psychologist will guide managers to enhance the possibility of employee empowerment and to reduce the prospect of stifling employees. Business health psychologists are particularly well equipped to help in sensitive situations, such as those in which managers lack confidence about their assessment of the root difficulties or are in persistent disagreement about them, where cultural habit limits perceptions about critical realities, or where painful past experiences cloud judgement and thereby inhibit necessary risk taking. This can be challenging as well as stimulating. If psychologists are asked to contribute in an organization where an employer displays to them the same lack of regard that he does to employees, they face the challenge of not losing their balance while making sense of the situation (Garratt, 2003).

Working within mainstream traditions of psychological interventions

Although the work of Ciara outlined above was on a relatively small scale, her interventions illustrate how a business health psychologist can operate within the three mainstream traditions of psychology, noted in Figure 29.1.

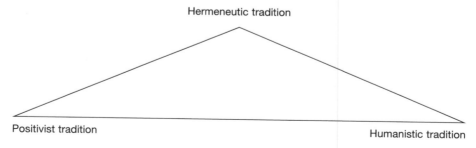

Figure 29.1 Mainstream traditions of psychological interventions.

Hermeneutic tradition

Whatever the approach management adopt to employee health, safety and development, their actions and communications construct a story that creates opportunities and sets limits for employees (Allan et al., 2002). The character of the strategy they adopt gives direction and indicates priorities at the same time as they pass on management interpretations of how failures, accidents, errors and even violations (Reason, 1990) present opportunities for learning. In this case study, part of the 'look ahead' included not only the introduction of automation and restructuring of the logistics department, but also different use of the accident book and the innovation of auditing the management of stress and musculo-skeletal disorders (Duignan, 2004). From the perspective of the evolution of psychology, this lies in the 'hermeneutic' tradition of the discipline, whose grandfather was Sigmund Freud (Stevens, 1983; Kelly, 1992; Weick, 1995; Stevens, 1998; Garden, 2000; Cziksentmihalyi, 2003).

The choice of the organization's storyline is largely determined by senior management. It may be about a change of business strategy, about resilience under pressure or about relationships at work. In Ciara's case study, the storyline framework was introduced by the board but Ted was not aligned to it. As she wrote her report, and during the meeting when it was discussed, this gap was something Ciara had to address very sensitively.

How might she have influenced a shift in thinking of Ted, the logistics manager? One way could well have been to draw on personal construct psychology (Dalton and Dunnette, 1992; Kelly, 1992), which is explicitly grounded on a fundamental postulate that people channel their attention, energy and other psychological processes according to stories that they construct to anticipate and steer events. In contrast with the emerging story of company commitment to 'world-class facilities', Ted's dominant story appeared to emphasize a mix of amiability, inertia and concentration on demands of the moment. Ciara's approach to the apparent gap in management stories reflected an important emphasis of personal construct psychology, namely on 'commonality' – that is to say, themes or values shared in common by different people. In facilitating the reframing of Ted's story so that it was aligned to that of the board, Ciara emphasized the shared values to the extent that Ted acknowledged the relief he felt as he adjusted to the changing demands on him; in an environment where it is necessary to reconcile shifts in management thinking with trade union expectations, bridge-building by a business health psychologist may save an enormous amount of management time and defuse unproductive conflict.

Positivist tradition

As a psychologist contributes to the story of business health, she may dwell on technicalities required for adjustments to situations or to people, such as changes in equipment, furniture and procedures that Ciara recommended to reduce the hazards associated with musculo-skeletal disorders.

In this way, she draws on the positivist scientific tradition that has found applications in the fields of safety, health, curative development and personal development (Krause et al., 1990; McSween, 1995; Smith Benjamin, 1996; Sutherland et al., 2000; Snyder and Lopez, 2002), and whose grandfather was Ivan Pavlov, the Russian laboratory scientist who uncovered laws of behaviour through experiments with animals. Working in this vein, the business health psychologist needs to be able to interweave psychological understanding with a good working knowledge of ergonomics (Pheasant, 1991; Oborne, 1995; Kroemer and Grandjean, 1997) as well as relevant law (Kloss, 1998; Earnshaw and Cooper, 2001; Firth and Nickson, 2002) and sufficient grasp of statistical methods to test models used in interventions should clients wish for such rigour.

A wise business health psychologist tends to apply positivistic approaches with awareness of how others interpret such interventions, avoiding impressions of mechanistic control in so far as possible through thoughtful communication at all times. Ciara's proposal to automate 70% to 75% of the flow of goods through the goods inwards section of the department included much more than improvements to the knives, seats and desks of check-in control staff. Her approach reflects the creative coordinations of a psychologist who undertakes observation-based consultation (Garden, 2000), in her efforts to contribute to the 'flywheel effect' that Eric remarked on – where a flywheel takes a long time to gather momentum but eventually achieves a breakthrough into a holistically energizing culture (Collins, 2001). This very painstaking approach is usually greatly appreciated where it is practised.

Humanistic tradition

Too often stories of intervention in the field of health and safety at work are limited in scope to *ad hoc* adjustments, which appear to be legalistic afterthoughts, if not mere cover-ups for past employer neglect, and show no regard for the human relationships intimately involved in effective working. Where management invests the time and thought to coordinate attention to employee health and safety with care for human relationships, business strategy is enriched. In such situations, an employer needs guidance on insight into the behaviour, thinking, values and feelings of managers and other employees.

The business health psychologist's most valuable contribution can be to stimulate and support the gradual emergence of alternative organizational stories of sustainable success. They do so in two ways. One is through facilitating the development of reality-centred conversations about the safe, healthy implementation of these stories or directing attention to indications of underperformance, illness or injury (Meineger, 1973; James, 1975; Herman and Korenich, 1977; Jongeward and Seyer, 1978; Nevis, 1987; Merry and Brown, 1987; Dalton and Dunnette, 1992; Kelly, 1992). Acting in this sphere, they take part in a humanistic phenomenological tradition, whose psychological grandfather was the Austrian Jakob Moreno, best known for his innovations in psychodrama, who directed attention to the value of the experience of every person who participates in any social or organizational process.

The other way is also often influenced by the humanistic tradition; as Clarkson and Shaw (1995) explain, fruitful consulting interventions require the consultant to engage at several levels of a working relationship. This was apparent from the levels of Ciara's working relationship with Ted. Even in a relatively brief set of interactions, Ciara indicated two levels of relationships. One was a task-centred alliance focusing on the results the company expected of her and Ted; the other concerned Ted's distinctive pattern of strengths. This other level of relationship management involved generating sufficient trust with Ted and his section leaders to enable them to converse candidly and constructively, in a context where they started with the uncontested view that 'boredom' was the only thing management and staff shared.

The humanistic tradition of psychological interventions actually interweaves with the other two traditions. Its commitment to promoting and supporting relationships marked by mutual understanding and trust facilitates skilful work in either of the other two traditions. It is more appropriate, really, to regard these three traditions less in terms of contrast than in terms of the interacting forces represented by sides of a triangle, as in Figure 29.1.

Business health psychologists work in the same physical and cultural environment as their clients. What they offer is distinctive by virtue of their observations along with the methods and tools they use for gathering data and communicating them. They may conduct risk assessments and research through survey methods, audits, statistical modelling, repertory grids and other quantitative tools. However, their more distinctive contributions come from a relative emphasis on qualitative tools of intervention and through facilitating managers to enrich their decision making by integrating understanding of human behaviour, motives and emotions with data from diverse other disciplines, especially through conversations (Kegan and Laskow Lahey, 2001).

CHAPTER 30

Psychological principles and the online evaluation environment

JOANNE SHARE-BERNIA

The phenomenal growth of the World Wide Web and its application is having an enormous impact upon all aspects of business. This trend, and the importance of using the Internet as a business tool, has made it necessary for business psychologists to ask the question: how can psychological principles be applied to this medium to add further value to its already enormous capability?

Having a website alone is not enough. Making pages self-evident is like having good lighting in a store; it just makes everything seem better. Using a site that doesn't make us think about unimportant things feels effortless, whereas puzzling over things that don't matter to us tends to sap our energy, enthusiasm and time. This acts against the medium's potential.

So how must we really use the web? When we examine this, we find that it is important to make a person *not* think about how they are using it. This is fundamental to the successful application of psychology to improve a website's performance. Currently, most people are likely to spend much less time looking at the designed web pages and considering their content than we would want or like.

Research evidence for achieving maximum usability in system design is growing. The evidence exists in several professional domains of psychology, human factors and ergonomics, physiology, management science and computer science.

Using these concepts, and the value inherent within them, as a reference can help us when undertaking specific contract assignments. They can serve as a starting point in developmental discussions and dialogue on usability. Moreover, combining evidence with ideas from those professionals actually undertaking the design can bring together an overall richer source of information that can be applied to the business issue in question.

Webdesigners and usability professionals have spent a lot of time over the years debating how many times you can expect users to click to get what they want without them getting too frustrated. Psychology and its application commercially has particular relevance to resolving this question.

Design rules generally state that it should never take any more than a specified number of clicks – three, four or five – to get to any page in the site. However, what really matters is how 'hard' each click is; that is, how much thought is required and the amount of uncertainty that is involved about making the right choice. A 'rule of thumb' might be 'three mindless, unambiguous clicks equals one click that requires thought'. So, how can webdesigners improve an application's effectiveness?

When undertaking Internet or intranet design, it needs to be borne in mind that the user will be outcome orientated. For example, any design seeking to sell should incorporate aspects of emotion such as trust to engage customers and stimulate their motivation to buy.

From a purely psychological perspective, there are certain facets that can greatly improve the attractiveness of a website, increase business success and which show how applying psychology can add real value to business in an online environment.

Cognitive load and interactivity

Cognitive load refers to the use or handling of knowledge, how individuals neurally process and code signals from the eye and then subsequently draw subtle analogies, explanations and pictures from the environment.

Interactivity is achieved by ensuring that the system can perform an interaction with the user that is similar to having a conversation, playing a game of tennis, dancing a salsa or dressing a child. That is, having a set of reciprocal acts that require cooperation and where the system and user must coordinate their activities.

There is a huge amount of research evidence, from attention theory to memory, neural networks and colour perception, which is applicable to systems design.

Relevant points to consider in the webdesign process are linked to left- or right-brain hemisphere functioning and the selective attention that human beings exercise in the preparation, exploration and maintenance of their environments. Laboratory observations here have concentrated on how interfaces can be reshaped to make environments (including the web) more cognitively congenial.

Usability is a central concern. Users will lose interest in a system where they experience excessive cognitive load. Users do not read pages, they scan them and excessive cognitive load occurs when there is too much information on any one page or screen. However, interactivity between the human and computer becomes closer and more intense when time delay decreases between any action–reaction–action.

There are some key design issues that should therefore be taken into account to reduce cognitive overload.

Key design points

- Ensure that any actions that need to be taken are clearly visible to the user.
- Allow users to discover what they want to do rather than do what they want to do. It is important to remember that users do not always have their goals fully formulated.
- Reducing the number of options at any one point to a maximum of seven.
- Avoid overuse of buttons and menus as these can result in the loss of engagement and cause the user to rush through a page.
- Consider that users have multiple levels of cognitive coding styles. It is important, therefore, to appreciate and understand that the population for whom a system is being designed will vary in terms of its ability to use it.
- A system should encourage users to externalize their thinking – for example, by the use of text annotations. This will allow them to be creative and engage with the system.
- Options that are unlikely to be needed by most users should be either hidden or have a lower profile to negate unnecessary investigation.
- Provide strong visual cues to aid navigation.
- Reduce the number of links to other sites.
- Break informational elements into manageable chunks (via separate screens) through which the user can navigate, thus reducing complexity and allowing them to more easily form a functional mental model of both the task and the task environment.

The function of emotion

'We don't figure out how things work. We muddle through.'

Emotion can play a critical part in behaviour. Studies indicate that the various types of feelings all influence judgement and decision making in a similar manner. Examples include:

- *Trust*. An important emotion in the domain of human–computer interaction is the feeling of trust that a user places in the system, as trust has a significant impact on the way people use a computer system. If individuals do not trust a decision, they might either reject it or manipulate it. Essentially any interaction must cause the user to stop thinking and, instead, to engage fully, so that time and consciousness disappear. This maximizes interactivity because the user then trusts the system.

- *Informative feelings*. One study in e-commerce research (Kirsh, 1997) showed that the feelings induced by customer interfaces can enhance the quality of the customers' experience by triggering informative emotions that can aid decision making. Atkinson and Kydd (1997) found that if users enjoy an activity, they would be more motivated to use it either for pure pleasure or for a particular purpose.
- *Universal emotions*. Research evidence has found that films have a high degree of ecological validity insofar as emotions are often evoked by dynamic visual and auditory stimuli designed to engage the user directly in the interaction. Accordingly, human–computer interfaces also have the potential to elicit universally common emotions in their users, justifying the attempt to design the customer interface to elicit certain target emotions.

Key design points

As a consequence of these factors, it would be beneficial for any designer to do the following:

- Carefully consider any delays users will experience as they view the web, for example, reduce downloads to essentials only and within finite time scales.
- Ensure that graphics are expected and accepted by users only if delays are relatively short. Remember, however, that text-only web interfaces are likely to be disappointing.
- If delays become longer, users will prefer functionality over aesthetics and may prefer just plain text. If a user experiences a negative perception of the site, they will blame the graphics for the delay.
- Research by Ramsay, Barabesi and Preece (1998) shows that subjects' perception of the quality of site information is significantly influenced by site presentation and the minimizing of download delay length.

Engagement and functionality

Depending on how 'expert' a user is, any site should allow for exploration and browsing to give users a high level of control over their experience. The rationale here is to allow for different user knowledge levels. When purchasing online, for example, experts will want to browse and have more control over some areas. Requiring less expert customers to browse

extensively will result in anxiety and a possible reluctance in decision making or closing a sale. Browsing can also take inordinate amounts of time.

There are other factors that can create motivation for web users and, if
included in the design, can enhance a website's performance:

- The added value attached to completion of a sale – for example, a gift;
  air miles; database benefits.
- Catering for the multiple levels of cognitive coding of the various users
  of the site, for example:

  - experienced/inexperienced;
  - elderly/young/middle aged;
  - male/female;
  - ethnicity;
  - at work or at home.

- Enabling the user to be active in the buying process – the more interactions between user and the task, the better, taking into account the
  design points above.
- The need for an appropriate level of mismatch between what users
  know and what the interface and task require, so that users can use
  their own creativity whilst feeling and remaining in control.

Key design points

There are, therefore, some basic rules of engagement:

- All 'happy talk' must go.
- Instructions must go.
- Reduce the 'noise' level of the page by omitting redundant words.
- Create prominent and useful content.
- Make the pages shorter, allowing users to see more of each page at a
  glance without scrolling.

User control and navigation

Given that users 'muddle through', rather than structuring where they
want to go, a challenge is to place enough scaffolding in the web environment to guide learners in useful directions and to satisfy the principle
of visibility. It is essential therefore to ensure that:

- Users are able to see the actions that are open to them at every point
  of choice or selection.
- They receive immediate feedback about any actions they have just

instigated and taken – few things upset computer and web users more than not knowing what the computer is doing or when it seems to be churning unexpectedly.
- They receive timely and insightful information about the consequences of their actions.

User control involves those aspects of interface and instructional design that provide users with the functions that enable them to choose:

- the nature of the feedback they receive;
- the navigation paths through content;
- the content to be engaged in;
- the pace of that engagement.

Key design points

- A major 'stress factor' is system response time; therefore make sure that any response time is no more than 6 seconds.
- Spell out the big picture on the home page.
- Use a good tagline that is personable, lively and clever, next to the site ID.
- Use as much space as is necessary, but not more.

Play, motivation and engagement

Psychologically, playing has been described as 'flow' activity where total immersion takes place, self-consciousness and time disappear and the experience is so gratifying that the individual will undertake it for its own sake.

Research in laboratories and universities into webdesign has shown that to engage the customer effectively in the buying process the notion of *play* should be an inherent part of any design to some extent.

Research by Atkinson and Kydd (1997) tested playful activities embedded in the design process. They showed that notions of fun and enjoyment in using a system result in satisfying intrinsic and extrinsic human motivations. Extrinsic motivation refers to performance of an activity because it is believed to be instrumental in achieving valued outcomes, whereas intrinsic motivation is the inner enjoyment of an activity for its own sake.

Finally, Atkinson and Kydd (1997) posited that, whereas people with introverted personalities would not exhibit playfulness in person when with others, the web engages and taps into their playful nature. This emphasizes the importance of the play factor in webdesign.

Key design points

- Research evidence shows that the characteristic of playfulness is positively correlated with web use. Play should therefore be incorporated.
- Intrinsic motivators such as animation, colour and screen balance, which have elements of fun and enjoyment and enhance ease of use, are powerful facets of webdesign and use.
- Designers should consider extrinsic motivators when undertaking intranet/Internet designs. Outcome-oriented users will seek information that is linked and instrumental to their job or position at work.
- Evidence suggests that games, quizzes, immediate feedback and familiarity will attract users browsing the web even though they may have no particular outcome in mind.

Visual design factors

Visually there are a number of elements that are affected by psychological considerations and that can be exploited in the design process to take account of how human beings like and respond to symmetry. Generally, the more important something is, the more prominently it should be placed on the screen.

- *Creating a clear visual hierarchy*. In one research study (Dos Santos and De Moraes, 1996), subjects were shown 26 interfaces and then asked to draw those that they could remember. These free recall tests were done at random intervals. Subjects were then expected to remember the features they had paid most attention to, either consciously or subconsciously, in judging the intensity of feelings elicited by a particular interface. Results showed that only some of the main features were remembered, that drawings were symmetrical and that any needless objects in the screen design were not remembered.
- *Colour layout* is important in enhancing the emotion of trustworthiness when using a system. Research (Kim, Moon and Yonsei, 1998) has shown that the preferable tone of colour for the interface should be cool rather than warm and that its main colour should be a moderate pastel colour. At the same time the colours used in an interface should be of low brightness and used symmetrically because, neurologically, we are attracted to symmetry. An interface that has a bright colour background and uses an asymmetrical colour scheme will induce a feeling of untrustworthiness.
- *Balance*. The same study examined the balance on screen, or symmetry. Evidence here suggested that the users engage more effectively when the objects on screen are distributed symmetrically. Other

research by Tannen (1991), into left-brain hemisphere laterality shows that, biologically, we want to view objects symmetrically and logically. People do not read pages; they scan them. Reports from subjects who viewed different styles of layout showed preferences for symmetry in screen design.

Key design points

- Ensure that the most important headings are either larger, bolder, in a distinctive colour, offset by more white space, or nearer the top of the page – or some combination of the above.
- Information that is related logically should also be related visually. Information can be shown to be similar by grouping it together under a heading, displaying it in a similar style, or putting it all within a clearly defined area.
- Break up pages into clearly defined areas to make apparent what is 'clickable' to instigate further action.
- Use balanced figures, toolbars, colours in screen design to make the screen symmetrical – do on one side what you do on the other.
- Use pastel colours to ensure that the brightness of colour is not too vivid.
- Do not overuse animation.
- Have a home button in sight at all times to offer reassurance that, no matter how lost users may get, they can always begin again.

Text and language

Research by Tannen (1991) into conversational planning shows that one of the goals is to maintain utterance-by-utterance coherence – that is, seeing to it that the conversation is sustained by having a bearing on what the other has said.

A related and considerate communication style of using language therefore gives a greater ability to pick up non-verbal and emotional cues. Work by Deborah Tannen, a sociolinguist, into the effect of symmetry and asymmetry in language construction has shown that there are competitive and collaborative ways of building language. A competitive (asymmetrical) style involves a closed objective statement, whereas a collaborative style uses a more subjective statement that encourages/invites the listener to respond. The optimum linguistic repertoire is believed to be the subjective approach. For example, calling a person by his or her name or addressing the user with familiarity.

To achieve a motivating dialogue with consumers in a web setting means that using a collaborative style is important.

Key design points

- Use open questions such as those which begin with 'W' – 'Who?' 'What?' 'Where?' 'Why?' 'When?' 'How?' (an honorary 'W').
- Use metaphors to illustrate the topic.
- Understand the power of emotive words, such as the use of a person's first name.

Develop a customer journey

Creating a process through which a user can pass will maintain interest. For example, the close of sale process could take into account all of the preceding points. However, if coaching from a sales assistant and scaffolding to develop a formal process takes place, effectiveness increases. This contrasts with unstructured browsing, which for some users/buyers can decrease the motivation to buy. An example here is where use is by a less 'expert' individual.

It is important, therefore, that a web journey is pitched at the ability level of the user to make it emotionally and viscerally appealing. To do this the site should be based on a theme that suits both the information being presented and users themselves – the culture/s of any buyers, for example. Pertinent points here are:

- Who are the buyers?
- What are the features of the established and existing customers?
- Who else do we want to come on board?

Any identified theme should have a real-life context. This allows for the application of psychological theory to a variety of actual situations. Customers then use the situation context to maximize usability and/or buying behaviour and remember their experience for future business activity.

Key design points

- Replicate a real-life context; for example, a store or the bank in a buying process.
- Research typical user characteristics and demographics, bear these in mind, and incorporate them, when carrying out design.
- Be mindful of designing for cross-cultural users and the use of appropriate language.
- Take a strategic approach to web development. Ensure that your product fits within the organization's strategy and future vision.

The decision cycle model

As well as psychological investigations into usability, scientific investigations into interactivity (including web-based interactivity) are in the early stages of developing a theoretical model. The received theory in human–computer interaction – the decision cycle model – is based on a sense of interactivity that cognitive engineers have in mind when they say that an interface is 'interactive'. It falls somewhere between the social sense and the agent and its environment. The process is interactive because the environment reacts to users' actions and, if well designed, leads them into repeatedly looping through the decision sequence in a manner that tends to be successful. As the environment is made more responsive to the cognitive needs of any user, it moves towards a more social sense of interaction.

Don Norman, a management guru, has proposed a decision cycle model that uses a seven-stage process. The stages are:

1. Form a goal – the environmental state that is to be achieved.
2. Translate the goal into an intention to do some specific action that ought to achieve the goal.
3. Translate the intention into a more detailed set of commands – a plan for manipulating the interface.
4. Execute the plan.
5. Perceive the state of the interface.
6. Interpret the perception in light of the expectations.
7. Evaluate or compare the results to the intentions and goal.

Accordingly, any interaction is seen to be analogous to a model-driven feedback system; a user would have a mental model of the environment and so formulate a plan internally.

This makes visibility very important in the design of any interface and the decision cycle model has been invaluable in reminding interface designers that immediate feedback via visibility is essential.

However, it is an incomplete theory. One central idea is missing in the model: the notion that goals are often not fully formed in the user's mind. There is an interactive discovery characteristic in how we engage with environments; we are contributing architects to our own environments as we go along. As described previously (in design implications to reduce cognitive load), users like to discover what they want to do and to feel involved.

Conclusions: benefits of best practice

Adopting and incorporating best psychological practice brings several benefits to designers and to the performance of web-based products. The main considerations for designers are:

- Understand and consider the psychological aspects of design and assist in the formulation of cutting-edge web developments so as to inform strategic direction.
- Follow the principles of usability by incorporating psychological principles that make design easier as well as more effective.
- Work more creatively by bringing design teams together to present their ideas and how they can integrate psychological principles. Enhanced communication and motivation is an added benefit to design teams who normally spend a great deal of time working independently.
- Last but not least, good design ensures the users' ease of use – through enjoyment of using the product – which can only have a positive effect on the bottom line by bringing in business and securing repeat business. Implementing psychology principles and incorporating them into the design process can only enhance this outcome!

PART 6
ORGANIZATIONAL CHANGE

CHAPTER 31

Introduction

PAULINE GRANT

Only the brave, and perhaps those lacking in imagination, venture into the field of large-scale organizational change. Here we move into chaos, where key players move on just when we relied on them to champion the next stage, where groups experience a crisis of confidence from time to time, where priorities shift, the share price drops, and where people don't always do what we expected them to do. By all means, take comfort from a linear multi-stage process that seems to chart a path from where we are to where we want to be, but don't rely on it being the path that will actually be followed!

'The most exasperating thing about big corporations in crisis is that they got there by doing what once made them big.' This observation by Roger Martin in 1998 is as true now as it was then. Carrying on as before can be a risky choice, as high street retailers like Marks & Spencer have discovered to their cost. Emotional investment and genuine confidence in the way things have traditionally been done can be potent forces for achieving great performance but there is a thin, almost invisible line between that and blind faith, complacency and over-optimistic projections.

Of course, whilst a crisis is sometimes the driver for change, more frequently we notice change to align a company with a new strategy, to respond to market developments, to take opportunities offered by new technologies or cheaper resources, to counter competitive threats or to embrace the philosophy espoused by the new CEO. This presents challenges in itself, for although most people will eventually see a burning platform and accept the need to do something about it, when things seem to be going smoothly people tire of yet another change.

> We tried hard – but it seemed that every time we were beginning to form up into teams, we would be reorganised. I was to learn later in life that we tend to meet any new situation by reorganising, and a wonderful method it can be for creating the illusion of progress while producing confusion, inefficiency and demoralisation.

This familiar tale (strangely, but wrongly, attributed to Petronius two millennia ago) is a poignant reminder that change initiatives can sap the motivation of people who would otherwise be committed, hardworking and perhaps imaginative employees.

Enter the business psychologists, who in some ways are taking over from the business process re-engineers as the consultants of choice in times of change, although, as Drew notes, they are not always welcomed wearing a psychology hat. A growing minority of business psychologists operates in this field; for them, the possibility of making a difference to multiple lives, even whole communities, is a compelling attraction. However, to gain credibility in this area of work and give clients confidence that we can help them through their change journey can be, and probably should be, a challenge. Nevertheless, business process re-engineering left some organizations cynical about costly interventions that made them dependent on external agents to effect the required changes, and failed to deliver the hoped-for benefits. They are therefore more appreciative of approaches that target and work with the people who will be the change designers, drivers, champions, implementers and adjusters – in other words, the employees who will make it work rather than watch and see if it works. It is this orientation towards respecting employees' contribution throughout the process that characterizes contemporary thinking.

Thompson begins with a history of organizations as we know them and the development of research in that environment. He provides a quick jog through the social and academic roots of current thinking about 'change' and thereby sets the scene for the later chapters. Throughout, he draws attention to some of the major studies over the years that provide the platform for contemporary practice. Brewerton then describes an approach to culture analysis and diagnosis that takes us to the point of reporting on required change. He warns, though, that a consultant who backs out after delivering such a report is leaving an unfinished job.

Drew's chapter offers the theoretical and philosophical background to his approach to change, and provides a detailed case study illustrating the approach in practice. Although an 'underground' psychologist, it is clear from his account that a deep understanding of people is a key ingredient to his methodology. Storey's case study invites us to look more specifically at the role of the psychologist and she concentrates attention at the implementation end. Not surprisingly, like Brewerton, she emphasizes the importance of communication and engagement.

Finally, Plenty takes us on a journey through the history of thinking about change in practice, showing how these models have developed. Indeed, he speculates as to whether change itself is changing, which relates directly to the importance of learning as an organizational coping mechanism. He draws on diverse disciplines, as well as being informed by social and economic development. He gives insight into the difficulties with some more traditional paradigms, particularly where change is seen as an event. This leads him to thinking more holistically about organizational interventions. His short case examples show how two different interventions and paradigms have played out.

The contributors to this section have in common an emphasis on what employees feel about change, why they might resist it and what can be done about it. This section is rich in practical experience. It steers us to learn from the past by gaining awareness of what has informed current thinking, and it encourages us to have the humility to recognize that change interventions are learning experiences for consultants too.

focus on: what employees FEEL @ Δ;
WHY might they resist it?
WHAT can be done

CHAPTER 32

Organizational change – an historical overview

David Thompson

Early organizations

It was really the industrial revolution in Britain that gave birth to employing organizations as we now know them. Most of the early entrepreneurs were associated with small businesses, which were handed down from one generation to the next as if they were landed estates. The latter part of the nineteenth century and the early twentieth century saw the rise of large organizational structures; for example, William Lever's small soap enterprise led him to the jungles of west Africa and his successors joined hands with the Dutch in the huge Unilever concern of 1929, the first great European multinational. Germany and the US went through their own industrial revolutions and came to challenge Britain, yet in 1913 Britain still accounted for a quarter of the world's trade in manufactured goods (Briggs, 1983). This period also saw the rise of trade unionism and collective bargaining. There was a heated debate about Britain's relative decline. Some blamed management, others blamed the inflexibility of the unions and a failure to adopt 'American manufacturing practices'. The seeds were thus sown for what has become a continuing debate about the challenges associated with organizational change.

'Organizations' become a subject for study

It was not until after the Second World War that social scientists began to study organizations. The first seminal work was by Elliot Jaques (1951), published as *The Changing Culture of a Factory*, in which he commented upon the changing roles and relationships within the Glacier Metal Company. This created considerable controversy at the time and stimulated new ways of thinking about organizations. Perhaps better known, though, is the study by Trist and Bamforth (1951) on the coal mining industry – also sponsored by the Tavistock Institute and still quoted in

MBA courses today. It was from this study that two key concepts emerged: that of the organization as an open socio-technical system, and the idea of adaptive work organizations. These had a significant impact on what developed in the 1960s as organizational psychology. During the 1960s, Britain developed worldwide pre-eminence in the academic study of organizations with notable contributions from sociologists such as Woodward (1965) and Burns and Stalker (1961). In America there was little interest in 'theory' but an increasing interest in the practice of 'planned organizational change', which gave rise to the term 'organizational development' (OD) (Bennis, Benne and Chin, 1969).

More recent organizational agendas and interventions

During the1970s, Britain had an appalling record for working days lost through both official and unofficial industrial action and it became known as the 'sick man of Europe'. Setting aside disputes about pay, the majority of these disputes had at their heart opposition to change. Britain is now much less strike prone. In fact, since the mid-1990s it has had only half of the days lost of other OECD countries. Most commentators put the change down to the dramatic decline in union membership, caused by the structural changes in the economy – essentially a reduction in large employing organizations in the UK. The decades from the 1970s to the 1990s were characterized by massive organizational downsizing. It was against this broad canvas of activism by organized labour and changes in the economy in the late twentieth century that theorists studied organizations. Business psychologists along with other organizational development practitioners attempted to support business managers with the effective implementation of organizational change.

The 1980s saw the rise in interest in the concept of employee stress and the development of stress management interventions aimed at the individual. Many of the courses on offer were designed to help people cope with organizational stressors such as role conflict, role ambiguity and organizational change. The critics of this at the time (see Murphy, 1984) pointed to the need to focus more on prevention than remediation, by developing a better understanding of the causes of stress, often created by poor organizational design or change processes. The 1980s also saw the rise in acquisitions and mergers and of the multinational company, and with it an associated interest in how people of different nationalities behave in organizations. Some such companies succeeded, but others did not, this most frequently being attributed to failures to integrate either different organizational cultures or national cultural groups.

Peter Senge made a major contribution to our thinking about organizations in the 1990s with the notion of the learning organization. He argued that organizations should be helping their people to embrace change rather than just cope with it. He saw people in learning organizations reacting more quickly to change because they were anticipating change and also creating their own change, as they knew what change they wanted. Senge's *Fifth Discipline Fieldbook* (1994) brimmed over with practical suggestions for how OD specialists and managers could marry individual personal development and economic performance.

Bringing us up to date

At the beginning of the twenty-first century organizations were still downsizing in order to save cost and hence remain competitive, or as in the case of the public sector to provide value for money services. But the change agenda was, and still is, often bigger than this. It was about: redistributing internal resources, particularly to the front line; increasing levels of efficiency; refocusing upon customers; making managers more 'professional' or 'strategic'; increasing effectiveness by using technology more widely, and sharing services such as human resources or IT. Consequently, there was plenty of scope for well thought through OD interventions such as the ones described later in this section.

For some employees the process of change represents a violation of the personal psychological contract (see Herriot, 1992) that they have with their employer. Emotions invariably run high and employee behaviour can seem to be irrational when change is under way. Nor does the story end there. Those coming out the other side of significant change programmes often suffer from 'survivor syndrome' (see Konovsky and Brockner, 1993), which is typically characterized by lower levels of motivation and risk taking – just the opposite to the behaviours that the change programme could have been aiming to foster. Disconcertingly, those with the highest pre-existing levels of organizational commitment can be the ones most adversely affected by perceived injustices in how their co-workers are treated in a downsizing process (Brockner et al., 1992) and suffer considerable loss of motivation. It is therefore very clear that there is much that business psychologists can contribute to the change process, even at the simple level of assisting in reducing some of the negative impacts on the people affected.

The early 2000s saw the rise amongst employees of the search for meaning in their working lives (see Holbeche and Springett, 2004), with the fear amongst human resources professionals that those who feel that their work lacks meaning would be more difficult to manage during change, because of their cynicism. So the various challenges associated with change metamorphose and move on; for the future the increase in global competition is likely to figure significantly. The rest of Part 6 provides fascinating insights into attempts to wrestle with the challenges.

CHAPTER 33

Using culture and climate profiling to drive organizational change

PAUL BREWERTON

Introduction

As Blue Edge, a business psychology consultancy specializing in culture/climate profiling, organizational and executive development, we are often asked to present to company executives on the topic of organizational culture. The questions come thick and fast. Questions such as . . .

- How are we going to measure our culture?
- What is the link between culture and leadership in our organization?
- How do we link our brand values to our organization's culture?
- What is the relationship between culture and climate? Is there a difference?
- Does setting a culture only come from the top of our organization? What about our employees – don't they have a role?

For many executives, there is a fascination with organizational culture as something traditionally seen as ethereal, difficult to conceptualize, tie down and measure – but nonetheless something that they believe can give them a competitive advantage and can add real value to their bottom line. If only they could get a handle on what 'it' really is.

Of course, we meet just as many executives with a healthy scepticism about such ideas. Their questions are more likely to challenge directly the worth of culture and climate in large-scale organizational change and development:

- Surely, I'm better off spending my budget on something that's going to have an immediate impact on our profits?
- Isn't it just another fad?
- By asking the staff, aren't we just going to get a whole load of people letting off steam but not really know much more about the company at the end of it all?

300

- It sounds all well and good, but there must be more important things for us to focus on?

For these executives, the business case for addressing and assessing culture is hazy at best. Like their colleagues, they too see culture as '. . . difficult to nail to the wall' (Schneider, 1987). But they are also more inclined to see the concept as somewhat of a distraction from the task at hand, rather than as a potential long-term benefit.

As business psychologists, our role at this early stage is often to put forward an appropriate business case and to support management teams in deciding on the true value of culture for their own organization. If they decide that actively measuring, managing and changing their culture will be of use to them in the long term, our company will become more closely involved in shaping that process.

In this chapter, I would like to present a suggested process for applying organizational culture and climate measurement to organizational change programmes. I will include specific examples based on real consulting experience, as well as pointing out problems and pitfalls in the process, many of which are also drawn from experience.

Definitions

Before presenting an introductory model, I should put forward some working definitions of organizational culture and climate. For us, organizational culture is concerned with the *meaning* that people invest in organizations, organizational structures, memorable events, noteworthy people, processes and procedures. This 'meaning' provides a set of core beliefs or values each individual holds about their organization (for example, 'we are a young, dynamic company, encouraging innovation and new ideas', or 'our organization is structured and ordered – everyone knows what to do and when to do it'). When these beliefs and values become articulated and shared with other organizational members, culture begins to come alive. The fact remains that culture is often difficult for employees to articulate as it is concerned with deeply held assumptions, often based on a long-term relationship with their organization.

Organizational climate describes those aspects of organizational life, which are more tangible, observable and measurable both to organizational members and, partly, to outsiders such as customers and suppliers (including consultants!). In our experience, observing and assessing climate can take us part way towards an understanding of the culture of an organization. An open-plan workspace, for example, where people are encouraged to chat and converse, while surrounded by stimulating architecture and décor (all very observable features of an organization's *climate*) might suggest a culture that its employees believe promotes creativity, collaboration and innovation. Of course, this assumption may be inaccurate and we must go further in our assessment to gain a more comprehensive picture of culture. Climate, on the other hand, is more straightforward to see, hear and touch.

Interested readers are referred to Schein (1990), who takes a similar approach to that outlined above with his multilayered model of culture. Denise Rousseau (1995) builds on this conceptualization and her model is outlined in Figure 33.1. For me, the only real point of contention in defining culture and climate comes when trying to identify the point at which the crossover from the *psychological* nature of culture (values, beliefs, assumptions) to the *behavioural* and *observable* aspects of climate (work environment, organizational artefacts) takes place.

[handwritten margin note: Culture = Values, beliefs, assumptions. Climate: more tangible]

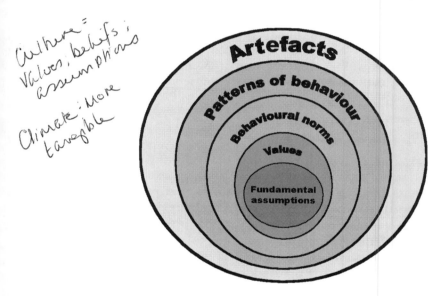

Figure 33.1 Adapted from Denise Rousseau's (1995) 'onion-skin' model of culture.

Our approach

Blue Edge's approach to culture/climate measurement and intervention is shown in the Gantt chart in Table 33.1. For each stage described, I will outline the primary purpose and activities taking place, drawing on real-world examples from time to time.

Month	1	2	3	4	5	6	7	8	9	10	11	12
1 Workshop with executive team	▲											
2 Agree blueprint of culture	—											
3 Agree assessment/intervention plan including method	----											
4 Roll out staff communications plan	·····-···											
5 Organise logistics; run assessment project			·····-··-··-···									
6 Interpretation, analysis and reporting						—						
7 Presentation and action planning						▲ ▲						
8 Taking action							·····-····-····-····			·····-····-		····
9 Monitor and measure							·····-····-····-····-····			·····-····-		····

Key
▲ Milestone
·-···- Part time activity
——— Full time activity

Table 33.1 Blue Edge's preferred approach to organizational culture/climate assessment and development

Workshop with executive team

Outputs

The consultant's goal at this stage may be simply to 'fact find' in order to decide on a subsequent course of action, for example:

- Is more research needed?
- Will further sessions be required with the management team?
- Is the organization actually ready for change?

Another important goal will be to build commitment to the need for cultural change. This may then be supported by submitting a business case or proposal outlining the key stages to follow.

Rationale and approach

There are various reasons for making initial contact with the organization's executive or management team:

- These people are principally responsible for creating and implementing the company's strategy and so will be best placed to assess the value of culture as regards their business strategy. They also wield the greatest power to make change happen.
- They will provide useful business context, to allow the consultant to more fully understand their existing culture and what cultural changes may be needed to help the organization achieve its strategic goals.
- The management team will need to understand right from the start of the project that engaging in any kind of diagnostic process, no matter how small scale, will raise employee expectations for something to

happen as a result. It is also important to point out the potential implications of cultural change programmes and how 'resource intensive'
these may be.

Depending on the nature of the audience and on the consultant's intentions at this stage, it may be appropriate to ask open questions of the
management team. This will allow the consultant to find out more about
specific issues currently facing the organization, glean information to construct a sound business case/proposal and help the consultant identify
advocates and sceptics within the management team. Questions for consideration might be:

- Where are you now as a business? What is the history of the business?
- What do you see as the greatest challenges facing you in implementing
  your corporate strategy?
- What metaphor(s) would others use to describe your organization?
- What do you feel differentiates your company's culture from the cul-
  ture of its competitors?
- What could your organization usefully learn from other companies'
  cultures that it doesn't have now?

With some clients, we have also run initial exploratory focus groups with
employees, to surface key issues and provide a focus for subsequent
research. This also sends out a clear message at the start of the process
that employees' views are important at all stages and will be heeded.

Pitfalls/obstacles

Perhaps most importantly, the consultant's message to the management
team needs to be clear and should focus on the pragmatic rather than the
academic, in order to build credibility around the important role of culture. Presenting a series of theoretical models may not be appropriate for
this audience and may undermine the message that culture has practical,
bottom-line implications.

Agree diagnostic model or blueprint of culture

Outputs

This will be a working model of culture against which the client organization can assess its current performance and benchmark aspirations for
the future.

Rationale and approach

This stage involves gaining agreement from the management team and other key stakeholders, such as human resources, for the model or 'blue-print' of culture that they wish to drive towards. This will guide the research methodology, the specification of any metrics to be used or designed, giving a focus for the entire programme, and is particularly helpful if it can be conceptualized in a neat and understandable way.

In our experience, flexibility is needed at this stage. The consultant will need to build on the data gathered at Stage 1, describing the culture to which the organization and management team aspires and stating why this is important.

Real-world examples

One of our clients was interested in growing and developing its culture to gain competitive advantage in its sector. By the time we were brought into the project, considerable work had already been done by the marketing team to rebrand and rebadge the organization. A senior manager had also conducted a brief piece of research around current perceptions of the organization's culture according to other senior managers. We were provided with a list of brand values, public relations /marketing materials and output from the survey of top managers' opinions about the business culture, and asked to formulate a cultural model based on these base data.

Another client had taken the decision to build a 'global' culture for its many businesses around the world. They had already run focus groups with senior executives describing what they saw as the future for the organization, what they thought of the current culture and what it meant to be a leader within the organization. We were provided with the summarized output from these focus groups and asked to support the culture team in developing a framework describing the organization's aspirational culture.

In both cases, we built substantive models of culture that used their data sources as a start point. We also drew on the output from discussions with other stakeholders and our knowledge of the culture/climate research field to 'flesh out' the framework and ensure its consistency with the company's business strategy while providing academic robustness.

Other clients have been keen to use existing models of culture and climate (such as our own Performance Culture Audit© model, linking culture and climate with individual attitudes/behaviours/performance – see Figure 33.2), which can provide them with a pre-existing framework for assessing/improving their own culture and corporate performance. In cases such as this, the management team can use the model to stimulate discussion and pinpoint areas of particular interest for the future of their organization.

Pitfalls/obstacles

The consultant needs to pitch these discussions appropriately so as to engage and enthuse as many of the executive team as possible. Some companies will favour pre-existing, off-the-shelf models; others will feel that a bottom-up, bespoke approach is needed truly to capture their vision for the future culture of their business; and many will require a hybrid approach, combining features from each. Our advice is to 'listen between the lines' to find out what the client is really looking for. Beware of taking a 'one-size-fits all' approach as this is seldom appropriate.

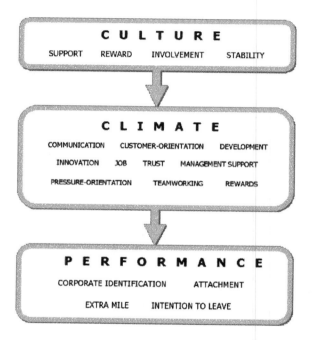

Figure 33.2 Blue Edge's Performance Culture Audit© model.

Agree assessment/intervention plan, including methodology and metrics

Outputs

Creation of a concrete project plan, to be agreed by the management team and all project stakeholders, as well as the piloting of a metric/method to assess culture.

Rationale and approach

By this stage, the consultant will have a firm idea of the likely scope of the project and the most appropriate methods to obtain relevant data from the client organization, within any budgetary constraints. The management team will need to agree to the scope and methodology used, although they are likely to rely on the consultant's judgement to make their final decision.

Approaches to choose from are varied and might combine some or all of the following.

1. Questionnaire

Off-the-shelf culture profiling instruments include, for example, the Performance Culture Audit© or the Organizational Culture Inventory (Cooke and Szumal, 1993). If the project requires a bespoke approach, this will involve careful consideration of the elements of culture and climate to be measured and how these can be assessed via a questionnaire (see Oppenheim, 2000, for more on questionnaire construction).

Real-world example

We were asked by a client to produce a culture questionnaire to very specific parameters: the questionnaire should be fun and quick to complete, should combine qualitative and quantitative questions and should reflect the organization's current brand values (young, innovative, friendly).

Of course, we had to balance these design criteria against the requirements for a valid, robust psychometric instrument that could deliver a comprehensive picture of the culture of the organization. We chose to combine a variety of question types (forced choice, graphical/text rating scale, open ended, sentence completion) within an attractive design, and piloted various versions of the questionnaire with around 100 members of the organization, checking and adjusting its psychometric properties as we went.

The questionnaire was able to deliver maximum value for the client by providing an objective, reliable and valid analysis of culture across 10 separate dimensions, while at the same time being short, fun to complete, attractive and user friendly.

2. In-depth interviews

These can draw on techniques such as behavioural interviewing, repertory grid, and critical incidents (see Furnham and Gunter, 1993; Breakwell, Hammond and Fife-Schaw, 1999; and Brewerton and Millward, 2001, for culture assessment methods and for more generic psychological research methodology). The purpose here is to ask key stakeholders to describe their culture by describing events, processes, policies, procedures, and key figures. Of particular value are 'myths and legends', perhaps people, events or situations that capture the essence of the organization's culture for different organizational members. The methodology adopted is primarily qualitative although it can include quantitative elements, especially if interviews are structured and behaviourally based.

3. Focus groups

We have found focus groups to be enormously useful for:

- generating ideas for improvement;
- capturing the essence of an organization's culture (particularly bearing in mind the notion that culture exists at a group level, so questioning groups about it can provide a useful extra perspective);
- clarifying local and organizational issues.

The sessions need to be well structured and carefully managed to ensure that all members are included in the discussion and that any lack of consensus between participants is identified and discussed.

Pitfalls/obstacles

An unpiloted or flimsy metric (in terms of its measurement properties), or an inappropriate assessment method, can be a recipe for disaster if it is unable to provide a sufficiently comprehensive and useful assessment of the company's culture.

Another pitfall is for the consultant to limit the scope of the project to include only activities up to and including the presentation of survey findings, but no more. Although this provides a tidy 'cut off point' for the client, it gives a false impression that the project will end when the management team have the findings in their hands. It is in fact far more likely that this presentation will represent the *first* step on a long road to improving the organization's culture.

A point to consider is that of 'competing' methodologies. Culture and climate research has long been dogged by debate around the merits of adopting *either* qualitative *or* quantitative research methods when assessing culture.

- Qualitative cultural researchers argue against what they perceive as the inherently reductionist perspective of quantitative research, suggesting that psychometric techniques employed in such studies are fundamentally at odds with the nebulous and implicit nature of the construct (for example, Martin et al., 1983).
- On the other hand, quantitative researchers regard culture measurement as crucial for understanding relationships between factors of interest, arguing that in order to generalize findings across organizations, comparable measures must be developed to allow valid

investigation of cultural differences and their relative impact on other organizational factors (for example, Xenikou and Furnham, 1996).

See Martin and Frost (1996) for an eloquent debate on this topic. We believe that all methodological approaches have something to offer. It is the role of the consultant to select appropriate methods based on time and budgetary restrictions, which will provide best value for the client and will deliver on the client's needs. Our experience is that combining elements of qualitative and quantitative methodology can provide a thoroughly comprehensive picture of culture (see Rousseau, 1990, for more on this).

Build interest through communications plan

Outputs

The requirement here is for a clear communications plan including key tasks, timings and responsibilities, drawing on various communication modes as appropriate.

Rationale and approach

I cannot overstate the importance of employee communications to the overall success of a cultural assessment/development project. For many clients, we have constructed a specific 'communications plan' to ensure that this is carried out as effectively as possible. Communications with staff should start early to build interest, be clear and straightforward and continue throughout the initial research portion of the project.

Following presentation of findings to the management team, communications take on an even greater importance. Actions taken as a result of staff feedback during the cultural assessment phase should be communicated. Indeed, the link in employees' minds between their feedback and subsequent changes/improvements plays a vital role in the process. It can encourage participation in subsequent surveys and build positive perceptions of management and organizational initiatives.

The consultant will need to probe the client to identify the most appropriate modes of communication to use at each stage of the project. Emails, memoranda, team briefings, newsletters, the intranet, departmental meetings, and so forth, can all lend themselves to building interest and enthusiasm for the project.

Real-world example 1

Figure 33.3 illustrates an overview communications plan that we put together for a client to ensure that communications for their cultural assessment project were timely and user friendly.

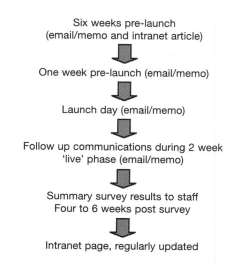

Figure 33.3 Communications plan.

Pre-launch communications would focus on generating interest in the staff population, by communicating:

- What has happened since previous surveys. (For example, 'Since the previous survey and the feedback provided by staff, we have: overhauled the staff appraisal system; put in place a development planning system; introduced a management development programme; and a formal means for staff to feed back information to the board'.)
- The purpose of the current survey. (For example, 'The current survey will allow us to assess how far we have come since the last time we ran the survey. Your feedback will allow us to make further improvements to our company's culture in an effort to improve the working lives of all our staff.')
- How the information will be used and confidentiality/anonymity of responses. (For example, 'All data collected will be reported back to the board in summary form, so no individual responses will be traceable. In addition, the survey is being managed by an external company to ensure that confidentiality is absolutely guaranteed.')
- Why it is important that employees contribute. (For example, 'By participating in the survey, staff can have a direct impact on future decisions made about our company's culture. It is vitally important that you participate, so that we understand the views of as many staff as possible across our company.')
- How and when they can expect feedback on their contribution. (For

example, 'A summary of the project findings will be made available to all staff in X months' time, along with an action plan as to the board's plans for improvement based on staff feedback.')
- Any form of incentive. (For example, contribution to local charity, entry into prize draw, and so forth.)
- The sponsor(s) of the research, preferably outlining the sponsorship of senior staff. (For example, 'Signed by Bill Gites, CEO.')

This would be supported by setting up a dedicated intranet page, which would provide more detail on some of these topics, giving further information on some of the remedial actions taken since the previous survey.

Follow-up communications during the live phase would be used as reminders and would stimulate response in particular groups if required.

Following the presentation of results to the steering committee and subsequent decisions on action (approximately 4 to 6 weeks post-survey), summary findings would be disseminated to all staff via the intranet, email, team briefings, or other suitable forums. If using team briefings, staff would be given the opportunity to question and challenge findings. This would require the individual chairing the briefing session to be fully familiar with the final report and to be able to answer potentially detailed questions.

Real-world example 2

To maximize interest from their workforce prior to a web-based culture survey, one of our clients went to great length to bombard its staff with relevant communications, as well as related merchandise (pens, stress balls, and so forth) to build credibility and interest. Partly as a result of this focus on positive communications in the pre-diagnostic phase, the survey response rate across seven European countries exceeded 95%.

Pitfalls/obstacles

Failing to build enthusiasm and buy-in from staff at this stage can result in poor participation, low response rates, suspicion of management and/or the project (generating biased results) and a lack of interest/trust in subsequent actions/improvements. The communication modes and content must be appropriate to the audience to achieve maximum interest and buy-in.

It is particularly important to engage the middle manager level, as these staff are well positioned to either encourage or discourage their teams' participation in the project. Specific communications or group briefings may be required for this group to explain the purpose, value and logistics of the project, including their role within it.

Organize logistics of research process and run research

Outputs

The goal here is a well-managed, smooth and glitch-free cultural assessment project where comprehensive, representative data are obtained from the organization and participating staff feel engaged in the process as 'part owners' of it.

Rationale and approach

Taking the correct decisions at this stage will provide accurate, comprehensive data on the culture/climate of the client organization and if handled appropriately, will build a positive feeling among staff that their views are being heeded. These decisions include:

- *How to apply an appropriate sampling frame.* If the project adopts a questionnaire-based approach, will this be distributed to all employees or targeted at particular departments? Will a representative *sample* of a large workforce be asked to respond?
- *How to organize communications inviting staff to attend focus groups or interviews.* These should be handled carefully in order that staff trust the research project and the way in which they have been selected to participate.
- *How to distribute and collect questionnaires (if used).* The client may prefer a survey to be run online (either intranet or Internet based) or on paper. Either way, suitable channels need to be identified for participants to receive the survey and return it to the company analysing the data. Distribution may be via internal mail, external mail to home addresses, or email. Collection could involve online databasing of responses, or returning questionnaires to the survey hosting company via external or internal mail.
- *Where to hold interviews/focus groups.* It may be appropriate to hold interviews or focus groups off site if this will provide more accurate data. When held on site, quiet, secure accommodation will be needed to ensure that participants feel that their contributions remain confidential.
- *When to distribute questionnaires, run focus groups and interviews.* When using a multi-method research approach, the consultant will need to decide when to run each research phase. Would it be more useful to collect questionnaire data first, and run preliminary analyses to provide specific question areas for subsequent focus groups? Or could interview/focus group data usefully feed into the formulation of questions to be used in interviews/questionnaires?

Pitfalls/obstacles

The potential for error at the research implementation stage is substantial. Possible pitfalls include (but are not limited to):

- Applying a faulty sampling frame, for example using a 'convenience' sample (those staff who are easiest to access or most motivated to participate) rather than a random or quota sampling approach – clearly this will limit the accuracy of the data.
- Selecting the wrong medium for a culture questionnaire – for example email, or Internet when not all participants have easy access to a personal computer.
- Failing to follow up participants after distribution of their questionnaire, which can result in poor response rates and limited accuracy of data obtained.
- Allowing the perception of anonymity or confidentiality to be compromised. We have experienced organizational research projects where line managers have opened 'confidential' return envelopes or have even asked to see what employees have written in their questionnaires before returning them to the survey host. Any action that is likely to be interpreted as compromising participants' anonymity or confidentiality of responses is likely to undermine the research process, reduce accuracy of data and raise suspicion about the findings.

Interpretation, analysis and reporting

Outputs

A comprehensible, credible, user-friendly interpretation of the culture assessment data collected. This should facilitate the executive team's understanding of where they are now and which areas need greatest work to get them to where they want to be.

Rationale and approach

Let us assume, then, that the culture assessment phase is complete and the data obtained are useable, representative and as free from bias as possible. We feel that it is now the consultant's role to turn this information into user-friendly, understandable messages with high impact. As a company, we are passionate about this and have made it part of our strategy to deliver clear, straightforward, meaningful information to our clients. The information presented back to the project sponsors should describe the current culture of the client organization and how this compares with its 'aspirational' culture and/or other organizations' cultures (if a normative approach has been used). It should identify areas of strength as well as areas for development and improvement within the organization.

Real-world example

Blue Edge's Performance Culture Audit© reports organizations' cultural profiles as shown in Figure 33.4 (slightly modified from our base model). An example of a *bespoke* model that we have created for a client is shown in Figure 33.5.

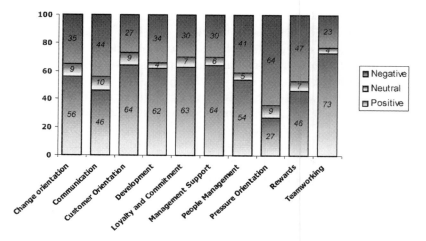

Figure 33.4 Blue Edge's Performance Culture Audit© cultural profile.

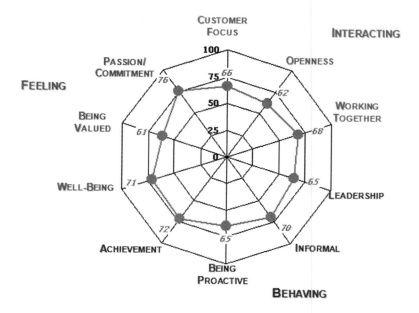

Figure 33.5a Output from bespoke models.

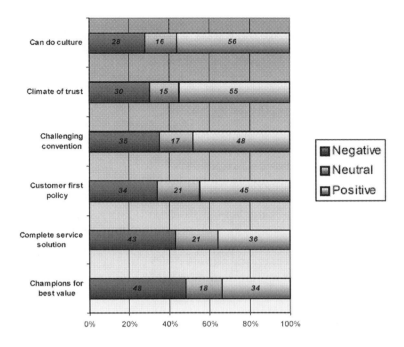

Figure 33.5b Output from bespoke models.

Pitfalls/obstacles

The greatest challenge here is in distilling down research findings to the basics. There is an urge amongst most researchers in the field of psychology (ourselves included) to provide more, rather than less, information to clients to give them the 'full picture'. While this is fine (as long as much of this detail is 'appended' to the main report), we feel that the focus should be on driving an accurate message home as strongly as possible. Extraneous information can dilute this message and potentially confuse or distract the reader from the key information. Our advice, therefore, is to present the research findings in a written form that communicates a clear message to the reader.

Presentation to executive and action planning workshop

Outputs

The output from the presentation and action planning session should at the very least provide the project stakeholders with a clear picture of the strengths of their organization assessed against their initial cultural 'blue-print', and an appreciation of areas that might need further work. At best, this session can mark the start of the executive team deciding on subsequent actions they wish to take to improve their organization's culture.

Rationale and approach

Presenting findings to the project's stakeholders (often the executive team) provides another opportunity to get the message across in a clear, powerful and credible way. It also offers the opportunity for:

- the consultant to gain direct feedback from the management team, responding directly to any challenges on the research findings and clarifying any misunderstandings – our advice is to be well prepared for *any* possible questions, particularly around sampling and negative findings;
- the consultant to facilitate management decisions on targeting specific areas of culture in order to deliver greatest gains for the organization in terms of staff satisfaction, morale, performance and productivity;
- project stakeholders to start action planning in light of survey findings. In this regard, the consultant might take a facilitative role, only providing recommendations or ideas for improvement if necessary, but encouraging the executive team to take full ownership of the subsequent cultural development programme by generating their own ideas for initiatives.

The format and length of the presentation will depend largely on the availability of the executive team and the 'air time' given to hear the results of the research.

Real-world example

We have been asked to present results from our cultural assessment research within a 20-minute time slot. We have also been given a whole day to talk through the detail of a diagnostic study and to start to generate actions for cultural development and improvement.

The overall aims of shorter and longer presentations necessarily differ. For shorter presentations, our focus is on driving home the key message in order that the management team starts to recognize and acknowledge which areas are currently positively perceived and which areas might need more work. For longer presentations (half a day and more), in addition to getting across key messages from the research, it may also be possible to start 'unfreezing' the management team's thinking and encouraging them to generate ideas and actions for change.

Typically, our presentations last between 1 and 2 hours and, given the choice, we prefer to run separate sessions for presenting results and generating actions. The audience often needs time to digest the results and to acknowledge and accept them (and for some, to go through the full process of 'SARA': Surprise, Anger, Rationalization and Acceptance), so a second session for action planning, perhaps 2 to 4 weeks later, can be a good approach.

Pitfalls/obstacles

As with the written research report, there is often a tendency for consultants to overcomplicate the message at presentations, or to be distracted into a debate about detailed aspects of the research findings. However, it is by repeatedly putting across the key messages throughout the presentation that the audience starts to focus on the big picture coming out of the research.

Feeding back universally negative results can be a challenge. Of course, accuracy is important in all parts of the presentation to maintain the credibility of the research. Our advice (to reduce the chances of denial or flat-out rejection of findings from the audience) is to present as balanced a picture as possible, while making sure it is accurate and comprehensive. This might mean drawing the audience's attention to some positive findings from time to time just to show that it's not all 'doom and gloom'.

As a point of interest, within the last few years we have stopped including recommendations in our cultural research reports. We have found that it is far more beneficial to take a facilitative approach and ask management teams to generate *their own* ideas for improvement rather than 'impose' our views on what will work best for them. This facilitative approach has its risks but, in our view, the reward of ensuring the management team's total ownership of the results and subsequent actions substantially outweighs those risks. Failing to gain 'buy in' to the research findings or to the need for subsequent action can be very damaging; it can lead to inaction on the part of management and therefore a failure to deliver on the raised expectations of employees, potentially affecting future management and OD initiatives for years to come.

Decisions on action, communication to staff, roll out interventions

Outputs

The output here will be a clear statement of planned changes and improvements and the process to achieve them, agreed by the management team and communicated to staff.

Rationale and approach

The executive team should now be at a stage where it is ready to decide upon and commit resources to the next stage of the cultural change programme. This is the time for management to decide on how the programme will be managed, what it will involve and how its success will be gauged. It is also the stage to inform the workforce about decisions taken and the actions that will follow. Actions, it should be emphasized, which have been derived in part from the staff's own feedback through the earlier cultural diagnosis.

The approach taken to implementing change will depend on a number of factors including budget, time scale and, of course, the current culture within the organization, so some approaches will be more appropriate/more likely to succeed than others. Issues for consideration include:

- *Which areas will be targeted for improvement?* This will depend on the cultural diagnosis and on the priorities for the organization in terms of improvements required.
- *How will the change programme be implemented?* Will it be managed centrally but implemented at local level? Will 'action groups' comprising members of different departments and from different levels be set up to generate ideas for improvement? Will 'change champions' be appointed throughout the organization to take responsibility for change initiatives?
- *How will change be reinforced and embedded within the culture?* Is there a case for aligning the change initiative with the company's performance management system, so that new ways of working and behaving can be linked to appraisal, training, selection and promotion systems? The link between leadership and culture may need to be explored, so that the executive team recognizes the importance of the organization's leaders 'role modelling' new ways of working and behaving at work
- *How will the relative success of the programme be assessed?* Will success be assessed by benchmarking current staff perceptions with the perceptions of staff in 12 or 24 months' time? What sort of shifts in perception will define 'success'? Changes in behaviour in line with the aspirational culture could be assessed via 360-degree behavioural assessment – but will this work within the current culture and climate of the organization?

Pitfalls/obstacles

For some consultants in this field, the delivery of a cultural diagnosis via written and verbal reports represents the end-point of the project. The danger of this is that it can also represent the project conclusion for the management team. In our experience it is at this point and in the months that follow the cultural diagnosis, when the support of consultants can be very beneficial. Perhaps by drafting in a consultant to manage the change process (although in some cases, this can be an expensive option which may lead to a 'dependent' relationship between client and consultant – see Schein (1987) on the dangers of consultant dependency), or perhaps by providing support by phone and in person, allowing the client to play with ideas about how change may best be implemented and what might and might not work in their organization. Having someone as an external 'sounding board' with experience of successes and failures in other companies can be a real help to change teams during this implementation phase.

A potential pitfall here is a lack of communication with the workforce as to what will happen next. We have encountered many businesses that have made various positive changes to their organization as a result of cultural research findings but have failed to tell staff that (a) these things are happening at all and (b) that they are happening *as a direct result of their (staff's) feedback.* I cannot overemphasize the importance of keeping this link fresh in the minds of employees if an organization wishes to maintain commitment to and enthusiasm for change across the workforce.

Maintain interest, monitor and measure success

Outputs

The overarching goal is to implement an ongoing and continuous process of change and development, punctuated by objective assessments of success in targeted areas.

Rationale and approach

For the change programme to have lasting impact, interest needs to be maintained in its outcomes. One way this can be achieved is by providing ownership of different areas targeted for change to staff groups and/or 'change champions' within the organization. Communication will once again be essential to ensure that staff are informed of ongoing changes and improvements and where the ideas for change came from. The success of different initiatives also needs to be measured and there are various methods that can help to achieve this.

Real-world example

A bold example of an attempt to change a culture of poor vertical and horizontal communication and of a historical 'command-and-control' management style was demonstrated by one of our clients. Following our objective assessment of its culture, it decided to focus on the four distinct areas perceived least positively by their workforce. These were 'teamwork', 'transparent leadership', 'focus on the customer' and 'commitment to excellence'.

They created 'action teams' to generate ideas for each of the four targeted areas of culture, each team comprising one member of the board, two senior managers, two team leaders and five staff members, all from different parts of the business. Each action team took responsibility for generating two 'SMART' (Specific, Measurable, Achievable, Relevant, Time-limited) targets in their area of culture. For example, in the area of 'focus on the customer', one team arrived at two goals: (1) ensure that all senior managers spend a day managing one of our shops within the next 6 months and feed back what they find to the board; (2) devise a method for all staff to capture new product/service ideas and reward the best new innovation each month. These goals were then communicated and implemented across the organization.

This approach visibly demonstrated the management team's commitment to changing the company's culture towards more knowledge sharing and greater involvement of staff in decision making.

Pitfalls/obstacles

As with all OD initiatives, culture-change programmes can lose their shine and interest can wane unless active steps are taken to insure against this. If progress on the culture-change programme starts as an afterthought for management team meetings, it won't take long before it disappears from the agenda altogether. It is of great benefit, therefore, to have an advocate of culture change either as a member of the executive team or central to the organization but with credibility at board level. Either way, it is important to ensure that culture as a discussion topic remains 'current' and continues to be taken seriously as the months go by.

A further issue to be aware of is communication: again, this needs to be kept current and relevant if staff are to maintain an interest in the change programme. Perhaps a dedicated portion of the intranet, a 5-minute slot at quarterly team briefings, a dedicated newsletter or section of the corporate newsletter could be used to communicate achievements and successes. Above all, maintaining interest, commitment and enthusiasm for culture change programmes requires hard work and dedication.

So, why do we work as business psychologists in this area? For us, it is a fascinating proposition to gain an understanding of what makes an organization 'tick' and to better understand what that organization *means* to its workforce. Our work also gives us the chance to provide employees with a feedback route to their management team, so that they can let management know where things are going well and not so well within the business. Finally, it is very rewarding to see organizations take up the challenge of changing and improving their culture, particularly when this begins to make a real difference to individual, departmental and corporate performance.

In our minds, there is no doubt that organizational culture and climate do make a difference to organizational change initiatives, but in choosing to develop an organization's culture, the management team and any consultants working with it should acknowledge that the journey will be a long one, requiring persistence and commitment to make substantial gains.

Further reading

Schein EH (1985) Organizational Culture and Leadership: A Dynamic View. San Francisco: Jossey-Bass.

Schneider B (1987) The people make the place. Personnel Psychology 40: 437–53.

Schneider B (1990) Organizational Climate and Culture. San Francisco: Jossey-Bass.

CHAPTER 34

Designing and implementing strategic change programmes

ROY DREW

Introduction

For years I have found myself practising psychology undercover, using the mask of management consultancy.

My passion is organizational effectiveness, working within organizational development (see Beer, 1976; Pugh, 1978) and focusing on the task of helping companies to design and implement strategic change programmes.

Large-scale change assignments with British Airways, Royal Ordnance, various electricity companies and British Nuclear Fuels provided an early opportunity to practice and develop approaches and methodologies.

A scan through any strategic management process literature shows strategy subdividing into formulation and implementation (Mintzberg and Quinn, 1991; Johnson and Scholes, 1993). The issues associated with formulation relate to alternative business visions. Those of implementation are clearly of more direct interest to a business psychologist.

Strategy implementation is discussed in terms of *organization design* and whether this provides the capabilities appropriate to the pursuit of strategic ambitions (Miles and Snow, 1978; Mintzberg, 1983; Porter, 1980, 1985). Concepts such as paradigm set and strategic drift (Johnson, 1989) are also introduced and culture examined for relevance to corporate performance (Kotter and Heskett, 1992). Schein (1985) suggests how to define and change culture. These are clearly important areas of contribution to our understanding of strategy implementation.

Implementation is also discussed in terms of *managing the process of organizational change* and in this the organizational development practitioner or business psychologist should be on firm ground. The work of Alexander (1989) has shown how difficult implementation really is. Pettigrew and Whipp (1993) describe change as a source of competitive advantage to those who do it well. Kotter and Schlesinger (1989) show us different approaches to take depending on how rapid change needs to be and Beer, Eisenstat and Spector (1993) show us the critical path to the successful implementation of change.

Furthermore, if the practitioner works within the theoretical framework offered by the Tavistock Institute (Miller, 1993), or for that matter Argyris (1970) and Habermas (1971), then by embracing the relationships within organizations between rational and social systems and individual employees, they are well placed to provide optimal solutions to corporate strategic change needs.

Understanding the rational system of organizations may require help from other disciplines but being able to keep the whole organization in view is a potential major advantage on offer from the business psychologist.

Going undercover to contribute to corporate strategy implementation comes from experience. Psychology does not appear, in the eyes of senior executives, to add value to such mainstream management activity. For most executives, psychology is associated with the tools and techniques used in addressing human resource administration needs, such as the selection and development of individuals, and hence is irrelevant to top table issues.

The case study illustrated here was such a situation. The CEO bought into the concept of management consultants, not psychologists, with a primary focus on the rational system of organizations, as a means of securing his strategic ambitions. What was in practice delivered was an organizational-development led approach to the design and implementation of a strategic change programme.

Key strategic issues

The company was a subsidiary business unit of a trade association, providing a range of services to members consisting of various types of transactions with a menu of prices.

The financial goals were to provide a service to members at a cost lower than if they did the work themselves, and to break even as a business unit.

The environment in which it operated provided a number of threats to its longer-term survival:

- First, transaction processing volumes had been falling by 12% per annum over a number of years, as the market in which its association members operated shrank owing to the successful entry of foreign competition. There had also been some structural consolidation among member firms that had an effect on total transaction volumes.
- Secondly, the legitimate need for the business was based on cost and

service. The financial goal of breaking even, and charges for transactions lower than members performing the work themselves created a bind for the CEO of the business. Facing declining volumes, it could not widen its market appeal or reposition itself to growth markets because it was tied to the service of association members.

- Thirdly, significant cost reduction was most likely to be achieved by information technology applications. This would require considerable financial investment for a business geared to low-cost operation and breaking even. Any investment funding would need to be provided by association members, requiring them to invest in their own company systems, in some form of unison association-wide, for any benefit to become viable. This was seen as unlikely in the medium term.
- Finally, budget forecasts for the following year were based on a loss on trading, leading to price increases for members. Service levels, based on a 5-day turnaround standard for processing activity was rarely achieved and the CEO faced persistent calls from managers for more staff, although the CEO had an internally produced report that in transaction processing staff were only 50% efficient.

The CEO had a future vision of attaining growth by breaking out of the constraints imposed by membership of the trade association, to reach new markets and develop new products and services for both existing and new market sectors.

This would require funding in product–service development and information technology, and options being contemplated were a management buyout, strategic partnerships and acquisition by a third party. Through growth, economy of scale and technical development, his belief was that low-cost, high-quality services could be provided to clients – both members of the association and others. However, at the time of our entry, executives of the association were somewhat ambivalent about these goals.

For the CEO, current levels of organizational performance constituted a barrier to these aspirations, and the lack of finance to invest in IT prevented the development of any new service capabilities to present to the association, or potential new markets.

With these concerns and ambitions in mind, the CEO invited us into the business to explore the issue 'how do we achieve a step-change in processing performance and an improvement in efficiency levels, whilst at the same time enhancing customer service?'

Approach and orientation

For the CEO, the issues focused on organizational capability and effectiveness. We approached these issues from an open systems perspective, with a focus on the linkage between systems behaviour, performance and perceived environmental demands.

We started with a modest knowledge of systems performance (50% efficiency level, missed service level targets), some information that influenced or constrained performance from the environment (falling volumes, association requirements), and the CEO's aspirations for the future (management buyout, and so forth), but knew almost nothing about internal systems capability and behaviour, or how far others in the organization shared the CEO's strategic ambitions.

Theoretically, we could make a number of deductions:

- Firstly, any improvement in organizational capability and effectiveness would need to result in managers and staff behaving differently in some way – in the boardroom, within management and on the shop floor.
- Secondly, this difference would most probably evoke change – perhaps in what they did, in how they perceived and related to their task, and how they related to colleagues and the organization as a whole. Change would also be needed in what they valued and gave priority to, and the commitments, beliefs and attachments they would be expected to hold.
- Thirdly, if behavioural change was to be the end-result of improvements in organizational capability and effectiveness, it was appropriate to start our analysis from this point of view. That is, to discover and feed back to the company the characteristic behaviour of managers and staff and its relationship to current levels of effectiveness, and how this would need to change or be adapted, to achieve superior performance.

The analysis of characteristic organizational behaviour displayed by individuals provides a window through which we can access those things shaping it (rational system elements), those things influencing it (social system elements) and how both will need to change and adapt to bring into being different strategically relevant behaviours and performance.

Characteristic systems behaviour

The findings from a review conducted over 3 weeks revealed some interesting patterns based on observation, semi-structured interviews, and discussion groups:

- A lack of consensus at all levels of management about the need for, or the desirability of, the change proposed by the CEO, and for staff, and indeed association members' ambivalence towards it.

- Little recognition that existing performance was problematic or less than ideal and, apart from service levels, no other metrics on systems performance existed at an operational level.
- Managerial roles were based on operating tasks and activity, rather than managerial function, and their value and indeed career progression was based on social competency. The framework of business operation was limited to annual budgetary routines.
- Transaction processing technicians selected and managed their own work and, given that flexi-time working operated, could decide when to build and take it. This rarely seemed to relate to workload, or service level, but rather was driven by personal desire.
- Teams were structured variously, such as 5 or 16 to a team, with no apparent rationale for the difference, apart from manager preference.
- Cross-team resource flexibility or capability did not exist and teams operated within defined silos. This led to an inability to cope with fluctuating workflow and demand, and an imbalance in workload across teams.
- A misplaced obsession with the 5-day service level. When failing to meet service level, teams worked overtime, built flexi-hours, or took on temporary staff. When workload was light, they reduced the pace of work to fill the time available to meet the 5-day standard. As a result, they could never meet the average standard.
- Personal alliances, social relationships and friendship cliques appeared to be both an organizing principle and the basis of determining daily priorities, within the very broad constraints of formal contracts of employment.
- From sample studies, efficiency levels appeared consistent at 50%, and productivity levels at 40%. That is, 3 or 4 hours of work output for every 8 hours paid.

Assumptions, contrasts and change goals

The design of the rational system of this organization (its roles, structures, systems and processes) appeared to be based on the administration of tasks and activity to break even on trading, based upon assumptions of historic volumes, a transaction price menu and forecast operating costs. Within this framework, the dominant ideology appeared to be providing some unarticulated value to its parent company, the association, rather than its own status as a thriving business.

This design was reflected in the social system of the organization, the dominant values and beliefs about good and bad, right and wrong, more-or-less appropriate ways of relating to one's role, task and relationships. After Harrison and Stokes (1992), this appeared to have the hallmark of a person-centred culture.

The result was the display of characteristic individual and group behaviour and resultant systems performance at odds with the future strategic aims of the CEO.

Changes in systems performance can be brought about by changing characteristic organizational behaviour through a redesign of rational system elements. Through the process of adaptation to this, new values and beliefs will emerge to support and rationalize change and underpin superior systems performance.

The contrasts of change appropriate to the aims and ambitions of the CEO are shown in Tables 34.1 and 34.2.

Table 34.1 Rational system

Factor	From what is it?	To what will it need to be?
Roles	Specified activity	Specified performance
Structure	Fit to individual	Fit for purpose
Decision making	Centralized	Decentralized
Resource planning	Annual budget forecast	Daily workload balance
Information flow	Historic	Real time
Control systems	Monthly reviews	Hourly, daily, weekly
Work allocation	Self-selection	Supervisor allocated
Human resources policies in terms of hours worked, when to work and when to take holidays	Self-decided	Production contingent

Table 34.2 Social system

Factor	From what is it?	To what will it need to be?
Key sentiments	Parental authority	Self-determination
Legacy of control	Acceptability	Knowledge and skill
Work orientation	Social enjoyment	Results achievement
Basis of reciprocity	Personal satisfaction	Task necessity
Good managers are	Responsive to me	Meritorious
Good workers are	Popular	Best at task
People who do well are	Personally sponsored	Most competent
Company treats people as	Interesting individuals	Co-worker to a goal

These descriptions arise from observing people in the workplace and focused investigation into how management is practised in the organization. The future view is derived from an extrapolation of the strategic change needed by the CEO.

A discussion was held with directors and departmental managers about whether the change in structural configuration from what was, given the dominant culture in the organization, should be based on semi-autonomous work groups or direct supervision. In the end, direct supervision was considered more appropriate to promote the changes required.

Bipolar descriptions were inferred from the stories, illustrations, and incidents given by interviewees of working in the organization. The future view was an interpretation of key values and beliefs appropriate to perceived change in the rational system elements. These profiles represented hypotheses for discussion and debate with teams, supervisors, managers and directors in the attempt to give visibility to factors that may lie beneath the surface of cognition. In process consulting terms, this was an attempt to negotiate the reality of a situation.

Characteristic behaviour

How the above shape and influence the characteristic behaviour of individuals and groups is shown in Table 34.3.

Table 34.3 Characteristic behaviour

Factor	From what is it?	To what will it need to be?
Priorities are given to	Individual preference	Production need
Conflicts are	Contained and politicized	Surfaced and resolved
Orientation to the day is	Undertaking a task	Achieving a result
The pace of activity is	Inconsistent	Regular
Cooperation between teams is	Closed	Reciprocal

These descriptions formed the content of a debate with supervisors, managers and directors about the validity of what existed, and the desirability of what would be required. It also provided a means for exploring with those who would lead change, the symbols, routines and rituals in the organization that may reinforce the past rather than the future.

The fundamental change proposition

The proposition visualized for managers and staff is shown in Figure 34.1.

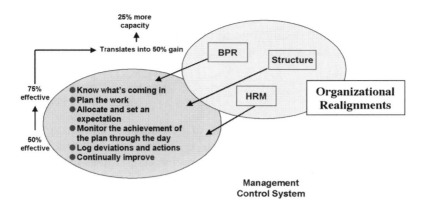

Figure 34.1 The fundamental change proposition.

Change management

The hypothesis on the nature and direction of required change in this organization was based on a short situational review of the enterprise. In an attempt to understand the organization through the eyes of those who worked in it, surfacing politically incorrect issues, confronting and challenging contradictions in the accounts and explanations of employees, and negotiating realities therein, the process of change was already begun.

In the process of engaging staff in the design and implementation of an ensuing change programme the process model shown in Figure 34.2 was adopted.

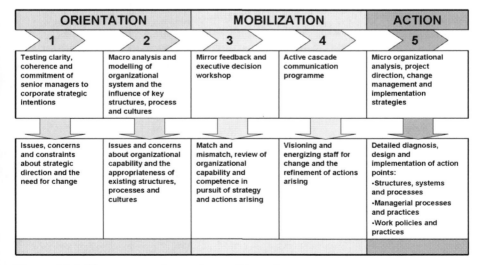

Figure 34.2 The process of engaging staff in a change programme.

Through this model, initial findings were verified and issues defined and agreed, and the detailed work of designing appropriate solutions for implementation into everyday practice was begun.

Achievements

Table 34.4 shows the achievements of this organization in terms of systems performance. Data are shown in terms of achievements at our point of entry, at the end of facilitating the process of change (4 months) and at an audit point, 24 months later. Figures represent average weekly attainments over a 12-week window.

Table 34.4 Achievements of the organization in terms of systems performance

Factor	At project start	At project end	Twenty-four months later
Efficiency	52%	73%	80%
Productivity	40%	43%	70%
Backlogs (vol.)	2700	961	zero
Service (days)	6	4.5	2

At the company's financial year-end following the change programme, the CEO was able to report to his parent organization:

• An increase in volume of 10%, rather than a forecast 12% decline.
• A 33% staff reduction in relative terms.
• A profit turnaround of £1.5 million, rather than a forecast loss.
• The creation of a results- and achievement-based organizational culture, which appeared improbable at the start of the change programme.

Postscript

Twelve months after the 24-month audit point, the CEO did, in fact, achieve his original strategic ambition. A tripartite agreement between a financial investor and the merger with a former competitor provided a new and enlarged organization, establishing a foundation for growth.

CHAPTER 35

The role of psychology in implementing large-scale change with diverse cultures

SYLVANA STOREY

Introduction

This case study concerns the 'roll-out' of a service segmentation strategy throughout a region within the oil industry and serves to illustrate the role of psychology in achieving business objectives and meeting organizational needs.

This strategy embraced, from the beginning, an integrative approach to change that stemmed from three marked campaigns – political, marketing and 'military'. Through these campaigns this case focuses on some of the key characteristics of implementing large-scale change and illustrates the use of psychological techniques and tools that aid in the execution and facilitation of strategic transformation.

Each section identifies elements of the change programme where the specific contribution of business psychology was particularly pertinent and from which learning points are derived. These elements are:

- Articulating the need for change that embraces elements of a marketing campaign.
- Addressing organizational culture, diversity and dynamics through a military campaign.
- Relationships – external and internal – which embrace elements from a political campaign.
- Supporting strategy implementation where evidence of all three campaigns can be found.

Background

The customer service segmentation strategy was developed and implemented with the sole rationale being to differentiate the company from its competitors whilst adding value for the customer. It took the activity of

331

market segmentation a step further by analysing service segments. These newly identified service segments would create new customers (stimulate customer growth) as well as 'locking-in' existing customers (customer retention).

This strategy was developed and deployed in the following stages:

1. Identification of markets.
2. Scoping of markets.
3. Identification of service segments.
4. Identification of customers within those service segments and interviewing them.
5. Understanding the customers' value-chains, competition factors and logistics.
6. Developing the 'distinctive offer'.
7. Costing the offer and examining capability of the organization to deliver it.
8. Redesign of the organizational structures, systems and processes that embrace the offer.
9. Introduction and implementation of change initiatives (see below).
10. Distinctive offer presented and delivered to the customer.
11. Evaluation and monitoring.

Given the range of market characteristics within the region, markets were firstly divided into 'emerged', 'emerging' and 'hidden' and the location of the customer into 'urban', 'rural' and 'remote'. It was also vital to understand where the business was won – that is, internationally, regionally, locally or through the community. Armed with this information the strategy then evolved into the analysis of service segments and value-enhancing services using value-chain logic. The end-result was the 'distinctive offer'. To be distinctive, the offer had to be at least one step further up the service ladder compared to the competitor's offer in that service segment.

Simultaneously the organization's capability to deliver in terms of financial, marketing, technological and organizational resources was also assessed, cross-functional multidisciplinary teams deployed and the change programmes launched. The distinctive offer was then presented and delivered to the customer by these teams, having been aligned to the strategy and trained with the capability and skills to deliver the service offer.

 # Change programmes

Anticipated changes to structure, systems and processes meant that a series of change initiatives that would build organizational capability throughout the region were developed and rolled out. These included:

- Training trainers to deliver programmes to every employee of the organization that would upskill and develop them.
- A communication strategy that focused on both external and internal customers and stakeholders.
- Workshops and launches that built upon the theme and thus encouraged a sense of excitement, involvement and team spirit.
- Implementation of customer relationship management systems.

Articulating the need for change

The strategy aimed to promote integration of service for the customer. In this vein, the structure of the organization was changed, so that offer delivery within the given service segment would be seamless, coherent, accessible and consistent regardless of the country in which the customer was located.

However, this entailed significant upheaval within the organization with regard to structures and skills that would support and deliver the offer. From a psychological perspective, the main issues to address were:

- overcoming resistance to change;
- changing attitudes and behaviour to support the theme of 'distinctiveness';
- gaining 'buy-in' that would increase motivation and job satisfaction.

Primarily, these issues were addressed through one method – involvement underpinned by the marketing campaign: involvement of employees and customers in workshops, training programmes, launches and a communication strategy. It was vital to gain and sustain the attention of employees by inviting them to participate all the way through the process, so that they felt they 'owned' and contributed to the changes. This extended to actively seeking the opinions of employees who previously would not have been involved in a strategic change process from initiation.

The communications strategy had a clearly articulated, high-level theme that employees at all organizational levels could respond to – that of distinctiveness. It was in everyone's interest to be a *distinctive* person who was part of a *distinctive* organization. This had the effect of creating unity amongst colleagues.

Learning points

- Explore the rationale for the change by thoroughly understanding the market conditions.
- Identify critical success factors that would highlight 'quick-wins' and thus gain and sustain momentum for the process.

- Don't pretend to know 'everything' about the organization – allow key workers to guide and inform you, so that change is both credible and sustainable. For example, the drivers who had responsibility for delivering the product to the customer were able to meet the customer and cite specific examples of obstacles they faced during the course of transporting the product to their premises.

Addressing organizational culture, diversity and dynamics

This change programme was unique, in that it involved eight different countries all with their individual languages and cultures and as such 'their way of doing things'. To obtain buy-in for uniformity with regard to service delivery was an uphill battle. One of the key ways of winning was to tap into the very diversity that made each distinct, and subsequently enable and forge alliances bringing into play aspects of the political campaign.

To support this, diversity workshops were held that employed the skills of a facilitator who used a variety of comic and sporting analogies to explain the strategy through differing contexts and cultures. Employees from different countries were grouped together in different locations at different times. This aided in appreciating others' cultures as well as creating friendships and bonds. Thus upon implementation alliances had been forged which broke down the 'them and us' barriers.

In parallel with this, the organizational structure was redesigned so that the emphasis weighed on service delivery and segment performance rather than individual delivery and country performance. Roles within the organization were reassigned via performance feedback and employees indicating their preferred role in the acknowledgement that the best person won the job. This created a paradoxical aspect – that of a sense of competition underpinned by admiration for one's colleagues.

Learning points

- Strengthening cultural awareness is an asset to both the organization and the individual's personal development as they develop cultural sensitivity.
- The focus on 'distinctiveness' through 'offers', systems, processes and people as a theme, created a feeling of unity – 'we're all in this together' – and an acknowledgement that what 'someone does will affect how I am perceived and have bearing on my performance outcomes'.
- Align the organization's structure in accordance with the strategy, so that the best possible results are achieved.

Relationships – external and internal

One of the most important parts of the strategy was creating a customer relationship based on forming 'business partnerships'. To attain this, one had to become conversant with the language of interpersonal skills, such as non-verbal communication, active listening and engaging and obtaining pertinent information. Employees were trained in these skills.

An appreciation and respect of group dynamics was also relevant and the 'politicking' that is part and parcel of organizational life was brought to the fore through open debate in workshops and through elements of the communications strategy. The leadership, senior management, and cross-functional teams learned to exhibit certain behaviours that employees could emulate such as increased openness, honesty and commitment to promises made and actions undertaken.

The customer was also invited to participate in certain activities so as to gain an in-depth understanding of how the company was implementing change in culture as well as service delivery.

Learning points

- Build business partnerships that both 'engage' and 'lock-in' the customer through inviting continuous feedback and practising 'active listening'.
- Emphasize differentiation by creating value-adding and bespoke offers for the customer. For example, installing Internet capability in remote areas so as to engage consistently with the customer.
- Respect and seek to understand each person's role in the process through frank and open discussion employing consistent, clear communication across divisions.
- The champion(s) of the process must both lead by behaviour and serve with respect. For example, a segment director visiting the customer with front-line team members.
- Be wary of politicking between various individuals/functions/divisions. Aim for a shared purpose with sustained collaboration amongst all key individuals. (This was provided through the creation of the 'distinctiveness' theme.)

Supporting strategy implementation

In order to implement the strategy, a number of initiatives were rolled out that linked all three campaigns to build organizational capability and sustain the strategic imperatives.

- A training needs analysis was undertaken that determined training programmes best suited to facilitate the roll-out of the strategy. Training served to bring to the fore elements of a marketing campaign that would brand and engage the strategy.

  - Programmes such as interpersonal skills, change management, problem solving, and pipeline coordination. In total, 23 programmes were developed and delivered.
  - Linked to these were personal development plans.
  - Trainers were trained and they in turn then rolled out the programmes to every employee in their respective countries. This was supervised by the human resources function.
  - A series of workshops was conducted, beginning with the development of the strategy to the roll-out of the offer to the customer. This is where elements of a military campaign were used.
  - Each workshop had a representative from each country, function, division and level.
  - The concluding workshop was the launch, which was conducted in each of the eight countries undertaking two or three of the service segments.
  - Senior management throughout the region, every employee in that country and selected customers who had been involved in the process thus far, attended it. These were customers the company had recently won via the process, or who had been retained but increased their orders as a consequence of the offers.
  - This enabled integration of relationships and understanding of the overall process. Indeed, the launch (a two-day event over a weekend) was presented by employees themselves.

- A communication strategy – developed so as to engage the 'hearts and minds' of all employees, so that 'buy-in' and commitment to the process would be achieved, as well as promoting an understanding of business processes and encouraging involvement.

  - This represented the opportunity for transformation.
  - A variety of media was employed to gain attention at many sensory levels. For example, intranet, newsletters, conference calls.
  - Continuous feedback from both customers and employees was encouraged through the communications strategy.
  - The communications strategy enabled coalitions to be formed and others' views to be understood, bearing close resemblance to political campaigns.

- Lastly, as a company would do when conducting marketing research, a customer relationship management database was created that sought details on every aspect of the customer from order requirements to children's birthdays. This had the psychological advantage of making the customer feel special.

Learning points

- Patience is of the essence in implementing any strategic transformation programme – practise patience and remember that you are in it for the long haul! As such, flexibility and adaptability are essential.
- Stretch employees – encourage emotional development, support entrepreneurship and be tolerant of failure. Embrace fear of the unknown.
- Be sensitive to employees during structural change. Seek to engage employees' hearts and minds by giving them the opportunities to add value to the process.
- Invite continuous feedback and communicate envisaged processes and outcome consistently.

Conclusion

An integrative approach to change is much more likely to be successful and sustainable as it achieves engagement of all involved. Throughout this transformation process, three distinct but linked campaigns were identified:

- A political campaign to create a coalition strong enough to support and guide the initiative.
- A marketing campaign tapping into employees' thoughts and feelings and effectively communicating the strategy's theme and benefits.
- A 'military' campaign that deployed executives' scarce resources of attention and time and managed resistance.

Naturally, there were many challenges along the way; however, they were dealt with immediately and openly through mentorship; active listening, participation, support and encouragement. This all contributed to what really made the company distinctive in the end:

- From front-line teams to board members, all were involved in the process gaining an in-depth understanding of the customer's experience. This led to a shift in mindset and consequently behaviour for employees. They all understood that they each could make a distinctive contribution both to meeting the company's objectives and the customers' business needs.
- This significant level of participation from the development of the strategy culminating in its delivery, served to create a culture of shared

experiences and goals and subsequently increased work motivation, job satisfaction and commitment.

• Lastly, a greater understanding of performance management issues was created.

It was recognized that at the end of the day 'nothing endures but change'. With the organization's new culture of flexibility, adaptability and comradeship, the 'distinctiveness' of the organization and its people came unique customer relationships and increased profitability.

CHAPTER 36

'Why won't they do what we tell them?'

RICHARD PLENTY

Introduction

It's not deciding *what* to do that's the problem for many of today's leaders – it's understanding *how* to get their people to do it that increasingly keeps them awake at night. To survive in business, change is more necessary than ever, but research consistently shows that most change efforts fail. Why? The reasons given are many and varied, but the top obstacles to successful change are rarely related to technical difficulties and nearly always related to people:

- misunderstanding of what change is;
- lack of planning and preparation;
- no clear vision;
- goals set but too far away;
- tendency for the quick fix;
- poor communication;
- legacy of previous change;
- 'the way we do things around here';
- fear of failure and losing control;
- employee resistance at all levels;
- disregarding the domino effect;
- ill-prepared employees.

In fact, recent research indicates that the top obstacle to successful change is generally perceived to be 'employee resistance' – not just with front-line staff, but at all levels, including middle and even senior managers. Typically, there are difficulties in gaining sponsorship and support, getting people on board, gaining their commitment, and persuading them to do things differently from before. A lack of awareness and understanding of the change, comfort with the status quo, fear of the consequences and the existing heavy workloads of many employees all contribute to the difficulties.

This list hardly looks like rocket science, and it's difficult at first sight to see why, if it is so obvious, there should continue to be such difficulties in getting change implemented. It is not as if the topic of change management is a new area. There are now many academic courses dealing with the topic, articles about it abound in learned journals, and there is no shortage of information – over 600,000 references on Google in February 2004. And change management is now seen in many organizations as a key leader competency.

The problem lies deeper. Despite our knowledge of people and change management, there remains a tendency to ignore people issues until resistance is met, and then to attempt to isolate the issues and address or remove them as directly as possible. For example, even the excellent '6-sigma' website, which is devoted to process management, talks about tips for 'overcoming' people resistance to change. This approach works sometimes, but not always, and certainly does not work well with complex strategic change.

Somehow, when it comes to thinking about organizations and change, many leaders seem to dispense with their intuition, common sense and personal experience about people and still continue to view business and organizations primarily as a 'mechanical system', with people as cogs in the machine who can be manipulated at will. They know that 'people do not so much resist change, as being changed' (Beckhard and Harris, 1979), but prefer to gloss over that. This perspective can be traced back to the late nineteenth century through disciplines such as time and motion study, and arguably extends through to current methodologies such as business process re-engineering. These disciplines are useful and effective but do not tell the whole story about organizations, and unfortunately too often crowd out and subjugate other equally valid and useful perspectives.

The end-result is that those who are really interested in the human side of change, and have something genuinely useful to offer, generally have to fight for their place at the table with those whose primary focus is on problem solving and making direct improvements to processes, systems and structure as a way of improving business performance. What seems to be happening as a consequence is that not enough knowledge and experience of change management is being applied in a systematic way. Change management is too often an afterthought rather than a discipline considered from the outset.

If this process is to be reversed, there is a need for more people to understand just what specialists with an in-depth knowledge of people and change issues – business psychologists, and related professionals in the area of people-centred change – can offer organizations and their leaders. To appreciate this, it is helpful to go beyond the 'tip and techniques' courses on 'overcoming resistance' to understand in more depth both the individual and organizational impact of change, which requires an appreciation of the various paradigms on change which have influenced thinking in the field.

The impact of change on the individual

The impact of change on the individual has been extensively researched. People differ in their responses on the basis of previous life experience, personality and resilience, and their current circumstances and likely personal consequences for them. There are, however, a number of common factors that make an enormous difference to people's reactions to change and the extent to which they are likely to resist it.

First, do they really understand what the change is about and why it is necessary? The extent to which people feel committed to the overall purpose and values of the change can depend to a large extent on whether the organization has bothered to explain it to them. It is surprising how little effort some organizations make in explaining the basics.

Secondly, are they sufficiently involved in the change process? Being involved in change, a 'player' rather than a 'victim', has a hugely positive effect on how stressful the experience is likely to be, something that has been recognized by the UK Health and Safety Executive in its guidelines on stress.

Thirdly, is there enough understanding and support for people throughout the change process? Change in organizations can be very fast but people take time to adapt and typically go through a number of reasonably predictable phases of individual transition (see Figure 36.1).

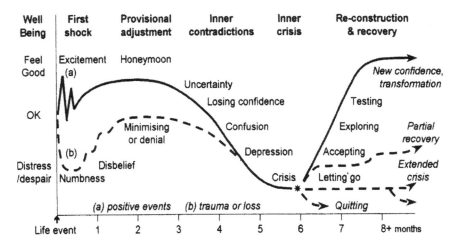

Figure 36.1 People take time to change.

Bridges (2003) has developed a number of strategies that can help people through their personal transitions – for example, he talks of the need to recognize and mark 'endings' (for instance, with ceremonies, symbolism and recognition of past achievements) rather than just to focus on new ways of working.

Lastly, is there enough training provided for people to learn the new skills and capabilities required? The 'soft' investment in the time and resources required to train people to develop new skills may be harder to justify than harder investments in systems, capital equipment and process design.

Frameworks for thinking about organizational change

There are a number of different paradigms that have influenced thinking on organizational change. Unfortunately, their practical implications differ and hence there is a need to understand in which circumstances each is the most appropriate.

The change pioneers

The change 'pioneers' of the second part of the twentieth century built on the realization that change as a topic in its own right was an important consideration in effecting organizational improvement. Whilst there had been insightful philosophers on change from Greek and Roman times (such as the *Book of Changes* by I Ching), the change pioneers were able to articulate and describe change in the detail, which made it possible for practical interventions to facilitate the process.

For example, Richard Beckhard, known as the father of organization development, developed an approach based on understanding the change 'gap' between the current reality and future vision, thinking that underpins most of the subsequent work in this area; Kotter (1996), a Harvard Business School professor, later developed an approach to change that took into account the political dimension, and the need for a 'guiding coalition' to help bring about major change.

These change models are generally rather mechanistic, linear and top down in character, and are typically concerned with the implementation of major, 'one-off' strategic change. They help in overcoming resistance to change by forcing leaders to articulate current reality and a future vision, to clarify the steps needed to close the change gap in a systematic way, to identify the engagement required of stakeholders, and to define the actions and resources that need to be committed. This paradigm is a good fit with major change involving project implementation, such as organizational restructuring, project management, and downsizing. It is less appropriate for change that is more iterative in nature.

Change as learning

By the 1980s and early 1990s the limitations of the change models developed by the change pioneers were increasingly evident. Change was not always linear, and very often a vision that was developed would itself undergo substantive modification as the change process unfolded. Chief executives such as John Harvey Jones in ICI achieved considerable success by getting their organizations moving, and adapting the vision as they went, taking into account input from their people. Practitioners such as Arie De Geuss (1997) from Shell also forcefully articulated the idea that strategic planning and change involved a substantive degree of adaptation and learning.

In his seminal publication *The Fifth Discipline: The Art and Practice of the Learning Organization,* Peter Senge (1994) helped give voice to that wave of interest. There was no recipe for success, but a number of areas were shown to be important: systems thinking and seeing the world in an integrated way; personal mastery, which focused on individual behaviours and developing approaches that facilitate learning; the importance of understanding and articulating different mental models through interaction and conversation skills; the development of shared vision and alignment of people with organizational strategies; and the importance of team as well as individual learning.

Where this approach works well, it is possible to see greatly enhanced levels of commitment as people genuinely begin to understand others' perspectives and have the opportunity to come up with solutions that will enhance both their own and the organization's performance and capability. This can have a very beneficial effect on levels of resistance. However, there is a risk that only lip service is paid to communication, involvement and engagement because ultimately all the really important decisions are reserved for those at the top.

Performance management systems

Perhaps the most widely used approaches to bringing about change in practice in large organizations at the present time, particularly those in American companies and the public sector, are those based on the systematic application of performance management frameworks. The approach starts from the basis that any strategy needs to be translated into actionable and operational reality if it is to be effective and deliver on its objectives.

In its simplest form, this implies that the corporate goals or objectives need to be clearly stated; these in turn need to be translated into operational plans and targets, which translate into personal and performance goals. The targets used can be benchmarked both internally and externally to provide objective standards and cover market, social, environmental and financial measures as part of a balanced scorecard. There is then a clear line of sight for the individual from his/her personal contribution to the achievement of corporate objectives. Not only that, but there is generally a feedback loop at all levels that communicates progress against objectives, rewards progress, and highlights and attempts to remedy deviations.

The origins of the performance management approach lie in quality management, but the impacts on behaviour at the team and individual level are such that it can also be viewed as a form of behaviour modification. Goals are set and agreed, plans are drawn up and rewards – positive and negative – are given depending on results. The processes work best when there is an environment in place that is conducive to learning, and where both positive and negative feedback is available. The psychology of this approach is usually reinforced by a vigorous and systematic alignment of reward systems with performance outcomes. Those who meet their targets do better than those who don't.

Performance management has gained popularity as it provides a straightforward way for senior leaders to feel they are connecting with their organizations, particularly in environments where they do not have direct control. From the employees' point of view, a good system can provide clarity, focus, and the opportunity to understand how their role fits into the bigger picture. It also provides a ready agenda to facilitate dialogue and discussion with supervisors. By providing a real sense of meaning and understanding, as well as extended opportunities for involvement, performance management systems can help to get people on board with change led from the top down.

Performance management systems do not, however, come without their risks. It is critical that the targets set are realistic and achievable. The approach can also become an 'empty shell' if targets are simply imposed and dialogue and communication is absent, with people feeling that there is 'management by numbers' rather than a genuine effort to help them achieve their goals.

Emergent change

Since the 1990s, lessons from research in fields such as physics, information theory and biology into complexity, 'complex adaptive systems', and emergence, has greatly influenced thinking about organizational change and transition. As with the organizational learning paradigm, this is built on systems thinking and represents an organic rather than mechanistic approach; however, it also reflects a belief in natural self-organization, and recognizes that change does not start only at the top of organizations but may begin anywhere. Authors such as Ralph Stacey et al. (2000) have provided an intellectual underpinning in this area.

In this view of the world, the job of leaders is to design an organizational infrastructure and environment that will facilitate and accelerate the natural processes of emergent change. The role of leaders in storytelling, helping to 'frame' and explain situations and make sense of the environment, becomes critical and it is essential to develop shared meaning through conversation and dialogue. Leaders focus on setting clear boundary conditions and challenging objectives, and providing the context and support for people to develop solutions for themselves. At the same time, they must resist the temptation to drive and control change, which can be an uncomfortable experience for managers used to more traditional management styles.

An interesting implication of this approach to change is that it turns on its head the conventional approach to change of 'unfreeze, change, and refreeze'. Since change is assumed to be always happening, the job of the leader is to recognize existing pockets of innovation occurring anywhere in the organization (freeze), work with that energy and shape it (adjust) and then set the organization free again (unfreeze).

Emergent change provides an excellent paradigm for bringing people on board because it builds on the energy that exists rather than assuming that all change must be imposed. However, it can be difficult to apply in circumstances where fast change is required that is driven by external necessity.

Leadership change

Last but not least, there are those who believe that it is only through people and structural change at the top leadership level that the energy can be provided for fundamental radical and energized change. In this view of the world, the organization is seen as a political system rather than a homogeneous entity and there is recognition of different interests and interest groups. Power is of the essence, symbolic change is important, and new leaders are chosen for their values and their loyalty, as well as their capability. The leader typically needs to take a rapid grasp on the levers of power, and the 'first 100 days' becomes of great significance.

This perspective of change owes more to Machiavelli than more recent thinkers, but remains nevertheless extremely relevant to large organizations today. The key roles of the top leader are to set the agenda for change, and to appoint and dismiss the leaders who report to him or her.

Revolution can at times be very effective – but the approach does run the risk of longer-term failure if fundamental cultural, structural and process issues are not addressed and the change in leadership becomes a way of avoiding dealing with deeper issues. There is also the risk of alienating key staff and leaders who do not fit into the new framework, as well as the (considerable) practical difficulty of finding enough new leaders of the right calibre in the first place. In this paradigm, resistance to change is simply overpowered, but this may have only a short-term effect.

Is change changing?

There is some evidence to suggest that the nature of change itself is changing. Up to the 1980s, the business environment was comparatively stable, and organizations were generally hierarchical in nature with clear lines of command and control. However, since the mid-1980s the business environment has evolved rapidly. Technology, particularly IT and Web technology, has created new possibilities for globalization. Waves of change affect most organizations: no sooner has one change been initiated than another seems to be necessary. Organizations have downsized and there are greater demands on the staff remaining. In these circumstances, people no longer accept what they are told to do without question; they increasingly need to be convinced that what they are asked to do makes sense both for them and the organization.

Change may also have complex psychological consequences. More change than ever is 'landing' on organizations from the outside – imposed change that is not necessarily welcomed and where the key psychological link between performance and reward is broken. Consider, for example, workers who find their jobs outsourced to another country for global economic reasons, despite consistently high standards of local performance. In these circumstances there is a political dimension, which needs to be understood, communicated and managed.

From the individual's perspective, more is being demanded. The speed of change is faster and, given the high and incessant workloads many people experience, it is hardly surprising that change fatigue then becomes a real possibility, with people simply worn out, cynical and apathetic about anything new. On the brighter side, as experience with change increases, some people are becoming more resilient as they develop experience, capability and new skills in dealing with uncertainty and ambiguity.

The shifting environment has meant that each change needs to be viewed as unique, and every situation and set of circumstances viewed in their own right. Rarely do real-life changes fall neatly into any one of the frameworks described earlier. In practice, change can be very messy. There is always more than one story about what is really happening and unanticipated problems, chaos rather than order, political infighting, unplanned events, turf wars and fear for the future often characterize much of what passes for normality. These circumstances do not lend themselves easily to a prescriptive mindset based upon a particular model of change.

There has also been a realization that stability can also be helpful, and that some things do not or should not change. Organizations that keep to core values but are flexible have been shown to outperform others over periods of time. It is important that organizations do not act in a way that cuts across their brand reputation, as brand financial values have become so high – up to $70 billion in the case of leading brands such as Coca-Cola and Microsoft. In order to preserve brand value, it is essential that the culture of organizations inside the company is as consistent as possible with that portrayed to the outside world.

Last but not least, the search continues for the Holy Grail of real commitment, for people who are driven to do what organizations want not because they are told to, but because they themselves passionately believe in it, has never been more intense. Apart from anything else, it represents a less expensive alternative than the supervision, control and reward systems required to enforce compliance, which is a difficult option to implement with educated staff who have the freedom to leave if they wish. Arguably, the most successful organizations in this respect to date have not been found in business but in networks of volunteers, religious groupings, and political activists where a deep belief in a common cause has been allied with emergent models of organization and change.

Leading and supporting change

Leaders of change increasingly need to concentrate on getting their people on board through real engagement, as well as building the organization's ability to deliver change for itself. A preoccupation with driving change, developing detailed project management plans, and regularly reviewing and monitoring progress is no longer enough. People treated as pawns in a game will usually dig their heels in.

Leaders' personal behaviour will be under intense scrutiny. They need to demonstrate personal commitment to the changes they advocate. They must stay focused and have the will, courage and faith to persevere through inevitable difficulties. They are role models whose personal commitment to change is communicated not just through formal plans, but also through their everyday personal behaviour and actions.

Leaders must also have a passion for communicating and explaining what is going on. Their role in 'framing' change, so that it can be understood, so that links with business strategy are clear, and so that the implications for people at all levels are properly considered, is very important (Higgs and Rowland, 2003). Painting the overall picture, and then giving people the space and time to work things out for themselves is an effective approach providing there is sufficient challenge and people have genuine choice (Bruch and Ghoshal, 2002). Creating a desire for change, rather than using a 'burning platform' scenario, provides a better way of gaining genuine commitment.

The good news for leaders is that once they have grasped, understood and accepted these basic concepts, the skills required are not overly technical and can be developed on the basis of personal experience, provided there is a will to reflect thoughtfully on what has worked and what has not. Intuition, insight and personal experience can count for a lot, provided that leaders are sufficiently open minded and ready to adapt their own behaviours. The 'not so good news' is that not all leaders are prepared to do this.

The other side of the coin is to invest in the resources and structures required to build change capability in the organization, so that the efforts of people at all levels are properly supported. This requires clear definitions of accountabilities, providing transparent tracking and monitoring systems, so that progress is visible, and using surveys, focus groups and 360-degree feedback, so that organizations have the infrastructure in place to learn from their experience, transfer learning and 'autocorrect' when things go wrong. Individual leaders, teams and individuals may need support in their personal 'transitions' as they review their ways of working and behaving. On a longer-term basis there is a need to align the people systems including (leader) selection, assessment and reward with the desired culture.

Business psychologists, and people-centred change specialists, are well equipped to support this type of change. The emerging role is one of change coordinator, whose role is to help choreograph change (see Figure 36.2). The coordinator acts as a consultant to the leader and the system, has a strategic focus, and co-designs the engagement, learning and implementation strategy. Typically the consultant will help to identify pressure points, and specific areas to intervene. He or she will work to help build and align the people systems required to support change, which may include assisting the organization in leader assessment and selection. At times it may be necessary for the consultant to confront leaders with evidence that shows their own behaviours are part of the problem, a task that requires considerable skill – and in some cases courage – to do effectively. The role may not be full time, and the profile of jobholders differs substantially from more conventional change managers, who often have a background in technical or project management and are generally used operationally to drive change.

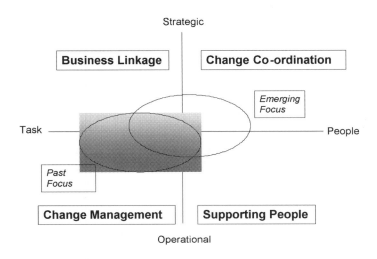

Adapted from Dave Ulrich, 'Human Resource Champions'

Figure 36.2 The ideal role for change specialists.

In summary, an earlier and more systematic incorporation of the thinking on the human side of change can be a great help to leaders struggling with how to implement change. Leaders need to focus on the 'how' as much as the 'what', designing processes for genuine engagement and building the organization's capability to manage change for itself. External support can be very useful in helping to orchestrate these activities. People may not do what they are told – but they will pursue what they really believe in.

Case study 1: organizational learning in the oil industry in the 1990s

The degree of change in the oil industry in the 1990s was very high as a consequence both of intense international competition and the fluctuations in oil prices that made it essential for organizations to be robust enough to survive in bad times as well as good. Cost cutting was essential. Globalization, restructuring, downsizing and the introduction of new technologies were typical responses but these solutions generally required considerable cultural change to be effective. People needed to do things differently if the businesses they worked in were to continue to survive and prosper.

In Shell, change paradigms based on organizational learning were used in many parts of the organization in an effort to develop the understanding and commitment required for people to adopt new ways of working. Companies such as Shell Oil in the US adopted organizational learning as a key strategy and invested heavily in sophisticated leadership training and training facilities. Newly formed global organizations such as Shell Chemicals built organizational learning concepts right from the start into their leadership team building, and management and communication processes.

The simplest examples of organizational learning in action were however generally in manufacturing sites where the intense pressure to cut costs and hence manpower meant that people simply had to work differently if they were to be successful. A good example was Stanlow Refinery in the UK, where a radical downsizing and cost-cutting programme in 1992 (from approximately 1,800 to 1,200 staff) was allied to a cultural change programme, which achieved considerable success over a period of 5 to 6 years, winning a Management Consultants Association award in 1998.

The author worked in conjunction with the top leadership team at the manufacturing site to co-design the initial phases of the engagement strategy. The style of working was very much as a 'choreographer' rather than 'project manager' of change. Liaising closely with the refinery manager, human resources manager and training coordinator, an ambitious programme of learning was sketched out, and the considerable investment required in resources and time 'guesstimated', then sold to the top management team.

The programme involved two principal stages. In the first phase, all members of staff attended off-site events at which the current business environment and the reasons for restructuring and downsizing were explained. There was ample opportunity for staff to talk about the issues, come up with ideas, and vent their feelings about aspects of the change over which they had little control. The second phase of the programme was more proactively engaging – it was designed to allow people in different parts of the plant to take time away from their jobs, and get involved in redesigning their own work and work processes to fit the new realities. A search was made for consultants who could help with this programme, and Coverdale consultants were selected to carry this out in a systematic manner, whilst being required to build change capability internally. The programme as a whole turned out to be a highly involving, developmental and performance-enhancing process that lasted a number of years.

Over time, the sense of ownership for the facility and its performance changed dramatically from a few people in management, to people at all levels in the plant. This is one of the most difficult things to achieve in organizational terms. The economic realities were widely understood, and staff began to take the initiative to improve performance and keep costs competitive. There was a realization that the plant would have to close if the organization could not keep improving – and that required commitment at all levels. For example, a shopfloor level group that identified and resolved an oil-spillage issue by itself saved over a million pounds.

Over the same period, management attention was focused on making changes to infrastructure, policies, and leadership/communication styles that were consistent with this new approach.

The improvement programme survived many changes in top leadership over the years as it became institutionalized in systems, processes and, just as important, values and behaviours of the whole system. The refinery itself has already survived many years longer than might have been initially expected, and the original investment in involving staff and giving them the space and time to work things out for themselves has been repaid many times over in productivity gains and plant improvements.

Case study 2: emergent change in the World Bank

Successful examples of emergent change in business are just beginning to be properly documented, and a case study in the *Harvard Business Review* of October 2002, written by Robert Chapman Wood and Gary Hamel, provides a very interesting example of many of the principles in action.

Wood and Hamel describe how the World Bank has developed an 'innovation market' to identify and fund new ideas that will combat poverty around the world. The traditional approach to funding projects was to evaluate new proposals and ideas through a bureaucratic top down process typical of most large organizations. Unfortunately the process was not working well, as no one at the top was able to properly evaluate more than a tiny proportion of proposals. Those few projects that did emerge were often highly capital intensive, and were not always successful in practice.

The process designed by the World Bank relied on a much more entrepreneurial market-based approach, and incorporates many of the principles of emergent change:

- New ideas were encouraged from all levels of the organization worldwide, and processes were set up to encourage people to talk with each other and engage in conversations about their ideas. The idea was to increase the surface area of experimentation, building on the fact that ideas tend to evolve and expand through conversations.

- A 'development marketplace' was held, at which over 700 people in 270 cramped booths competed with each other for funds. This provided an ideal forum for assessing the merits of various proposals to ensure that the most worthy received funding, and ensured that a measure of 'risk' was allowed, which would be unlikely if traditional executives were given control of the budget.
- Only projects that didn't require huge investments to succeed were supported. The philosophy was that investing thousands rather than millions of dollars let the World Bank fund many unproven but promising projects, which could ultimately produce more breakthrough ideas than central resource allocation.

The combination of grassroots innovation, a market-based approach to innovation and loosening the grip of traditional decision makers has proved a very successful strategy.

Acknowledgements

Ideas in this chapter were based on a lecture originally given to post-graduate students at King's College London in the Department of Organizational Psychiatry and Psychology. The author acknowledges the influence of conversations and communication with members of the Virtual Academy for Organizational Change, organized by the Association of Business Psychologists and YSC Ltd; Carol Cole of Carole Cole Associates; Terri Morrissey of Accomplish; Eric Burrows of The Work Foundation; John Smythe, Organizational Fellow with McKinsey & Company; Jim Cannon of Cannon Associates; Deborah Rowland of RFLC; and Paul Haken of Atkins Management Consultants. He thanks them all for their input.

PART 7
EPILOGUE

CHAPTER 37

Business psychology – the key role of learning and human capital

DAVID A LANE, AMIN RAJAN

The challenge for business psychology

As the contributors to this book demonstrate, there are a number of key challenges facing business psychologists as we seek to add value to organizations:

- the need to understand that consulting is itself changing – not offering product, but really developing service that reflects what clients want and need; how to ensure that different models of consulting meet their requirements, overt and covert;
- the need to challenge conventional thinking on measurement and prediction and look differently at how we view assessment centres and talent assessment at a senior level;
- the need to recognize that releasing talent is about development and includes a pivotal role for coaching;
- the need to understand why so many initiatives fail, by recognizing the key role of the business environment, its internal workings and culture;
- the need to look at the psychological input to areas such as the supply chain, including the consumer angle;
- the need to recognize that organizational change will contain larger-scale interventions but also small-scale narratives that emerge and impact in ever increasing circles of influence.

Underpinning much of this is the way we use human capital within an organization and the key role of learning. This concluding chapter is concerned with that underpinning: how we can use and develop the capital within organizations through learning and how we as business psychologists can develop ourselves.

The contributors to the book in different ways raise two central issues:

- Effective measurement. An effective measure must relate to the integration of human with business issues, employee values and stakeholder

355

interest. Human capital is not embedded in the heads of people; it is lived in the interactions between people where there is a shared value in collaboration. How an organization generates the shared values between its stakeholders and draws upon that entire capital, to sustain value, is the most interesting measure that can be employed.

- The role of learning. We see the critical issue in how learning is embedded, how it is developed, and then applied to generate value. This requires a detailed account of how learning is modelled in the organization rather than an emphasis on the training spend. Effective evaluation of development is absent in many organizations and limited in others. Some make considerable efforts and are able to report on the value that returns.

These two themes permeate the rest of the chapter.[1]

Leveraging the business through human capital development

Does the organization have as a core purpose the enhancement of human capital of all its stakeholders?

The approach taken to this question provides a framework to create and nurture intellectual capital in order to enhance the readiness of organizational leaders to take on the greater challenge of realizing their strategic options.

A company that can provide a coherent account of how it gives current and future executives space and resources to develop themselves and be innovative in growing the business and how that is translated into a development process for all employees will be more likely to sustain future value. In measuring human capital, therefore, there is a need to consider such accounts.

One approach provides for a company to create a narrative on its approach to human capital and support this narrative with evidence

1. Our chapter draws upon two studies. The National Employability Research Forum was a joint endeavour between PDF, the Chartered Institute of Personal and Development, the Cabinet Office, Department of Education and Skills, CBI, TUC, CREATE and some 30 leading UK organizations. Data were collected from over 900 organizations, public and private, large and small. This provided a detailed account of the relationships between employers and employees in generating high levels of employability. The report was authored by Amin Rajan, David Lane, Robert Wylie, Pat Cleverly, Penny van Eupen, Kirsty Chapple and Angela Puri, and published by CIPD, Create and PDF in 2000 as *Employability: Bridging the Gap Between Rhetoric and Reality*. The second study for the Work Foundation builds upon the first and considered further data on knowledge management within organizations and some 50 case studies to identify effective practices in human capital development. The study is in progress and is authored by David Lane and Amin Rajan.

appropriate to the account. This process parallels that used by professional bodies or universities when considering how to judge the experience of someone applying for advanced standing. The narrative then generates questions that form the basis of a human capital development process capable of measurement and report.

An example of a narrative and the questions it generates is:

We believe that as a responsible organization and corporate citizen we have an obligation to maximize leverage on our financial capital. Similarly, we all have a duty to release and maximize the intellectual capital and capability of our people and ourselves.

Executives have the biggest leverage potential. They have the freedom required to innovate through reconceptualizing the business, developing themselves through the experience and achieving quantum shifts in raising shareholder value. However, this organization enables all its employees to recognize that the relationship between their own commitments and development and the success of the organization represents the core mechanism for converting intellectual capital into shareholder value. Therefore we are committed as an organization to acknowledge, celebrate and develop all of our stakeholder relationships. Our potential for leverage of human capital is thereby multiplied.

We commit ourselves to:

- fully assessing the potential of all our people;
- building and leveraging the human capital in our organization;
- ensuring an effective developmental process that:
    - provides for individual preparation for development;
    - creates a range of development solutions matched to need;
    - generates opportunities to apply learning to key projects in the organization.
- Through experimentation and reflection on our learning we will create the link between our people and business growth.
- We will strive to align our people, their expectations and aspirations within the needs of the business and our stakeholders, to ensure that:
    - human capital is leveraged for business success;
    - our culture is supportive of the development of human capital;
    - our brand is viewed by customers and staff alike as supportive of their aspirations.
- These commitments will be reflected in our systems of operation to deliver our values and will be demonstrated in our day-to-day behaviours, so that we ensure shareholder returns and stakeholder satisfaction.

If this represents the company narrative, then a series of questions emerges. Thus the key questions of human capital development and its measurement become:

- Assessment – how does the organization assess its human capital and link this to development options relevant to personal and business growth?
- What are the processes for building the human capital base of the organization and how is that capital leveraged to achieve outstanding business results?
- How does the organization prepare individuals for development, apply learning to leverage work in progress, and develop them for future challenges?

Example of a development framework comprising three separate but interrelated components

Individual preparation – a process that will deliver an appropriate range of personal development support opportunities and interventions, which will be configured to optimize the development of the individual.

Application – identification of actual work-related learning and development opportunities, where the individual will (a) achieve real business results, and (b) be encouraged to use experience to derive learning that could be turned into case examples for contribution to development solutions.

Development solutions – a mechanism that will provide access for the individual to a range of personally 'customized' developmental tools and knowledge, including case studies, internal and external programmes, taught or experiential learning, leading expertise and world-class leadership material.

- What process does the organization use to experiment with alternative ways of leveraging human capital, reflect on that experience and apply the lessons learned to business growth?
- What attempts are made to understand the aspirations and hopes of all stakeholders and how does the organization capture and leverage these to build and sustain the future?
- What process does the organization use to align the aspirations of their people with business needs?

Organizational process questions to align personal aspirations with business needs

- What are the key competitive drivers for the business and how is the human capital marshalled to address these drivers?
- To what extent does the culture of the business place a premium on the development of human capital and the well-being of all its stakeholders as part of its business model?

- What does the brand stand for – exploitation, intellectual drive, burned-out executives, stakeholder inclusion, profit at all cost, short-term gain or long-term sustainability?
- Do the people in the organization feel that they are encouraged to share ideas, and have their ideas acknowledged? Are they proud to work for the organization?
- What do people expect of the organization and what does it expect of them? How are these expectations aligned?
- What aspirations do people have for themselves, their colleagues, their families and the organization and what aspirations does it have for them? Are these aspirations conducive to the development of human capital – do they encourage excellence, development, new ideas, and collaboration?
- Are the values in the organization supportive of the development of human capital? Do people (particularly leaders) behave in ways that encourage the sharing and use of knowledge, and are there systems in place to encourage the sharing, capturing, leverage and use of human capital?

Where there is a coherent account it is possible to ask questions that create the basis for a human capital measure. Outside of an account (or narrative) that is relevant to that organization in its market, any evidence quoted will be historical and not live.

Thus the key starting point for any viable measure of human capital must be the narrative account by the organization of its values, behaviours and systems for human capital development. Evidence in support of that narrative can then be provided. Those reading that account can then consider the coherence of the evidence compared with the narrative.

To establish such a process requires us to understand three key areas.

1. The social contract between employer and employee to ensure that staff acquire the competence they need to stay employable and the organization achieves the results it needs to stay ahead of the competition.
The recognition that lifelong learning is a key building block in the creation of a viable economy has led many nations to promote it as a tool of economic policy. Unfortunately, it has become increasingly clear that the major users of learning initiatives at work and elsewhere are those who have already benefited from the educational system.

Globalization and the rapid pace of technological change have increased the pressure on businesses to remain competitive, both nationally and internationally. Britain, it is argued, needs to differentiate its uniqueness in ways that competitors find hard to imitate. The assets for this differentiation are increasingly in the form of knowledge, skills and creativity.

To keep ahead:

- people must continue to learn and update the skills they need throughout their working lives and obtain the tools to grasp the opportunities generated in a modern, knowledge-driven labour market;
- organizations must leverage that learning to ensure sustainable competitiveness – hence the importance of human capital in the current debate.

The importance of this learning and competitiveness link is widely believed and drives much of the policy agenda in different countries. That it is important seems not to be doubted although the claim may be seriously overstated and the impact of spending on development activities may be less than commonly assumed. Companies committed to a learning agenda argue strongly for its value. Motorola, for example, estimates that it receives a return of $33 for every dollar it spends on education, and it believes that 5% of an employee's time should be spent on development activities.

In a study for the Chartered Institute of Personnel and Development of 300 small and medium sized enterprises (SME) the link was apparent and has since been increasingly recognized (Lane, 1994):

> A new social contract between employer and employee is emerging in which continuous development is seen as the key to ensuring that staff acquire the competence they need to stay employable and organisations achieve the results they need to stay ahead of the competition.

However, it was notable that commitment to training in SMEs was much higher in companies where managing directors were committed to their own learning. The question of how such commitments can be achieved generates a broad range of possible solutions.

This has filtered down into a large number of initiatives at government, union, and employer level. When we look at the impact of various measures, it seems that most employees feel that their employer is already strongly committed to improve their skills and qualifications. Commitment is not an issue. And yet they also indicated that time off for training was a major impediment to development – therefore access was an issue. Looking behind those positive findings reveals a problem in linking learning to employment prospects. The majority do not feel that access to training will improve their sense of job security. In particular, a study by the MSF Union (quoted in the Lane and Rajan Study) indicated that most employees felt employers were providing training for skills they already had but not for their future skill needs. Other research quoted indicates that employees feel that commitment to both current and future training needs is something that employers should provide.

What we had was a mismatch between the employees' and employers' views of what training was needed, when it needed to be provided and the ability to access it, although they agreed these were important. This resulted in reluctance by many employees to engage in a training agenda where they could see no benefit to their immediate or longer-term employment prospects.

Consequently, it is not training spend that reveals value in the company. It is how the social contract for employability (competitiveness and development) operates in the business that provides the key information.

2. Ensuring that learning offered makes sense for the business and the recipient of the offer in terms of skill, confidence, timing and learning process to create the commitment to self-directed lifelong learning.

Now imagine for a moment that you work for a company, that seriously values learning:

- it is committed to overcome all the barriers that get in the way;
- it ensures that you are well informed about the options available;
- it creates time off from work, so that you can learn without impact on your domestic responsibilities;
- it expresses interest in your learning and will support it even if the topic you choose has no direct relevance to your work role;
- it will even pay you extra for your trouble.

What would you say about such an offer?

Overwhelming, participants in the companies surveyed expressed high levels of satisfaction with such systems when they were available. Yet, the companies involved found that they *still could not persuade staff to take up development options.* Many companies also expressed disappointment with the outcome of their training expenditure even where they could persuade staff to undertake it. Evidence that staff (beyond the basic skill level) applied their training to work situations was limited.

As you look behind these somewhat depressing findings a picture emerges to indicate what it takes to convert these reluctant learners into committed students. There is no simple solution, but our case studies revealed some similarities within the more successful efforts to sustain human capital development.

The research identified five critical elements that underpin successful interventions. These are:

- the role of learning myths, beliefs and support systems;
- the understanding that work-based learning is more than learning located at work;
- the importance of a learning coach;
- the creation of a commitment to self-directed lifelong learning;
- the relevance and timing of the learning offer.

In order to appreciate why these elements matter, a number of barriers to learning need to be explored. Subsequently, we can consider the process of getting it right.

Those who see themselves as highly employable and effective self-directed learners see all events that happen to them as learning opportunities even under difficult circumstances. The less effective think of learning as something that happens in particular designated training events. Thus a series of myths can build up about their learning and their own capacity, which gets in the way.

Where individuals were exposed to managers who themselves are excited about learning, convey that excitement, and put in place support systems, they woke up to the possibility of a broader view of learning. Such managers challenged the accompanying learning myths that individuals developed in childhood.

- They used their 'own sense of self as a learner' to promote learning in others.
- They exposed their staff to people or events that opened a prospect of an alternative way.
- They provided or accessed a support structure to make it possible.
- They engaged in frequent learning conversations.
- They sought to use and underpin significant learning moments.

It is clear that access to opportunities to learn and apply that learning vary within the same organization. Some evaluate and grasp appropriate opportunities and, again, the role of the line manager within a supportive environment appears important. Some managers are natural learning coaches because they are themselves dedicated to lifelong learning. Others have come to understand the importance of becoming a learning coach to ensure high levels of performance from their staff. Even within the same organization, where there is a set of values favouring learning uptake, they proclaim themselves to be a learning organization and win all the prizes, the application of learning varies widely. The presence of a manager who acts as a learning coach makes the difference.

If improving employability is about changing the employee mindset, then central to its development is personal responsibility for learning. This is reflected in what employers saw as the main avenues of training and development over the next three years.

The top five were:

- individual learning and development plans;
- in-house formal courses;
- coaching by line managers;
- use of NVQ/SVQ and modern apprenticeships;
- involvement in different work-based projects/assignment.

However, it was also apparent that employees felt well trained when:

- they understand how their performance is assessed;
- they think their performance has been assessed fairly;
- there are sufficient opportunities for them to receive training to improve their skills in their current job;
- there are systems in place where they work to evaluate the effectiveness of the training they receive;
- they have enough flexibility in their job to do what is necessary to provide good service to their customers.

That is, *they understand the performance needed and the gaps in their performance, receive training to address them and can apply learning to client benefit.* The key themes of trust, recognition, access to information and support, the role of management and the opportunity to apply learning to accomplish something worthwhile at work, appear in each of the subsamples when internal company data are analysed. Consequently, decisions about learning involved a broader set of decisions about the company. *Individuals commit to development to the extent that the company commits to them.* Those who had a definite intent to engage in learning did so because:

- they needed to develop their current skills further;
- they felt that it was important to keep their skill base up to date;
- it was important to them that they do a good job;
- they felt that they could learn a great deal in their present job;
- they felt that to be employable these days you need skills, personal attributes and commitment to customer goals;
- they felt that their manager was willing to shield the group from the wider organization, so that it can try out ideas in a supporting and trusting atmosphere.

Whatever source of learning is identified the central part played by managers was emphasized throughout the study. This makes it important to understand what it is that managers believe and what their staff believes. Staff believed that 'my manager really encourages me to learn' if they also stated that:

- they have plenty of opportunities for training in their current workplace;
- their ideas are valued by their employer;
- it is important to them that they do a good job;
- they work in an environment that encourages them to learn;
- they feel that they are consulted about workplace changes;
- they are encouraged to share useful ideas with others;
- the opinion of their employer regarding their learning matters to them.

It is clear that a new employer–employee relationship at work is evolving. Individuals recognize the scale and complexity of the changes in culture, structures and behaviours that confront them. They felt the pain and for many their worldview was shattered.

The concept of employability was supposed to offer an alternative to the job security of the past. It was about developing committed and motivated individuals who aligned themselves to the employer's business goals while meeting their own personal goals. Creating models of work-based learning that equipped the individual for future challenge was the central theme. Some have bought into this idea and expect their employers to deliver on the promise. Some remain confused and feel disenfranchised. It is clear, however, that employability is about far more than offering individual skills training.

Employability is about engaging with the worldview of the individual rather than the imposition of top-down initiatives. If you do not take into account the worldview of the individual, you will not deliver internal or external employability. Your best people go elsewhere to find employers who value their energy, creativity and commitment to delivering results.

In pursuit of this new worldview, a number of individuals have ceased to view their career as a number of hierarchical steps. Rather, career is viewed as a series of projects in pursuit of their own employability. Individuals view employability as a process of balancing the various drivers impacting on them with the mechanisms they have available to prepare themselves. This requires that employers seek to understand how individuals form the intention, commit themselves, undertake and evaluate their learning. It is not about the provision of more training based on the outcome of appraisal or personal development planning that lacks credibility. It is this more elaborated view of employability, as a process of continuous learning and active decision making, not as the acquisition of set skills, that drives individuals.

Most employers have yet to recognize this worldview and the complexity of the decision process that employees use to decide on their commitment to the training on offer.

3. Managers living the values, demonstrating the behaviours and using the systems to enable their people to find personal expression in the corporate vision.

Individuals make it clear that the failure of many learning, development and knowledge management offerings reflects the failure to incorporate personal learning into the corporate direction. Exemplar companies show that four issues impact on individual motivation:

- Organizational direction: where are we going? Individuals want to feel consulted about the impact of work-based changes, belief in the direction of the organization and the credibility of its leadership.

- Personal direction: where am I going? This is about alignment of personal to business goals and the ability to see how personal 'interests at hand' can be satisfied in the current role.
- Incentives: what's in it for me? Incentives are now viewed in broad terms. A range of drivers is important, most particularly balancing life and work aspirations.
- Development risk: can I achieve my objectives? All learning involves risk of failure. Some organizations stress the culture of performance but do not provide the safety net necessary to enable people to achieve. Individuals assess the risks that any development involves and seek feedback on the consequences of any action taken. Organizations that stress the importance of learning but fail to measure its impact convey the message that development does not matter. This is especially so if business targets are rigorously assessed.

Even in organizations that profess a commitment to best practice and see themselves as 'investors in people', individuals claim that there is a gap between rhetoric and the reality. They identify this gap in the difference between those things they feel are important and the performance of their managers in delivering them. This applies at all levels within organizations and is particularly evident when individuals can point to exhortations to engage in learning by senior managers who themselves are not engaged in any personal development.

The models a company uses to develop business excellence need to make it possible for individuals to answer those four questions. At the very basic level, individuals want to be able to see the connection between personal goals (such as doing a good job) and the responses that the above questions generate.

Individuals wish to engage in learning that delivers benefits to their personal development, career prospects, and skills acquisition. They will make the extra effort in the organization if they believe they receive recognition for work well done and see their efforts rewarded through promotion, support and encouragement and are fairly remunerated.

To a limited extent best practice organizations are now striving to deliver the promise of employability. That promise was, 'in return for high performance we will improve your future prospects for employment here or in the broader labour market'.

In order to help individuals form an intention to improve their employability and in turn commit to lifelong learning, organizations need to recognize and support individual efforts in four main areas:

- Managing self: primarily understanding the expectations and values that drive people's approach to their life and work. For many it involves a sustainable interesting job, career opportunity either through upward progression or varied work experiences, work–life balance and financial security.

- Managing others: understanding the key relationships that matter to individuals. This will involve the individual's family and community but is certainly influenced by a good line manager who promotes confidence and self-esteem. To maintain employability it is critical for individuals to use their personal networks of contacts to help them manage their career.

- Managing results: understanding the requirements for effective performance and managing the processes for achieving them out of the desire to do a good job. It is also about personal recognition for a job well done and, for some, a sense of personal legacy to leave a lasting impact.

- Managing consequences: the feedback mechanisms that enable individuals to make judgements about the commitment they are prepared to make to their job, to their development and to achieve work–life balance. The feedback received, through the consequences that impact upon them, determines the extent to which individuals are prepared to make that extra effort to deliver outstanding results.

Learning and development offerings that promote 'learning conversations' that enable individuals to manage themselves, others, results and consequences, do, it seems, have a greater chance of being accepted.

- Managing self-
  expectancy/values

- Managing others
  significance/norms

- Managing results
  perceived control

- Managing consequences
  behaviour modified by
  feedback

Figure 37.1 Learning conversation to create an intention to improve employability.

The conversations enable individuals to make connections between:

- what matters to them – their values and expectations;
- what matters to those who matter to them – their families, bosses, peers, companies;

- what matters if they are to deliver results – standards, performance, sense of control;
- what happens when they take action that matters to them – recognition, satisfaction.

Commitment to develop and share learning

Individuals vary in their commitment to develop and share their knowledge. For some the prospect of engagement with like-minded learners is enticing; they will willingly develop their human capital and share with others in the creation of new knowledge. If the commitment to lifelong learning is not generated at school, it can be generated later, but the models that were found to generate inclusion at school also apply later in life.

Individuals are selective in using opportunities for learning and development to improve their employability. In so far as external and internal employability depends upon training, development and other experiential learning to promote transferable skills and attributes, six groups have been identified. Two of these groups (franchise builders and career builders) are receiving more attention than others.

'Franchise builders' have a strong commitment to their craft or profession and are keen to build a strong personal brand that helps them in the internal market-place. They make use of support systems in their organization to help them develop but will find them elsewhere if necessary. Their loyalty is to their craft but, while preferring to make their mark and leave a personal legacy, they will switch employment in pursuit of better opportunities. They prefer flexibility in their working arrangements and enjoy being judged by results rather than having their performance managed for them. They are 'innovators' in their approach to development.

'Career builders' stress the importance of the partnership between themselves and their employers for training and development. They make use of the systems that exist within the organization to help them improve their performance. They work well with performance management systems and can adapt to meet changing circumstances. They are prepared to consider their role in its wider context and adapt their way of working to achieve results. They show loyalty to their organization and aspire to progress in the existing workplace. They are 'adaptors' who use existing development offerings to meet their needs.

'Career satisficers' want a career but perceive it in narrow terms. They expect their development to be supported by their employers but tend to wait to be asked rather than actively seek opportunities. Unlike the first two groups who have skills and abilities that their organizations both value and develop highly, this group tends to be trained to do their job.

Their worldview tends to be 'me and my job'. They value clear systems and procedures and particularly quality standards that enable them to fulfil their objective to do a good job. They accept development scripts written by others and try to 'act' in accordance with them to the best of their ability.

Career satisficers and the other three groups tend to receive less support since they are perceived as wanting a job not a career. Some of them who enjoy making an impact, *portfolio workers* in particular, see this as shortsighted. They may be working on contracts alongside other groups but are denied access to the training that would enable them to improve delivery of contracted services. They would welcome the opportunity to develop through experience in leading-edge contexts but will do what it takes to develop themselves where it improves their marketability. They tend to become dissatisfied with their current job. *Flexible workers* are often denied training access but are increasingly finding development opportunities through the agencies that manage their employment. *Job satisficers* have little sense of their own skills or prospects and believe that they miss out on training and development opportunities.

For those who are not so committed, inclusion in lifelong learning comes through systems of support and exposure to a manager who takes their role as coach seriously. Within such a structure if the offer is timely and appropriate staff will accept it. We saw far too many examples of offers that were neither.

People have to feel that they are part of a safe, valued learning environment that respects their worldview and the place of learning within it. Skills can then be acquired through key people, events and moments, but those in a position to assist others also need the values and competence to be a learning coach. The lack of such competence was one of the clearest concerns expressed to us by managers who were committed to the values. Organizations talked much and often invested heavily in learning but did not understand what it took to engage their staff in the process. Even the companies that won all the prizes quietly admitted dissatisfaction with the take-up of their offers.

So what is the way forward?

First, employers need a view that is broader than knowledge alone. They need at a minimum to think of learning and employability as a process not as training for a specific set of competencies. It goes beyond training courses and remunerating people, so that they are motivated to deliver results. It is about engaging with people's worldviews and helping them to balance their commitment to delivering business results with their own personal agenda. This requires an educational model (a pedagogy) for work-based learning. If we want to promote learning at work, discussion on those educational roles must take place. Individuals are more prepared to experience new learning opportunities if they see that their organization is open in its communication with them, so it is important to encourage openness.

Second is ensuring that individuals can prepare for the future by helping them to have the tools that they need to plan, respond to current pressures, recover from periods of difficulty, and mitigate the effect of events outside their control. A few organizations are striving towards offering their employees help at that level of preparation. A curriculum for employability and lifelong learning is needed, which genuinely delivers employability.

Third is the need to have leaders at all levels with the skills, values and behaviours consistent with the business culture they are seeking to develop. If learning is central to that culture, leaders and managers in schools and public and private sector organizations need themselves to be actively engaged in their own ongoing development. They also need coaching skills to assist others. Managers identify assisting others' learning as one of their key concerns. Creating programmes to enhance coaching/mentoring skills is a priority to create educational role models. Such initiatives need to be encouraged.

Finally, what are the implications for our learning as professionals in this field? We need to:

- Understand our own profile as a learner, are we franchise builders?
- Integrate our understanding of psychology with our understanding of learning in business – what social contract exists for us?
- Adopt a continuing commitment to inquiry – what is the evidence base on which we stand?
- Demonstrate our commitment as both scientist and reflective practitioners drawing upon the knowledge base and our own searching within ourselves.
- Be actively engaged in personal development, not course attendance, but as this chapter argues, in the development of our human capital.
- Base this knowledge in our understanding of the business environment in which we work – how our own development is aligned to our role – and to ask of our self and our profession the questions we ask of others.

References

Adair J (1975) Action Centered Leadership. New York: McGraw-Hill.

Adams S (1998) The Joy of Work. New York: HarperCollins.

Ajzen I, Madden JT (1986) Prediction of goal-directed behaviour: attitudes, intentions, and perceived behavioural control. Journal of Experimental Social Psychology 22: 453–74.

Alexander AD (1989) Successfully implementing strategic decisions. In D Asch, C Bowman (eds) Strategic Management. Buckingham: Open University Press.

Allan J, Fairclough G, Heinzen B (2002) The Power of the Tale. Using Narratives for Organisational Success. Chichester: Wiley.

Andrews Munro Ltd (2000) Is Talent Enough? A Survey of the Career Tactics of UK Managers. Chipping Norton: Andrews Munro Ltd.

Appelbaum E et al. (2002) Manufacturing advantage: why high performance systems pay off. Ithaca NY: ILR/Cornell University Press.

Appelbaum SH, Harel V, Shapiro B (1998) The developmental assessment centre: the next generation. Career Development International 2(4): 5–12.

Argyle M (1969) Social Interaction. London: Methuen.

Argyle M, Henderson M (1985) The Anatomy of Relationships. Harmondsworth: Penguin Books.

Argyris C (1970) Intervention Theory and Practice. Reading MA: Addison-Wesley.

Atkinson M, Kydd C (1997) Individual characteristics associated with World Wide Web use: an empirical study of playfulness and motivation. The Database for Advances in Information Systems 28(2): 53–62.

Bahn C (1979) Can intelligence tests predict executive competency? Personnel (July–August): 52–8.

Bandura A (1986) Social Foundations of Thought and Action: A Social Cognitive Theory. Englewood Cliffs NJ: Prentice-Hall.

Barham K, Willis S (1993) Management Across Frontiers – Identifying the Competencies of Successful International Managers. London: Ashridge Management Research Group.

Baron H, Chudleigh P (1999) Assessment: is bias in the eye of the beholder? Selection and Development Review 15(4): 10–14.

Baron H, Janman K (1996) Fairness in the assessment centre. International Review of Industrial and Organizational Psychology 11: 61–114.

Baron RA (1989) Impression management by applicants during employment interviews: the 'too much of a good thing' effect. In RW Eder, GR Ferris(eds) The Employment Interview: Theory, Research, Practice. Newbury Park CA: Sage Publications.

Bartram D (2002) Assessment in organizations. In R Hambleton, T Oakland (eds) Applied Psychology: An International Review. Oxford: Blackwell.

Baruch Y, Peiperl M (1997) High flyers: glorious past, gloomy present, any future? Career Development International 2(7): 354–8.

Bass BM (1985) Leadership and Performance Beyond Expectations. New York: The Free Press.

Bateman B, Wilson FC (2002) Team effectiveness: development of an audit questionnaire. Journal of Management Development 21(3): 215–26.

Beard D, Lee G (1990) Improved connections at BT's development centres. Personnel Management (April): 61–3.

Beckhard R, Harris RT (1997) Organizational Transitions: Managing Complex Change. Reading MA: Addison-Wesley.

Beer M (1976) The technology of organization development. In M Dunnette (ed.) Industrial and Organizational Psychology. Chicago: Rand McNally.

Beer M, Eisenstat RA, Spector B (1993) The critical path to effective change. In C Mabey, W Mayon-White (eds) Managing Change. Buckingham: Open University Press.

Bennis W, Benne KD, Chin R (eds) (1969) The Planning of Change. New York: Holt, Rienhart & Winston.

Bennis W, Nanus B (1985) Leaders: The Strategies for Taking Charge. New York: Harper & Row.

Bentley T (2001) The emerging system. Gestalt Review 10(1): 13–19.

Bentley T, Clayton S (1998) Profiting From Diversity. Aldershot: Gower.

Berne E (1973) What Do You Say After You Say Hello? New York: Sigma Books.

Berscheid E, Walster E (1978) Interpersonal Attraction. Revised edition. Reading MA: Addison-Wesley.

Bevan S, Thompson M (1992) Performance Management in the UK: Analysis of the Issues. London: Institute of Personnel Management.

Bhote KR (1996) Beyond Customer Satisfaction to Customer Loyalty. New York: American Management Association.

Borman WC, Bush DH (1993) More progress towards a taxonomy of managerial performance requirements. Human Performance 6: 1–11.

Boyatzis RN (1982) Accurate Self-assessment in Managers. The Competent Manager: A Model for Effective Performance. New York: Wiley.

Boyle S, Fullerton J, Yapp M (1993) The rise of the assessment centre: a survey of usage within the UK. Selection and Development Review 9: 1–4.

Bray DW, Grant DL (1966) The assessment center in the measurement of potential for business management. Psychological Monographs 80(17): 1–27.

Breakwell GM, Hammond S, Fife-Schaw C (1999) Research Methods in Psychology. London: Sage.

Brewerton PM, Millward LJ (2001) Organizational Research Methods. London: Sage.

Bridges W (2003) Managing Transitions: Making the Most of Change. Cambridge MA: Perseus.

Briggs A (1983) A Social History of Britain. London: Weidenfeld & Nicolson.

Briscoe DR (1997) Assessment centers: cross-cultural and cross-national issues. Journal of Social Behaviour and Personality 12(5): 13–52.

Brittain S (2002) The Use of Assessment Centre Data in a Financial Services Organization – HR and Line Manager Perceptions. Unpublished research report.

Brittain S, Ryder P (1999) Get complex. People Management (November): 48–51.

Brittain S, Yeung R (2002) Beyond the interview. In J Pickford (ed.) Mastering People Management. London: Financial Times/Prentice-Hall.

Brockner JB, Tyler TR, Cooper-Schneider R (1992) The influence of prior commitment to an institution on reactions to perceived unfairness: the higher they are, the harder they fall. Administrative Science Quarterly 37: 241–61.

Brogden HE (1949) When testing pays off. Personnel Psychology 2: 171–83.

Brown SA (2000) Customer Relationship Management – a Strategic Imperative in the World of E-Business. New York: Wiley.

Bruch H, Ghoshal S (2002) Beware the Busy Manager. Harvard Business Review 80(2): 62–9.

Buckley N, Williams R (2002) Testing on the Web – response patterns and impression management. Selection and Development Review 18(1): 3–8.

Burns T, Stalker GM (1961) The Management of Innovation. London: Tavistock Publications.

Burrough B, Helyar J (1991) Barbarians at the Gate. New York: Harper.

Butler P et al. (1997) A revolution in interaction. McKinsey Quarterly 1: 8.

Cabrera FC, Raju NS (2001) Utility analysis: current trends and future directions. International Journal of Selection and Assessment 9: 92–102.

Capelli P (1999) The New Deal at Work: Managing the Market-Driven Workforce. Boston MA: Harvard Business School Press.

Carey D, Ogden D (2000) CEO Succession: a Window on How Boards can Get it Right when Choosing new Chief Executives. Oxford: Oxford University Press.

Carron A et al. (1982) Cohesion and performance in sport: a meta analysis. Journal of Sport and Exercise Psychology 24(2): 168–88.

Carter SM, West M (1998) Reflexivity, effectiveness, and mental health in BBC-TV production teams. Small Group Research 29(5): 583–601.

Chan D et al. (1998) Applicant perceptions of test fairness: integrative justice and self-serving bias perspectives. International Journal of Selection and Assessment 6: 232–9.

Chartered Institute of Personnel and Development (2001) Performance through People: the New People Management. The Change Agenda. London: CIPD.

Chartered Institute of Personnel and Development (2002) Sustaining Success in Difficult Times. London: CIPD.

Clarkson P, Shaw P (1995) Human relationships at work in organisations. In P Clarkson (ed.) Change in Organisations. London: Whurr Publishers Ltd.

Clayton S (2001) Simply People. Gloucestershire: The Space Between.

Coch L, French J (1948) Overcoming resistance to change. Human Relations 1(4): 512–32.

Cohen BM, Moses JL, Byham WC (1974) The Validity of Assessment Centers: a Literature Review. Pittsburgh PA: Development Dimensions Press.

Cohen DS (2001) The Talent Edge: a Behavioural Approach to Hiring, Developing and Keeping Top Performers. Toronto: John Wiley & Sons.

Collins J (2001) From Good to Great. Why Some Companies Make the Leap and Others Don't. London: Random House.

Collins JM, Schmidt FL, Sanchez-Ku M, Thomas L, McDaniel MA, Le H (2003) Can basic individual differences shed light on the construct meaning of assessment centre evaluations? International Journal of Selection and Assessment 11(1): 17–29.

Conforti M (1999) Field, Form and Fate. Woodstock CT: Spring Publications.

Conger JA et al. (1999). The Leader's Change Handbook: An Essential Guide to Setting Direction and Taking Action. San Francisco CA: Jossey-Bass.

Constable A (1999) cited in Lee G (2000) The state of the art in development centres. Selection and Development Review 16(1): 10–14.

Cook M (1998) Personnel Selection: Adding Value Through People. Chichester: Wiley.

Cooke RA, Herche J (1992) Assessment centres: an untapped resource for global salesforce management. Journal of Personal Selling and Sales Management 12(3): 31–8.

Cooke RA, Szumal JL (1993) Measuring normative beliefs and shared behavioural expectations in organizations: the reliability and validity of the organizational culture inventory. Psychological Reports 72(3): 1299–330.

Cooperrider D, Whitney D (2001) A positive revolution in change: appreciative inquiry. In: D Cooperrider et al. (eds) (2001) Appreciative Inquiry, an Emerging Direction for Organisational Development. Champaign IL: Stipes Publishing LLC.

Cooperrider D et al. (eds) (2001) Appreciative Inquiry, an Emerging Direction for Organisational Development. Champaign IL: Stipes Publishing LLC.

Covey SR (1989) The Seven Habits of Highly Effective People. London: Simon & Schuster.

Cziksentmihalyi M (2003) Good Business. Leadership, Flow and the Making of Meaning. London: Hodder & Stoughton.

Dalton P, Dunnette G (1992) A Psychology for Living. Personal Construct Theory for Professionals and Clients. Chichester: John Wiley & Sons.

Dany F, Torchy V (1994) Recruitment and selection in Europe: policies, practices and methods. In C Brewster, A Hegewisch (eds) Policy and Practice in European Human Resource Management: The Price Waterhouse Cranfield Survey. London: Routledge.

Dawkins R (1976) The Selfish Gene. New York: Oxford University Press.

De Geuss A (1997) The Living Company. London: Nicholas Brealey Publishing.

De Waal F (1989) Chimpanzee Politics. Baltimore MD: Johns Hopkins University Press.

Denning, S (2001) The Springboard. Oxford: Butterworth Heinemann.

Dixon N (1994) On the Psychology of Military Incompetence. London: Pimlico.

Doorewaard H, Van Hootegem G, Huys R (2002) Team responsibility structure and team performance. Personnel Review 31(3): 356–70.

Dos Santos RLG, De Moraes A (1996) Graphic Interface for Automatic Teller Machine. Proceedings of the Silicon Valley Ergonomics Conference and Exposition. Palo Alto, CA: Silicon Valley, pp. 53–9.

Dubey B, Agrawal A, Palia R (2001) Personality profile and HRD intervention in a telephone cables company. Journal of Projective Psychology and Mental Health 8(2): 127–34.

Duignan K (2004) Proper Order? The Organisational Stress Self-Assessment Audit. Croydon: Enabling Space.

Dulewicz SV (1994) Personal competencies, personality and responsibilities of middle managers. Competency Journal 1(3): 20–9.

Dulewicz SV, Haley G (1989) A long-term assessment centre validation in a major UK company. Guidance and Assessment Review 5(6): 1–5.

Dulewicz V (1989) Assessment centres as the route to competence. Personnel Management (November): 56–9.

Dulewicz V (1991) Improving assessment centres. Personnel Management 23(6): 50–5.

Dulewicz V, Higgs M (2000) Emotional intelligence: a review and evaluation study. Journal of Management Psychology 15(4): 341–72.

Earnshaw J, Cooper C (2001) Stress and Employers' Liability. 2nd edn. London: Chartered Institute of Personnel and Development.

Fandt P, Ferris G (1990) The management of information and impressions: when employees behave opportunistically. Organisational Behaviour and Human Decision Processes 45: 140–58.

Feldman DC (1988) Managing Careers in Organisations. Glenview IL: Scott, Foresman.

Feltham R (1988) Justifying investment. Personnel Management 20(8): 17–18.

Ferris G, Judge T (1991) Personnel/human resource management: a political international perspective. Journal of Management 17: 447–88.

Ferris G, Kacmar K (1992) Perceptions of organisational politics. Journal of Management 18 (1): 93–116.

Ferris GR, Russ GS, Fandt PM (1989) Politics in organisations. In RA Giacalone, P Rosenfield (eds) Impression Management and Organisations. Hillsdale NJ: Erlbaum.

Firth J, Nickson S (2002) Health and Safety at Work. Legal Essentials. London: Hammond Suddards Edge/Chartered Institute of Personnel and Development.

Fleenor JW (1997) 360-degree feedback systems. Personnel Psychology 50: 1084–8.

Fleishman EA, Wetrogan LI, Uhlman CE, Marshall-Mies JC (1995) In NG Peterson, MD Mumford, WC Borman, PR Jeanneret, EA Fleishman (eds) Development of Prototype Occupational Information Network Content Model, 1, 10.1-10.39. Salt Lake City UT: Utah Department of Employment Security.

Fletcher C, Williams R (1992) Organisational Experience. Performance Management in the UK: an Analysis of the Issues. London: Institute of Personnel and Development.

Fox S, Caspy T, Reisler A (1994) Variables affecting leniency, halo and validity of self-appraisal. Journal of Occupational and Organizational Psychology 67: 45–56.

Francis RD (1999) Ethics for Psychologists: A Handbook. Leicester: BPS Books.

Furnham A, Gunter B (1993) Corporate Assessment: Auditing a Company's Personality. London: Routledge.

Furnham A, Stringfield P (1994) Congruence of self and subordinate ratings of managerial practices as a correlate of supervisor evaluation. Journal of Occupational and Organisational Psychology 67: 57– 67.

Galbreath J, Rogers T (1999) Customer relationship leadership: a leadership and motivation model for the twenty-first century business. TQM Magazine 11(3): 161–71.

Gandz J, Murray VV (1980) The experience of workplace politics. Academy of Management Journal 23: 237–51.

Garden A (2000) Reading the Mind of the Organization. Chichester: John Wiley & Sons.

Gardner T (2002) The role of discretionary behaviour in mediating the HR firm performance relationship. Paper presented at the Academy of Mangement conference, Denver.

Garratt B (2003) Thin on Top. Why Corporate Governance Matters and How to Measure and Improve Board Performance. London: Nicholas Brealey.

Gary L (2002) How to think about performance issues now. Harvard Management Update 2(2): 1–4.

Gattiker V (1990) Predictors of career achievement in the corporate hierarchy. Human Relations 43: 703–26.

Gaugler BB, Rosenthal DB, Thornton GC, Bentson C (1987) Meta-analysis of assessment center validity. Journal of Applied Psychology 72: 493–511.

Goffman E (1961) Asylums. Garden City NY: Anchor, Doubleday & Co.

Goleman D (1996) Emotional Intelligence: Why it Can Matter more than IQ. London: Bloomsbury Publishing.

Goleman D (1998) Working with Emotional Intelligence. London: Bloomsbury.

Grams WC, Rogers RW (1990) Power and personality: effects of Machiavellianism, need for approval and motivation on use of tactics. Journal of General Psychology 117: 71–82.

Green PC (1999) Building Robust Competencies: Linking Human Resource Systems to Organizational Strategies. San Francisco CA: Jossey-Bass.

Griffin D (2002) The Emergence of Leadership. London: Routledge.

Griffiths P, Goodge P (1994) Development centres: the third generation. Personnel Management 26: 40–4.

Guest D et al. (2000) Employment Relations, HRM and Business Performance: an Analysis of the 1998 Workplace Employee Relations Survey. London: CIPD.

Habermas J (1971) Towards a Rational Society. London: Heinemann.

Handy C (1995) Gods of Management. London: Arrow.

Hardy C (1994) Managing Strategic Action: Mobilizing Change: Concepts, Reading and Cases. London: Sage.

Harris MM (1989) Reconsidering the employment interview: a review of recent literature and suggestions for future research. Personnel Psychology 42: 691–726.

Harrison R, Stokes H (1992) Diagnosing Organisational Culture. Amsterdam and London: Pfeiffer.

Hatfield M.(2000) More is most often not the best. Selection and Development Review 16(6): 3–7.

Health and Safety Commission (1999). Management of Health and Safety at Work Regulations. Guide and Approved Code of Practice. London: HSE Books.

Herman SM, Korenich M (1977) Authentic Management. A Gestalt Orientation to Organizations and their Development. London: Addison Wesley.

Hermelin E, Robertson IV (2001) A critique and standardization of meta-analytic validity coefficients in personnel selection. Journal of Occupational and Organisational Psychology 74: 253–77.

Herriot P (1992) The Career Management Challenge. London: Sage.

Herriot P, Anderson N (1997) Selecting for change: how will personnel and selection psychology survive? In N Anderson, P Herriot (eds) International Handbook of Selection and Assessment. Chichester: Wiley.

Heskett J, Sasser E, Schlesinger L (1997) The Service Profit Chain. New York: The Free Press.

Higgs M, Rowland D (2003) Is Change Changing? An Examination of Approaches to Change and its Leadership. Henley-on-Thames: Henley Management College.

Hofstede G (1992) Cultural dimensions in people management: the socialization perspective. In V Pucik, NM Tichy, CK Barnett (eds) Globalizing management: Creating and Leading the Competitive Organisation. New York: Wiley.

Hogan R, Hogan J (2004) Assessing leadership: a vision from the dark side. Selection and Development Review, 20: 1.

Holbeche L, Glynn C (1999) The Roffey Park Management Agenda. Roffey Park: Roffey Park Management Institute.

Holbeche L, Springett N (2004) In Search of Meaning in the Workplace. Horsham: Roffey Park.

Hough LM, Oswald FL (2000) Personnel selection: looking toward the future – remembering the past. Annual Review of Psychology 51: 631–64.

Hough LM, Ones DS, Viswesvaran C (1998) Personality correlates of managerial performance constructs. Paper presented at the thirteenth annual conference of the Society for Industrial and Organisational Psychology.

House RJ et al. (1999) Cultural differences on leadership and organisations: Project GLOBE. Advances in Global Leadership 1: 171–233.

House RJ, Javidan M, Dorfman PW (2001) Project GLOBE: an introduction. Applied Psychology: An International Review 50: 479–88.

HRM Software (2000) Survey of Succession Planning Practices in Major UK Organisations. London: HRM Software.

Huck JR, Bray DW (1976) Management assessment center evaluations and subsequent job performance of white and black females. Personnel Psychology 29: 13–30.

Human Qualities (2001) Selection and Development of Top Executives Survey. www.humanqualities.co.uk.

Human Qualities (2002) Management Development Survey. www.humanqualities.co.uk.

Hunter JE, Schmidt FL (1996) Intelligence and job performance: economic and social implications. Psychology, Public Policy and Law 2: 447–72.

Hunter JE, Schmidt FL, Judiesch MK (1990) Individual differences in output variability as a function of job complexity. Journal of Applied Psychology 75: 28–42.

Huy Q (2002) Emotional balancing of organizational continuity and radical change: The contribution of middle managers. Administrative Science Quarterly 47(1): 31–69.

Iles P, Robertson I, Rout U (1989) Assessment based development centres. Journal of Managerial Psychology 4: 11–16.

International Test Commission (2001) International guidelines on test use. International Journal of Testing 2: 93–114.

Jackson C (2002) Predicting team performance from a learning process model. Journal of Managerial Psychology 17(1): 6–13.

James M (1975) The OK Boss. New York: Bantam Books.

Janis IL, Mann L (1977) Decision Making: a Psychological Analysis of Conflict, Choice and Commitment. New York: Free Press.

Jaques E (1951) The Changing Culture of a Factory. London: Heinemann.

Jaques E (1989) Requisite Organisation: A Total System for Effective Managerial Organisation and Managerial Leadership for the Twenty-first Century. Arlington VA: Cason Hall & Co.

Jaques E, Stamp G (1993) Wellbeing at work: aligning purposes, people, strategies and structures. International Journal of Career Management 5(3).

Jehn KA, Chatman JA (2000) The influence of proportional and perceptual conflict composition on team performance. International Journal of Conflict Management 11(1): 56–73.

Johnson G (1989) Rethinking incrementalism. In D Asch, C Bowman (eds) Readings in Strategic Management. Buckingham: Open University Press.

Johnson G, Scholes K (1993) Exploring Corporate Strategy: Text and Cases. Hemel Hempstead: Prentice-Hall.

Jongeward D, Seyer P (1978) Choosing Success. Transactional Analysis on the Job. Chichester: Wiley.

Kakabadse A (1984) Power, Politics and Organizations: A Behaviour Science View. Chichester: Wiley.

Kakabadse A, Parker C (1984) Towards a Theory of Political Behaviour in Organizations. In A Kakabadse, C Parker (eds) Power, Politics and Organizations: A Behavioral Science View. Chichester: Wiley.

Kanter RM (1989) The new managerial work. Harvard Business Review (November–December): 85–92.

Kazerounian N (2002) Stepping Up. Women's Guide to Career Development. Maidenhead: McGraw-Hill International.

Kazimer-Shockley K, Bergert S (2001) The customer rules. Intelligent Enterprise (July) 4(11): 31.

Kegan R, Laskow Lahey L (2001) How the Way We Talk Can Change the Way We Work. Seven Languages for Transformation. San Francisco CA: Jossey-Bass.

Kellogg WA, Richards JT (1998) The Human Factors of Information on the Internet. In J Nielsen (ed.) Advances in Human–Computer Interaction. Vol. 5. Norwood NJ: Ablex.

Kelly G (1992) A Psychology of Personal Constructs. Vols 1 and 2. London: Routledge.

Kiger PJ (2002) Why Customer Satisfaction Starts with HR, http://www.workforce.com.

Kim J, Moon JY, Yonsei IJ (1998) Designing towards emotional usability in customer interfaces–trustworthiness of cyber banking system interfaces. Interacting with Computers 10(1): 1–30.

Kipnis D, Schmidt SM, Wilkinson I (1980) Intraorganizational influence tactics: explorations in getting one's way. Journal of Applied Psychology 65(4): 440–52.

Kirsh D (1997) Interactivity and multimedia interfaces. Instructional Sciences 25: 79–96.

Klemp GO Jr. (1980) The Assessment of Occupational Competence. Report to the National Institute for Education, Washington DC.

Kloss DM (1998) Occupational Health Law. Oxford: Blackwell Science.

Kohn A (1993) Why incentive plans cannot work. Harvard Business Review (September–October): 54–63.

Kolb DA (1984) Experiential Learning: Experience as the Source of Learning and Development. Englewood Cliffs NJ: Prentice-Hall.

Konovsky MA, Brockner J (1993) Managing victim and survivor layoff reactions: a procedural justice perspective. In R Cropanzano (ed.) Justice in the Workplace. Hillsdale NJ: Erlbaum.

Kotter JP (1996) Leading Change. Boston MA: Harvard Business School Press.

Kotter JP, Heskett JL (1992) Corporate Culture and Performance. New York: Free Press.

Kotter JP, Schlesinger LA (1989) Choosing strategies for change. In: D Ash, C Bowman (eds) Readings in Strategic Management. London: Macmillan Education.

Krause TR, Hidley JH, Hodson S (1990) The Behavior-based Safety Process. Managing Involvement for an Injury-free Culture. New York: Van Nostrand Reinhold.

Kroemer KHE, Grandjean E (1997) Fitting the Task to the Man. A Textbook of Occupational Ergonomics. 5th edn. London: Taylor & Francis.

Lane DA (1994) Human Resource Management in Small and Medium Enterprises. Wimbledon: CIPD.

Lawrence P (1994) 'In another country' or the relativization of management learning. Management Learning 25(4): 543–61.

Ledwith S, Colgan F (1996) Women in Organisations: Challenging Gender Politics. Basingstoke: Macmillan.

Lee G (2000) The state of the art in development centres. Selection and Development Review 16(1): 10–14.

Leslie JB, Van Velsor E (1996) A Look at Derailment Today. Greensboro NC: Centre for Creative Leadership.

Leverick F et al. (1998) Using information technology effectively, a study of marketing installations. Journal of Marketing Management 14(8): 927–62.

Lievens F, Harris MM (2003) Research on Internet recruitment and testing: current status and future directions. In CL Cooper, IT Robertson (eds) International Review of Industrial and Organisational Psychology. Chichester: John Wiley & Sons Ltd.

Lievens F, Klimoski RJ (2001) Understanding the assessment centre process: where are we now? In CL Cooper, IT Robertson (eds) International Review of Industrial and Organisational Psychology 16. Chichester: John Wiley & Sons Ltd.

Locke E, Latham G (1990) A Theory of Goal-Setting and Task Performance. Englewood Cliffs NJ: Prentice-Hall.

Loh L, Ong YS (1998) The adoption of Internet-based stock trading: a conceptual framework and empirical results. Journal of Information Technology 13: 81–94.

Longenecker C, Ludwig D (1995) Ethical dilemmas in performance appraisal revisited. In J Holloway, J Lewis, G Mallory (eds) Performance Measurement and Evaluation. London: Sage.

Lowman RL (ed.) (1998) The Ethical Practice of Psychology in Organisations. Washington DC: American Psychological Association.

Lucier C, Spiegel E, Schuyt R (2002) Why CEOs Fall: the Causes and Consequences of Turnover at the Top. McLean VA: Booz Allen Hamilton Inc.

Luthans F, Yodgetts R, Rosenkrantz S (1988) Real Managers. Cambridge MA: Ballinger.

Macan TH, Highhouse SH (1994) Communicating the utility of human resource activities: a survey of I/O and HR professionals. Journal of Business and Psychology 8: 425–36.

Maccoby M et al. (2003) Ego Makes the Leader. 2nd edn. Boston MA: Harvard University Business School Press.

Martin J et al. (1983) The uniqueness paradox in organizational stories. Administrative Science Quarterly 28: 438–53.

Martin J, Frost P (1996) The Organizational Culture War Games: a Struggle for Intellectual Dominance. In SR Clegg, C Hardy, WR Nord (eds) Handbook of Organization Studies. London: Sage.

Martin R (1998) Changing the Mind of the Corporation. Harvard Business Review on Change 71: 81–94.

Martinez MN (1997) The smarts that count. HR Magazine 42(11): 72–8.

Maslow AH (1943) A theory of human motivation. Psychological Review 50: 370–96.

Maurer TJ, Mitchell RD, Barbeite FG (2002) Predictors of attitudes toward a 360-degree feedback system and involvement in post-feedback management development activity. Journal of Occupational and Organizational Psychology 75: 87–107.

McCall MW Jr (1998) High Flyers: Developing the Next Generation of Leaders. Cambridge, MA: Harvard Business School Press.

McCall MW Jr, Hollenbech GP (2002) Developing Global Executives. Cambridge MA: Harvard Business School Publishing Corporation.

McCall MW Jr, Lombardo MM (1983) Off the Track: Why and How Successful Executives Get Derailed. Technical Report 21. Greensboro NC: Center for Creative Leadership.

McCall MW Jr, Spreitzer G, Mahoney J (1994) Identifying Leadership Potential in Future International Executives: a Learning Resource Guide. Lexington MA: International Consortium for Executive Development Research.

McClelland DC (1985) Human Motivation. Chicago IL: Scott Foresman.

McClelland DC, Burnham DH (2003) Power is the great motivator. Harvard Business Review 81(1): 117–26.

McGregor D (1960) The Human Side of Enterprise. New York: McGraw-Hill.

McKinsey & Co (2000) War for Talent Corporate Officer Survey. In E Michaels, H Handfield-Jones, B Axelrod (2001) The War for Talent. Boston MA: Harvard Business School Press.

McSween TE (1995) The Values-Based Safety Process. Improving Your Safety Culture with a Behavioral Approach. Chichester: Wiley.

Mead GH (1934) Mind, Self and Society from the Standpoint of a Social Behaviourist. Chicago IL: University of Chicago Press.

Meineger J (1973) Success through Transactional Analysis. New York: Signet Books.

Merry U, Brown G (1987) The Neurotic Behaviour of Organizations. London: Gardner Press.

Miles E, Snow CC (1978) Organisation Strategy, Structure and Process. New York: McGraw-Hill.

Miller E (1993) From Dependency to Autonomy, Studies in Organisation and Change. London: Free Association Books.

Mintzberg H (1983) Structures in Fives. Hemel Hempstead: Prentice-Hall.

Mintzberg H (1985) The organization as political arena. Journal of Management Studies 22: 133–54.

Mintzberg H, Quinn JD (1991) The Strategy Process: Contexts and Cases. Hemel Hempstead: Prentice-Hall.

Mirabile RJ (1997) Everything you wanted to know about competency modelling. Training and Development (August): 73–7.

Morgan G (1986) Images of Organisations. Bristol: JW Arrowsmith.

Mozenter J (2002) Recent links macro forces, emerging trends and OD's expanding role. Organization Development Journal 20(2): 48–58.

Murphy KR (2000) Impact of assessments of validity generalisation and specificity on the science and practice of personnel selection. International Journal of Selection and Assessment 8: 194–206.

Murphy L (1984) Occupational stress management: a review and appraisal. Journal of Occupational Psychology 57: 1–15.

Murray RB, Mount MK, Judge AJ (2001) Personality and performance at the beginning of the new millennium: what do we know and where do we go next? International Journal of Selection and Assessment 9: 9–30.

Murray V, Gandz J (1980) Games executives play: politics at work. Business Horizons (December): 11–23.

Nadler D, Tushman M (1999) The organization of the future: strategic imperatives and core competencies for the 21st century. Organizational Dynamics 28(1): 45–60.

Nevis EC (1987) A Gestalt Approach to Organisational Consulting. New York: Gestalt Institute of Cleveland Press.

Newman GA, Wright J (1999) Team effectiveness: beyond skills and cognitive ability. Journal of Applied Psychology 84: 376–89.

Newton T, Findlay P (1996) Playing God? The performance of appraisal. Human Resource Management Journal 6(3): 42–58.

Nilsen D, Campbell D (1993) Self-observer rating discrepancies: once an overrater, always an overrater? Human Resources Manager 32(2–3): 265–81.

Nobble CA, Bozionelos N (2001) The utilisation of 'sophisticated' selection techniques: results from a case study in a large organisation. Selection and Development Review 17(5): 12–14.

Noe RA, Steffy BD (1987) The influence of individual characteristics and assessment centers evaluation on career exploration behaviour and job involvement. Journal of Vocational Behaviour 30: 187–202.

Nyfield G (1998) The Consultant Perspective: How to Consider Cultural Context in Adapting Selection Practices Across Borders. Thames Ditton: SHL Group.

Nyfield G, Gibbons P, MacIver R (1993) Practical Implications of Assessing International Managers. Paper presented at 1993 International Assessment Conference.

Oborne D (1995) Ergonomics at Work. Human Factors in Design and Development. Chichester: Wiley.

Olea MM, Ree MJ (1994) Predicting pilot and navigator criteria: not much more than g. Journal of Applied Psychology 79: 845–51.

Ones DS, Viswesvaran C, Schmidt FL (1993) Comprehensive meta-analysis of integrity test validities: Findings and implications for personnel selection and theories of job performance. Journal of Applied Psychology Monograph 78: 679–703.

Oppenheim AN (2000) Questionnaire Design, Interviewing and Attitude Measurement. London: Continuum.

O'Reilly CA, Chatman JA (1994) Working smarter and harder: a longitudinal study of managerial success. Administrative Science Quarterly 39: 603–27.

Palmer I, Hardy C (2000) Thinking about Management: Implications of Organizational Debates for Practice. London: Sage.

Parlett M (1991) Reflections on field theory. British Gestalt Journal 1(2): 69–81.

Pearce CL, Sims HP (2002) Vertical versus shared leadership as predictors of the effectiveness of change management teams: an examination of aversive, directive, transactional, transformational, and empowering leader behaviours. Group Dynamics 6(2): 172–97.

Peters G (1978) Air Traffic Control: A Man Machine System. Systems Behaviour. Module 2, Open University T241. Milton Keynes: Open University Press.

Peters T, Waterman R (2004) In Search of Excellence. London: Profile.

Pettigrew AM (1973) The Politics of Organisational Decision Making. London: Tavistock.

Pettigrew A, Whipp R (1993) Understanding the environment. In C Mabey, W Mayon-White (eds) Managing Change. Buckingham: Open University Press.

Pfeffer J (1992) Understanding power in organisations. California Management Review 34(2): 29–50.

Pheasant S (1991) Ergonomics, Work and Health. Basingstoke: Macmillan.

Phillips JM (2001) The role of decision influence and team performance in member self-efficacy, withdrawal, satisfaction with the leader, and willingness to return. Organizational Behaviour and Human Decision Processes 84(1): 122–47.

Pirsig R (1979) Zen and the Art of Motorcycle Maintenance. New York: Morrow.

Porter ME (1980) Competitive Strategy. New York: The Free Press.

Porter ME (1985) Competitive Advantage. New York: The Free Press.

Potter RE, Balthazard PA (2002) Virtual team interaction styles: assessment and effects. International Journal of Human-Computer Studies 56(4): 423–43.

Power M (1997) The Audit Society. Rituals of Verification. Oxford: Oxford University Press.

Prahalad C, Hamel G (1990) The core competence of the corporation. Harvard Business Review (May–June): 79–91.

Price RE, Paterson F (2003) Online application forms: psychological impact on applicants and implications for recruiters. Selection and Development Review 19(2): 12–19.

Prinsloo M (1992) Cognitive Process Profile Manual. Gauteng, South Africa: Magellan Consulting (Pty) Ltd.

Pritchard J, Stanton N (1999) Testing Belbin's team role theory of effective groups. Journal of Management Development 18(8): 652–65.

Pugh DS (1978) Understanding and managing organisational change. London Business School Journal 3(2) 29–34.

Ramsay J, Barabesi A, Preece J (1998) A psychological investigation of long retrieval times on the World Wide Web. Interacting with Computers 10(1): 77–86.

Reason J (1990) Human Error. Cambridge: Cambridge University Press.

Reicheld FF, Sasser WE (1990) Zero defections: quality comes to services. Harvard Business Review (September–October): 105–11.

Reinartz W, Kumar V (2002) The mismanagement of customer loyalty. Harvard Business Review (July): 86–94.

Ritchie RJ, Moses JL (1983) Assessment centre correlates of women's advancement into middle management: a 7-year longitudinal analysis. Journal of Applied Psychology 68: 227–31.

Robertson IT, Makin PJ (1986) Management selection in Britain: a survey and critique. Journal of Occupational Psychology 59(1): 45–57.

Robertson IT, Smith M (2001) Personnel selection. Journal of Occupational and Organizational Psychology 74: 441–72.

Rosa EA (1998) Meta-theoretical foundations for post-normal risk. Journal of Risk Research 1: 15–44.

Rousseau DM (1990) Assessing organizational culture: the case for multiple methods. In B Schneider (ed.) Organizational Climate and Culture. San Francisco CA: Jossey-Bass.

Rousseau DM (1995) Psychological Contracts in Organizations: Understanding Written and Unwritten Agreements. London: Sage.

Russell CJ (2001) A longitudinal study of top-level executive performance. Journal of Applied Psychology 86: 560–73.

Ryan AM, McFarland L, Baron H, Page R (1999) An international look at selection practices: nation and culture explanations of variability in practice. Personnel Psychology 52: 359–92.

Salgado JF, Ones D, Viswesvaran C (2001) Predictors used for personnel selection: an overview of constructs, methods and techniques. In N Anderson, DS Ones, HK Sinangil, C Viswesvaran (eds) Handbook of Industrial, Work, and Organisational Psychology 1: 165–99.

Schein EH (1985) Organization Culture and Leadership. San Francisco CA: Jossey-Bass.

Schein EH (1987) Process Consultation. Volume II: Lessons for Managers and Consultants. Reading MA: Addison-Wesley.

Schein EH (1990) Organizational culture. American Psychologist 45(2): 109–19.

Schippmann JS et al. (2000) The practice of competency modelling. Personnel Psychology 53: 703–41.

Schmidt FL, Hunter JE (1998) The validity and utility of selection methods in personnel psychology: practical and theoretical implications of 85 years of research findings. Psychological Bulletin 124: 262–74.

Schmidt FL, Hunter JE, McKenzie RC, Muldrow TW (1979) The impact of valid selection procedures on work-force productivity. Journal of Applied Psychology 64: 609–26.

Schmitt N, Gooding RZ, Noe RA, Kirsch M (1984) Meta-analyses of validity studies published between 1964 and 1982 and the investigation of study characteristics. Personnel Psychology 37: 407–22.

Schneider B (1987) The people make the place. Personnel Psychology 40: 437–53.

Sears A, Jacko JA, Borella MS (1997) The Effect of Internet Delay on the Perceived Quality of Information. Chicago IL: School of Computer Science, DePaul University.

Seligman MEP (2003) Positive psychology, fundamental assumptions. The Psychologist 16(3): 126–7.

Senge PM, Kleiner A, Roberts C, Ross RB, Smith BJ (1994) The Fifth Discipline Fieldbook. London: Nicholas Brealey Publishing.

Shackleton VJ, Newell S (1991) Management selection: a comparative survey of methods used in top British and French companies. Journal of Occupational Psychology 64(1): 23–36.

Sheldrake R (1988) The Presence of the Past. London: HarperCollins.

SHL (1999) OPQ32 Manual and Users' Guide. Thames Ditton: SHL Group.

SHL (2002) Guidelines for Best Practice in Assessment and Development Centres. Thames Ditton: SHL Group.

Skinner BF (1938) The Behaviour of Organisms: An Experimental Approach. New York: Appleton-Century.

Skinner BF (1953) Science and Human Behaviour. New York: Free Press.

Skinner BF (1969) Contingencies of Reinforcement. New York: Appleton-Century-Crofts.

Sloan Wilson D, Near D, Miller RR (1996) Machiavellianism: a synthesis of the evolutionary and psychological literatures. Psychological Bulletin 199(2): 285–99.

Smith Benjamin L (1996) Interpersonal Diagnosis and Treatment of Personality Disorders. 2nd edn. London: Guilford Press.

Snyder C, Lopez S (2002) The Handbook of Positive Psychology. Oxford: Oxford University Press.

Somers, MJ (2001) Thinking differently: assessing nonlinearities in the relationship between work attitudes and job performance using a Bayesian neural network. Journal of Occupational and Organisational Psychology 74: 47–61.

Spreitzer GM, McCall MW, Mahoney JD (1997) Early identification of international executive potential. Journal of Applied Psychology 82(1): 6.

Spychalski AC et al. (1997) A survey of assessment center practices in organizations in the United States. Personnel Psychology 50: 71–90.

Stacey R (2001) Complex Responsive Processes in Organizations. London: Routledge.

Stacey R (2003) Strategic Management and Organisational Dynamics. 4th edn. London: Financial Times/Prentice-Hall.

Stacey R, Griffin D, Shaw P (2000) Complexity and Management: Fad or Radical Challenge to Systems Thinking. London: Routledge.

Stern E, Sommerdale E (1999) Workplace Learning, Culture and Performance. London: CIPD.

Stevens J, Ashton D (1999) Underperformance appraisal. People Management 5(14): 31–2.

Stevens R (1983) Freud and Psychoanalysis. An Exposition and Appraisal. Milton Keynes: Open University Press.

Stevens R (1998) Trimodal theory as a model for inter-relating perspectives in psychology. In R Sapsford et al. (eds) Theory and Social Psychology. London: Sage.

Sutherland V, Makin P, Cox C (2000) The Management of Safety. Chichester: John Wiley.

Syer J (1986) Team Spirit. London: The Kingswood Press.

Syer J, Connolly C (1996) How Team Work Works. Maidenhead: McGraw-Hill.

Tannen D (1991) You Just Don't Understand. London: Virago Press.

Tarleton R (2002) Motivation Comes from Within the Individual, so How Can it be Assessed? Treos: Arkadia Research.

Teel KS, DuBois H (1983) Participants' reactions to assessment centres. Personnel Administrator (March): 85–91.

Terrior JL, Ashforth BE (2002) 'I' to 'we': the role of putdown humour and identity in the development of a temporary group. Human Relations 55(1): 55–88.

Tett RP, Jackson DN, Rothstein M (1991) Personality measures as predictors of job performance: a meta-analytic review. Personnel Psychology 44: 703–42.

Thompson JE, Stuart R, Lindsay PR (1996) The competency of top team members: a framework for successful performance. Journal of Managerial Psychology 11(3): 48–66.

Thornton GC (1992) Assessment Centers in Human Resource Management. Reading MA: Addison-Wesley.

Townsend R (1970) Up the Organisation. London: Michael Joseph.

Trist EL, Bamforth KW (1951) Some social and psychological consequences of the Longwall method of goal setting. Human Relations 4: 3–38.

Tuckman BW (1965) Developmental sequence in small groups. Psychological Bulletin 63: 384–99.

Ulrich D (1997) Human Resources Champions. Cambridge MA: Harvard Business School Press.

Ury W, Fisher R (1992) Getting to Yes. London: Random House Business Books.

Vandermerwe S (2000) How increasing value to customers improves business results. Sloan Management Review 42(1): 27–37.

Vandewalle D, Cron WL, Slocum JW (2001) The role of goal orientation following performance feedback. Journal of Applied Psychology 86(4): 629.

Vecchio RP, Sussmann M (1991) Choice of influence tactics: individual and organizational determinants. Journal of Organizational Behaviour 12: 73–140.

Voight M, Callaghan J (2001) A team building intervention program: application and evaluation with two university soccer teams. Journal of Sport Behaviour 24(4): 420–31.

Walley L, Smith M (1998) Deception in Selection. Chichester: John Wiley & Sons.

Weick KE (1995) Sensemaking in Organizations. London: Sage.

Welch J (2001) Get Better or Get Beaten! Twenty-nine Secrets from GE's Jack Welch. New York: McGraw-Hill.

West M, Borrill CS, Dawson J, Scully JW, Carter M, Anelay S, Patterson M, Warring J (2002) The link between management of employees and patient mortality in acute hospitals. International Journal of Human Resource Management 13(8): 1299–1310.

West M, Patterson M (1998) Profitable personnel. People Management 8 (January): 29.

Williams D (1997) Life Events and Career Change: Transition Psychology in Practice. British Psychological Society Symposium, Jan 1997. http://www.eoslifework.co.uk/futures.htm.

Wilson DS, Near D, Miller RR (1986) Machiavellianism: A Synthesis of the Evolutionary and Psychological Literatures. Psychological Bulletin 199(2): 285–99.

Wolf S (1998) The role of caring behaviour and peer feedback in creating team effectiveness. Dissertation Abstracts International, A (Humanities and Social Sciences). University Microfilms International, volume 59.

Wood R (1998) High Flyers, High Potentials, Fast Tracks, Fast Streams – What is Going on? Croner Recruitment, Selection and Induction Briefing 46 (June).

Wood R, Payne T (1998) Competency-based Recruitment and Selection. Chichester: Wiley.

Wood RC, Hamel G (2002) The World Bank's Innovation Market. Harvard Business Review 80(6): 104–12.

Woodruffe C (1993) Assessment Centres: Identifying and Developing Competence. London: Institute of Personnel Management.

Woodward J (1965) Industrial Organisation: Theory and Practice. London: Oxford University Press.

Wright R (1994) The Moral Animal. London: Abacus.

Xenikou A, Furnham A (1996) A correlational and factor analytic study of four questionnaire measures of organizational culture. Human Relations 48(3): 349–71.

Yukl G, Falbe CM (1990) Influence tactics and objectives in upward, downward and lateral influence attempts. Journal of Applied Psychology 75: 130–140.

Zinker J (1994) In Search of Good Form. Cambridge MA: GIC Press.

Index